AF659849

ENVIRONMENTAL MANAGEMENT

ENVIRONMENTAL MANAGEMENT

G.N. Pandey
Ph.D.

Director
Institute of Engineering and Technology
Lucknow

VIKAS® PUBLISHING HOUSE PVT LTD

VIKAS® PUBLISHING HOUSE PRIVATE LIMITED
E-28, Sector-8, Noida-201301 (UP), India
Phone: +91-120-4078900 • Fax: +91-120-4078999
Registered Office: A-27, 2nd Floor, Mohan Co-operative Industrial Estate, New Delhi-110044
E-mail: helpline@vikaspublishing.com • Website: www.vikaspublishing.com

SALES AND MARKETING OFFICES OF VIKAS® AND S CHAND AND COMPANY LIMITED

Chennai	:	Ph: 044-2363 2120, chennai@schandpublishing.com
Guwahati	:	Ph: 0361-2738 811, 2735 640, guwahati@schandpublishing.com
Hyderabad	:	Ph: 040-4018 6018, hyderabad@schandpublishing.com
Jalandhar	:	Ph: 0181-4645 630, jalandhar@schandpublishing.com
Kolkata	:	Ph: 033-2335 7458, 2335 3914, kolkata@schandpublishing.com
Lucknow	:	Ph: 0522-4003 633, lucknow@schandpublishing.com
Mumbai	:	Ph: 022-2500 0297, mumbai@schandpublishing.com
Patna	:	Ph: 0612-2260 011, patna@schandpublishing.com

All rights reserved. No part of this publication may be reproduced or copied in any material form (including photo copying or storing it in any medium in form of graphics, electronic or mechanical means and whether or not transient or incidental to some other use of this publication) without written permission of the copyright owner. Any breach of this will entail legal action and prosecution without further notice.

***Jurisdiction**: All disputes with respect to this publication shall be subject to the jurisdiction of the Courts, tribunals and forums of New Delhi, India only.*

Environmental Management
ISBN: 978-81259-0292-8

Product Code: V8EVM60ENVS10ENAA97O

First Published 1997
Reprinted several times between 1997 and 2022
Reprint 2023

VIKAS® is the registered trademark of Vikas Publishing House Private Limited
Copyright © Vikas Publishing House Private Limited, 1997

PRINTED IN INDIA
By Vikas Publishing House Private Limited, Plot 20/4, Site-IV, Industrial Area Sahibabad, Ghaziabad-201010 and Published by Vikas Publishing House Private Limited, E-28, Sector-8, Noida-201301

Disclaimer: The publishers have taken all care to ensure highest standard of quality as regards typesetting, proofreading, accuracy of textual material, printing and binding. However, neither they nor the author accept responsibility for any loss occasioned as a result of any misprint or mistake found in this publication.

Preface

Even though environment and development are considered as two sides of the same coin, the impact of development on environment has unfortunately not been fully appreciated. Industrialization is considered as the barometer of civilization. Industrialized nations enjoy the best facilities available in the world and, due to favourable trade balance, they attract not only the resources available in the developing countries but also the best talents from them. The first chapter, "Impact of Development on Environment", indicates the interdependency of environmental degradation and development. The second chapter, "Engineering Ethics", indicates the need for engineering practices based on ethics to ensure minimal environmental degradation. Chapters 3, 4, 5, 6 contain background material on water, air, and noise pollution and control. Chapters 7 and 8 are on treatment of sewage and solid waste disposal which are direct contributions of Socio-Economic activities, especially urbanization, industry and transport, to environmental degradation

Even today, for the developing countries, pesticides and fertilizers for agriculture, tannery, textile, sugar, distillery, etc., are relevant and, naturally, cause concern for the control of pollution produced by their effluents. Power generation, especially through conventional systems, is largely based on thermal processes, where coal and petroleum are used as fuel. This contributes significantly to environmental degradation. Hence, the need for renewable energy resources and the conservation of energy have been discussed separately. In the end, a chapter has been devoted to environmental management.

The purpose of this book is to educate the planners as well as the executives, working in the industry, especially for developing a feel for the necessity of integrating environmental protection with development for balanced environmental management. The importance of simultaneous implementation of developmental activities and environmental protection is very well appreciated at the time of planning. Both should receive the same importance in the process of implementation also. The book will be useful to graduate and postgraduate students in Civil, Mechanical, Chemical, Biochemical and other disciplines of Engineering and Technology, as all of them will have a core course in Environmental Science and Engineering.

The assistance provided by Dr. Alka Tripathi and Dr. S.K. Singh, IET, Lucknow, at the initial stage of preparation of the manuscript, is gratefully acknowledged.

The author will greatly appreciate being informed about errors and receiving constructive criticism which may be of use when the book is reprinted.

G N Pandey

Contents

1

Impact of Development on Environment

Environment and Development are considered as two sides of the same coin. The environmental degradation, in fact, started with the propagation of human race, e.g., considering the mythological suggestion that the process of Adam and Eve who ate an apple and threw away the peels, which led to the beginning of the environmental degradation. This process of environmental degradation was accelerated with the development of socio-economic activities, e.g., agriculture, industrialization, drugs and Pharmaceuticals, transport, civil construction including roads and buildings, etc., with growing population, the requirements of food grains and other consumer items increased greatly, leading to further environmental degradation. As long as the assimilation capacity of receiving water system, land, air, etc., was more than the pollution load, the importance of environmental degradation was not really appreciated. But today there are places where rivers are polluted to the extent that they have practically no assimilation capacity due to domestic waste and trade effluents, e.g., river Ganga at Kanpur, river Gomti at Lucknow, etc.

In India, beginning 1951–52 when the first Five Year Plan was initiated, production of total food grains was about 52 million tonnes. This was raised to 66.85 million tonnes in 1955–56 when the first Five Year Plan terminated and during the successive plans, the production of total food grains was increased to 138.41 million tonnes in 1987–88. The production of rice was increased from 21.3 million tonnes in 1951–52 to 56.43 million tonnes in 1987–88, wheat production was increased from 6.18 million tonnes in 1951–52 to 45.1 million tonnes in 1987–88. This exponential increase was possible due to the increasing input of fertilisers- nitrogenous, phosphatic, and potashic, and also with proper irrigation, contributed by major irrigation through canal system and minor irrigation through tubewells. The use of increasing amount of fertiliser to increase the productivity of land, contributed to water pollution through soil pollution as well as air pollution. The production of pesticide to meet the requirement of agriculture, in order to remove the effect of pest on agriculture, also led to water pollution as well as air pollution. The development of large scale canal system led to deforestation; water logging, around canal system, led to barren lands. Thus, it is clear that on the one side agriculture was intensified with the input of fertilisers and irrigation, and on the other side the environment was degraded. However, during this period the population increased from 235.9 million in 1891 to 361 million in 1951 and further to about 800 million in 1988. As shown in Fig. 1.1 (a, b, c), the per capita net availability of total cereals remained at about 400 grams/ day and pulses at about 40 grams/day.

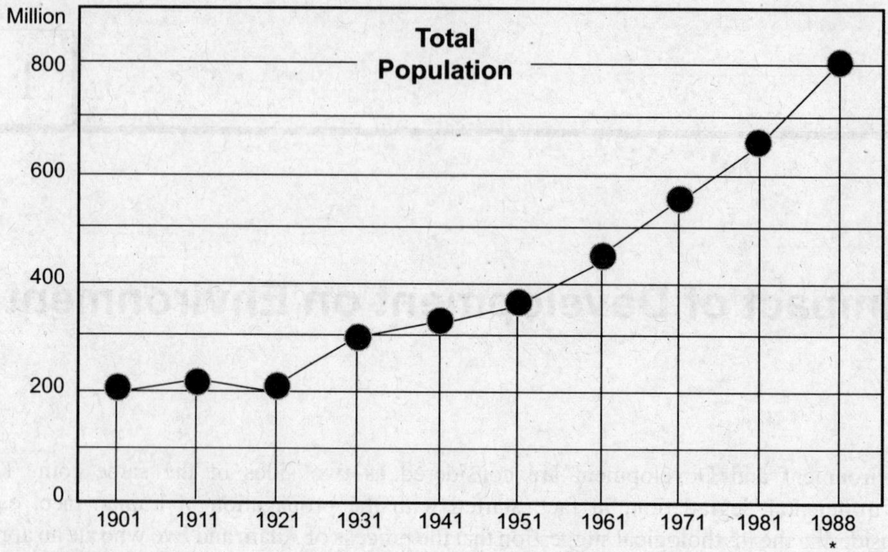

Fig. 1.1(a) Growth of Population

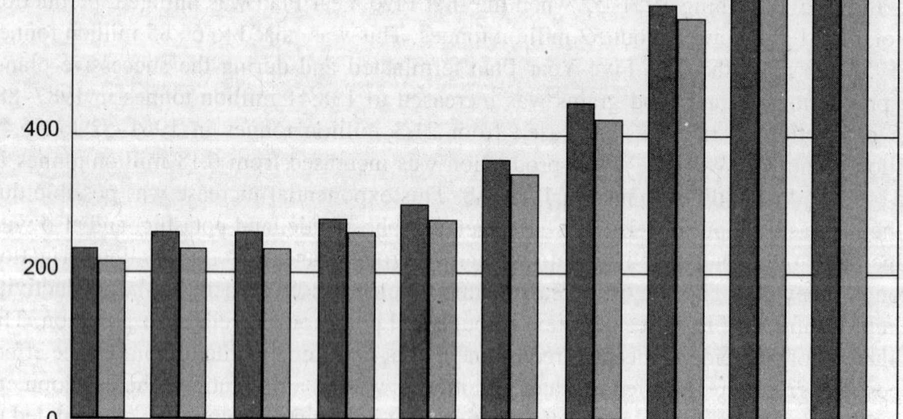

Fig. 1.1(b) Growth of Population

* Estimates

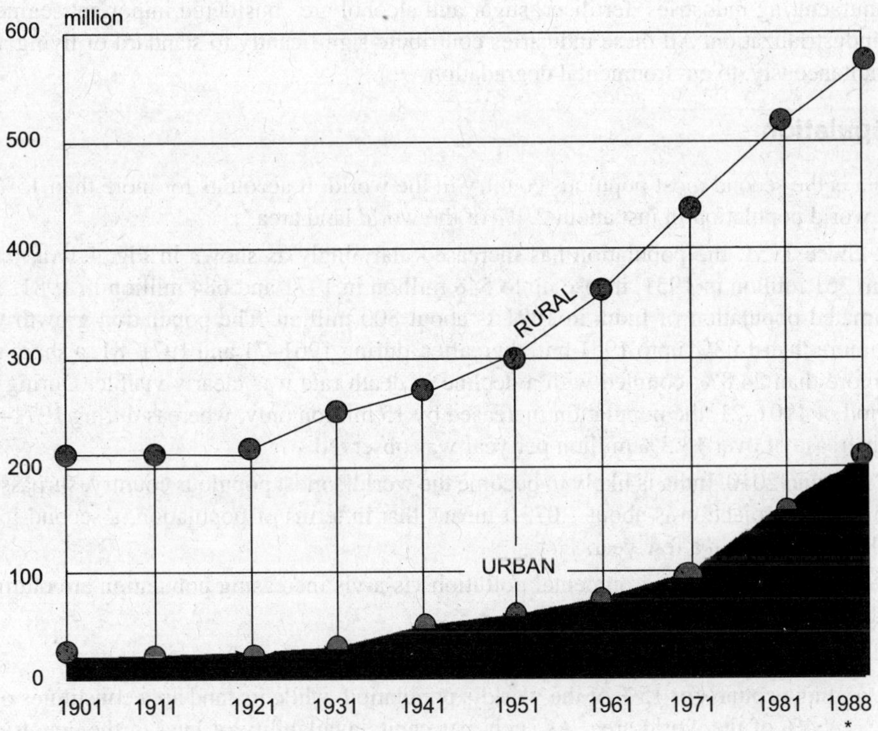

Fig. 1.1(c) Growth of Population

* Estimates

Industrialization

Similarly, in industrial production, the index number of wholesale price for manufacturing products went up from 51.4 in the year 1951–52 to 411.9 in the year 1988–89 with the base as 100 for the 1970–71, in the case of textiles, it went up from 59.5 to 329.6, in the case of paper and paper products from 75.7 to 430.2, in the case of leather and leather products from 81.9 to 611.1, in the case of rubber and rubber products from 73.3 to 414.8, in the case of machinery and transport equipment from 51.8 to 413.0, in the case of foodgrain from 51.0 to 3 89.9, in the ' case of edible oils from 38.6 to 423.1, in the case of sugar and Khandasari gur from 58.7 lo 429.7 during the same period., i.e., from 1951–52 to 1988–89, with the base as 100 for 1970–71. Similarly, die index number of the wholsale price index of crude petroleum shot up from 100.0 in 1970–71 in 1988–89. It went up from 54.1 in 1952–53 to 656.6 in 1988–89. in the case of electricity and for building materials, it went up from 50.2 in 1951–52 to 587.5 in 1987–88 with the base as 100 for 1970–71. Thus, it is clear that there has been substantial increase in the production of consumer items, including manufacturing products, textiles, paper and paper products, leather and leather products, rubber and rubber products, machinery and transport equipment, foodgrain, sugar and khandsari gur, crude petroleum, electricity and building material. Obviously, industrialization which has been responsible for increasing availability of consumer item, has contributed significantly to environmental degradation. Even today, for a developing country like India, the pulp and paper industry, leather and leather products, manufacturing industries, fertiliser, sugar and alcohol are considered important segments of industrialization. All these industries contribute significantly to standard of living and, simultaneously, to environmental degradation.

Population

India is the second most populous country in the world. It accounts for more than 15% of the world population in just about 2.4% of the world land area.

Since 1951, the population has increased alarmingly as shown in Fig. 1.1 (a, b, c), from 361 million in 1951, it rose up to 548 million in 1971 and 684 million in 1981. The estimated population of India in 1991 is about 800 million. The population growth was not more than 14.3% upto 1951,but, thereafter, during 1961–71 and 1971–81, a sharp rise of more than 24.8%, coupled with a decline in death rate was clearly visible. During the period of 1901–21, the population increased by 15 million only, whereas during 1971–81, an increase of over 13.5% million per year was observed.

Around 2010, India is likely to become the world's most populous country, surpassing China. The projection is about 1.07. It means that in terms of population, a second India will be emerging in a few years.

Some aspects of environmental pollution vis-a-vis increasing population are outlined in the following sections:

(*i*) *Availability of Land*

India counts for 15% of the world's population, while its land area constitutes only 2.4% of the world area. As such, per capita availability of land in the country, is 0.48 hectare as against 4.41 hectares in the USA, 8.43 hectares in the USSR, and 0.98 hectares in China. Furthermore, the population in India is concentrated in well-watered plains, creating further problems.

(*ii*) *Urbanisation*

Judged by the international standards, in 1984, our urbanisation rate of 24% is rather lower than those of Philippines and Brazil, where it is 39% and 72%, respectively. But the economic and social strains of the urban life in India, particularly in metropolitan centres, have already reached such frightening proportions that few would advocate further massive urbanisation in India.

The urban population in the 1981 census was 156 million which represented 24% of the total population. According to an estimate, the urban dwelling population will reach a figure of 350 million by 2000 A.D. doubling from present figure which would then place India in the first position, with regard to the size of its urban population. The result is over-crowding of built-up areas and growth of unauthorized colonies, leading to slum formation. At present, 20% of India's urban population lives in slums.

In the big cities, it ranges, from 10% in Bangalore, 37% in Kanpur, 38% in Bombay to 42% in Calcutta; 40% of all slums' population lives in the metropolitan cities.

(*iii*) *Water Supply and Sanitation*

Notwithstanding the improvements over the years, lack of potable drinking water continues to be a serious problem for a large part of our population. In 1947, the percentage of rural population, having access to potable water, was only 6%; it rose upto 31% in 1980. In urban areas, the percentage was 60% in 51.75% and

1977 in 1988. On a national level, 41% of the total population had access to potable water as compared to 17% in 1970. As such, more than half of our population, i.e., 59%, is still to be provided with the basic need of potable water supply.

Clean air, clean drinking water and clean nourishing food are the three pre-requisites of a decent existence. These require conservation of soil and water and sufficient vegetative cover. Management of our land and water resources must reccive highest attention. Greening our common lands could be a major employment generating programme. Reducing pests in agriculture must be attended to by resorting to organic measures of pest control and providing soil nutrients to the soil. Poor returns in agriculture, with increasing cost of input, is giving rise to fanner unrest in areas, which were responsible for green revolution. Stalling feeding of cattles to conserve biomass and to prevent overgrazing of common lands especially in hills, must be promoted. Every habitation in the country should have its own woodlot to meet the fodder, fruit, fuel and biomass needs of that habitation. Every road should be lined with tress to counter the pollution caused by the exhaust of motor vehicles.

In the hill regions, tourism based on trekking needs to be encouraged. Instead of multistorey five-star hotels to come up in future, it would be advisable to promote small tourist lodges as extension of existing houses of the local residents. Hill areas, where further road construction is not an economic necessity, should not be subjected to dynamite blasting, which does irreparable damage to the local flora and fauna. Gentler methods of landscape development need to be resorted to in the Himalayan regions, lest our sentinel, the Himalaya is washed down the rivers into the Bay of Bengal. Cultivable lands in areas higher than 4,000 meter, above sea level, should be used primarily for fodder cultivation to stall-feed all the cattle there. Growing of vegetables and herbs may also be encouraged as cash crops at high altitudes. Employment generation in the hills should come out primarily from government sponsored tree-plantation programme to cover bare hills. All prominent hill stations should develop satellite hill stations to prevent overcrowding and insanitary conditions during peak tourist seasons.

In areas of water scarcity can rainfall on roofs be conserved for use as drinking water? Every village and town should be geared to store rain water for irrigation aid for water supply systems. Our town are using potable water for flushing their lavatories and irrigating their parks and lawns while large areas of our country are short of drinking water.

Existence of waste of all kinds is a prominent feature of our landscape. If we want to make our environment livable, proper management of waste seems to be inescapable. Can we not generate employment in the cottage-industry sector by using the locally available waste as raw material? Thus, restoration of the ecosystem, and management and recycling of waste should be the two prominent areas to generate employment in future.

As regards sanitation, only 27% people of the urban population were provided sanitation facilities upto March 1981.

Thus, it is clear that with growing population, the need for increasing food grains, consumer items and other materials, not only to maintain proper standard of living but also to have better standard of living, compared to those of developed nations, will be there for some time to come. At the same time, with increasing socio-economic activities, there will be further degradation of environment. Hence, in order to have proper environmental protection, a balanced approach, with built-in provision for pollution control, with each development activity will be essential.

Projected Impact of Environmental Pollution in the World

There has been an all out effort to intensify the pace of industrialization even in developing countries on the pattern of industrialized nation. Added to this, is the serious problem of dwindling resources, specially of crude oil. In fact, the availability of resources, even increasing population, increasing environmental pollution due to rapid industrialization and total food requirement, are being given serious thought in the world. The figures given in this chapter project the position of these four important considerations over the next 30 years. These figures should serve as guidelines for those who are interested in an overview of the problem. Economic activities such as food production, industrial production and energy generation and environment should be considered as two sides of the same coin. In fact, due to their close interactions, it is essential to have an integrated approach to resource utilisation, economic activities and environment. This fact has become more important lately. The interactions between resources, food per capita, population, industrial output and pollution have been shown in Figs. 1.2, 1.3, 1.5 and 1.6 respectively. The impact of nuclear energy and recycle on such interactions is shown in Fig. 1.4 while Figs. 1.7 and 1.8 indicate the same interactions when proper pollution control and effective birth control are introduced. The interaction between the same parameters is shown in Fig. 1.9 except when the resources for non-renewable energy are developed and consequently industrial activities are affected. Figures 1.10-1.13 indicate suitable models with control on resources, food production, population, industrial production and pollution. It is, therefore, essential to have development with appropriate control on economic activities, proper birth control to check growing population, and appropriate utilisation of resources. The-efforts are already on in this direction and, hopefully, by the turn of this century, the results will be obvious.

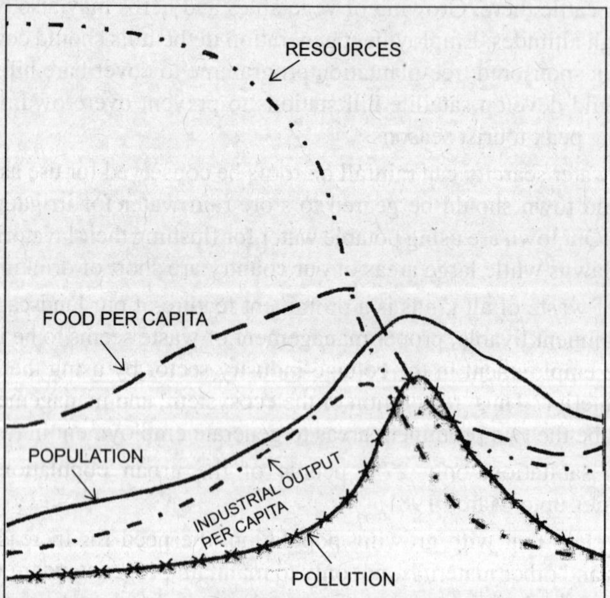

Fig. 1.2 World Model Standard Run

CONDITIONS: With no major change in the physical, economic or social relationship; food, industrial output and population grow exponentially ; population growth is balanced by rise in death rate

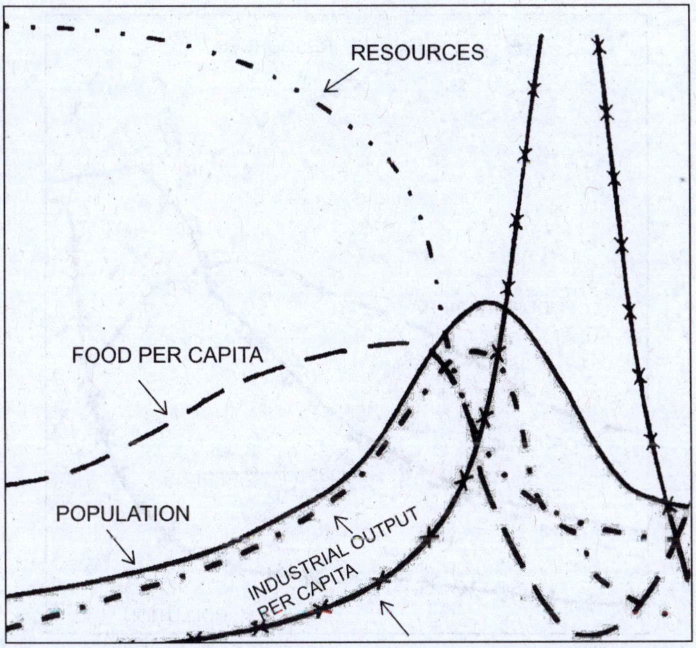

Fig. 1.3 World Model with Natural Resource Reserves Doubled

CONDITIONS: Industrialization reaches a higher level as resources are maintained.

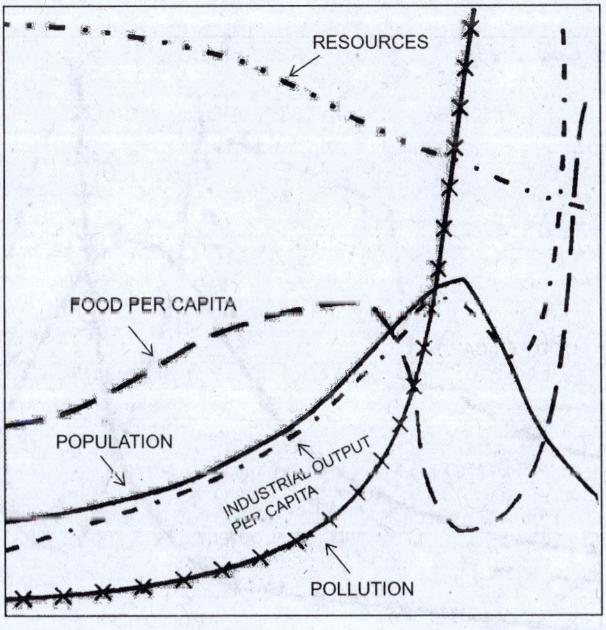

Fig. 1.4 World Model with "unlimited" resources

CONDITIONS: With the resource depletion problem eliminated by (a) Unlimited nuclear power that will double the resources ; (b) Possibility of recycling and substitution by nuclear energy; growth is stopped by rising pollution

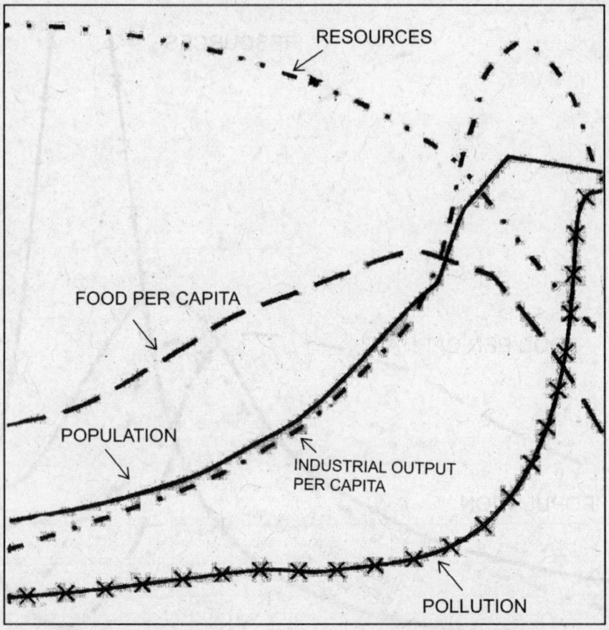

Fig. 1.5 World Model With Unlimited Resources and Pollution Controls

CONDITIONS: When pollution generation of per unit of industrial and agricultural output can be reduced to 25 per cent and food per capita declines and industrial growth is slowed

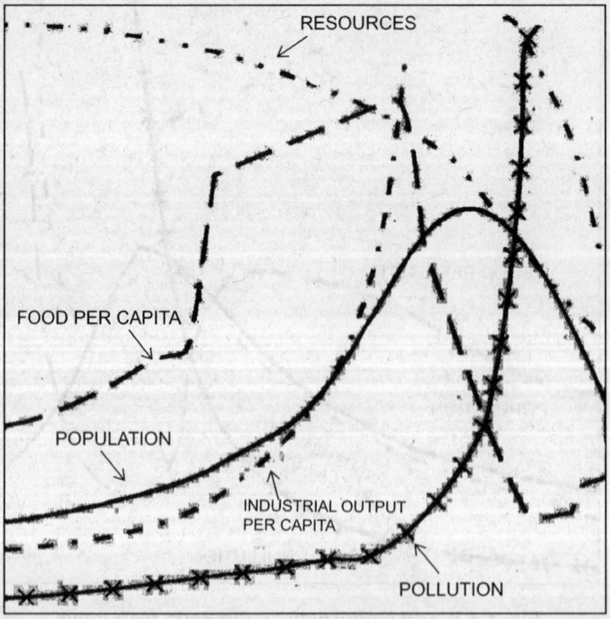

Fig. 1.6 World Model with Unlimited Resources, Pollution Controls, and Increased Agricultural Productivity

CONDITIONS: When a average land yield is doubled in addition to pollution and resources policy and industrial production generates much less pollution.

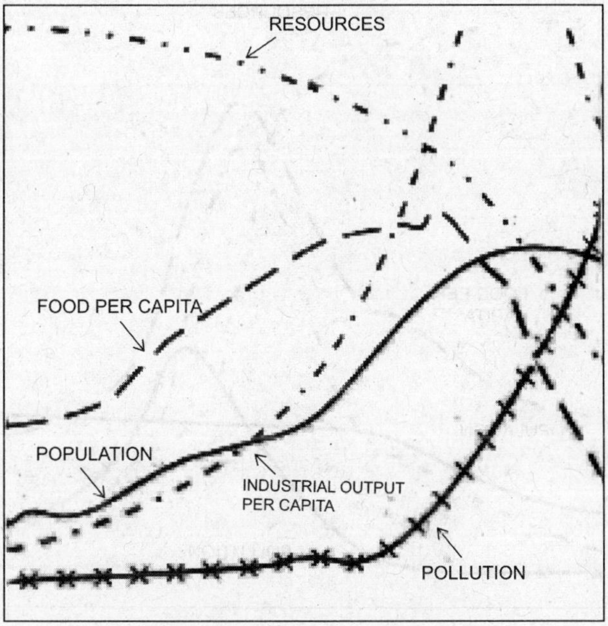

Fig. 1.7 World Model with "Unlimited" Resources Pollution Controls, And Perfect Birth Control

CONDITIONS: When resources are fully exploited and 75 per cent of those used are recycled; pollution generation is reduced to 25 per cent; land yields are doubled and effective methods of birth control are made available and temporary achievement of a constant population with a world average income per capita

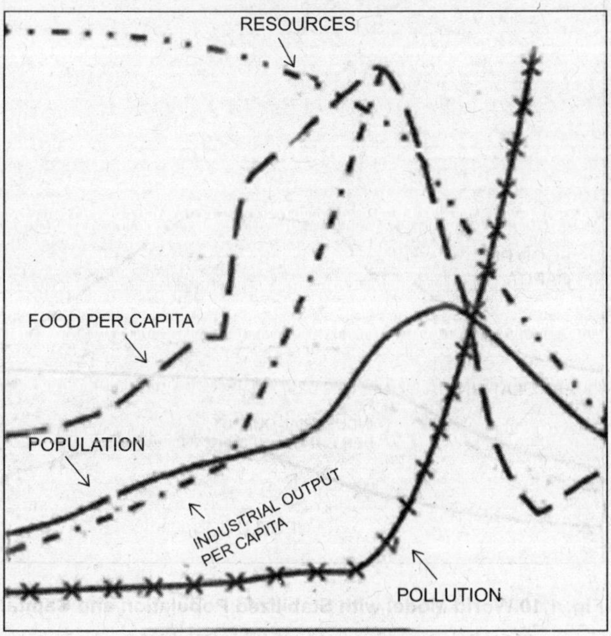

Fig. 1.8 World Model with "Unlimited" Resources

CONDITIONS: Pollution control, increased agricultural productivity and perfect birth control

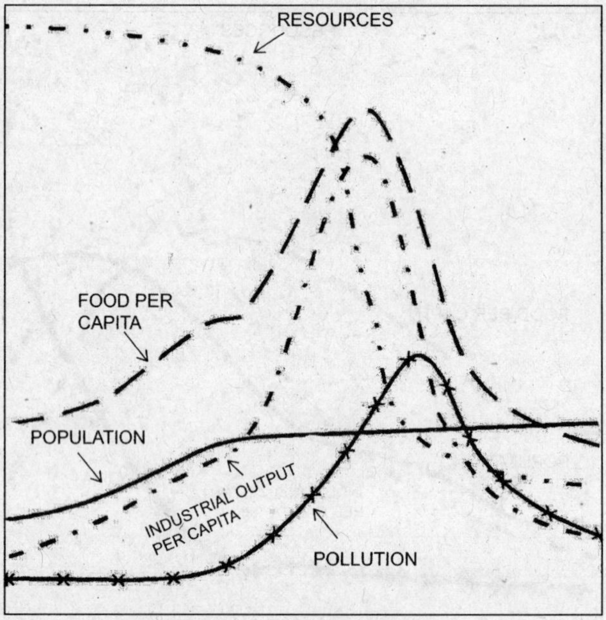

Fig. 1.9 World Model with Stabilized Population

CONDITIONS: When industrial capital continues to generate exponential growth of industrial output and depletion of non-renewable resources brings a sudden collapse of industrial system

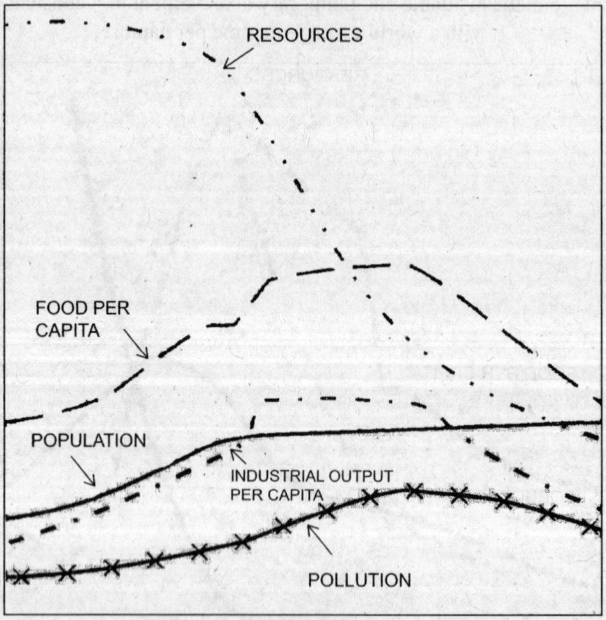

Fig. 1.10 World Model with Stabilized Population and Capita!

CONDITIONS: When population level and capital is sufficiently high to deplete resources rapidly and industrial output decreases and efficiency of capita! goes down

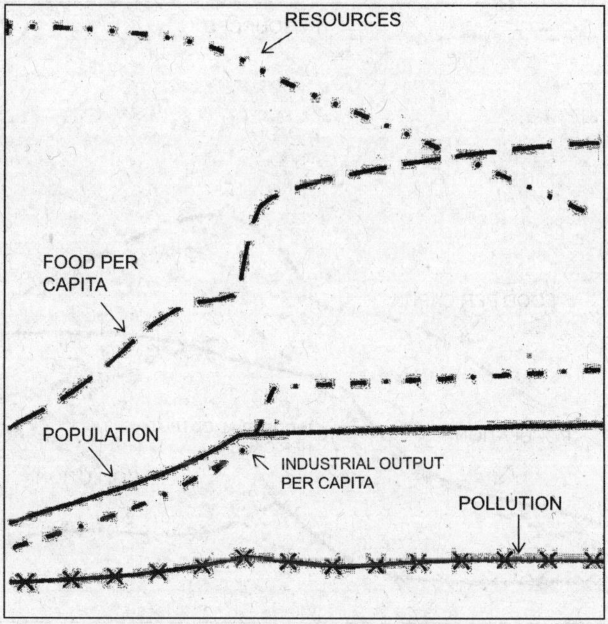

Fig. 1.11 Stabilized World Model I

CONDITIONS: When resource recycling, pollution control device, increased lifetime of all forms of capital are added to growth regulating policies.

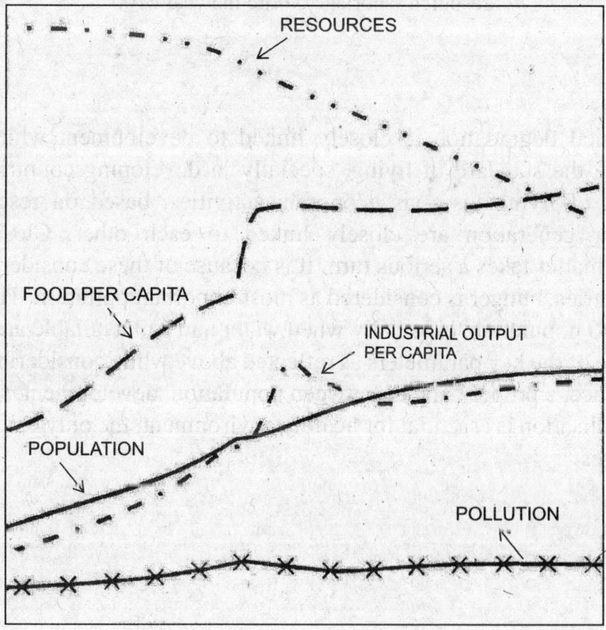

Fig. 1.12 Stabilized World Model II

CONDITIONS: When effective birth control and an average desired family size of two children are achieved and the birth rate slowly approaches the death rate

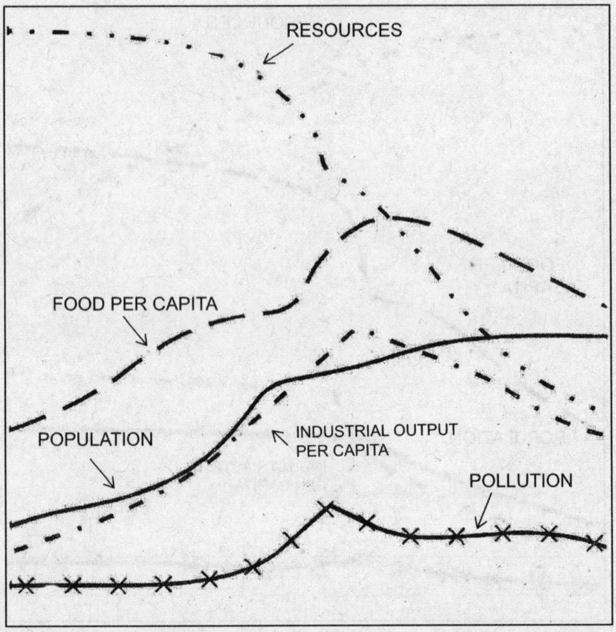

Fig. 1.13 World Model with stabilising policies introduced in the year 2000

CONDITIONS : When all the policies are delayed until 2000 AD the equilibrium state is no longer sustainable and population and industrial capital and industrial capital may create food and resources shortage before the year 2100

Conclusion

The environmental degradation is closely linked to development which is considered essential to raise the standard of living, specially in developing countries. As indicated above, standard of living vis-a-vis economic activities, based on resources available, transport, power generation are closely linked to each other. Closely linked with population, this matter takes a serious turn. It is because of these considerations that in the developing countries, hunger is considered as most important pollution. This hunger is also directly related to population, especially when water and soil available are limited. Hence, population is one of the key parameters as reflected above while considering environmental degradation. Hence, a proper balance between population, development, standard of living and resources utilisation is essential for healthy environment, the only environment that we have for ourselves.

2

Engineering Ethics

Ethics and morality are among the most difficult subjects to define and discuss. Opinions concerning these matters are frequently automatic, held on an a preconceived notions and are never subject to verification until after the fact, and, often, not even then. To some critics, any use of technology leads to increasing alienation and dehumanization ; therefore, technology is considered far from moral. However, most people recognize the great improvement in the quality of human existence which has been possible only with the input of technology. For them, the issue is to maximize the gains and minimize the losses, stemming from technology. Hence, they focus upon the principal practitioners of technology, the engineers, and wish to examine the moral nature of the decisions made by these practitioners.

In the United States, much of the moral concern of the nation has been with how to avoid damage to the welfare of minorities who may, otherwise, lose out in an elective process that depends upon majority rule. Most ethical systems seek to reduce the distress level in a society. In primitive societies, the notions of duty arise in response to the desire to avoid causing suffering or inconvenience to other members of the community. Ultimately, these duties are crystallized in taboos and are observed automatically. Thus, are ethical codes of behaviour born. And so, it is with us today. Ethics constitute the basic codes of civilized hehaviour, without which our environment, as we know it, would be impossible. Such rules embody the basic constraints each of us agrees to practise in relationships with others. We consent to these constraints in the knowledge that, in so doing, we make the existence of all, including ourselves, more agreeable.

Ethical codes can be of help in most instances that confront us, but dilemmas do arise in which it seems there are no suitable alternatives. In such a case, all external guides are helpless, and it is, indeed, necessary to resort to one's own internal values.

The greatest moral dilemmas, in society, are those related to war. Engineers, say some, are immoral if they work on weapons, because their clear moral duty is to oppose war by refusing to be involved in those activities which support it.

It has been said that medicine has given people health, that the humanities have given people pleasure and that technology has given people the time to enjoy both. Since the mid-1960, there has been a growing concern over the legal responsibility of manufacturers for product safety. The landmark event which is generally accepted as the beginning of this trend is the case of Greenman V. Yuba Power products, Inc., which established the principle of strict product liability. Under this principle, a manufacturer is held liable for a product which proves to have a defect resulting in injury, even though there may be intervening sellers During about the same period of time, there has also been a mounting debate over the moral obligations of engineers, not only with regard to safety, but also relating to other matters such as pollution, nuclear weapons and war.

Undoubtedly, the best known critic of product safety (and of engineers) is Ralph Nader. It is his thesis that engineers identify their personal objectives too closely with those of the companies for which they work. He feels that the professional creed of engineers should require them to be independent of corporate directions.

A more militant approach is that taken by the committee for social responsibility in engineering (CSRE). CSRE seeks to challenge the present orientation of engineering and declares that its objectives are to ';end unemployment and pollution and provide adequate medical care, housing, education, transportation and communication systems for all people". To implement these objectives, engineers are to be organized in groups to oppose corporate power.

These are difficult and important matters. The crux of the matter is: What is the engineers' role in a company? Is it proper to adapt to the corporation's directions? Or, is it proper to assume a role of independence, reach a moral judgement on an issue, and, then, to demand that the corporation accept that judgement, while not relinquishing any claim to a salary? Presumably, if the latter course is chosen, the engineers in a company will have to organise themselves into something like a union, withholding their services (that is, going on strike) if their wishes are not met. Implicit in this arrangement is the existence of a mechanism for reaching a collective moral judgment on an issue. However, to be honest, in reading the works of those who propose such measures, there appears to be an automatic expectation in the proposals that the groups, once formed, will adopt the moral views of the proposers. Such an expectation may be unrealistic.

Nuclear diplomacy on the world stage is beyond the scope of action of most engineers. Product safety is another matter. Virtually all engineers become involved with safety as a regular part of their professional activities. Few engineers would knowingly design unsafe devices. But safety frequently comes at increased cost; the engineer must inevitably balance safety against cost.

If, to make a product safer, it must be made stronger and heavier, or must be equipped with extra devices, or made of superior materials, to the point that it is so much more expensive that few will buy it, what has been accomplished? The manufacturer may have to close his doors if he can not sell product, but it is hard to see how morality has been served thereby. A result of the company's closure may also be that some useful products have been denied the public. Corporations are neither as perfect as portrayed by some, nor as evil as portrayed by others. They are simply the economic units in our society that are necessary to supply the goods and services, we need. No better means to serve this purpose has yet been found. While corporations obviously would prefer to market safe products rather than unsafe ones, they feel justified in asking why they should voluntarily increase the safety of a product if the result is that sales suffer. The provision of safety belts in autos is a good example.

The levelling effect of governmental action is indispensable in producing improvements in product safety and pollution reduction. It does little good to exhort engineers to insist that their ideas on safety or pollution be adopted, if the effect would be to jeopardize their employer's welfare. If such actions result in damaging their employers, have they properly fulfilled the ethical obligations they assumed when they accepted employment? In return for a salary, there is an implied obligation that an employee will help advance the employer's interests.

The individual engineer can not be expected to assume a hard line moral position that moves very far ahead of public opinion. If engineers as a group presumed to take on themselves the authority to act as moral judges for the rest of the society and to provide or withhold certain items from the public, such action would be to assume totalitarian powers over others. The justification for applying the word totalitarian in this context lies in the fact that a small group—the engineers would be making decisions for the society, which were not subject to review by elected officials or by the functioning of the market system. This arrogation of power would act to cancel the authority of the body politic, which is supposed to decide the questions of public policy. Furthermore, engineers posses no special qualities which make them superior moral authorities, to justify such a presumption of power. Engineers have an obvious ethical obligation to the public when out and out violations of the law and /or safety codes occur or when known safety hazards are concealed. Even if moral obligations were to be set aside for a moment and the most selfish personal motive invoked, engineers should ask whether their own long range interests are well served by continued employment with a company which would knowingly conceal a safety hazard or violate the law. The appropriate course of action for the engineer is best phrased by the Board of Ethical Review of the National Society of Professional Engineers (NSPE).

The engineer should make every effort within the company to have the corrective action taken.

Some have insisted that engineers aim for no less than 100% safety, or that society should allow no new technological undertakings unless it can be guaranteed that there will be no undesirable side effects. Neither of these conditions is achievable, of course. Life cannot be made 100 percent safe, nor can any human being guarantee the future. We are always going to be faced with the presence of a certain amount of risk, although engineers, with their special technical knowledge of materials and the like, are in a better position to reduce risks than almost any other group. Furthermore, an engineer who is constantly thinking about matters such as safety and pollution is much more likely to produce designs that excelled the categories that one who does not think about them.

The preceding material on Engineering Ethics has been developed as it is practised in U.S.A.

The Institution of Engineers, a professional body in India, has its own Code of Ethics for its corporate members. The same is reproduced below :

Code of Ethics for Corporate Members

The Code

1. A Corporate Member will co-operate members in his profession by the free interchange of information and experience, and will contribute to the work of engineering institution to the maximum effectiveness he is capable of.
2. A Corporate Member will endeavour to protect the engineering profession from misrepresentation and misunderstanding
3. A Corporate Member will refrain from expressing publicly an opinion on an engineering subject unless he is informed as to the facts relating to that subject.

4. A Corporate Member will express an opinion only when it is founded on adequate knowledge and honest conviction if he is serving as a witness before a court or commission.
5. A Corporate Member will not divulge any confidential findings or actions of an engineering commission or committee, of which he is a member, without obtaining official consent.
6. A Corporate Member will take care that credit for engineering work is given to those to whom credit is properly due.
7. A Corporate Member will not offer his professional services by advertisement or through any commercial advertising media, or solicit profession work either directly, or through an agent, or in any other manner derogatory to the dignity of the profession.
8. A Corporate Member will not submit a proposal for an engineering engagement unless he is invited to do so.
9. A Corporate Member will not directly or indirectly injure the professional reputation or practice of another Corporate Member.
10. A Corporate Member will exercise due restraint in criticizing the work of another Corporate Member and remember that the proper forum for technical criticism is an engineering society or the engineering press.
11. A Corporate Member will not try to supplant another Corporate Member in a particular employment.
12. A Corporate Member will not compete unfairly with another Corporate Member by charging fees below those customary for others in his profession practising in the same field and in the same area.
13. A Corporate Member will not associate in work with an engineer who does not conform to ethical practices.
14. A Corporate Member will act in professional matters for his client or employer as a faithful agent or trustee.
15. A Corporate Member will not misrepresent his qualifications to a client or employer or to the profession.
16. A Corporate Member will not disclose information concerning the business or technical affairs of his client or employer without his consent.
17. A Corporate Member will present clearly the consequences to be expected if his professional judgement is overruled by a non-professional authority where he is responsible for the professional adequacy of the work.
18. A Corporate Member will act with fairness and justice between his client or employer and the contractor when dealing with contracts.
19. A Corporate Member will not be financially interested in the bids as or of a contractor on competitive work for which he is employed as an engineer unless he has the written consent of his client or employer.
20. A Corporate Member will not receive any commission, discount or other indirect profit in connection with any work with which he is entrusted.

21. A Corporate Member will make his status clear to his client or employer before undertaking an engagement if he may be called upon to decide on the use of inventions or equipment or any other thing in which he may have a financial interest.
22. A Corporate Member will immediately inform his client or employer of any i Merest in a business which may compete with or affect the business of his client or employer.
23. A Corporate Member will not allow an interest in any business to affect the engineering work for which he is employed or may be called upon to perform.
24. A Corporate Member will engage or advise engaging engineering experts and specialists when in his judgement such services are to the interests of his client or employer.
25. A Corporate Member will not review the work of another Corporate Member for the same client, except with the knowledge of the second Corporate Member, unless such engineering engagement or the work which is subject to review is terminated.
26. A Corporate Member will not accept financial or other compensation from more than one interested party for the same service, or for services pertaining to the same work, without the consent of all interested parties.
27. A Corporate Member will subscribe to the principle of appropriate and adequate compensation for those engaged in engineering work, including those in subordinate positions.
28. A Corporate Member will endeavour to provide opportunity for the professional development and advancement of engineers in his employ.
29. A Corporate Member, if he considers that another Corporate Member is guilty of unethical, illegal or unfair practice, will present the information to the Council of the Institution for action.
30. A Corporate Member who is engaged in engineering work in a country abroad will order his conduct according to the professional standards and customs of that country, adhering, as closely as is practicable to the principles of this Code.

3

Effects of Pollutants on Living System, Effluent Guidelines and Standards

In order to generate a deep sense of real concern about the urgent necessity for pollution abatement, it is essential to know the effects of pollutants on the human body. Once the impact of each pollutant on the human body is understood, it would automatically provoke interest in the continuous monitoring of pollution at strategic points to determine its extent vis-a-vis the desired limit.

In any discussion on the effects of pollution on the population, one should, perhaps, begin by estimating how much ill-health or how many deaths can be attributed to the discarded wastes of an industrial society. Though no accurate quantitative information exists, a number of relatively well-defined syndromes, caused by particular substances, are known and, in general, the fact that health may be diminished by living in an area of substantial industrial pollution has been established. To put this in perspective, it should at once be pointed out that, in statistical terms, the effects on mortality is minor compared with the damage done by the motor car and the cigarette. The reason that no formal estimate of effects of pollution on health can be given lies in the complexity of population, the varying exposure and response of the individuals at risk, and the difficulty of proving cause and effect.

A relatively straightforward illustration of this is the need to conduct elaborate surveys to determine the side-effects of therapeutic drugs, where one is testing the reaction of humans to strict doses of defined chemicals, under relatively standard conditions. If an effect takes some time to develop or only occurs in a minority of cases, it may take a prolonged study to reveal it. When one looks at a more complex case, demônstration becomes even more difficult. For example, it has long been believed that cigarette smoking is bad for lungs. It has, however, taken elaborate statistical investigation to prove that there is a strong link between smoking and lung cancer. Even now there is considerable uncertainty about which of the possible carcinogens, in a cigarette is most harmful. Similarly, when one takes environmental variables, often themselves, poorly quantified, it becomes even more difficult to prove an effect. However, even if we cannot always calculate total damage, a number of 'pollution syndromes' is known and precautions may be taken accordingly.

Those who are at risk to pollutants fall into three main categories : those who are exposed to the highest concentrations, those who have impaired health, and the very young. The highest concentrations of pollutants are commonly found at their source, and so workers in the industries concerned are most likely to suffer ill effects. It is, indeed, by examining occupational associations of disease that suspicion may first be aroused. One of the first such cases was noticed by Sir Percival Pott in 1775, when he noticed that chimney sweeps were especially prone to develop cancer of the scrotum. In those days, chimney sweeps suffered long exposure to soot, frequently hot soot, under conditions which allowed little hygiene. Since then, many other occupational cancers have been discovered among workers, for example, tar, shale-oil and asbestos industries and in factories where workers suffer prolonged contact with certain kinds of lubricating oils. Lest it be presumed that such risks are totally remote from any general problem of effluent control, it may be pointed out that only recently has skin cancer been found among gardeners, apparently caused by the habit of spreading soot by hand. Industrial illnesses are carefully investigated then, no only to protect workers, but also to prevent their products or wastes from threatening other members of the population.

A second group, at risk, consists of those who are, in some way, less fit. During the heavy London fogs that are now happily infrequent, it was found that mortality and sickness rates increased dramatically. Those affected were mostly the old or the ill. Similarly, it was noted that those suffering from the heart disease 'angina' were liable to deteriorate if exposed to the smog-laden atmosphere of a Los Angeles freeway. In the same environment, when assured a supply of uncontaminated air, they remained in relatively good health. The control of general industrial smoke and car exhaust pollution, then, can be justified, in particular, on grounds of protection of the ill, and in general, for die rest of the population on whom there may be lesser effects.

The young, too, are specially at risk from pollution. Many noxious substances greatly affect rapidly growing and developing tissues, particularly of the yet unborn child. Although the absolute threshold levels, for the poisoning by heavy metal, has not been determined, it is clear that the required doses are less for children than for adults, and the effects are much more likely to be permanent. Also, if an environmental hazard takes some time to manifest its effects, the young are clearly those most at risk. When there is a long latent period, the elderly are hardly in danger, but the young are, since they alone will live long enough to develop the syndrome.

Air Pollution

Industrial processes and car exhaust release into the atmosphere gases, liquids in the vapour phase, and dust particles. The most generally released gases include carbon dioxide, carbon monoxide and sulphur dioxide. Carbon dioxide is least likely to pose a problem as it is a normal metabolite. If the body absorbs a metabolic, the body has a mechanism for its disposal, into the atmosphere from where it is removed by vegetation. Carbon monoxide, at the levels found in heavy traffic areas, does not build up in the blood in high concentrations. A survey of non-smoking London taxi drivers, for example, showed that carbon monoxide only replaced oxygen in their blood to about 2–3 percent, a small figure, when compared to the levels that may be found in inhaling heavy smokers. A small amount of carbon monoxide may well exacerbate a pre-existing lesion, cause discomfort or a slight impairment of athletic achievement, but it has yet to be proven to cause serious disease. Sulphur dioxide has, however, been more incriminated as a health hazard and its level, in the air, has correlated well with the incidence of acute attacks of bronchitis, a respiratory disease. Mortality rates are higher than in countries having a similar climate but less sulphur dioxide pollution, and recognition of this relationship has been the main impetus behind the drive to reduce the release of this gas by the combustion of sulphur-containing fuels.

Of the liquids liberated in a vapour phase by an industrial society, probably, the hydrocarbons predominate. Although atmospheric pollution is reduced by natural processes, and although the hydrocarbons as a group are usually toxic only at high concentrations, there are slight health effects associated with their excessive release. This factor can be minimized by ensuring that petrol is fully burnt. Some hydrocarbons can react photochemically in the atmosphere to produce toxic substances which, for example, irritate the eye. Petrol, however, also contains additives such as tetraethyl lead which will be discussed later.

Grit and dust particles are generated by a wide range of industrial processes. When large particles (over about 10 pm in diameter) are inhaled, they are usually trapped in the mucus of the upper respiratory tract and readily eliminated from the body. Smaller particles, however, frequently reach the lungs, where some will be trapped in mucus, but others will be engulfed by cells, the phagocytes, which serve to remove foreign bodies. In this case, the effects on the body depends on the nature of the dust absorbed. In the case of biologically inert particles there will be no damage, even if the lungs accumulate some amount of material, as is the case with city dwellers. Although coal dust particles are fairly inert, high concentrations of dust are not in public interest, and prolonged exposure to massive amounts can lead to the potentially disabling pneumoconiosis, sometimes, found in coal miners. More general health hazards are produced by silica and asbestos dusts. Silica particles are liberated into the atmosphere by quarrying stone working and abrasive processes, and inhalation for some years may result in a condition in which lung tissue is replaced by cancerous tissue. Asbestos dust can cause a somewhat similar disease, and with some types of asbestos, a form of lung cancer is caused. Here, the required exposure is so low that the environmental risks are apparent : this cancer has been found not only in asbestos workers or dockers alone, but also in their wives, whose main contact is presumably through the handling of clothes which have been contaminated with particles. Beryllium dust is responsible for another lung disease, which is, however, fortunately not malignam. Although commonest amongst the workers directly involved, occasional neighbourhood cases occur through pollution.

Water pollution

The spread of infectious disease by water pollution is a well-known hazard which is controlled by public health authorities in advanced countries and need not concern a discussion on industrial effluents, except to point out that microbiological growth is dependent on the concentration of certain trace elements. Whether or not these elements, in any way, influence the geographical variations in the prevalence of certain infectious diseases, is unclear. Investigations are presently under way, and these could eventually be reflected in changes in the practice of water treatment, just as dental recommendations have, sometimes, led to the adjustment of fluoride levels. Similarly, research on heart and blood vessel diseases has shown that they seem to be more prevalent in soft water regions.

Of far more concern to most engineers is the need to control toxic materials in water effluents. Radioactive isotopes are obviously a danger, although not immediately toxic in any likely doses. The pathological effects depend on the chemistry of the isotope : Strontium 90, for example, is dealt with by the body as if it were calcium and becomes localised in the bones, while phosphorus 32 is treated as if it were the stable isotope phosphorus 31 and may get incorporated into the chromosomes of dividing cells, possibly causing mutation or cancer. Toxic ions are currently receiving much attention, since cyanide, lead, cadmium, arsenic, mercury, mangnese and chromium are all among the industrial wastes which may be released. Although heavy metal may be discharged in highly diluted form, they can come back to man in a concentrated form if they are absorbed and retained by plants or animals and these creatures serve as food for other animals. The metals, thus, pass up the food chain, becoming progressively more concentrated as each predator eats many prey. That is why heavy metals, dumped in the sea, are especially likely to be found in the largest amounts in large predator fish like the tuna. The other animals, responsible for concentrating toxic metals, are shellfish which filter large volumes of sea water and may retain some constituents.

The dangers to health from, heavy metals, depend, to some extend, on the form in which they occur. Mercury, for example, is not accumulated by animals as a metal or ion, bat in organometallic form, such as methyl or dimethyl mercury. Methylation of mercury by microorganisms occurs readily in the environment, especially at the bottom of lakes and seas, and, thus, there is always a danger that wastes discharges, as relatively inert, may reappear in a more alarming form.

Another type of water pollution occurs when chemicals persist in the environment. An immense number of synthetic compounds are now made and used ; many of these, if discharged, are readily metabolised by micro-organisms, and cause no health danger unless present in high concentrations. Some, however, are not degraded and persist with the potential to build up in concentration if their discharge is continued. Examples of these include some plastics, the halogenated hydrocarbon, pesticides and some types of detergents. The latter can become an indirect public health danger, if allowed to build up to levels, that impair the efficiency of water purification plants. At one time or another, humans have been poisoned fatally by each of the common pesticides, though (his has resulted from the deliberate or accidental ingestion of large amounts. Through pollution, people, now, contain a few parts per million of chlorinated hydrocarbons in their fat tissue, but no adverse effects on health have been detected at this level. If only medical aspects were considered, it would be concluded, in general, that pesticides have greatly increased health throughout the world through control of disease bearing pests and augmentation of food production.

Some Pollution Syndromes

Among the most striking of the diseases that can be caused by heavy pollution are those involving heavy metals. Between 1953 and 1960, a large number of Japanese, living in the villages around Minamata Bay, were taken ill with a strange neurological disease, and over a 100 people died. 'Minamata disease' is, now, known to have been caused by eating lethal amounts of mercury which had accumulated in the fish and shellfish caught in that bay. The polluter was eventually traced : a vinyl chloride and acetylaldehyde plant that had used organic mercurials as catalysts and had dumped the wastes in the. bay. The symptoms of chronic mercury poisoning include damage to some parts of the brain, which leads to a feeling of dumbness and blurred vision. There may be difficulty, experienced when accomplishing tasks involving a sense of balance, such as walking. Mental symptoms include difficulty in following complicated conversations and episodes of excitement, followed by depression. Since these acute symptoms only appear after moderate to high doses of mercury poisoning, some fear that lower doses may have some cumulative effects, which are only manifested but do not regenerate nerve cells. It is a reasonable fear that results of poisoning with low levels might appear in old age, when the brain is suffering from life-long wastes of nerve cells without replacement. A low intake of mercury showed no obvious effect on pregnant women, but, when their children were born, they exhibited clear symptoms of poisoning.

The most obvious way to limit the effect of mercury on health is to monitor the amount found in food, notably in fish, and to restrain the sale of any commodity found to have too high a level. Now, an absolute value can be given to the permissible level. Taking a likely level, it appears to be possible to get mercury poisoning by eating about fifteen pounds of tinned tuna a week. Since this is a singularly unlikely diet in any country, and especially in Britain where less than, an ounce of tuna, per person, per week, is sold, it is presumed that no immediate risk exists. How much industry is, indeed, to blame for the accumulation of mercury in tuna is, in itself, debatable, since museum specimens of fish, caught long ago, have been analysed and found to contain almost as much as those caught today. The danger to health arises when there is intensive local pollution as can occur near mercury-cell-chloralkali plants or some plastics factories which use mercury catalysts. Since the Minamata Bay episode, considerable control, often voluntary, has been exercised, and one would like to believe that careful plant operation and supervision will eventually eliminate the danger of serious concentrations of mercury being released into the environment.

Lead Pollutants

There has recently been considerable discussion on the risk from lead pollutants. The effects of direct poisoning are well-known, such as occur when children chew lead toys or paints, resulting in abdominal pain and vomiting, drowsiness, perhaps, leading to coma, paralysis or convulsions, and possible brain damage. In adults, suffering from severe poisoning, lead has usually been absorbed at work, and, at first, it causes only colic, constipation and malaise, but continued exposure can lead to cramps, paralysis of some muscles and various neurological effects, including loss of concentration, poor memory, increased excitability, insomnia and impotence. Since the most drastic and obvious effects are on children, a great stress has been laid on the control of products, likely to contain large doses of lead, but much less is known about the results of chronic low exposure on either children or adults. The earliest symptoms are rather vague, and so, it has been suggested that those, at risk, should be regularly monitored, since there is a fairly straightforward test—a blood enzyme is very sensitive to lead poisoning, and shows changed activity before there are any obvious clinical signs.

This kind of survey clearly has a role to play in the control of lead smelters, with respect to those who work in them, and those who live nearby. There is, however, another more controversial issue. A substantial amount of lead is released into the atmosphere, as organic or inorganic lead by petrol engines, using tetraethyl lead as anti-knock additives, and while there is no question of this being present in severely toxic doses, it has been suggested that the current levels might themselves cause some detriment. A notable protagonist, in this field, Professor Biyce-Smith of Reading, has forcefully argued that lead pollution may already be having long term adverse effects on human behaviour. Available evidence may be summarized briefly. First, Russian research work has shown that conditioned reflexes (a standard test in the country of Pavlov) are slowed down by imbibing very small amounts of lead, and, as a result, smaller levels of atmospheric lead are tolerated there than in the test. Secondly, children who have suffered acute lead poisoning, but subsequently recovered, may have a later history of poor education progress, and exhibit behavioural difficulties like violent tendencies. Thirdly, a survey in Switzerland has shown that inmates of a reformatory prison had abnormally high blood lead levels. Clearly, very much more work needs to be done to establish an association between current intake of lead and behavioural disturbances, as the symptoms, being complained of, are rather general, and the fact that behaviour is affected by a large number of social and medical factors cannot be discounted. Nonetheless, however ill-established the connection between lead poisoning and anti-social activity is, the matter is worthy of investigation. It has even been suggested, though speculatively, that plumbism may have been a factor in the decline of the Roman Empire after lead conduits were introduced to carry drinking water.

Other Elements

Characteristic ailments are associated with various other elements, though no clear-cut conclusions have been reached. A high intake of selenium causes bad teeth, skin discoloration and gut problems, but this element is widespread in nature and industrial use cannot be presumed to contribute to any pollution, and, indeed, small amounts of selenium arc beneficial in reducing the toxicity of some other heavy metal. If anything, there seems to be a slightly lower incidence of cancer in high selenium areas, but since animal studies show a narrow threshold between beneficial and toxic concentrations, no direct recommendations can be madc. Mangnese poisoning is sometimes found as an occupational disease but, as with many other trace elements, it is essential in small amounts for life processes. At present, there is no reason to consider moderate mangnese pollution as a cause of disease although, like lead and mercury, chronic low does may lead to rather vague nervous symptoms which can be confused with other syndromes. A number of metals has been implicated in carcinogenesis, including arsenic, chromium, nickel, cobalt, lead, iron and cadmium, but statistical studies of a complicated environmental situation are as yet imperfect. Some simple compounds too cause certain diseases and are, therefore, controlled in drinking water supplies, such as nitrates which can reduce the hemoglobin of infants. Again, however, absolute standards are not known and the level to which the nitrate is controlled is somewhat arbitrary.

Effects of Low Dose

Besides straightforward clinical syndromes, general comfort is an important aspect. Noise pollution is a good example of this: high levels are required to effect any physical damage, but lower levels cause discomfort, and can disturb the well-being of an individual while ordinary sounds are part of normal life. The same is true of many minor pollutants, and any general conclusion of a survey of medical aspects of pollution can merely be that as yet we can only speculate about the effects of low doses of many industrial wastes. Many industrial products are inert or readily degraded and most unlikely to be a major factor in illness. Others are suspect, but it is difficult to establish any real association with disease. To end this review as it began, one can only say that the effect of industrial pollution on human mortality is, as far as can be seen, less harmful than that caused by cigarette smoking or transport accidents.

Dispersal of Heavy Metal Pollutants Around Industrial Complexes

In the following account, particular emphasis will be placed on cadmium. There will be reference also to mercury. These two metals have in common the fact that they both have been the cause of serious human poisoning as the result of industrial pollution. Much information is available regarding the way in which they enter the diet and the body. The damage done to the body is usually slow in its action because the concentration in the environment or the food is usually very low, and, hence, it takes a long time to reach toxic levels in the tissues. For the same reason the correct identification of the cause of this kind of poisoning can take months or years.

It is particularly important in developing countries that due regard is paid to the history of these two slow-acting poisons. The lessons learned can be equally applied to other waste products of industry.

How Metal Enter the Environment

Cadmium: This metal is usually found in association with zinc. In fact, the ancient name for cadmium ore was "cadmia". Cadmium is more volatile than zinc and, when the latter is extracted by smelting, cadmium comes over in the first products of distillation. Unlike zinc, it is highly toxic and has to be trapped to avoid atmospheric pollution. A study of the history of zinc smelting shows that enormous improvements have been made in controlling the escape of cadmium in 'die fumes. Spokesmen for the industry have said (with some justification) that environmental contamination, as attributed to zinc smelting, is a legacy of the "bad old days" and that the present levels of contamination are insignificant.

Sometimes, cadmium escapes into the environment through air, probably in the form of small particles which have escaped the trapping process at the smelter. Although the present- day emission from a modern smelter may be immeasurably small at the source, it is, often, being released on a twenty-four hour basis.

Large zinc smelters caused local pollution in Toyama, Japan, and Bristol, England. In both the cases, the air-borne contamination could be identified in the plants and soil in the surrounding district. In Japan, unfortunately, some of these plants happened to be rice, which is a principal constituent of tire diet of the local people in the city of Toyama. In Britain, the surrounding area was not agricultural land and, hence, cadmium effects on humans have not been observed. It is not always possible to separate air-borne and. water-borne pollution in the case of cadmium when the principal source is a smelter. In Toyama, for example, much of the cadmium in the rice came from the irrigation water which, in turn, came from a river which passed close to the smelter. Turning again to Britain, another example concerns a small village called Shipham, near Bristol. It lies below an area which used to be intensively mined for lead. Lead ore also contain some cadmium. The water which drains from the mineral area contains, in addition to lead, significant amounts of cadmium which, over hundreds of years, have accumulated in the soil around the village. Vegetables, grown there do contain cadmium but no definite effects on the population have been observed. This is due to the fact that most of the food for the village comes from outside the contaminated area.

Cadmium can also enter the environment from many different industries. The most obvious of these is the electroplating industry. In these days, when brass is so expensive, it has been found that it is cheaper to plate steel with cadmium and, thus, provide corrosion resistance The liquid effluent from this process is potentially very dangerous. Harder to identify are the many other liquid sources associated with other industries. For these reasons, the effluent, from any industrial city, is almost certain to contain some cadmium whether or not zinc smelting is earned out. An example of this is seen in the results of work carried out by the Institute of Science, Bombay, on the aquatic environment of the Kalu river. Here, the cadmium concentration in the water was at an acceptable level (under 50 ppm). There was evidence, however, that the cadmium concentration was much higher in the leaves and roots of plants growing near the river. A biological concentration of over one thousand fold was reported. Thus, after it enters the environment, this metal can slowly accumulate in sediments and sedentary organisms, like animals or plants.

Mercury: Once again, for the most serious example of human poisoning, we must turn, to Japan. In this case, it was in the coastal town of Minimata, which is just south of Nagasaki, that large numbers of people died or were permanently crippled, mentally and physically.

This later became known as the "Minimata Disease", caused by mercury which had accumulated in the bodies of fish which constituted an important part of the human diet in that area. Mercury differs from cadmium in one respect, i.e., it can be converted by microorganisms into alkyl compounds. Such a compound, methyl mercury, is actually more toxic than mercury itself. This conversion can take place in the sediment of river beds where the mercury compounds can enter the food chain. The worms which live in this mud are the main diet of many fish which are used for human consumption. An analysis of thirty species of fish from the Bombay and Thane areas showed that many species, in particular, Tilapin, Lates, Wallago, Mugil and Elops, carried mercury burden which approached or slightly exceeded the permissible level of 500 pgm//. Once again, we see here, an example of toxic- metal pollution, originating from a highly populated and developed area.

Beneficial Effects of Metals on the Human System

Metals are unique environmental and industrial pollutants in that they are neither created nor destroyed by humans but are only transported and transformed into various products.

Since our civilization is heavily dependent on the use of heavy metals, particular attention must be paid to control the contamination, caused as a result of large dispersal of metal in the land and environment. If we continue to allow the soil to be contaminated on a long term basis with toxic trace elements which can pass into plants and, hence, into the food chain, we might run a risk of creating biochemical difficulties for ourselves. It becomes, therefore, necessary to review the behaviour and impact of metal toxicity not only in healthy adults but also in young organisms, growing in an environment which has changed much from the ancient times.

On the contrary, humans need metals for growth, health and survival. In view of the concept of origin and evolution of life, mammals owe their present development to many metals. Metals such as calcium, sodium, potassium and magnesium are, essential to maintain physiological milieu essential for life. Micro quantities of other trace metals such as Mn, Cu, Fe, V, Co, Zn and Ni, affect their influence on enzymes and help to maintain the structural integrity of genetic materials. Trace metals also enhance the vitality of an organism by stimulating the development of immunity.

Thus, it is evident that while a certain amount of trace metals is necessary for proper functioning and survival of the organism, the same trace metals can assault the organism in toxic levels.

Toxicity

At this point, the principles of toxicology should be reviewed briefly. Toxicology covers the entire range of harmful interactions of chemicals on any biological system. It has a different meaning, depending on the context of its usage—chemical, clinical, experimental, biochemical, forensic, industrial or environmental. It could be defined as the capacity of the chemical to affect adversely any activity of the organism.

Toxicity studies are normally described in terms of dose-response curves. The dose-response curve could be defined as the response of a defined species under controlled experimental conditions. The essentiality, deficiency and toxicity can be depicted as a continuum in a wide-range dose-response curve.

The plateau region of concentration depicts optimum growth, health and reproduction. Beyond the plateau region, all metals (essential or non-essential) become toxic and eventually lethal.

The toxicity of heavy metals and their compounds, in mammalian systems, is influenced by the following factors:

1. Electrochemical character and the state of oxidation of the metal.
2. The stability, reactivity, and solubility of the metal compounds in body fluids and tissues.
3. The rate of absorption versus clearance.
3. The transport of metal compounds in blood, their distribution and retention in the tissues.
5. The ability of these heavy metals to chelate with ligands of biological macromolecules and tissue components, and the stability of these metal chelates.
6. The efficiency of the enzymatic and homeostatic mechanism which controls the absorption, excretion, distribution and retention of the toxic metal ions or compounds

The criteria for metal toxicity in mammals are growth retardation, decreased health and intellectual capability, detrimental changes in reproductive cycle with mortality of offspring, increased morbidity, pathological changes, appearance of tumors and chronic disease symptoms and decreased longevity.

The adverse effect of a metal on biological systems could be the result of an interaction of the metal with protein, leading to denaturation, an interaction with DNA, leading to a mutation, effect upon cell membranes, effect on regularity enzymes, involved in the metabolic disposition of a variety of endogenous and exogenous chemicals or even a change in the ecological system.

Environmental contamination is largely endangered by man himself and presents both cultural and genetic hazards. Just how great the potential for genetic damage is, has become evident only in very recent years. It is also now well-established that the human species pays a large price for genetic variability. Approximately one-third or all spontaneous abortions, or five per cent of all recognizable conceptions, carry a genetic abnormality. But nature reduces the number of major genetic errors in new-borns by ten-fold or approximately one in every 200 births.

Those defects (mutants) which survive, however, impose not only an economic load upon society but also bring untold human suffering, both physical and emotional. Fortunately, one half of these are sterile, and does not pollute the genetic pool.

Possible gene-influenced disorders include

1. Diabetes
2. Dwarfism
3. Hypoglycemia
4. Obesity
5. Pubertal variations
6. Hematological disorders
7. Asthma
8. Cancer of breast, lung, etc.
9. Neurological disorders.

How can we cope with this problem? In order to inhibit the increase of mutagenic in the environment, planners in environmental health sciences should ban those chemicals which are known or suspected to harmful to be human beings and which are being produced and marketed at an increasing rate, unless their safety can be ascertained. Detrimental mutations can be easily induced in the laboratory in a variety of biological systems, attesting to the occurrence of induced genetic effects in all life forms.

"About five percent of babies in West Germany have genetic defects" says a specialist on treating the handicapped. This means that, of the average 600,000 births per year in the past 20 Years, 30,000 babies are born with disorders, says Prof. Gerhard Wendt of the Foundation for the Handicapped Child. Marburg.

Chelation Therapy

The recent surge in the clinical use of chelating agents in animals and humans can, perhaps, be considered a major triumph in combating metal poisoning. The harmful effects of heavy metals have been minimized or prevented, by chemically modifying the activity of the metal, by binding it with the chelating agent. It is mandatory that physicians must be familiar with the potential dangers of these powerful agents. Therefore, toxic manifestation of the chelating agent must be taken into account. For a chelating agent to be useful in medicine, it must, of course, be non-toxic, soluble, diffusible and readily excreted.

State of World Environment

Man does not deliberately damage his own environment any more than a rational person would purposely destroy his own house. However, the results of his activities damage the environment, e.g,

1. Release of materials in the atmosphere causing ozone disbalance.
s. Effect of uranium on workers in uranium mines
3. Effect of radium on workers involved in radium work
4. Consumption of intoxicants
5. Water pollution
6. Drug abuse

All environmental pollutants which enter the human body bring about a change in the essential metabolic processes.

Man's inherent desire to improve the quality of life has led to rapid industrialization. Besides other things, it has resulted into remarkable achievements in the fields of modern chemistry and the chemical industry. The use of chemicals, whether organic or inorganic, during the past 200 years, has made possible many of the benefits which modern society enjoys. But chemicals are among the chief pollutants, and pose considerable risk to man and his environment.

Protection and Improvement of the Environment

In order to protect and improve the environment, stress must be laid on;

1. Population control
2. Inculcation of a civic sense in children at an early stage so that anti-pollution attitudes are strengthened

3. Prescription of mandatory course on environment at the school level
4. Development of a morality of consciousness.
5. Strict legislation (famous carrot and stick approach)
6. Planting of more trees which absorb environmental pollutants
7. The National Committee on Environmental Planning and Coordination, broadening its activity, rather than bringing in so many laws and not paying adequate attention to their implementation in a proper sense.

Mode of Action o! Cadmium Poisoning

Because of its known toxicity to animals, a large amount of research has been carried out to find out how and why this metal is poisonous. For this reason, this chapter will be largely devoted to cadmium. For comparative purposes, reference will also be made to other toxic metals. It is hoped, however, that by presenting the information discovered about cadmium, the reader will be able to see ways in which similar approaches could be used to examine the effects of other metals.

Cadmium enters the body through diet and by breathing air containing dust particles which themselves contain cadmium. It is a surprising finding that less than 3 percent of the cadmium in the diet is taken up by the body. This is due to a remarkable ability of the intestine to avoid absorbing this metal. The situation in the lungs, however, is quite different —here about 30 percent of the inhaled cadmium is taken up by the body. This, at once, suggests that in the case of this metal, air pollution is far more dangerous than water pollution.

Once taken up by the body, the cadmium at first circulates in the blood. The blood, however, soon interacts with two important organs, the liver and the kidneys. The cells of these organs respond to the presence of cadmium by producing a protein which binds the metal. After this, the metal is not free in solution but trapped inside the cells. This is because the protein cannot diffuse out of the cells. The protein, called thionine, is unusual, in that it contains much more sulphur than ordinary cell proteins. When combined with a metal, it is called metallothionine. It seems that the same protein can combine with metals other than cadmium too. Zinc, for example, combines with a protein which can also bind cadmium.

The presence of these protein molecules in the liver and kidney means that the cadmium inside the body is not easily excreted. In humans, this amounts to a very serious condition—accumulation. It is believed that over 20 or 30 years, very small traces of cadmium in the environment can gradually build up in the liver and the kidney tissue until finally the protein binding mechanism can no longer provide any protection. At this point, the first signs of illness begin to show up as other parts of the body become affected. The arterial portion of the blood circulation undergoes certain changes, which results in an increase in blood pressure. This is called hypertension. The chemistry of the blood itself gets altered. The concentration of glucose becomes higher. This has been proved in the experiments with mammals in the laboratory. It has even been reported in marine organisms which live in a cadmium contaminated environment. Returning to humans, it has been found that cadmium poisoning is also associated with abnormalities in bone structure due to some interference with the proper deposition of calcium in the bones.

It is important at this point to mention that in Japan (where cadmium poisoning was studied in great detail) it was mainly women who showed the symptoms. Most of these women were over 40 years old and had several children. The reason for this is that pregnancy places an additional strain on the calcium metabolism of the body. Thus, as a woman becomes older, she accumulates more and more cadmium and pregnancy results in symptoms which otherwise might be absent or much less serious.

The presence of cadmium in organs and tissues is usually detected by atomic absorption spectroscopy. This is a time-consuming method and usually involves careful digestion of the tissue samples in strong acid. In competent hands, this method can reliably measure cadmium at concentrations as low as 0.05 ppm. The equipment for the atomic absorption technique is very expensive and requires a skilled operator. It is, therefore, important to find out that cadmium can also be measured by a colorimetric method, needing only a spectrophotometer to take the final measurements. Such a method is the Dithizone method which has been used successfully for cadmium measurements on marine organisms. It remains a useful technique where atomic-absorption equipment is not available.

Much research has been carried out on the effects of cadmium within living cells. It has been found that it is potentially capable of affecting many processes in cells, simply by inactivating enzymes. The disturbance to the glucose level in the blood is possibly due to the reverse effect, the stimulation of certain enzymes. For example, some evidence has been obtained, which suggests that four enzymes which control the synthesis of glucose (by gluconeogenesis) increase their activity in the presence of cadmium.

The cells obtain their energy by the combined effects of glycolysis (glucose breakdown) and aerobic respiration in the particles, called mitochondria. Both of these processes could be inhibited by cadmium. Research in this field is hampered by the fact that in order to study the processes, the cells must first be broken up. When cadmium is added to such a system, we are dealing with artificial situation, which might not apply to the whole cell condition. For example, the protein binding mechanism may operate effectively when whole cells are exposed to cadmium.

In spite of these difficulties, evidence is being gathered which shows that respiring mitochondria are less efficient in making ATP when cadmium is added to the preparation. Whether this accurately reflects the situation in the cadmium-poisoned animal, remains to be seen. Perhaps, the more promising approach is to measure the important biochemical processes in tissues of known cadmium content, which have been taken from animals which have been feeding on a low cadmium diet. These would contain enough cadmium to produce poisoning symptoms after several weeks. Results obtained, using this approach, are more likely to provide information which applies in a real life situation.

Much has been 'earned about the cadmium-binding protein itself. The procedure here is to homogenise the tissue and, then, subject them to differential centrifugation, the tissue fragments being dispersed in a suitable solution such as isotonic saline. The various fractions are separated and the final supernatant, after the high speed centrifugation, is usually found to contain the most cadmium. This technique is best used with radioactive cadmium (^{109}Cd). When the final supernatant is treated with a protein precipitant, such as trichloracetic acid, then centrifuged, it is usually found that most of the radioactivity is in the precipitant.

If instead of precipitating the protein, we subject it to gel filtration, much more information can be obtained. In this method, the protein solution is allowed to slowly pass down a column of a substance like sephadex G-75. The mixture of protein is, thus, separated on the basis of molecular weight. The results of this type of research show that the cadmium is bound by one or two protein with a molecular weight near 10,000.

The radioactive tracer technique has shown that marine animals, which have previously encountered cadmium in their environment, have a different cadmium binding capacity when compared with similar animals from a cadmium-free environment. Another advantage of this method is that it lends itself well to autoradiography, a procedure by which a thin slice of tissue is placed in contact with a photographic film in the dark. After a period of, exposure the film is developed and the site of location of cadmium, within the tissue, is revealed by dark areas in the film. This technique requires practice and can be applied at the microscope level for proteins of tissue. For small organisms, the whole animal can be sectioned.

Most of the approaches and techniques described here can be equally applied to other heavy metals or even pesticides. In the latter case, a protective device is needed before using radioisotopes. This is because the originally labelled compounds may undergo metabolic changes and different derived compounds will confuse the results. There are fewer such problems with metals. Isotopes with reasonable half-lives are ^{51}Cr, ^{103}Hg, ^{109}Cd, ^{65}Zn and ^{210}Pb.

Plants differ in one important respect from animals, in that their heavy metal burden may be in the form of external contamination such as in dust on leaves. This may have very little effect on the plants. Damage to foliage doses, of course, take place and, here, we have a situation which is complicated by the coexistence of photosynthesis, respiration and active transport processes, all of which are interdependent to some extent. Plants have a remarkable ability to avoid taking up many toxic heavy metals from the soil. On the other hand, many multi-cellular and uni cellular aquatic plants actually concentrate these substances.

In the case of uni cellular plants, laboratory experiments are carried out to find out their tolerance levels. Their ability to take up metals is best studied by the radioactive method because, unlike the case with animals, experiments have to be conducted in a short time. Again, with uni cellular plants, the rate of photosynthesis, and respiration can be measured, using an oxygen electrode method as described for B.O.D. (Chapter 3).

The effect of adding controlled amounts of the heavy metal in solution can be observed and the amount required to inhibit or stop respiration for photosynthesis can be determined. This type of approach, using uni-cellular plants, bypasses the transport mechanisms which would complicate the interpretation of experiments using multi-cellular higher plants.

Research with multi-cellular land plants is still possible but is made more difficult because of the many interacting systems. The metabolism of plants is very much dependent on photosynthesis. To study this process in land plants requires equipment which can reliably monitor the gas exchange with the atmosphere. The special knowledge and equipment required to do this result in fewer experiments being carried out at any one time. If the metabolic effects of heavy metals on plants are disregarded, then much useful research remains to be carried out for finding the binding sites for these metals in those plants which actively take them up. This is the topic of increasing importance because plants of this type may be used to remove toxic metals from effluents.

The relevant pollutant for important industries are given in Tables 3.1 and 3.2, which indicate average values of different parameters. Some of the parameters indicated do not have any direct effect on living system, for example, BOD, which is so frequently mentioned. Biochemical Oxygen Demand (BOD) quantitatively measures the organic load on the receiving stream and very often, when an effluent with high BOD content is discharged into a river system, fishes in large numbers are found dead, due to lack of dissolved oxygen which is utilized in bio-degradation of organic matter. Similarly, suspended solids do not have any direct effect but these are considered as carriers for microbes and consequently help in spreading of water borne diseases.

Table 3.1
Characteristics of waste water from selected Industries in India

Industry	*pH*	*Suspended solids mg/l*	*BOD mg/l*	*COD mg/l*	*BOD/COD*	*BOD load per kg product*	*Other important characteristics*
1	*2*	*3*	*4*	*5*	*6*	*7*	*8*
Dairy	8.0	690	816	1340	0.6	5.7	Oil and grease, ready putrescibility.
Distillery	4.0–4.5	—	40,000	80,000	0.5	560	High TDS, Cl, SO_4 and putrescibility.
Cotton textile	7–10	375	350	525	0.66	8.75	TDS 300 mg/l, % sodium 90 and Colour.
Viscose Rayon	2.8–4.1	200	—	210	—	—	Zinc, 6-18mg/l polysulfides.
Tannery	8.0	1900	1700	3500	0.48	5.4	Cr^{+3} 0.35–0.45 kg/100 kg hide, Cl 4600 mg/l, tannin, colour.
Pulp and paper Craft process	6.5–8.2	375	160	610	0.26	50	Lignin, colour, suspended fibre.
Primary polymers	1.44–5.8	—			—		Solids.
Polythylene	1.44–5.8	—	200–4000		—		
Polypropylene	1.44–5.8	—	200–4000		—		
Polysterene	1.8–3.6	—	1000–3000		0.05–0.025		
Polyvinyl chloride	5.5–11	50–500	1000–2000		0.05–0.25		
Cellulose accetate	0.036–0.72	500–2000	1000–5000		0.4–0.5		
Butyl rubber	7.2–21.6	800–2000	2500–5000	—	0.32–0.4		

(Contd...)

(Table 3.1 *Contd.*)

Industry	*pH*	*Suspended solids mg/l*	*BOD mg/l*	*COD mg/l*	*BOD/COD*	*BOD load per kg product*	*Other important characteristics*
1	2	*3*	*4*	*5*	*6*	*7*	*8*
Miscellaneous sub-stances							
Cyanate	18.0–36	1000–2500	4000–8000		0.25–0.31		Nitrogen
Phenyl glycerine	18.0–36	1000- 2500	4000–8000		0.25-0.31		Phenol content
Parathion	10.8–28.8	1500- 3500	3000–6000		0.5–0.59		Solids, pH
Tributyl phosphate	3.6 –14.4	500–2000	1000–3000		0.5–0.67		Phosphorous
Coke oven	8.6–11.2	82	1200	2500	0.41	3.6	NH_3, phenol, CN, CNS, tar and oil.
Refinery		300	200			0.34	Free oil, 2500 mg/1 emulsified oil, 100 mg/1 mercaptane 115 mg/1
Phenol formaldehyde resin	4.0–7.0	—	23.600	32160	0.73	7.1	Phenol, 7900 mg/1 HCHO 4360 mg/1
Parathion	2.0	—	700	3000	0.23	—	TS 27000 mg/1 parathion 20 mg/1
Carbaryl	7.10	Nil	Nil	10,000	—	—	TS 40,000 mg/1, no carbaryl, low toxicity.

Table 3.2
Characteristics of waste water from some organic chemical industries

Industry	*Flow* m^3*/onne*	*BOD* *mg/l*	*COD* *mg/l*	*BOD/COD*	*Other important characteristics*
Dyes and pigments	180–900	200–400	500–2000	0.2–0.4	Heavy metals, solids, colour, pH
Primary petrochemical ethylene	0.18–54	100–1000	500–3000	0.2–0.33	Phenol, oil and pH
Propylene	0.36–7.2	100–1000	500–3000	0.2–0.33	Phenol, pH
Primary	*Intermediates*	300–2500	1000–5000	0.3–0.5	
Toluene	1.1–11.0				
Zylene	0.72–11	500–4000 ,	1000–8000	0.5	—
Methanol	1.1–11	300–1000	500–2000	0.5–0.63	Oil and solids
Ethanol	0.72–7.2	500–4000	1000–8000	0.5	Heavy metals
Ethyl benzene	1.1–11	500–3000	1000–7000	0.43–0.5	Heavy metals
Clorinated hydrocarbons	0.18–3.6	50–150	100–500	0.3–0.5	Oils solids pH
Secondary	*Intermediates*	1200–10000	2000–15000	6.63–0.67	Phenol, solids
Phenol	1.8–9				
Acetone	1.8–5.4	1200–5000	2000–10000	0.5–0.63	
Glycerine glycols	3.6–18	500–3500	1000–7000	0.5	
Terephthalic acid	3.6–10.8	1000–3000	2000–4000	0.5–0.77	Heavy metals
Urea	0.36–7.2	50–300	100–1050	0.29–0.5	
Acrylates	3.6–10.8	500–5000	2000–15000	0.25–0.33	Solids, cyanide and colour
Acetic anhydride	3.6–28.8	300–5000	500–8000	0.63	pH
Acrylonitrite	3.6–30	200–700.	500–1500	0.4–0.48	CN, colour, pH
Butadiene	0.36–7.2	25–200	100–400	0.25–0.5	Oil and solids
Styrene	3.6–36	300–3000	1000–6000	0.3–0.5	
Vinyl chloride	0.036–0.72	200–2000	500–5000	0.4	

Effluent Guidelines and Standards

The necessity for the development of realistic standards is obvious. Suitable relationships are established between the intensity, duration and frequency of exposure to pollution and the risk or magnitude of an undesirable effect occurring in the environment. Such information allows dose-response relationships to be devised. When exposure levels are low and long- term, it becomes extremely difficult to accurately develop such relationships. In the absence of scientific information, it becomes necessary to adopt other approaches based on experience and inspired guesses. Environmental health standards may be set by any of the following methods:

1. *Limit set for a pollutant taken up by an organism or a population*. These are, sometimes, known as primary protection standards. Examples are acceptable daily intakes (ADI) of toxic substances and maximum permissible index (MPI).
2. *Limit set for pollutant present in a specific environment medium or product (food or consumer products)*. Such limits are, sometimes, called desired working levels. These include standards for ambient air, and standards for water quality. When applied to products such as food, they are frequently referred to as 'product standards'.
3. *Limit set for discharges or emissions from Polluting Sources*. These Attempt to limit the release of pollutant into a medium. A well known example is the so-called royal commission standard set for sewage effluent in UK. Here, the effluent should have BOD of less than 20 mg/1 and a suspended solid content of less than 30 mg/1 and the river into which it is discharged should dilute it eight fold.

Modes of Disposal

The following paragraphs briefly review the important points of various widely practised modes of disposal of liquid effluents:

Disposal on Land

The disposal of liquid effluents on land is a common practice, but if any stagnation of liquid effluents on land is allowed, mosquitoes and flies will breed on these, resulting in health problems. The careful and well-designed disposal of liquid effluents on land helps to achieve economic drop-irrigation and soil filtration, depending on water-holding capacity of the soil, land topography, general climate and particular crop in question. Excessive application of nutrient-rich water on land, however, may pose the following problems:

1. Concentration of various constituents, causing deleterious effects on crop growth.
2. Decreased soil permeability.
3. Sewage sickness, and
4. Ground-water contamination.

With a view to maintaining the quality of effluents at par with irrigation water so as to avoid any adverse effect on the crop, soil and ground water, the industrial effluents discharged on land should not contain constituents that are likely to or do pollute ground water to an extent that it (the ground water) does not remain fit for human or animal consumption.

Disposal into Public Sewers

"The presence of certain constituents in industrial effluent may choke or damage sewers, impair the proper working of the sewage treatment plant, and where land irrigation is adopted for final disposal of the sewage, the vegetation and the soil may be adversely affected. Large amounts of sulphur compounds in effluents, for instance, would tend to form sulphuric acid under certain conditions, which would corrode the sewer. Toxic elements such as chromium, or others with a high acidity or alkalinity level and the high temperature of the effluents are, inimical to biological activity in the treatment plant. The presence of flammable and toxic volatile matter may cause explosions and be a serious hazard to the life of persons working in sewers or in the sewage treatment plants. Oils, tar and grease may stick to the sides of sewers and reduce their hydraulic capacity. It is, therefore, necessary to limit the concentration of such undesirable constituents in industrial effluents discharged into public sewers". The disposal of solids such as ash, cinder, sand, tar, lime residue, lime slurry, and garbage into public sewers is also inadmissible. In order to prevent such ill effects of untreated industrial effluents on sewers, sewage treatment plants and sewage forms, it is necessary to limit certain constituents present in the industrial effluents before allowing them to be discharged into a sewer.

Disposal into Inland Surface Waters

For the prevention and control of water pollution, the Indian Standards Institution, now called Bureau of Indian Standards (BIS), has prescribed "certain standards for the purity of water into which effluents have been discharged so that such receiving water courses could be safely used for various purposes". The water polluting contaminants of industrial effluent discharged into land surface water, may be an acid, alkali, oil or grease, a floating suspended or dissolved organic matter, a toxic or poisonous substance or a colour. As per definition hid down by the Indian Standards Institution, "By inland surface water is meant rivers, estranges stream, big lakes and reservoirs, including rivers liable to seasonal drying". The BIS further notes that "pollution of inland surface water with sewage, effluents and industrial water is important problem associated with industrial development and concentration of population in cities".

Tolerance Limits

The standards of tolerance limits have been adopted by different countries including India, depending upon each country's requirement.

India

Regarding water pollution, the standard values for some important parameters were prescribed in 1976. The values of different parameters were revised in, 1983. The characteristics with tolerance limits generally adopted in Indian, are given in Tables 3.3 and 3.4.

Table 3.3

Standards for sewage and trade effluent discharged into streams

S. No.	*Characteristics*	*General tolerance limit*	*Relaxation for specific industries*
1.	Total suspended solids, mg/1, max.	—	—
2.	Particle size of total suspended solids	Shall pass 850 micron I.S. sieve	—

(Table 3.1 *Contd...*)

S. No.	*Characteristics*	*General tolerance limit*	*Relaxation for specific industries*
3.	pH	5.5 to 9.0	5.5 to 9.0 for nitrogenous fertilizer industry
4.	Temperature	Shall not exceed 40°C in any section of the stream within 15 meters down stream from the effluent outlet	
5.	BOD for 5 days at 20°C, mg/1, max.	30	100 for existing distilleries and for existing Straw Board industry
6.	Oil and grease mg/1, max,	10	—
7.	Phenolic compounds (as C_6H_5OH) mg/1, max.	1.0	—
8.	Cyanides (as CN) mg/1, max.		0.2
9.	Sulphides (as S)mg/1, max.	2.0	—
10.	Insecticides	absent	
11.	Colour and odour	absent	absent as far as possible for paper industry
12.	Total Residual, chlorine mg/1, max	1.0	—
13.	Fluoride (as F) mg/1, max.	2.0	5 for phosphatic fertilizer industry
14.	Cadmium (as Cd) mg/1, max.	2.0	
15.	Copper (as Cu) mg/1, max.	3.0	
16.	Total Chromium (as Cr) mg/1, max.	0.5	—
17.	Hexavalent Chromium	0.1	5 for phosphatic fertilizer industry
18.	Lead (as Pb) mg/1, max	0.1	—.
19.	Mercury (as Hg) mg/1, max.	0.01	—
20.	Nickel (as Ni) mg/1, max.	3.0	—
21.	Selenium (as Se) mg/1, max.	0.05	—
22.	Zinc (as Zn) mg/1, max.	5.0	5 for phosphatic fertilizer industry
23.	Ammoniacal nitrogen (as N)	50	100 for Nitrogenous fertilizer industry
24.	Free ammonia (as NH_3)	5.0	—
25.	Total nitrogen (as N) mg/1, max.	100	150 for Nitrogenous fertilizer industry
26.	Chemical Oxygen demand, mg/1, max. 250		—
27.	Dissolved phosphate (as P) mg/1, max.	5.0	—

S. No.	*Characteristics*	*General tolerance limit*	*Relaxation for specific industries*
28.	Chlorides (as Cl) mg/1, ma:	1000	—
29.	Radio-active materials		—
	Alpha emitters mg/1, max.	10-7	—
	Beta emitters mc/ml, max.	10-6	—
30.	Arsenic (as As) mg/1, max.	0.2	1.0 for existing plants of nitrogenous fertilizer industry

Table 3.4
Standards for the effluents to be discharged on land

1.	pH	5.5-9.0	—
2.	Total dissolved (as SO_4) mg/1, max.	2100	—
3.	Sulphates (as SO_4) mg/1, max.	1000	—
4.	Chlorides (as Cl) mg/1, max.	600	—
5.	Per cent sodium, max.	60	—
6.	Biochemical Oxygen Demand for 5 days at 20°C	200	500 for existing distillery up to 1984 only
7.	Oil and grease mg/1, max.	20	—
8.	Boron (as B) mg/1, max.	2	—
9.	Cyanides (as CN) mg/1, max.	0.5	—
10.	Total chromium (as Cr) mg/1, max.	2.5	—
11.	Hexavalent chromium (as Cr), mg/1.	1.0	—
12.	Zinc (as Zn) mg/1, max.	10	—
13.	Ammoniacal nitrogen (as N) mg/1, max.	100	—
14.	Copper (as Cu) mg/1, max.	3.0	—
15.	Nickel (as Ni) mg/1, max	3.0	—
16.	Total mercury (as Hg) mg/1, max.	0.01	—
17.	Selenium (as Se) mg/1. max.	0.1	—
18.	Lead (as Pb) mg/1, max.	0.5	—
19.	Arsenic (as As) mg/1, max.	0.5	—
20.	Cadmium (as Cd) mg/1, max.	5.0	—
21.	Radio-active materials	10^{-9}	—
	Alpha emitters (μc/ml, max.	10^{-8}	
	Beta emitters μc/ml, max.		

It may be mentioned that the tolerance limit depends upon the ultimate disposal of liquid effluent, *e.g.*, soil/water stream. The values of different parameters are generally lower in case of water streams. Implementation has been rather slow both for trade as well as domestic effluents, but lately pollution control has been receiving greater attention in India.

Bureau of Indian Standards The BIS standards are intended to provide guidelines to the authorities of State and Central Governments, which would help decide on suitable restrictions on liquid effluents' disposal and to the industry for selecting an appropriate technology, suitable sites and the degree of treatment required for liquid effluents before their disposal. However, the local authorities of the State or Central Government may opt to enforce relaxed or more stringent standards depending upon the local conditions.

The BIS has prescribed standards for tolerance limits for liquid effluents of a chemical industry, including fertilizers, discharged on land for irrigation, into public sewers, into inland surface water including rivers, and into marine or coastal areas.

Table 3.5 shows the BIS standards for tolerance limits for inland surface water subject to pollution for (*i*) public water supply (*ii*) recreation and aesthetics (*iii*) fish culture, (*iv*) irrigation and (*v*) surface water (general).

Central Board for Prevention and Control of Water Pollution. The Central Board has so far not prescribed standards of tolerance limits for liquid effluents from industries. A committee has been formed to study the problems of pollution in the industry and suggest to the Central Board (*i*) suitable effluent standards for the industry and (*ii*) guidelines to take effective pollution control measures. In the meantime, the Central Board is using BIS standards to make specific recommendations and suggest guidelines for effluents standards and their disposal methods for liquid effluents from industries.

State Boards for Prevention and Control of Water Pollution. All the 14 State Boards are newly constituted and in the process of evolving their own standards of tolerance limits for liquid effluents, depending on the regional conditions related to the manufacturing units located in the respective states. Meanwhile, these boards have temporarily adopted ISI standards and recommendations, with minor changes in the effluents' standards in some cases, and issued the necessary guidelines to manufacturing units located in the respective states. Table 3.5 shows the standards of tolerance limits for liquid effluents set by some State Boards.

USA

Environmental Protection Agency (EPA) EPA of the USA has prescribed tolerance limits for liquid effluents, as given in Table 3.6.

Japan

The Environment Agency of Japan has prescribed separate standards for surface water for the protection of human health, the preservation of the living environment, (e g., rivers, lakes and waters), and liquid effluents discharged into inland surface water. Table 3.7 shows the Japanese standards for surface water and liquid effluents.

UK

There are no national standards for liquid effluents in the United Kingdom The effluents are controlled on a case-by-case system. Each discharge, from-a factory, is considered on its merits such as capacity of receiving waters to absorb the water, and the technology of abatement, and, finally, a constant, defining the allowed volume, and the concentration of the individual components (*i.e.*, water pollutants) is issued by the appropriate water authority. The tolerance limits for effluents to be discharged into sewers as prescribed by the North West Water Authority, are given in Table 3.8. The standards of tolerance limits for liquid effluents prescribed in Switzerland are given in Table 3.9.

Table 3.5
Standards for liquid effluent and inland surface water for prevention and control of water pollution

S. No.	Water quality	Type of water	Bureau of Indian Standards (BIS)	State Boards					
				Karnataka	Kerala	Maharashtra	Rajasthan	U.P.	West Bengal
1	2	3	4	5	6	7	8	9	10
1.	TSS mg/1, max.	A. Public water supply	—	—	–	—	—	—	100
		B. Recreation & aesthetic	—	—	—	–	—	100	~
		C. Fish culture	—	—	—	100	—	—	
		D. Irrigation	—	—	100	—			
		E. Surface water (general)	100	100	—	—			
		F. On land for irrigation	—	—	—				
		G. Public sewers	600	—					
2.	Particle size of TSC, micron, max.	A. Public water supply	—	—	—	—	—	—	—
		B. Recreation and aes-	—	—	—	—	—	—	—
		thetic	—	—	—	—	—	—	—
		C. Fish culture	—	850	—	—	—	—	—
		D. Irrigation	850	—	—	—	—	850	850
		E. Surface water (general)	—	—	—	—	—	—	—
		F. On land for irrigation	—	—	—	—	—	—	—
		G. Public sewers							
3.	TDS mg/1, max.	A.	—	—	—	—	—	—	—
		B.	—	—	—	—	—	—	—
		L.	—	—	—	—	—	—	—
		D.	2100	—	—	—	—	—	—
		Ei.	—	—	—	—	—	—	—
		F.	2100	—	—	—	—	2100	—
		G.	2100	—	—	—	—	—	—
4.	Temperature °C, max.	A.	—	—				—	—

(Contd. ...)

(Table 3.5 *Contd.*)

1	*2*	*3*	*4*	*5*	*6*	*7*	*8*	*9*	*10*
		B.	—	—	—	—	—	—	—
		C.	—	—	—	—	—	—	—
		D.	—	—	—	—	—	—	—
		E.	40	40	40	—	—	40	40
		F	—	—	—	—	—	—	—
		G.	45	—	—	—	—	—	—
5.	PH	A.	6.0-9.0	—	—	—	—	—	—
		B.	—	—	—	—	—	—	—
		C.	—	—	—	—	—	—	—
		D	5.6-9.0	—	—	—	—	—	—
		E.	5.5-9.0	5.5-9.0	5.5-7.0	5.5-9.0	—	5.5-9.0	5.5-9.0
		F.	5.5-9.0	—	—	—	—	5.5-9.0	—
		G.	5.5-9.0	—	—	—		—	—
6.	BOD mg/1, max.	A.	3.0	—	—	—	—	—	—
	(5 days at 20°C)	B.	—	—	—	I	—	—	30
		B.	30	30	30	100	—	30	—
		D.	500	—	—	—	—	500	—
		E.	500	—	—	—	—	—	
		F.							
		G.							
7.	COD mg/1	A.	—	—	—	—	—	—	—
		B.	—	—	—	—	—	—	—
		C.	—	—	—	—	—	—	—
		D.	—	—	—	—	—	—	—
		E.	250	250	250	250	—	—	—
		F.	—	—	—	—	—	—	—
		G.	—	—	—	—	—	—	—

1	*2*	*3*	*4*	*5*	*6*	*7*	*8*	*9*	*10*
8	Dissolved Oxygen mg/1, min	A.	—	—	—	—	—	—	—
		B.	—		—	—	—	—	—
		C.	—	—	—	—	—	—	—
		D.							
		E.				5			
		F.							
		G.							
9	Oils and greases mg/1, max.	A.	0.1						
		B.							
		C.							
		D.							
		E.	10	10	10	—	—	10	10
		F.	10					30	
		G.	100						
10	Ammonical nitrogen (as N) mg/1, max.	A.							
		B.							
		C.							
		D.							
		E.	50	50	50	50	—	50	50
		F.							
		G.	50						
11	Free ammonia (as NH_3) mg/1, max.	A.							
		B.							
		C.							
		D.							
		E.	—	102	12				
		F.							
		G.							

(*Contd. ...*)

(Table 3.5 *Contd.*)

1	*2*		*3*	*4*	*5*	*6*	*7*	*8*	*9*	*10*
12.	Nitrates (as NO_3)	A.		50						
	mg/1, max.	B.								
		C.								
		D.								
		E.								
		F.								
		G.								
13.	Sulphate	A.								
	(as SO_4) A. mg/1,	B.								
	max.	C.		1000						
		D.								
		E.		–	–	—	5	—	—	—
		F.		1000					100	
		G.		1000						
14.	Phosphate (as PO_4)	A.								
	A.mg/1, max.	B.								
		C.								
		D.								
		E.		15	15	5.0	—	—	—	—
		F.								
		G.								
15.	Sulphides (S)	A.								
	mg/1, max.	B.								
		C.								
		D.								
		E.		2.0	—	—	—	—	—	2.0
		F.						2.0		
		G.								

1	2	3	4	5	6	7	8	9	10
16.	Fluorides (F)	A.	0.5						
	mg/1, max.	B.							
		C.							
		D.							
		E.	2.0	2.0	2.0	1.0	—	2.0	2.0
		F.							
		G.							
17.	Chlorides (Cl)	A.	600						
	mg/1, max.	B.	600						
		C							
		D.							
		E.	—	1					
		F.	600	—	—	—	—	600	—
		G.	600						
18.	Cyanides (as	A.	0.01						
	CN)	B.							
	mg/1, max.	C.							
		D.							
		E.	0.2	0.2	—	—	—	0.2	0.2
		F.							
		G.	2						
19.	Lead (Pb)	A.	0.1						
	mg/1, max.	B.							
		C.							
		D.							
		E.	0.1	0.1	—	—	—	0.1	0.1
		F.							
		G.	1						

(*Contd. ...*)

(Table 3.5 *Contd.*)

1	*2*		*3*	*4*	*5*	*6*	*7*	*8*	*9*	*10*
20	Selenium (Se)	A.								
	mg/1, max.	B.								
		C.								
		D.								
		E.								
		F.								
		G.								
21	Zinc (Zn) mg/1,	A.		0.05						
	max.	B.								
		C.								
		D.								
		E.		0.05	0.05	—	—	—	0.05	0.05
		F.								
		G.								
22	Copper (Cu) mg/1,	A.								
	max.	B.								
		C.								
		D.								
		E.		5	5	5	—	—	5	5
		F.		1.5						
		G.								
23	Nickel (Ni) mg/1,	A.								
	max.	B.								
		C.								
		D.								
		E.		3.0	3.0	—	—	3.0	3.0	

1	*2*	*3*	*4*	*5*	*6*	*7*	*8*	*9*	*10*
		F.							
		G.	2						
24.	Hexavalent	A.	0.05	0.1	0.1	—	—	0.1	0.1
	chromium (Cr^{+S})	B.	0.1						
	mg/1, max.	C.	2						
		D.							
		E.							
		F.							
		G.							
25.	Cadmium (Cd)	A.	2.0	2.0	—	—	—	2.0	2.0
	mg/1, max.	B.							
		C.							
		D.							
		E.							
		F.							
		G.							
26.	Mercury (Hg)	A.	0.01	0.01	—	—	—	0.01	0.01
	mg/1, max.	B.							
		C.							
		D.							
		E.							
		F.							
		G.							
27.	Arsenic (AS)	A,	0.2						
		B..							

(Contd. ...)

(Table 3.5 *Contd.*)

1	2	3	4	5	6	7	8	9	10
	Arsenic (AS)	C.							
		D.							
		E.							
		F.	0.2	0.2	0.2	—	—	0.2	0.2
28	Sodium (Na) per cent, max.	A,							
		B.							
		C.							
		D.	60						
		E.							
		F.	60	—	—	—	—	60	60
		G.	60						
29	Phenolic compounds (C_6H_5OH) mg/l, max.	A,	0.005						
		B.							
		C.							
		D.							
		E.	1.0	1.0	—	—	—	1.0	1.0
		F.							
		G.	5						
30	Residual chlorine (Cl) mg/l, max.	A.							
		B.							
		C.							
		D.							
		E.	1	1	1	—	—	1	1
		F.							
		G.							

1	2	3	4	5	6	7	8	9	10
31.	Barium (Ba) mg/1, max.	A.							
		B							
		C							
		D.							
		E.	—	—	—	—	0.3	—	—
		F.	—	—	—	90	—	—	—
		G.							
32.	Iron (Fe) mg/1, max.	A.							
		B							
		C							
		D.							
		E.							
		F.							
		G.							
33.	Vanadium (V) mg/1, max.	A.							
		B							
		C							
		D.							
		E.	—	0.1					
		F.							
		G.							

Table 3.6
Tolerance limits for inland surface waters subject to pollution

S. No.	*Water quality*	*Type of water*	*State of*[†] *Washington USA*	*International*‡ *Water supply Association*	*Federal Water Pollution Control Act* ** *UK*
1	2	*3*	*4*	*5*	*6*
1.	pH	A. Public water supply	—	—	6.0-8.5
		B. Recreation and Aesthetic	—	—	5.0-9.0
		C. Fish culture	—	—	6.0-9.0
		D. Irrigation	—	—	4.5-9.0
		E. Surface waters (general)		—	—
2.	Dissolved solids	A. Public water supply	—	—	3.0 ppm
		B. Recreation and aesthetic	—	—	—
		C. Fish culture	—	—	4.0 ppm
		D. Irrigation	—	70% saturation	—
		E. Surface water (general)	85% saturation		—
3.	Bio-chemical Oxygen A.	A.	—	—	—
	—	B.	—	—	—
	—	C.	—	—	—
	Demand (5 days at 20"C) B.	D.	—	—	—
		E.	2.0 mg/l	4.0 mg/l	—
4.	Ammoniacal nitrogen	A.	—	—	—
		B.	—	—	—
		C.	—	—	—
		D.	—	—	—
		E.	0.5 mg/l	0.5 mg/l	—

1	*2*	*3*	*4*	*5*	*6*
5.	Chromium	A.	—	—	0.05 ppm
		B.	—	—	—
		C.	—	—	—
		D.	—	—	5-20 ppm
		E.	0.01 mg/l	0.05 mg/l	—
6.	Phenols	A.	—	—	0.001
		B.	—	—	—
		C.	—	—	—
		D.	—	—	—
		E	0.005 mg/l	0.001 mg/l	—
7.	Cyanides	A.	—	—	—
		B	—	—	0.20 ppm
		C.	—	—	—
		D	—	—	—
		E.	0.01 mg/l	0.01 mg/l	—
8.	Fluorides	A.	—	—	—
		B.	—	—	—
		C.	—	—	—
		D.	—	—	—
		E.	1.0 mg/l	—	—
9.	Chlorides	A.	—	—	—
		B.	—	—	250 ppm
		C.	—	—	—
		D.	—	—	—
		E.	20.0 mg/l	200 mg/l	—

(Contd. ...)

(Table 3.6 *Contd.*)

1	*2*	*3*	*4*	*5*	*6*
10.	Nitrates	A.	—	—	10.0 (N)Ind. NO_3 ppm
		B.	—	—	—
		C.	—	—	—
		D.	—	—	—
		E.	1.0 mg/1 above Natural	—	—
11.	Oils and greases	A.	—	—	—
		B.	—	—	—
		C.	—	—	—
		D.	—	—	—
		E.	None	None	—
12.	Lead	A.	—	—	—
		B.	—	—	—
		C.	—	—	—
		D.	—	—	—
		E.	0.02 mg/1	0.1 mg/1	—
					—
13.	Arsenic	A.	—	—	—
		B.	—	—	—
		C.	—	—	—
		D.	—	—	—
		E.	0.005 mg/1	0.2 mg/1	—
					—
14.	Selenium	A.	—	—	—
		B.	—	—	—

1	2	3	4	5	6
		C.	0.002 mg/1	0.05 mg/1	—
		D.			
		E.			
15.	Sulphates	A.	—	—	250 ppm
		B.	—	—	—
		C.	—	—	—
		D.	—	—	—
		E.	30 mg/1	—	—
16.	Temperature	A.	—	—	85°F
		B.	—	—	85°F
		C.	—	—	83°-96^{0}F for 6 h
		D.	—	—	55-85° F
		E.	Natural + 2 C	To be fixed (pending)	—
17.	Insecticides and pesticides	A.	—	—	0.001-0.1 ppm
		B.	—	—	—
		C.	—	—	Varies with organisms
		D.	—	—	—
		E.	—	—	—
18.	Electrical conductivity	A.	—	—	—
		B.	—	—	—
		C.	—	—	—
		D.	—	—	—
		E.	125% of natural	—	—

(*Contd. ...*)

(Table 3.6 *Contd.*)

1	*2*	*3*	*4*	*5*	*6*
19	Total dissoled solids	A.	—	—	550 ppm
		B.	—	—	—
		C.	—	—	—
		D.	—	—	0-5000 ppm
		E.	—	—	—
20	Boron	A.	—	—	—
		B.	—	—	—
		C.	—	—	—
		D.	—	—	—
		E.	0.3 mg/l	—	—
21	Sodium	A.	—	—	—
		B.	—	—	—
		C.	—	—	—
		D.	—	—	—
		E.	35% over natural	—	—
22	Alpha emitters	A.	—	—	—
		B.	—	—	—
		C.	—	—	—
		D.	—	—	—
		E.	USPHS.DWS	1/1	—

1	*2*	*3*	*4*	*5*	*6*	
23	Beta emitters	A. B. C. D. E.	— — — — USPHS.DWS	— — — — 10/1	1000/1 — 1000/1 1000/1 —	

† Rainbow, C. A. and R. O. Sylvester, "Methodology in Establishing Water Quality Standards", *J. Water Pollution Control Federation*, 39, (1967)

** Nemorrow, N. L., Liquid Wastes of Industries, Addison-Wesley Publishing Company, 1971 edn

‡Dr. P. K. Misra, Ph. D. *Thesis* submitted to Kanpur University.

Table 3.7

S. No.	Efficient characteristics	Surface water for protection of human health	Surface water for preservation of living environment													Liquid effluents discharged into inland surface water
			Rivers						lakes				Coastal water			
			AA	A	B	C	D	E	AA	A	B	C	A	B	C	
			Water supply class I conservation of natural environment and uses listed in A–E	Water supply class 2, fishery class I, bathing and uses listed in B–E	Water supply class 3, fishery class 2 and uses listed in D–E	Fishery class 3, industrial water class I and uses listed in D–E	Industrial water class 2, agricultural water and uses listed in E	Industrial water class 3, conservation of environment	Water supply class I, fishery class I, conservation of natural environment and uses listed in A-C	Water supply class 2 and 3, fishery class 2, bathing and uses listed in B–C	Fishery class 3, industrial water class I, agricultural water and uses listed in C	Industrial water class 2, conservation of environment	Water supply class I, fishery class I, conservation of natural environment and uses listed in A-C	Fisheries class 2, industrial water and uses listed in C	Conservation of environment	
1	*2*	*3*	*4*	*5*	*6*	*7*	*8*	*9*	*10*	*11*	*12*	*13*	*14*	*15*	*16*	*17*
1.	TSS, mg/l, max.	—	25	25	25	50	100	—	—	1	5	15	—	—	—	200
2.	pH	—	6.5	6.5	6.5	6.5	6.5	6.5	6.5	6.5	6.5	6.0	7.8	7.8	7.0	5.0
3.	BOD mg/l, max. (5 days at 20°C)	—	1	2	3	5	8	10	—	—	—	—	—	—	—	160
4.	COD mg/l, max.		—	—	—	—	—	—	1	3	5	8	2	3	8	160
5.	Dissolved oxygen mg/l, min.		7.5	7.5	5	5	2	2	7.5	7.5	5	2	7.5	5	5	

1	*2*	*3*	*4*	*5*	*6*	*7*	*8*	*9*	*10*	*11*	*12*	*13*	*14*	*15*	*16*	*17*
6.	Number of coliform groups MPN 100/1 max.	—	50	1000	5000	—	—	—	50	1000	—	—	N.D.	N.D.	—	3000
7.	Fluorides (as F) mg/1, max.	—	—	—	—	—	—	—	—	v	—	—	—	—	—	15
8.	Cyanides (as CN) mg/1, max.	N.D.	—	—	—	—	—	—	—	—	—	—	—	—	—	1.0
9.	Lead (as Pb) mg/1, max	0.1	—	—	—	—	—	—	—	—	—	—	—	—	—	1.0
10.	Cadmium (as Cd) mgA, max.	.05	—	—	—	—	—	—	—	—	—	—	—	—	—	0.1
11.	Hexavalent chromium (as Cr^{+6})	.05	—	—	—	—	—	—	—	—	—	—	—	—	—	0.5
12.	Mercury (as Hg) 1 mg/1 max.	0.0005	—	—	—	—	—	—	—	—	—	—	—	—	—	0.005
13.	Arsenic (As) mg/1, max.	0.05	—	—	—	—	—	—	—	—	—	—	—	—	—	0.5
14.	Organic phosphorus	N.D.	—	—	—	—	—	—	—	—	—	—	—	—	—	1.0
15.	PCB	N.D.	—	—	—	—	—	—	—	—	—	—	—	—	—	0.003
16.	n-Hexane extracts mg/1, max. (mineral oils)	—	—	—	—	—	—	—	—	—	—	—	N.D.	N.D.	—	5
17.	n-Hexane extracts (as oils and fats) mg/1, max.	—	—	—	—	—	—	—	—	—	—	—	—	—	—	30
18.	Zinc (as Zn) mg/1, max.	—	—	—	—	—	—	—	—	—	—	—	—	—	—	5

(Contd. ...)

(Table 3.7 *Contd.*)

1	2	*3*	*4*	*5*	*6*	*7*	*8*	*9*	*10*	*11*	*12*	*13*	*14*	*15*	*16*	*17*
19.	Copper (as Cu) mg/1, max.	—	—	—	—	—	—	—	—	—	—	—	—	—	—	3
20.	Iron (as Fe) mg/1, max.	—	—	— —			—	—	1—	—	—	—	—	—	—	10
21.	Phenolic compounds (as C_6H_5OH) mg/1, max.	—														5
22.	Chromium (as Cr) mg/1, max.	—	—	— —			—	—	—	—	—					2

N.D. — not decided

Table 3.8
UK Standards for liquid effluents discharged into sewers

Sl. no.	*Effluent characteristics*		*Tolerance limits*
1.	Temperature °C, max.		43.3
2.	pH		6 10
3.	Oils and grease mg/1, max.		50
4.	Nitrates (as N) mg/1, max.		20
5.	Sulphates (as SO_4) mg/1, max.		1000
6.	Sulphides (as S)		Zero
7.	Cyanides (as N) mg/1, max.		Zero
8.	Lead-nickel	individually or collectively mg/1, max.	10
9.	Copper-silver		
10.	Selenium (as Se)		
11.	Zinc (as Zn)		
12.	Copper (as Cu)		
13.	Chromium (as Cr)		
14.	Arsenic (as Se)		
15.	Vanadium (as V)		
16.	Cadmium (as Cd) mg/1, max.		Zero
17.	Mercury (as Hg) mg/1, max.		Zero
18.	Volatile/Toxic substances mg/1, max.		Zero

Finland

There are, at present, no consistent standards for the disposal of liquid effluents in Finland. According to the water law of Finland, the water courts set waste water standards for each plant separately and grant waste water permits for a fixed time. The criterion for Water Court permits is usually as maximum allowable amount concentration in waste water (mg/l) and/or maximum allowable amount per unit of time or of product (e.g., tonnes per day or per tonne of production). The permit may define the upper limit of noxious substances like CN, Hg, Cd, etc.

International Standards for Air Pollution Emissions

The need to harmonise national product and design standards in regard to air pollution emissions has been felt, but the establishment of a true international Emission Standard could be too restrictive. In some cases, the enforcement of certain set targets has proved impossible, resulting in extensive non-observance, and a consequent worsening of the situation.

The trend now appears to be towards the setting up of an universal air quality standard which could be related to local conditions (perhaps, based on the "best practicable means"), in order to retain the necessary flexibility, for continued improvement.

In 1972 a WHO Expert Committee on Air Quality Criteria and Guides for Urban Air Pollution reviewed all available information on air quality standards and suggested the following long-term goal. The recommendations were tentative and it was expected that they would be subject to change, as more data on dose-response relationships became available. Table 3.10 only indicates the limits below which the risk to health was considered negligible.

The ultimate aim is to achieve zero discharge of pollutants, a target which has been set, where practicable, by the Environmental Protection Agency in the USA.

Control of emission into the atmosphere is all important and not just a luxury to which developing countries cannot aspire. An attitude which considers control a luxury can prove both costly and dangerous when development escalates to the same levels as those prevailing in existing industrial countries.

Table 3.9
Swiss standard for water and liquid effluents

Sl. No	*Effluent Characteristics*	*Tolerance limits Effluent discharged into*		
		River water & industrial water	*Surface water*	*Open water Sea water*
1.	TSS, mg/1, max.	—	20	—
2.	Temperature °C, max.	25	30	60
3.	pH	—	6.5–8.5	6.5–9.0
4.	BOD (5 days at 20°C)	4	20	*
5.	COD mg/1, max.	not worth	*	*
6.	Dissolved oxygen (as 02) mg/1, min.	6	*	—
7.	Oils, fats and greases mg/1, max.	not worth	20	—
8.	Ammoniacal nitrogen (as N) mg/1, max.	0.5	*	—
9.	Free ammonia (as N) mg/1, max.	0.1	—	—
10.	Nitrates as (NO_3) mg/1, max.	25	—	—
11.	Sulphates (as SO_4) mg/1, max.	100	*	300
12.	Sulphides (as S) mg/1, max.	—	0.1	1
13.	Fluorides (as F) mg/1, max.	1	10	10
14.	Clilorides (as CI) mg/1, max.	100	*	1
15.	Cyanides (as (CN) mg/1, max.	0.01	0.1	0.5
16.	Lead (as Pb) mg/1, max.	0.05	0.5	0.5
17.	Zinc (as Zn) mg/1, max.	0.2	2	2
18.	Copper (as Cu) mg/1, max.	0.01	0.5	1
19.	Nickel (as Ni) mg/1, max.	0.05	2	2
20.	Cadmium (as Cd) mg/1, max..	0.005	0.1	0.1
21.	Mercury (as Hg) mg/1, max.	0.001	0.01	0.01
22.	Arsenic (as As) mg/1, max.	0.01	0.1	0.5
23.	Iron (as Fe) mg/1, max.	1	2	20
24.	Phenolic compounds (as C_6H_5OH) mg/1, max.			
	(*a*) with water vapour.	0.005	0.05	5
	(*b*) without water vapour	0.005	0.05	1
25.	Residual chlorine (as CI) mg/1, max.	—	0.05	0.5-3
26.	Barium (as Ba) mg/1, max.	0.5	5	*
27.	Tetravalent chromium (as Cr^4) mg/1, max.	0.01	0.1	0.5
28.	Trivalent chromium (as Cr^3) mg/1, max.	0.05	2	2
29.	Dissolved organic carbon substances-(as C) mg/1 max.	2	10.15	*

* Decided case by case

A major contributory factor to the present calmer and more thoughtful approach toward the problems of the environment has been the creation of the UN Environment Programme (UNEP), as well as the involvement of specialized UN agencies and non-governmental organizations such as the International Council of Scientific Unions (ICSU) and its Scientific Committee on Problems of the Environment (SCOPE).

Table 3.10

Pollutant	*Limit*
Sulpher oxides*	Annual mean 60 μg/m^3 98% of observations below 200 (μg/m^3
Suspended particulates*	Annual mean 40 μg/m^3 98% below 120 μg/m^3
Carbon monoxide (non-dispersive infra-red)	8 h average 10 μg/m^3 1 h max. 40 μg/m^3
Photochemical oxidants (as measured by natural buffered K1 method and expressed as ozone)	8 h average 60 g/m^3 1 h max. 120 μg/m^3

* Measured by method recommended by B.S. Institution (1963)

It is now recognized that well-designed, long-term research programmes are required to increase our understanding of environmental processes and the ways these may adversely affect certain activities. This understanding, by necessity, long in coming, is a prerequisite for effective environmental management. In the meantime, the potentially harmful effects of man's activities must be closely watched and limited in the most prudent way possible, albeit with incomplete understanding. Thus, the monitoring of the environment has two broad purposes:

* to produce data that are useful in advancing the understanding of ecosystems and their dynamics.

* to produce sufficient scientific data and information on pressing contemporary problems as are required by policy makers to assess environmental damage and contain it within generally acceptable bounds.

Environmental problems are of different magnitudes and occur on different geographical and time scales. At the global and regional levels, both UNEP and the UN agencies have an active role in monitoring. The work of the agencies is coordinated through UNEP's Global Environmental Monitoring System (GEMS) Programme Activity Centre.

The article by Munn and Cain on this issue outlines the objectives and activities of SCOPE and shows its connections with ICSU and the UN family. One of the major programme areas of SCOPE is environmental monitoring and assessment, and the focal point for this activity is the Monitoring and Assessment Research Centre (MARC) at Chelsea College, London. MARC is, in fact, a major link between UNEP monitoring activities and SCOPE and, thus, in a wider context, between the global monitoring systems being built upon the work of all the UN agencies, coordinated by UNEP/GEMS, and the relevant scientific work of ICSU unions and committees, coordinated by SCOPE.

The objective of MARC is to consolidate and advance the understanding of environmental processes and, thereby, aid in the design of monitoring systems for environmental management and research. The MARC programme provides scientific support to the foregoing programme of UNEP in general and of Earth watch/GEMS in particular.

The difficulties associated with the development of standards are very well-reflected by the wide variation of die standards, set in different countries. There is significant variation in the standards adopted by different states within the same country. This is specially true for larger countries, e.g., the United States, India, etc. The Standards accepted by the World Health Organization are also different from those which are prevalent in developing countries. While making statutory provisions for each pollutant, it is essential to consider total pollutional load vis-a-vis assimilation capacity of the receiving stream. The pollutional load depends upon the type of industries and the degree of industrialization. There is a classification of backward districts where suitable incentives, both financial and administrative, are given to encourage further industrialization. The adoption of different standards based on the principle of total pollutional load - vis-a-vis-assimilation capacity would suggest higher standards for backward region without affecting the health of the natural stream. This would encourage industrialization of such areas as per national priority.

The distribution of total pollutional load, by dispersal of industry, in case of further industrialization, and distribution of load, in case of those industries which are discharging similar effluent, also suggest the necessity for statutory provision for different industrial environment.

The next important point in this regard is the necessity for time-bound implementation of standards for each pollutant. Pollution abatement, to the extent required as per provision of the Act, may not be immediately possible due to various economical and technical reasons. Even in the case of the Environmental Protection Agency, there is such a provision. It should also be incorporated in the standards adopted in India.

4

Water Pollution and Control

A large quantity of water, used for domestic and industrial applications, requires certain specifications. The process industry, *i.e.*, the chemical and allied industry, requires a large amount of water for their condensers and coolers. The Engineering industry also requires a considerable amount of water for different applications including the generation of steam. In power houses too, water is used for generation of high pressure steam. Besides, water is used for recreation purposes.

The bulk of the water is drawn from natural stream, e.g., rivers, lakes, etc. These water reserves get contaminated due to the effluents received from industry. Sometimes its pH level is changed due to the acidic or alkaline nature of effluents. Generally, from some of the process equipments, *e.g.*, cooling towers, water emerges at an elevated temperature, causing thermal pollution. In most of these cases, water is discharged into natural stream. Many of the effluents, thus joining the river, are biologically degraded by the flora and fauna present in the river, but, then, the total pollution load should be only such that the undesirable organic load, thus received, is fully degraded biologically, *i.e.*, the total pollution load is within the assimilation capacity of the river. However, when the pollution load exceeds the assimilation capacity, the additional pollution load reduces the microbial activity and, thus, adversely affects the health of the rivers, flora and fauna. This process ultimately leads to a further reduction in the assimilation capacity and, eventually, a situation arises when the river cannot receive any more pollution load. This problems is equally important in both developing and developed nations. Water pollution has already reached serious dimensions at Kanpur, Varanasi, Delhi, Lucknow, Calcutta, etc.

This chapter deals with different sources of water pollution and their abatement. Foreign materials, either from natural or other sources, contaminate water supplies and may be harmful to life because of their toxicity and the reduction of the normal oxygen level of water. They also have aesthetically unpalatable effects and are responsible for the spread of epidemic diseases. The latter were prevalent in western countries until their cause and treatment were identified. In India, people have begun to realize the hazards of pollution and the Government is actively looking into pollution control. Many important cities and areas which, are badly affected by water pollution, are, however, still uncovered and water pollution, with industrial wastes, and particularly sewage, is still in use.

Pollutants which are directly attributed to industrial sources may be categorized as physical, chemical and biological in nature. The Government of India enacted, in March 1974, the Water (Prevention and Control of Pollution) Act to regulate water pollution in the country. A Central Board has been constituted with powers, with effect from September 1974, to take all necessary measures to effectively implement the programme.

Rapid industrialization in the country poses problems of environmental pollution and, consequently, adverse health effects. This growth, however, cannot be stunted or dwarfed.

It is, thus, a social obligation for industries to minimize pollution of water. It is also a great challenge to technologists to develop and provide feasible and economically viable equipment and techniques to industries for controlling pollution, irrespective of its location.

With regard to water pollution in India, the situation could be improved by a proper dispersal of industries, distribution of pollution load in the river and suitable physico–chemical/biological treatment of the effluents. Even good house keeping could contribute towards reducing the load to about 10–30 percent, specially in case of liquid and solid wastes. Another interesting observation is that, by and large, effluents are discharged into an aqueduct which either eventually joins the river or empties directly into it. This means that the entire quantity of effluents, discharged into the river, joins the laminar layer of the river where the flow remains minimal and naturally the dispersion is practically non–existent. Hence, the laminar zone of a river remains thoroughly polluted while the mid–stream remains almost fresh. However, the situation is different in the case of smaller rivers.

In India, during the monsoons (July–Oct), rivers are swollen and the bulk of water passing through them is considerably high. Therefore, with any amount of effluents, the dilution factor would be more than 500, which is considered satisfactory. Another point worth noting is that water during the rainy season is turbid due to the presence of dissolved solids and unsuitable for direct consumption and recreation. These points could be used to the fullest advantage while considering, pollution abatement in India.

Source of Pollution

Polluting substances in natural sources of water have their origins in a great variety of places. For convenience, these sources of contamination of natural waters are classified here as natural, agricultural, mining, municipal and industrial.

Natural Pollution

This type of pollution is either accidental or occasional. Aerial contaminants, like gases and dusts, get transferred to a body of water in the form of rainfall, soil silt, stripped from the land by heavy rainfall, or melting snow, or as soluble salts, leached from the earth by surface streams. Leachates from animal excreta, decaying bodies of plants and animals, and the decay of large quantities of organic matter as in swamps or deep ponds also introduced appreciable quantities of microorganisms.

Agricultural Pollution

Soil and silt–washings from land surfaces were mentioned earlier as a form of natural pollution; agricultural development of land may multiply the quantity of such pollution many fold. Use of fertilizers, insecticides, herbicides and weed killers, in agricultural practices, poses serious pollution problems as most of them are resistant to natural degradation. Warrick has described stream pollution that resulted in a series of fish kills, caused by the use of insecticides in the cotton fields of northern Alabama during the late summer of 1950.

Mining Pollution

Fines or tailings from ore washing are disposed off in water suspensions, which are ultimately transferred to the natural stream and which, thus, gets polluted. Iri addition to inert suspended solids, mining operations, sometimes, produce soluble toxic materials. An outstanding example of this stream pollution which is today one of our major unsolved problems, is the acid drainage from coal mines.

Municipal Pollution

Municipal wastes, mainly domestic sewage, includes the discharges from toilets, wash rooms, kitchens and similar areas in dwellings, institutions, commercial and industrial buildings. Its principal pollutional characteristics are pathogenic bacteria, suspended solids and oxygen consuming organic matter. In urban areas, these are generally disposed of collectively, thus, overburdening the receiving water sources.

Industrial Pollution

Water is an essential raw material in almost all manufacturing plants, though only a small part of it may appear in the final product. The remainder becomes a waste material contaminant, to a smaller or larger degree, depending on its usage in the plant. After entering the natural water resources, it contaminates them. Industries which are considered the principal sources of pollution may be classified as apparel, food and drugs, chemicals, materials and energy.

Effect of Effluent Natural Sources of Water

Pollution of natural waters by sewage and industrial wastes is objectionable and damaging for many reasons. Of primary importance is the possible hazard to public health and safety. Of lesser consequence but still very real are damage to aesthetic and intangible attributes of the stream and destruction of the economic value of clean natural waters. Considering all these ill aspects of water pollution, different pollution control agencies in the world have proposed limits in relation to various pollution parameters for different uses.

Effects of pollution on public health and safety, effect on aquatic and other life, damage to property and other economic losses are now briefly described.

Effect on Public Health and Safety

The principal hazards to public health, from polluted streams, are mainly due to the presence of pathogenic bacteria from domestic sewage, toxic materials (acids, alkalis, specific poison like cyanide and heavy metals, salts), and materials from industrial wastes. Danger to public health from polluted waters comes not only from direct use of the water but also from consuming food, for example, fish, that have lived in the polluted stream. Many poisonous substances are absorbed by fish, often in a concentrated form. Hence, eating of fish from polluted water may be even more hazardous than drinking the–water.

Effect on Aquatic and Other Life

Pollution of natural waters may be disastrous to fish and other organisms naturally inhabiting the stream. Organic wastes under the influence of bacterial action deplete the dissolve oxygen by consuming it in biochemical oxidation reaction. This may suffocate the fish and other aquatic animals which require the presence of an appreciable concentration of dissolved oxygen. With mild pollution, fish may acquire a flavour that renders their flesh unfit for use as food; whereas with more severe contamination; the fish sicken or die. The latter may also be a result of the presence of substances that are not in themselves toxic but cause asphyxiation by injuring the gills. Suspended solids such as silt and coal have been particularly troublesome in this respect.

Damage to Property

Discharge of acids and occasionally of other industrial wastes leads to damage of property through corrosive attack. Corrosion of steel objects such as ships, damage to concrete structures in the stream and corrosion of piping, pumps, valves and other equipments in plants, using contaminated water as cooling water, are quite common.

Other Economic Loss

Polluted streams which are used as the only source of municipal or industrial water require substantial treatment at considerable cost for the removal of suspended solids, taste, odour, color, hardness and specific chemicals present. If hot streams are used as a source of water supply, the cost of cooling is also added.

Waste Water and its Treatment

Waste water from human habitations is harmful to the environment from several points of view:

1. Spread of disease caused by bacteria, viruses and parasitic organisms.
2. Removal of oxygen from the water of rivers or lakes which receive the waste–water.
3. Poisoning of the lakes or rivers by chemicals and metals originating from industry.
4. Enrichment of the natural waters by salts such as nitrates and phosphates which, then, cause abnormal growths of algae and other plants, with undesirable results.

If untreated waste–water is allowed to enter a river, problems from most of these categories can be expected. The severity of the problem will, of course, depend on the volume of effluent and the size of the receiving river. In an extreme case, where the receiving body of water is the sea, waste–water from quite large cities, can be disposed of completely untreated. Surprisingly, few problems are encountered where this is done due to the large dilution factor involved and the tendency of sea water to kill most organisms which cause human disease. Some people do not entirely agree to this statement but, in view of economic considerations, waste–water, including sewage, continues to be disposed off in this way by coastal cities in most parts of the world.

Inland towns and cities, of course, do not always have the opportunity to dispose off their waste in a large body of water. An interesting case is that of Calcutta where a large proportion of the sewage is passed along an open ditch for many miles before eventually reaching the sea. The authorities there do not regard this as an ideal solution but alternatives are likely to be very costly.

Further inland, the treatment procedures vary from complete (primary and secondary) measures to no treatment at all. Where there is little or no treatment, the harm done to the environment is bound to depend on the size of the population centres and the size of the river which is receiving the effluent. Of course, it is the size of the river, especially in the dry season, which is important. This goes against the opinion, sometimes, voiced that a flood– plain river Ganga can receive large amounts of pollution because it is all washed out each rainy season.

This point of view may apply, to some extent, to inorganic pollutants such as some metals which require years to build up to toxic levels. One could, then, expect the flooding to slow down their accumulation in the river's environment. The situation is quite different, however, with biological pollutants. Here, we are dealing with infectious agents which can produce their effects (in the spread of disease) within hours of entering the drinking water. Though the danger will be reduced, in the rainy season, due to dilution, this could be more than offset by the danger of contamination of drinking water by flood water.

One of the most obvious and immediate effects of pollution from a town or city sewage is the removal of oxygen from the waters of the receiving stream. Oxygen measurements upstream and, at some distance, from any sewage, inlet down stream, will demonstrate this quite clearly. In fact, city effluents, which can be described as a suspension or solution or organic materials, and living organisms contribute to a heavy organic load. The organic material provides an unlimited supply of food for micro–organisms existing in the river. Unfortunately, in order to consume the organic material, the majority of these micro–organisms require oxygen which they consume at a faster rate than its rate of diffusion into the river from the atmosphere. Thus, the oxygen content is depleted, rendering it unsuitable for most forms of aquatic life. However, if no further organically rich effluents enter the river, it will gradually recover and its oxygen content will return to normal through the natural fortification mechanism for dissolved oxygen, *i.e.*, diffusion. The ability to recover is, of course related to such factors as the size of the river, compared with the volume of effluent.

Waste Water Treatment

The foregoing discussion has concentrated mainly on dissolved organic matter and its consequences for dissolved oxygen in the aquatic environment, which receives the efficient. Many other materials notably bacteria and dissolved inorganic salts may also be present which can cause problems in the environment. Methods are known, which can completed in purify waste water, even sewage, to such an extent that it can be safe for drinking. Such procedures are, however, only justifiable in the case of a large city with a limited supply of water, because the cost of the installation is extremely high. Also, expensive is the process for primary and secondary treatment, including activated sludge digestion. This involves the removal of nearly all particles and organic matter present but excludes the dissolved salts, many of which are plant nutrients. Bacteria, however, tepid to survive this treatment in enough numbers to constitute a possible health hazard in the seffluent. The same applies to viruses, in particular, the hepatitis virus. The high temperature anaerobic sludge digestion process, which can yield methane as a useful product is a desirable addition to a waste–water–treatment plant. It tends to kill the disease causing organisms. Once again, however, capital costs are considerable and high energy is required to make the plant function. Exceptions to this statement are plants where waste used as fuel to power the machinery.

The trickling filter is a surprisingly effective machine for treating waste water and sewage which has first passed through a primary settling tank. If properly designed, it required no power input and the rotating arms of the sprinkler are moved by momentum of the water. This requires a pressure of about 60 cms. The gravel bed, beneath the sprinkler, become colonised by a large number of organisms which effectively remove most of the matter. The effluent, however, after this process, will still contain large amounts of plant nutrients. Capital costs are also significant and the capacity of the system is not large enough for very large communities.

The stabilization pond or oxidation pond is another method of treatment. Compared with the methods describe above, these ponds have, somewhat, lower BOD loadings. They rely on the activity of micro–organisms in a large body of water, about 1 m deep. Particular use is made of microscopic plants. The organic matter is first consumed by aerobic bacteria and oxygen is supplied from both the atmosphere and plants during the day. The stabilization pond works best where temperatures are high and there is abundance of sunshine. Hence, their obvious advantage lies in India. The effluent can be quite low in organic matter but bacteria and parasite eggs remain a problem. This is a pity in view of the potential use of the nutrient–rich water for irrigation.

The health hazard, still present, in the stabilization pond–effluent, can be greatly reduced by growing crop, not used as food, cotton or crops grown on trees, including coconuts and citrus fruits. Much work of this kind has been carried out by N.E.E.R.I. at Nagpur. A good account of this has been given by Sundaresan[4]. The details of the rearing of edible fish, in the effluent from stabilization ponds, are also included. Other criteria for evaluating and comparing the performance of stabilization ponds in India are given by Bopardikar[5] and Dave and Jain[6].

The general opinion seems to be that their low cost, ease of maintenance and possible integration with some types of agriculture and fish production, makes the stabilization pond a practical choice. However, extreme care will be necessary to make sure that the potential disease causing organisms and parasites are kept in control. The complete treatment of waste water is usually divided into three stages. These are called primary, secondary and tertiary treatments. The final level of purity depends on the economics of the situation. It would naturally cost more to refine the water after the second and third stages so as to make the water fit for drinking.

Primary Treatment

Waste water usually contains large quantities of floating rubbish such as cans, cloth and wood. These larger objects are removed by metal bars which act like strainers as the water moves beneath them in an open channel. The velocity of the water is, then, reduced in a grit– settling chamber of a larger size than the previous channel. This results in most of the grit and sand settling at the bottom. Periodically, this settling chamber is disconnected from the main system and the grit is removed manually.

The smaller and lighter particles take longer time to settle under gravity. This slower process takes place in the primary sedimentation tanks. Such tanks are quite large and are usually circular with a bottom shaped like a shallow cone.

At the bottom of the cone, the sediment or sludge is drained away by a horizontal pipe. Rotating scrapers slowly scrape the sludge from the sloping sides, moving it gradually from the perimeter to the centre where it is drained off as described above. The disposal of this primary sludge can be a problem because of its offensive smell. It also has a water content of over 95 percent . It must be dried before it can be disposed of on land. Alternatively, it may be digested by the method described below under the heading "sludge digestion". The liquid effluent from the primary sedimentation tanks has now lost over half of its original suspended matter. This effluent may be drained directly into a river or the sea if other considerations permit this.

Secondary Treatment

The suspended particles, remaining after primary treatment, are too fine to be removed by a simple sedimentation process. This would take far too long and much of the material is colloidal and would never settle down. Most of this material is, however, organic and this means that certain micro–organisms can consume it as food. The carbon chains of the large organic molecules are, thus, broken down to smaller molecules such as carbon dioxide. This can be accomplished in a trickling filter or in an activated sludge digester.

A large area of land is required for trickling filters and they, sometimes, cause problems because they attract insects and emit an undesirable smell. They have the advantage, however, of needing very little maintenance once they are working. They also operate without electricity.

Incoming waste water (after primary treatment) is sprayed over circular filter beds by a rotating boom. This is a pipe with holes along its length and the water emerges in horizontal jets. The reaction to these jets causes the boom to rotate; thus, no additional power is required. The water is kept at the required pressure head by a type of siphon at the inlet.

The filter bed is usually about 1.5 m deep and surrounded by a circular brick wall. The filter consists of various combinations of stony material or even plastic material. The stones should, if possible, be round and between 3 and 10 cms in diameter. Stones of irregular shape can, however, be used. One of the problems which could be faced, if the organisms, which grow on the stones, eventually block the filters is too much effluent of high B.O.D. is applied. If the B.O.D. is too high at certain times in the days it can be diluted by recirculating some of the low B.O.D. effluent which emerges from the bottom of the filter. The bottom of the filter must allow free entry of air, and, for this reason, it is usually provided with a floor of perforated tiles under which the incoming air passes. This air makes its way up through the porous filter–bed to the upper surface.

It is important to note that trickling filters, like other forms of secondary treatment, require aerobic conditions. If there is lack of oxygen, the wrong types of organisms would develop and toxic materials would find their way into the final effluent. Under ideal conditions, the filter bed should provide a home for a wide variety of organisms including bacteria protozoa, fungi, worms and insects. The upper surface will also be colonized by algae.

The Activated Sludge Process

Where large volumes of effluent have to be treated and where more trained personnel are available, the output from the primary treatment is usually treated by the activated sludge process. The object here is to provide oxygen to a large volume of effluent after primary treatment. The aeration can be carried out by forced air or mechanical stirrers. The water is kept in constant turbulent motion, in concrete tank, which are 5 m deep and 10 m wide. The length is 50–100 m.

The result of this process is to suspend an enormous number of sludge particles and organic material in an aerobic environment. Each particle, then, becomes colonised by aerobic micro-organisms. There are also, of course, unattached micro-organisms of various kinds. If the system were non-aerated, the organisms would not flourish and the organic carbon would not be consumed. An anaerobic system would take over which, would be very undesirable.

It is important to note that the incoming water does not contain sludge. Therefore, the tanks must be constantly fed with sludge to provide the suspended particles without which the process would be much slower. Sludge from the final settling-tank is recycled to the extent of about 20 percent of the incoming volume to the aeration tank. Surplus sludge will eventually accumulate in the final settling-tank and this has to be disposed off, or can sometimes be used as fertilizer after drying. Alternatively it can be piped to a quay, and transferred to a special ship or barge. It is, then, dumped at sea. Sometimes, it is pumped directly into the sea through a pipe.

Sludge Digestion

An attractive alternative to sludge disposal is the digestion of sludge in the absence of oxygen at 35°C. Under these conditions (known as mesophilic), the micro–organism convert the organic matter, including the gas methane, into simpler compounds. About 2/3 of the sludge, in one batch, is consumed in this way, and the process is completed in about three weeks. The methane has fuel value and can be burned to provide the heat required to warm the digestion tanks. In large installations, there is sufficient methane to power generators which provide enough electricity to run all the installations, including the pumps and stirrers for the activated sludge digesters earlier.

The sludge which remains after digestion is inoffensive. Sludge digesters are not simple to operate and careful attention must be paid to the ingredients of the incoming material. Sometimes, it takes a long time for the correct conditions to be reached inside the tank and careful monitoring is needed to keep the biological conditions optimal.

Tertiary Treatment

This is aimed at removing dissolved materials which have survived the primary and secondary treatment. The most important solutes are compounds of phosphorous and nitrogen. Phosphorous is more important than nitrogen in causing eutrophication, which is the process which results in excessive and undesirable growth of plant life in lakes and harbours. Other toxic substances may also be present and special processes are used in each case. The end result should be water which is suitable for drinking.

Phosphorus can be removed by precipitation with coagulants such as $A1_2(S0_4)_3$ and $FeCl_3$. This is, sometimes, carried out in the activated sludge step of the secondary treatment, but, in true tertiary treatment, this precipitation is a separate process. Lime, as $Ca(OH)_2$, can also be used to precipitate phosphorus.

Nitrogen is more difficult to remove than phosphorus, but, where it is in the form of NH_3, it can be tripped by air at pH 11.0. This means that effluent, from the lime treatment, is particularly suitable for ammonia removal.

Apart from nitrogen and phosphorus, there are a variety of substances which contribute to the appearance and even the taste of the water. These can be removed by filtration through certain media, including activated charcoal. The charcoal can be reactivated and reused.

Many of the substances, which require removal by tertiary treatment, can theoretically be removed by biological processes, particularly in conjunction with the activated–sludge–step of the secondary treatment. Care must be taken, however, not to upset the chemistry to such an extent that the beneficial organisms are harmed. In conditions of adequate sunlight, plants such as algae can consume phosphate and nitrates. For this to be effective, the plants have to be removed at regular intervals. If successful, this method will have the added advantage when aquatic plants can accumulate, and, thus, remove toxic metals.

Industrial Waste Treatment and Disposal

As a consequence of rapid industrialization in the post–independence period, prior to which our economy was largely agrarian, the problem of industrial effluent has grown significantly. Since a large majority of industries are water–based, a considerable volume of waste–water emanates from them. As industrial effluents are as varied in nature as industries themselves, the problem gets further aggravated as no standard procedure for treatment can be recommended. For a variety of reasons, industrial effluents are generally discharged into water courses, either untreated or inadequately treated. This has created a problem of surface and subsoil water pollution. The pressure on our water resources is, therefore, two fold:

1. Requirement of a large volume of water for industry.
2. In availability of clear water, because of pollution, due to discharge of waste waters.

It, therefore, becomes imperative that industrial effluents are adequately treated so as to become largely innocuous. Industrial wastes, their origin and characteristics are given in Table 4.1.

Pollutional Characteristics of Wastes

The characteristics of waste water, from some important industries in India, are given in Tables 4.2 and 4.3. By preparing an inventory of industries, contributing to the pollution capacity of each unit, the total pollution load can be determined with the help of Tables 4.2 and 4.3. The inventory, thus, prepared will also indicate the contribution from each industry.

The pollutional characteristics of industrial wastes have been divided into three main categories: physical, chemical and biological.

Physical Characteristics

The most important physical characteristics of waste water is its total solids content, which is composed of floating matter, matter in suspension, colloidal matter and matter in solution. Other physical characteristics include temperature, colour and odour.

Chemical Characteristics

Most of the chemical pollutional characteristics are produced by dissolved materials; colour, taste, odour, pH, electrical conductivity, hardness, frothing, all of which are associated with chemical properties of the dissolved substances.

Biological Characteristics

Micro–organisms are mainly responsible for defining biological characteristics. The principal groups of organisms, found in surface and waste water, are classified as protista, plants and animals. The first category includes bacteria, fungi, protozoa and algae. Seed plants, ferns and liverworts are classified as plants. Invertebrates and vertebrates are classified as animals. Except for bacteria and fungi, other micro–organisms are absent in industrial effluents.

Treatment of Industrial Effluents

Industrial waste treatment should be handled in a systematic and planned way. The following steps are. necessary:

1. The analysis of each effluent with its rate of flow should be carried out to determine the daily, monthly and yearly average. Any proposed expansion of the plant should also be considered. While finalizing the capacity of the waste (treatment plant), average volume over a period of 24 hours should be taken. It is also essential to know the variation in concentration by repeated analysis of the waste.

2. Identification of pollutants, total pollution load with the assistance of flow rate and quantity should be determined.
3. The concentrated effluents should be separated and treatment programmes should be separately planned for concentrated as well as dilute effluents.
4. Material balance with regard to raw materials, intermediates and finished products should be used to verify the position.

The treatment methods can be classified into three main categories:

1. Physical treatment 2. Chemical treatment 3. Biological treatment.

Physical Treatment

This includes devices like

1. Coarse or fine screens as well as bar screens to remove bricks, wood pieces, paper, cloth, rags, etc.
2. Communicating devices like grinders, cutters or shredders which are employed to break up solid material.
3. Grit chambers are employed as the name suggests, to arrest sand, dust, stones, cinders and other heavy inorganic settleable material.
4. Grease traps are used to remove unemulsified oil and grease from the effluents.
5. Plain sedimentation tanks are employed to primarily remove suspended organic solids from the waste waters, prior to biological treatment. These tanks could be either rectangular or circular.

Chemical Treatment

This includes processes like neutralisation, coagulation and flocculation, and chemical destruction of toxic substances like cyanides.

Biological Treatment

As the name indicate, this process harnesses natural fauna and flora, both micro and macro, for the treatment of waste waters. Since most of the industrial effluents are deficient in one or the other essential nutrient, it is always advantageous to biologically treat them in conjunction with sewage, which provides not only the nutrients but also a heterogenous population of bacterial flora, required for the breakdown of the pollutants.

A variety of operations, either singly or in combination, may be employed for the treatment of effluent. Various methods of treatment are given in Table 4.4. The choice of the method of treatment is determined by the a conditions of each situation such as

1. The character of waste
2. Circumstances pertaining to the body of the water being used for final disposal
3. State Health Department requirement
4. The cost of the plant and its operation.

While selecting the final method, it is also essential to determine techno–economic feasibility. The approximate cost estimates for industrial waste treatment is given in Tables 4.5–4.8. For instance, the anaerobic treatment process has proved to be very effective for high–organic wastes like distillery wastes, tannery wastes, slaughter–house wastes, etc. The aerobic process is particularly useful for waste waters, which are not very rich in organic content, like municipal water, dairy wastes, etc. Quite often, the anaerobic process has to be followed by the aerobic process for complete or near–complete treatment of waste waters.

Table 4.1

Summary of industrial wastes: Their origin, character and treatment

Industries producing wastes	*Origin of major wastes*	*Major characteristics*	*Major treatment and disposal methods*
1.	*2.*	*3.*	*4.*
1. Textiles	Cooking of fibers, desizing of fabrics	Highly alkaline, coloured, high BOD and temperature, high suspended solids	Neutralisation, chemical precipitation, biological treatment, aeration and trickling filtration
2. Leather goods	Unhairing, soaking, deliming and bating of hides	High total solids, hardness, salt, sulfides, chromium, pH precipitated lime and BOD	Equalisation, sedimentation and biological treatment
3. Laundry trades	Washing of fabrics	High turbidity, alkalinity and organic solids	Screening, chemical precipitation, flotation and absorption
4. Canned goods	Trimming, cutting, juicing and blanching of fruits and vegetables	High in suspended solids, colloidal and dissolved organic matter	Screening, lagooning, soaking absorption or spray irrigation
5. Dairy products	Dilutions of whole milk, separated milk, butter milk and ghee	High in dissolved organic matter, mainly protein, fat and lactose	Biological treatment by trickling filtration, activated sludge
6. Brewed and distilled beverages	Steeping and pressing grain, residue from distillation of alcohol condensated from stillage evaporation	High in dissolved organic solids, containing nitrogen or their fermented products	Recovery, concentration centrifugation and evaporation, trickling filtration; used feeds, in feeds, digestion of slops
7. Meat and poultry products	Stockyards, slaughtering of bones and fats, residues of concentrates, grease and wash water, picking of chickens	High in dissolved and suspended organic matter, blood, other proteins and fats	Screening, settling and/or flotation, trickling filtration
8 Animal feedlots	Excreta from animals	High in organic suspended solids and BOD	Land disposal and anaerobic lagoons

Contd...

Table 4.1 (*Contd..*).

1.	*2.*	*3.*	*4.*
9. Beet sugar	Transfer, screening and juicing water, drainings from lime.	High in dissolved and suspended organic matter containing sugar and protein.	Reuse of waters, coagulation and lagooning.
10. Pharmaceutical products	Mycelium, spent filtrate and wash waters.	High in suspended and dissolved organic matter, including vitamins.	Evaporationand drying feed.
11. Yeast	Residue from yeast filtration.	High in solids (mainly organic) and BOD.	Anaerobic digestion, trickling filtration.
12. Pickles	Lime water, brine, alum and turmeric, syrup, seeds, and pieces of cucumber.	Variable pH, high suspended solids, colour, and organic matter.	Good house keeping, screening equalisation.
13. Coffee	Pulping and fermenting of coffee bean.	High BOD and suspended solids.	Screening, settling and trickling filtration.
14. Fish	Rejects from centrifuge, pressed evaporator and other wash water wastes.	Very high BOD, total organic solids and odour.	Evaporation of total waste; large remainder to sea.
15. Rice	Soaking, cooking and washing of rice.	High BOD, total and suspended solids (mainly starch).	Lime coagulation, digestion.
16. Soft drinks	Bottle washing, floor and equipment cleaning; syrup storage tank drains.	High pH, suspended solids and BOD.	Screening, plus discharge in municipal sewer.
17. Bakeries	Washing and greasing of pans; floor washings.	High BOD, grease floor washings, sugar, flour and detergents	Amenable to biological oxidation.
18. Water pollution	Filter, backwash, lime soda sludge, brine; alum sludge.	Minerals and suspended solids.	Direct discharge to streams or indirectly through hold lagoons.

1.	2.	3.	4.
19. Pulp and paper	Cooking, refining, washing of fibers, screening of paper pulp.	High or low Ph, colour, high suspended colloidal and dissolved solids inorganic filters.	Settling, lagooning, biological treatment, aeration, recovery of products.
20. Photographic	Spent solutions of developer and fixer	Alkaline, containing various organic and organic reducing agents.	Recovery of silver; discharge of wastes into municipal sewer.
21. Steel	Coking of coal, washing of blast furnace, fuel gases, pickling of steel.	Low pH, acids, cyanogen, phenol and ore, cokes, lime stone, alkali, oils mill scale, and fine suspended solids.	Neutralisation, recovery reuse, chemical coagulation.
22. Metal–plating	Stripping of oxides, cleaning and plating of metals.	Acid metals, toxic, low volume mainly mineral matter.	Alkaline chlorination of cyanide; reduction and precipitation of chromium; lime.
23. Iron–foundry	Wasting of used sand by hydraulic discharge.	High suspended solids, mainly sand, some clay and coal.	Selective screening, drying of reclaimed sand.
24. Oil fields and refineries	Dulling muds, salt, oil and some natural gas; acid sludge and miscellaneous oils from refining.	High dissolved salts from high BOD, oduor, phenol and sulfur compounds from refinery.	Diversion, recovery, acidification and burning of alkaline sludge. Leak and spill prevention, flotation.
25. Fuel oil use	Spills from fuel tank, filling waste; auto crank case oils.	High in emulsified and dissolved fats.	Diversion, recovery, acidification and burning of alkaline sludge. Leak and spill prevention, flotation.
26. Rubber	Washing of latex, coagulated rubber, exuded impurities from crude rubber.	High BOD and odour, high suspended solids, variable pH, high chlorides.	Aeration, chlorination, sulfonation, biological treatment.
27. Glass	Polishing and cleaning of glass.	Red colour, Alkaine non–settleable suspended solids.	Calcium chloride precipitation.

Contd...

Table 4.1 (*Contd..*).

1	*2*	*3*	*4*
28. Naval Stores	Washing of stumps, drop solution, solvent recovery, and oil recovery water.	Acid, high BOD.	By product recovery equalisation recirculation and trickling filtration.
29. Glue manufacturing	Lime wash, acid washes, extraction of nonspecific proteins.	High COD, BOD, pH, chromium periodic strong mineral acids.	Amenable to aerobic treatment and flotation.
30. Wood preserving	Steam condensates.	High in COD, BOD, solids, phenols.	Chemical coagulation, oxidation, pond and other aerobic biological treatment.
31.Candle manufacturing	Wax spills, stearic acid condensates.	Organic (fatty) acid.	Anaerobic digestion.
32. Plywood manufacturing	Glue washing	High BOD, pH, phenols, potential toxicity.	Settling ponds, incineration.
33. Acids	Dilute wash waters, many varied dilute acids.	Low pH, low organic content.	Upflow or straight neutralisation, burning when some organic matter is present.
34. Detergents	Washing and purifying soaps and detergents.	High in BOD and saponified soaps.	Flotation and skimming, precipitation with $CaCl_3$.
35. Com starch	Evaporator condensate or bottoms when not reused or recovered, syrup from final washes, wastes from bottling–up process.	High BOD and dissolved organic matter, mainly starch and related material.	Equalisation, biological filtration, anaerobic digestion.
36. Explosives	Washing TNT and gun–cotton for purification, washing and pickling of cartridges.	TNT, coloured, acid, odorous and contains organic acids and alcohol from powder and cotton, metals, acid, oils and soaps.	Flotation, chemical precipitation, biological treatment, aeration, chlorination. neutralisation, adsorption.

1	*2*	*3*	*4*
37. Pesticides	Washing and purification products such as 2, 4, D and DDT.	High organic matter, benzene ring structure, toxic to bacteria and fish, acid.	Dilution storage, activated carbon absorption, alkaline chlorination.
38. Phosphate and phosphorcus	Washing, screening, floatation rock, condenser bleed off.	Clays and slimes, low pH, high suspended solid, phosphorcus, silica and flouride.	Lagooning, mechanical clarification, coagulation and settling of refined waste.
39. Formaldehyde	Residues from manufacturing synthetic resins and from dyeing synthetic fibres.	Normally high BOD and HCHO, toxic to bacteria in high concentrations.	Trickling Alteration, absorption on activated charcoal.
40 Plastics and resins	Unit operations from polymer preparation and use; spills and equipment wash downs.	Acids, caustic dissolved organic matter such as phenols formaldehyde etc.	Discharge to municipal sewers, reuse; controlled discharge
41. Steam power	Cooling water, boiling blow–down coal drainage.	Hot, high volume, high inorganic and dissolved solid.	Cooking by aeration, store of ashes, neutralisation.
42. Coal processing	Cleaning and classification of coal, leaching and sulphur started with water.	High suspended solids, mainly coal, low pH, high H_2SO_4, and D_2SO_4.	Excess acid waste settling, froth flotation, drainage control and sealing of mines.
43. Nuclear power and radioactive materials	Processing ores, laundering of contaminated clothes; research lab wastes, processing of fuel, powder plant cooling waters.	Radioactive elements can be very hot 'acid'.	Concentration and containing of dilution and dispersion.

Table 4.2
Characteristics of waste water from selected Industries in India

Industry	*Flow*	*pH*	*Suspended solids (mg/1)*	*BOD mg/1*	*COD mgll*	*BOD COD*	*BOD load per kg product*	*Other important characteristics*
1	*2*	*3*	*4*	*5*	*6*	*7*	*8*	*9*
Dairy	7 m^3/m^3 milk	8.0	690	816	1340	6.6	5.7	Oil and grease ready putrescibility
Distillery	14 m^3/m^3 rectified spirit	4.0–4.5	—	40,000	80,000	0.5	560	High TDS, Cl, SO_4, and putrescibility
Cotton textile	25 m^3/1000 metre cloth	7–10	375	350	525	0.66	8.75	TDS 300 mg/11, % sodium 90 and Colour
Viscose rayon	570 m^3/tonne	2.8–4.1	200	—	210	—	—	Zinc, 6–18 mg/l, polysul–fides
Tannery	3.2 m^3/1000 kg hide	8.0	1900	1700	3500	0.48	5.4	Cr^{+3} 0.35–0.45 kg/100 kg hide, Cl 4600 mg/1, tannin, colour
Pulp and paper craft process	310 m^3/tonne	6.5–8.2	375	160	610	0.26	50	Lignin, colour, suspended fibre
Primary polymers polythylene	—	1.44–5.8	—	200–4000	—	—	—	Solids
Polypropylene	—	1.44–5.8	—	200–4000	—	—	—	—
Polystyrene	—	1.8–3.6	—	1000–3000	—	0.05–0.025	—	—
Polyvinyl chloride	—	5.5–11	50–500	1000–2000	—	0.05–0.025	—	—
Cellulose acetate	—	0.036–0.72	500–2000	1000–5000	—	0.4–0.5	—	—
Butyl rubber	—	7.2–21.6	800–2000	2500–5000		0.32–0.4	—	—

1	2	3	4	5	6	7	8	9
Miscellaneous substances								
Isocyanate	—	18.0–36	1000–2500	4000–8000	—	0.25–0.31	—	Nitrogen
Phenyl glycerine	—	18.0–36	1000–2500	4000–8000	—	0.25–0.31	—	Phenol conter
Parathion	—	10.8–28.8	1500–3500	3000–6000	—	0.5–0.59	—	Solids, pH
Tributyl phosphate	—	3.6–14.4	500–2000	1000–3000	—	0.5–0.67	—	Phosphorous
Coke oven	3 m^3/tonne of coke	8.6–11.2	82	1200	2500	0.41	3.6	NH_3, phenol, CN, CNS, tar and oil.
Refinery	1.7 m^3/tonne oil processed		300	200			0.34	Free oil, 2500 mg/1 emulsified oil, 100 mg/1 mercaptane 115 mg/1
Phenol–formaldehyde resin	30.0 m^3/tonne oil	4.0–7.0	—	23,600	32160	0.73	71	Phenol, 7900 mg/1, HCH0 4360 mg/1
Parathion	—	2.0	—	700	3000	0.23	—	TS 27000 mg/1, parathion 20 mg/1
Carbaryl	-------	7.10	Nil	Nil	10,000			TS 40,000 mg/1, no carbaryl, low toxicity

Table 4.3

Characteristics of waste water from some Organic Chemical Industries

Industry	*Flow* m^3*/tonne*	*BOD* *mg/l*	*COD* *mg/l*	*BOD* / *COD*	*Other important characteristics*
1	*2*	*3*	*4*	*5*	*6*
Dyes and pigments	180–900	200–400	500–2000	0.2–0.4	Heavy metals, solids, colour, pH
Primary petrochemical ethylene	0.18–5.4	100–1000	500–3000	0.2–0.33	Phenol, oil and pH
Propylene	0.36–7.2	100–1000	500–3000	0.2–0.33	Phenol, pH
Primary	*Intermediates*				
Toulene	1.1–11.0	300–2500	1000–5000	0.3–0.5	
Xylene	0.72–11	500–4000	1000–8000	0.5	
Methanol	1.1–11	300–1000	500–2000	0.5–0.63	Oil and solids
Butanol	0.72–7.2	500–4000	1000–8000	0.5	Heavy metals
Ethyl benzene	1.1–11	500–3000	1000–7000	0.43–0.5	Heavy metals
Chlorinated hydrocarbons	0.18–3.6	50–150	100–500	0.3–0.5	Oils, solids. pH
Secondary	*Intermediates*				
Phenol	1.8–9	1200–10000	2000–15000	6.63–0.67	Phenols, solids
Acetone	1.8–5.4	1200–5000	2000–10000	0.5–0.63	
Glycerine glycols	3.6–18	500–3500	1000–7000	0.5	
Terepthalic acid	3.6–10.8	1000–3000	2000–4000	0.5–0.77	Heavy metals
Urea	0.36–7.2	50–300	100–1050	0.29–0.5	
Acrylates	3.6–10.8	500–5000	2000–15000	0.25–0.33	Solids, cyanide and colour
Acetic anhydride	3.6–28.8	300–5000	500–8000	0.63	PH
Acrylonitrite	3.6–30	200–700	500–1500	0.4–0.48	CN, colour, pH
Buradiene	0.36–7.2	25–200	100400	0.25–0.5	Oil and solids
Styrene	3.6–36	300–3000	1000–6000	0.3–0.5	
Vinylchloride	0.036–0.72	200–2000	500–5000	0.4	

Table 4.4

Unit operations and their applications in environmental pollution control

Unit operation	*Principles involved*	*Application*	*Efficiencies and merits of the process*	*Remarks*
1	*2*	*3*	*4*	*5*
Sedimentation	Under the influence of gravitational force, suspended substances with higher specific gravity values get deposited to the bottom, while with lesser values float to the medium of suspension.	To remove suspended solids.	Rate of settling depends upon size and specific gravity (density) of the particles and viscosity and specific gravity of the medium of suspension.	Dissolved and colloided particles are not influenced.
Filtration (a) Screening	Particles when allowed to pass through screen of lesser pore diameter, get retained on the surface.	To separate solids with comparatively larger dimensions.	This operation is faster than sedimentation and the percentage of removal varies almost directly with pore size of the screen. Solids recovered are nearly dry.	Only coarser particles are separated.
(b) Bed filtration	Physical process of solid retention in a bed filtration, is a combination of at least three actions : i) Particles larger than the filter medium opening cling to the filter. ii) Particles, smaller than the openings in the filter medium, get absorbed into the filter. iii) Particles of different sizes cling to already filtered, caked material.	Drying of sludge.	Efficiency of process depends upon construction of bed, (absorptive property, size, packing and length of bed material), type of effluent to be filtered (pH) viscosity and surface tension, and pressure head.	Finite particles, and certain dissolved and colloidal substances are also removed.

Contd...

Table 4.4 (*Contd..*).

1	2	3	4	5
Flotation	By attachment of an air bubble to or inclusion in a suspended solid structure of liquid phase, the bulk density of the paired system may be less than the density of the parent system causing the agglomeration floated to the top.	To convert finite suspended solids and some colloidal emulsified and dissolved substances to floating matter.	Detention time and temperature are two important factors which define the effectiveness of the process. Satisfaction of immediate oxygen demand, associated with partially reduced compounds of the effluent, and minimization of odour nuisance are the merits of the process.	
Evaporation	Under the influence of heat, water and low boiling compounds of the effluent evaporate, leaving behind other dissolved and suspended solids.	To reduce effluent bulk, to concentrate toxic chemicals for their easy destruction, to separate low boiling liquids and to recover costly chemical.	Rate depends upon temperature difference between the effluent bulk and the surroundings, exposed surface area and rate of vapour removed from the surface.	
Dialysis	Solutes with unequal diffusion powers, when subjected to pass through membranes, get separated.	To separate costly toxic chemicals present in a dissolved state in the effluent.		
Ion Exchange	Certain compounds (mainly resins) possess a property to exchange one of their ions from the like ions of surrounding medium due to forces like electronegativity and ionization potential.	To separate costly chemicals present in, a dissolved state and also certain undesirable compounds.	Ease of replacement depends on the nature of the forces binding replaceable ions to the crystal, concentrations of exchanging ions in the liquid phase, charges on the ions, ion size and accessibility of the lattice ion.	Only ions or ionizable substances are removed.
Absorption	Under the influence of different surface forces many substances (e.g., clays, activated carbon, etc.) may retain certain type of compounds on	T o remove and/or recover toxic substances, colour producing compound, refractory organics and toxic metals	Capacity of a given (solid material) absorbant to absorb or extract is a complex function of several variables; Chemical and physical properties of	Absorbant bed in the form of the percolation bed, in addition serves as a filtration medium, while in the contact method as

1	2	3	4	5
	their exposed surface.	from the effluent bulk.	the solid absorbant, composition and concentration of the liquid phase, temperature of the system, type of contact and duration of contact.	coagulant for finely divided suspended solids. These services, however, interfere with the quantities absorbed.
pH–Control (a) Neutralisation	When alkaline or acidic materials are added to a solution, the medium gets correspondingly changed, due to neutralisation reactions.	To remove undesirable acidity or basicity of effluent and precipitation of certain unwanted compounds soluble in acidic or basic medium. To develop a medium for people biochemical activities.		
(b) Acidification		For breaking of emulsion, precipitation of colloids, removal of compounds volatile in acidic solutions such as cyanides and sulfides.		
(c) Causticisation		Byproduct recovery or salvage.		
Flocculation	Precipitates formed by reaction of coagulation chemicals, however ,have the property of forming large floes of high surface area. As these floes move through the liquid in the settling tank, they remove other suspended solids by absorption or mechanical agglomeration	To remove colloidal and finely divided particles and to reduce the organic load ofa waste.	Efficiency of the process gets considerably reduced in the presence of surface active chemicals like soaps, and detergents.	Dairy wastes due to presence of excessive detergent may not be flocculated.

Contd...

Table 4.4 (*Contd..*).

1	2	3	4	5
Chlorination	When chlorine gas is added to water, it hydrolyses to form hypochlorous. The reactions : $Cl_2 + H_2O — HOCl + HCl$ The acid produced, the alkalinity and the hypochlorite ion react with most reducing substances and oxidise them to a higher oxidation number. Electrical charges of colloidal particles are also affected thus aiding their coagulation.	Odour abatement, disinfection reduction of BOD or treatment of plant effluent, removal of gases to control bulking of activated sludge, to correct ponding on trickling filters are the main applications of the process.'	Chlorination reactions are not instantaneous, but proceed at a rate dependent on several variables; conc. of hypochlorous acid, dissolved chlorine and other compounds and temperature. An increase in temperature usually results in the acceleration of the chlorination reactions, although it may also cause considerable side reactions such as chlorate formation.	Chlorine solution with ammonia or with organic nitrogen compounds like protein amino acids for chloramines or the corresponding organic derivatives.
Electrolytic oxidation	Under certain pH, electrode potential and current density, some resistant organics are activised, which then get oxidised by the nascent oxygen produced at the electrodes during the process. Due to presence of highly active ionic species, neutralisation of charges on colloidal particles is also aided resulting in their precipitation.	For oxidation of toxic, colour producing and refractory organics, disinfection and precipitation of colloids.		
Oxidation	Substances containing elements at a low positive oxidation potential and with a strong tendency to change to a higher number, when brought into contact with oxygen, get oxidized.	To convert complex resistant organics to simpler non polluting compounds.		
(a) Aeration		To increase DO of the effluent, needed in oxidations both chemical or biological, and its degasing.		Breaking of emulsions and removal of volatile and odour producing substances is achieved in addition. ~

1	2	3	4	5
(b) Ozonization	Ozone when brought into contact with elements of low positive oxidation potential, also oxidises them.	For oxidation of resistant organics, disinfection, accelerated oxidation of organics and compounds producing colour and odour.	To achieve more efficient utilisation, batch treatment rather than continuous flow treatment may be preferred. Temperature is an important variable to define the efficiency of the process.	The end products and by products of oxidation with ozone are the same as those from air oxygen oxidation and are generally not objectionable.
Aerobic treatment	In the presence of dissolved oxygen and proper environmental conditions, certain micro–organisms utilise organic waste as food, converting it into simpler non–polluting compounds such as carbondioxide, nitrates, sulfates and water. Complex cell tissues and protein materials are also synthesised which are, then, agglomerated and removed from the waste by settling.	To remove organics.	Aerobic biological treatment operations for industrial wastes require, for their successful performance, a community of proper biological micro–organisms, food material, an appropriate environment and a supply of dissolved oxygen. Almost any organic matter with the possible exception of hydrocarbons and ethers may be oxidised by the process. Temperature influences the metabolic activities of the microbiological population (i.e., biological reaction rate constants), gas transfer rates and the settling characteristics of the biological solids, and, thus, plays a significant role in determining the efficiency of the process.	Germicidal and resistant organics like cyanides and phenols can be destroyed by special micro–organisms but after a prolonged period of acclimatisation.
(a) Activated sludge process	In this process aerobic oxidation of waste is performed by active growths created previously and an aerobic environment is achieved by the use of diffused or mechanical aeration. Organic matters from the wastes get absorbed on the gelled structure; by collision electrical attractions, chemical reactions of surface atoms	To remove dissolved, colloidals and coarse solid organic matter.	For optimum activity, the kinetics of activated sludge require a young flocculant sludge in the logarithmic growth state by controlled sludge wastage, continuous loading of the organisms and elimination of anaerobic conditions of any point with oxidation treatment.	Process is very susceptible to interference by toxic materials. However, tolerance may be built up over a period of time if concentrations are slowly and uniformly increased. Various degrees of efficiencies are obtained by controlling the contact period of the concentrations

Contd...

Table 4.4 (*Contd..*).

1	*2*	*3*	*4*	*5*
	and finally converted to simple compounds by oxidation enzyme systems.			of the active floe.
(b)Trickling filtration	In this process bacteria and other microorganisms are cultivated in a porous bed of some material with a large surface area and the entire system is maintained in aerobic condition by free passage of oxygen in the unit. The waste water is sprinkled over the bed and allowed to trickle through In during which the organics are oxidized. Gases produced are removed continuously in the effluent and solid residue of cell tissue that cling to the porous media for a time are finally sloughed off with the filter effluent.	Dissolved and colloidal organic matter.	Efficiency is affected both by waste and filter variables. Waste variables are the composition of the waste, strength of hydraulic loading, pH and temperature while filter variables include depth of filter, size and uniformity of filter medium, uniformity of waste distribution over the filter, and air availability. The trickling filter has more resistance to toxic waste than the activated sludge and also recuperates more promptly from an overdose.	A reasonable degree of tolerance to more toxic materials can be developed in the filter microorganisms by gradual building up of toxic concentrations, but shock load or sudden surges of concentrated poison may impair the efficiency of the filter temporarily or permanently.
(c) Lagooning	The process is essentially the same as the activated sludge process excluding the recycling of active growths from the treated effluent. Oxygen is supplied either through compressed air, mechanical surface aeration or by Photosynthetic aeration.	Dissolved colloidal and suspended organic matters	There is little or no decrease in the organic content of waste passing through an oxidation period. But putrescible raw wastes are converted into relatively stable algae cells. Temp, pH, dissolved oxygen concentrations sun light and presence of sufficient nutrient minerals are important variables to decide the efficiency of the process.	It is not suitable for use in populated areas because of its nuisance value from odour and insects.

1	2	3	4	5
Anaerobic treatment	Under anaerobic conditions, i.e., in the absence of gaseous or dissolved oxygen, certain groups of micro organism may carry out the digestion of complex organic wastes. These are mainly hydrolyte and methane forming organisms. Hydrolyte organisms by their action convert complex organic compound to a low molecular weight organic acids and alcohols. These are, then, converted to carbon–dioxide and methane by methane bacteria.	To remove complex organics and volatile solids.	A major advantage of the anaerobic treatment process is that reactions can be carried out in depth, without need for large surfaces or interfacial areas. It is less expensive but it has the limitations. that its final effluent is less satisfactory than from aerobic treatment because it is dark in colour, odorous and with a high residual BOD. It takes place in mixed or enriched cultures and hence may be maintained easily on a large scale. It is applicable to any type of substrate except lignin and mineral oil, and converts the entire substrate quantitively to CO_2 and CH_4. It produces lesser quantities of inoffensive sludge which may also dry quickly. Efficiency of the process depends on temperature, pH, waste loadings, presence of toxic materials and absence of oxygen.	The ultimate products of anaerobic decomposition are less oxygenated than products obtained under aerobic conditions.

Table 4.5
Cost estimates for industrial waste treatment

Industry	*Discharge into land surface water*		*Discharge on land for irrigation*	
	Capital cost	*Running cost per year*	*Capital cost*	*Running cost per year*
1	*2*	*3*	*4*	*5*
Dairy and milk bottling	₹1600–2500 per 1000 litres of milk	₹200–900	₹1000–2000	₹200–800
Brewery and distillery	₹50–100 per litre of alcohol	₹8–30	₹25–60	₹5–18
Tannery	₹25–58 per kg of hide	₹1.5–8.0	₹25–30	₹1–3.5
Pulp and paper	₹30,000 to 50,000 per tonne of paper	₹5000–6500	₹15,000–20,000	₹ 300–500
Coke oven by product	₹150 per tonne of coal	₹40	—	—
Explosive	₹250 per kg of cordite	₹300	—	—
Textiles	₹7–10 per meter length of cloth	₹5–6	₹4–5	₹2–3.5
Slaughter house	₹250–350 per animal	₹40–100	₹100–200	₹20–60
Fertilizer	₹1000–2000 per tonne of urea	₹500–800	—	—
Starch	₹2000–2500 per tonne of starch	₹300–500	₹1000–1200	₹160–280
Instant coffee	₹20–25 per kg of instant coffee	₹4–5	₹12–15	₹2.5–3.2

Table 4.6

Dairy and milk bottling plant

Wastage of milk from bottling plant:	2% of milk handled.
Volume of waste water produced:	4.5 litres/per litre of milk handled
BOD of whole milk:	1,32,600 mg/l
BOD of waste:	1,000 mg/1

Cost estimates for the treatment of dairy waste

	Discharge in land surface water	*Discharge on land for irrigation*		
	Anaerobic + Aerated lagoon	*Oxidation Ditch*	*Aerated Lagoon*	*Anaerobic Lagoon*
Expected BOD removal %	95–98	95–98	75	60
Capital cost per 1000 *l* of milk handled/day (₹)	1600–2500	1400–2500	1000–1400	85–150
Annual running cost for 1000 litres of milk handled per day (₹)	300–900	300–850	200–600	100–200

Table 4.7

Brewery and distillery

Flow = 1900 m^3/day; BOD load = 4000 kg/day

Scheme	*Capital cost million ₹.*	*Running cost million ₹*	*Land required hectares*
1. Anaerobic lagoon Aerated lagoon Oxidation pond	1.3	1,30,000	6.0
2. Anaerobic lagoon Oxidation pond	0.75	35,000	10.0

Table 4.8

Tannery Industry – Vegetable

1. Effluent quantity	3400 litres per 1000 kg of hide processed
2. Average BOD of effluent 5000 mg/l	
3. Desired effluent BOD:	(*i*) 500 mg/l for discharge on land;
	(*ii*) Below 100 mg/l for discharge into land surface water

Cost estimates for the treatment of wastes from vegetable tannery

Scheme	*Capital cost ₹/kg of hide processed*	*Running cost ₹/year/kg of hide processed per day*	*Effluent BOD mg/l*
1. Settling and anaerobic lagoon	20–30	1.2–3.5	500 mg/*l*
2. Settling, anaerobic lagoon and extended aeration	32–58	3.0–6.0	30 mg/*l*
3. Settling and aerobic lagoon	25–40	1.5–4.0	100 mg/*l*

Disposal of Industrial Effluents

The treated effluents can be discharged into surface water courses, sewers and on the land. The mode of disposal, however, has to be selected on the merits of each case to ensure that the problem of pollution can be minimized, if not totally eliminated. It is important to bear in mind that some of the stabilized industrial effluents have a good manurial potential which should be exploited. This practice will not only be beneficial for our soil but would also be a constructive step towards minimizing pollution. Nevertheless, it has to be ensured that the treated effluent is safe enough to be used for irrigation purposes.

References

1. Stack, V. T. (1972), *Water and Water Pollution Handbook*, 3 (Claccio, L. L. Editor), Marcel Dekker Inc., New York.
2. Lee, E. W. and W.J. Oswald (1954), *Sewage Ind. Wastes*, 26, 1097.
3. Clark, J. W, W. Viessmanand MJ. Hammer (1971), *Water Supply and Pollution Control*, 2nd ed, International Textbook Co., Scranton.
4. Sundaresan, B.B. (1977), *Seminar on Industrial Wastes*, Calcutta, Organized by N.E.E.R.I. and Calcutta Metropolitan Development Authority, Published by A.K. Basu.
5. Bopardikar, M. V. (1967), *Microbiology of a Waste Stabilization Pond for Water Treatment*, Environmental Health, 9,183.
6. Dave J. M. and J. S. Jain (1966), *"Status of Stabilization Ponds for Sewage Treatment," Environmental Health*, 3, 223.

5

Air Pollution and its Control

The atmosphere is used as a natural sink for gaseous pollutants. The assimilation capacity of the atmosphere, however, is limited and the dispersal of gaseous pollutants in the atmosphere depends upon the meteorological conditions prevailing. For example, gaseous pollutants may not pose a serious problem on rainy days, especially when the sky is overcast but the situation is complicated during the winter season when adverse conditions prevail in the atmosphere. Hence, from the point of view of dispersion of gaseous pollutants, it is essential to be constantly informed about the total pollution load, meteorological conditions, etc. It is, therefore, desirable to have some knowledge about the atmosphere and the related problems before deciding on suitable abatement techniques for gaseous pollutants. Inversion, the lapse rate and photochemical reactions in the atmosphere have also been briefly described in this chapter.

The Earth's Natural Atmosphere

A polluted atmosphere is generally considered an unnatural atmosphere. While it is true there are numerous natural materials in the earth's atmosphere that, at times, can prove quite objectionable, such as pollen and dust. However such materials are not usually referred to as air pollutants. To understand what man has added to the atmosphere, it is necessary to know something about the history and composition of the atmosphere as provided by nature.

The average composition of the earth's atmosphere, near the surface, is shown in Table 5.1. In addition to the constituents which occur in a more or less constant concentration in the atmosphere, there are a number of decidedly variable constituents of natural origin. Some of these are listed in Table 5.2.

Atmosphere weight is approximately 4.5×10^{15} metric tonnes. It presses down upon the earth with a pressure of 2,016 lbs/sq. ft (141.7248 kg/sq. m.). At the surface of the earth, it has a density of 0.0013 g/cu.m. It decreases in density as the distance from the earth increases. The atmosphere gradually thins out into space. At about 600 km and above, the atoms and molecules describe free elliptical orbits in the earth's gravitation field.

The proportion of the different components of the atmosphere remain essentially constant from the earth's surface to a height of about 10 miles (16 km). Above this height, gravitation separation probably begins, although it does not become important until above about 80 miles (128 km).

Table 5.1
Average composition of the atmosphere

Gas	Composition by volume ppm	Composition by weight ppm	Total mass $\times 10^{20}$ g
N_2	780,900	755,100	38,648
O_2	209,500	231,500	11,841
Ar	9,300	12,900	0.6555
CO_2	300	450	0.0233
Ne	18	12.5	0.000636
He	5.2	0.72	0.000037
CH_4	2.2	1.2	0.000062
Kr	1	2.9	0.000146
N_2O	1	1.5	0.000077
H_2	0.5	0.03	0.000002
Xe	0.08	0.36	0.000018

Table 5.2
Variable constituents of the earth's atmosphere of natural origin

Airborne soil	Pollen
Hydrogen chloride	Condensation nuclei
Hydrogen fluoride	
Meteoric dust	Ozone (formed photochemically and by electrical discharge)
Nitrogen dioxide (Electrical discharge)	Bacteria
Sodium chloride	
Sulphur dioxide	Spores
Water	Hydrogen sulphide (sulphide bacteria, volcanic origin)

The earth's atmosphere has not always had its present composition, although the latter has remained relatively unchanged throughout most of geological time. It is generally agreed that the predecessor of our present atmosphere consisted mainly of carbon dioxide, nitrogen and water. It may have been similar in composition to the gases emitted by present day volcanoes, which do not contain any oxygen. In some manner, life on earth started and the chlorophyll–containing plants converted some of the carbon dioxide and water into oxygen. Whether these phenomena occurred simultaneously or consecutively is probably immaterial at present. What is important is that changes have occurred and the probable nature of these changes helps us understand the chemistry of the atmosphere.

The hydrosphere and biosphere must be considered first in any discussion of the atmosphere. There is a constant shift of substances between these three spheres. The gases exist in the atmosphere; the hydrosphere contains all the waters of the oceans, the lakes, and the streams; and the biosphere comprises all living matter. Of the three, the biosphere has the least weight. They may be arranged in the following order according to their relative weights:

Biosphere	1
Atmosphere	300
Hydrosphere	69,100

There is a constant exchange between the earth's crust and atmosphere.

The common constituent gases of the atmosphere have been rather intensively studied. Much is known about the reactions in which such gases have taken part since the formation of the earth approximately three million years ago.

Oxygen

The atmosphere is constantly acquiring oxygen from chlorophyll bearing plants, which take up carbon dioxide and evolve oxygen. Some of the oxygen in the atmosphere dissolves in the hydrosphere. At the same time, oxygen is being removed from the atmosphere by the oxidation of the various reducing materials in the earth's crust such as sulphur, iron oxides, and mangnese salts. The amount of oxygen lost from the atmosphere by the oxidation of FeO to Fe_2O_3, MnO to MnO_2 and SO_2 to SO_3 has been estimated on the basis of the analysis of the ratio of ferric to ferrous iron in various types of rocks (Table 5.3) and on the weight of igneous rocks which have been eroded from the earth during geological time. Based on certain assumptions made in the calculation, the amount of "fossil" oxygen is between about 0.56 and 0.26 kg/sq. cm. of the earth's surface. The amount of oxygen in the hydrosphere is equivalent to 0.002 kg/sq. cm., and in the atmosphere to 0.230 kg/cm sq. Thus, the total free and fossil oxygen is between 0.79 kg/sq. cm. and 0.49 kg/sq. cm. In other units, about 2.5×10^{15} metric tonnes of oxygen has been produced by plants during the 3 billion years of the earth's existence, a large part of which, at present, is combined oxygen in sedimentary rocks.

Table 5.3

Ratio of Fe_2O_3 to FeO in various rocks

	Igneous rocks	*Shales*	*Terrigenous*	*Sandstones*
Percent Fe_2O_3	3.08	4.63	5.07	1.08
Percent FeO	3.80	2.46	8.30	0.30
Molecular quotient, $2Fe_2O_3/FeO$	0.73	1.47	1.98	3.24

It may be pointed out that there are, at least, two other hypotheses to explain the occurrence of oxygen in the atmosphere. One is that free oxygen was formed by thermal decomposition of water vapour while the earth and its atmosphere were very hot. However, it is difficult to refute the objection that the hydrogen and oxygen would later recombine on contact with the still hot surface of the earth. Another hypothesis is that photochemical decomposition of water vapour occurred, at a later and cooler stage, in the upper atmosphere. However, it is unlikely that there was ever sufficient water vapour at that high altitude to account for all the oxygen which was produced.

Carbon Dioxide

All living matter on the earth is involved in the rejection of the carbon dioxide in the atmosphere. Carbon dioxide is rejected into the atmosphere by volcanoes, by decay of organic matter, and by the combustion of fuels. It is also in equilibrium with the dissolved carbon dioxide in the waters of the earth. In addition, much is stored in limestones and dolomites; carbon which was once atmospheric carbon dioxide is stored in coal and petroleum. Goldschmidt estimated the following values for the weight of carbon dioxide per square cm.

Limestone and dolomite	6,560 g/sq. cm
Coal, bitumen, humus and the biosphere	0.67-3.1 g/sq. cm

Hydrosphere 20 g/sq. cm
Atmosphere 0.4 g/sq. cm.

The annual production of carbon dioxide by respiration and decay is approximately 0.040 g/sq. cm./year. Over the entire earth's surface of 5.1×10^{18} sq. cm., total CO_2 produced in one year is 2×10^{11} metric tonnes. The entire atmosphere contains approximately 2×10^{18} metric tonnes CO_2. In other words, decay and respiration are adding carbon dioxide to the atmosphere at the rate of approximately 10 per cent per year.

The combustion of fuels is also adding to the amount of carbon dioxide, but in a relatively insignificant manner. In 1951, the entire world had an energy consumption equivalent to 2.5×10^9 metric tonnes of coal. Approximately 20 per cent of this energy was hydroelectric power in Europe and, somewhat, less in the United States. If it is assumed that 15 percent of the total world's energy is hydroelectric power and that coal contains 90 percent carbon, then the combustion of coal to carbon dioxide would add only 7×10^9 metric tonnes of carbon dioxide per year or one-thirtieth of the amount produced by decay and respiration.

Geological evidence suggests that relatively little change has occurred in the concentration of carbon dioxide from archaeozoic times to the present. However, there must have been ceaseless minor fluctuations. Such data as exist show that the carbon dioxide content of the atmosphere has increased about 30 ppm in the last 50 years. The fact that it has not increased more is probably because of its consumption by plants and because the waters of the earth act as a huge reservoir which contain 50 times as much dissolved CO_2 as is mixed in our gaseous atmosphere.

Nitrogen

The amount of nitrogen that undergoes changes is small compared to that of oxygen or carbon dioxide. Nitrogen is removed from air by both organic and inorganic processes. Organic processes involve nitrogen fixing micro–organisms and some blue-green algae. The inorganic processes produce oxides of nitrogen by electrical discharges and photochemical reactions in the upper atmosphere. The amount of organically fixed nitrogen far exceeds that fixed by inorganic processes. It has been estimated that biological fixation adds 0.07 mg of nitrogen per square centimeter of the earth's surface per year and non-biological fixation adds not more than 0.005 mg/sq. cm./year. Much of this nitrogen is eventually returned to the atmosphere by the decay of organic matter. Adel, who suggested the presence of nitrous oxide in the atmosphere, concludes that it is supplied to the atmosphere as part of the earth's nitrogen cycle.

The presence of nitrous oxide has been confirmed by infrared spectroscopy and a mass spectrometer. It has been estimated that the average content of the combined nitrogen in sediments is 510 g/tonne. Multiplying this by Goldschmidt's figure of 170 kg/sq. cm., for the total amount of sediments formed during geologic time, gives 86.7 g/sq. cm. of fossil nitrogen.

Nitrogen is also a constituent of all igneous rocks, which contain an average of 0.04 cu cm of nitrogen per gram of approximately 0.005 percent by weight. It is evidently present in a combined form, since it may be released from the rocks as ammonia by means of fusion with soda ash. Ammonia is also a constituent of volcanic gases.

Ozone

A large gap exists in the present understanding of atmospheric ozone. The concentration at ground level is highly variable both at one locality and from place to place. Little is known about the effect of weather conditions on its concentration, particularly with reference to its vertical distribution. In most areas of the world where it has been measured, its concentration at ground level ranges between 0 to 5 ppm. However, there is considerable evidence to prove that the concentration near the ground is often considerably greater. Concentrations of ozone greater than 20 ppm in Alaska have also been reported. The concentrations of ozone, in Southern California, have been found to be as high as 20 to 50 ppm in the Los Angles area, on Mt. Wilson, and in the desert.

Aerosols

In our everyday life, visual perception plays an important role and dominates the other senses with which we are equipped. It is, therefore, not surprising that the average person associates the term atmospheric pollution with clouds of dust and palls of smoke. The word 'particle' is frequently used to describe the particles in aerosols. However, gas is also particulate; so aerosols really mean, at least, groups of molecules. Aerosols are set apart from gases such as nitrogen, oxygen, argon, carbon dioxide, and ozone as being present in larger groups than individual molecules of gases. Dust particles are larger than fume or smoke particles, and although they may be suspended in the atmosphere, they settle according to Stokes' law. The smaller fume or smoke particles on the other hand, may be either liquid or solid and exhibit Brownian motion.

When a liquid or solid is dispersed to form a cloud or a smoke, many of its properties are greatly altered. For example, the surface per unit weight (specific surface) is greatly increased and the nature of the surface may greatly influence the behaviour of the material. Typical diameters of a number of aerosols are shown in Table 5.4. It is assumed that the particles are spherical in shape and that their specific gravities are not changed by dispersion. These assumption are not strictly valid, nor are the typical diameters of the particles truly representative in all cases. Nonetheless, the figures provide a general indication of the size of such particles.

Table 5.4

Typical diameters of aerosol particles

Aerosol	*Diameter,* μ
Tobacco smoke	0.25
NH_4Cl smoke	0.1
H_2SO_4 mist	0.8–5.5
ZnO smoke	0.05
Coal mine air	10
Flour–mill air	15–20
Cement mill (kiln exhaust)	10
Grain elevator air	15
Fog	50
Talc dust	10
Pigments	1–4

As a result of the increase in surface area, the properties that depend upon the activity of the surface molecules are greatly enhanced.

Sources of Atmospheric Pollutants

Dusts

The atmosphere contains dust even in the absence of human activity. Meteoric dust from outer space settles at the earth at the rate of about 1,000 tonnes/year. However, this amount is exceedingly small compared to other sources. Volcanic eruptions and dust storms can contribute large amounts of dust to the earth's atmosphere. It has been estimated that the volume of fine ash thrown into the atmosphere by a strong volcanic eruption amounts to as much as 100 billion cu yd. A single dustfall in 1911 deposited 2 million tonnes of dust on the African desert and the continent of Europe. In February, 1903,10 million tonnes of red dust from northwest Africa was deposited over England. Dust from the American dust bowl was clearly visible in the city of Washington DC. Figure 5.1 shows a typical dust-fall gauge.

The dust in the atmosphere has a wide range of chemical composition. The composition of dust from natural sources varies as the various portions of the earth's crust.

Human activities, such as the manufacture of various products, introduce organic and inorganic particles into the atmosphere. These products include steel, rubber, lime and a variety of other items. In fact, almost all operations involving the burning of coal introduce some dust, i.e., soot and fly ash, into the atmosphere. A large quantity of rubber (50 tonnes/day in Los Angeles) is worn off tyres on city streets. Much of this is possibly injected into the atmosphere in the form of dust.

Condensation Nuclei

Vapours in general must be greatly supersaturated before condensation can occur in the absence of foreign particles. A supersaturation of about 4.2 times is required for water vapour. However, when the vapour contains particles which can act as nuclei for condensation, little supersaturation is required. Condensation nuclei are important because of the way in which they affect our everyday life. They are largely responsible for fogs and rain. Without them, condensation would occur mainly on the walls of buildings and other exposed surfaces of the earth.

Natural sources appear to be the main producers of nuclei. Such sources include volcanic eruption, ocean spray and natural combustion, e.g., forest fires. Man-made sources include many industrial operations, modern transportation facilities (locomotives, boats, automobiles, and aeroplanes) and domestic combustion processes. Enormous quantities of nuclei are often produced by a single source. An average grass fire extending over 1 acre produces some 20,000 billion–billion (2×10^{22}) nuclei. If these nuclei were distributed through a column of air, having a cross section of one acre and a height of 10,000 ft, there would still be a concentration of about two billion particles per cubic centimeter. Coste and Wright showed that a flame of commercial coal gas, lit for only 15 minutes, increased the number of nuclei in a chamber from 109,000–860,000 per cubic centimeter. Landsberg found that the concentration of nuclei in a ventilated kitchen containing a large operating gas range exceeded 500,000 nuclei per cubic centimeter while the outside air contained only about 25,000 nuclei per cubic centimeter.

Most nuclei range in size of about 0.0010 m. Their weight has been estimated at 10^{-1} to 10^{-15}g or an equivalent aggregate of about 106 molecules. It is interesting to note that water vapour is supersaturated enough to be self-nucleating, *i.e.*, when water condensation occurs in the absence of foreign nuclei, the nuclei consist of aggregates containing only about 80 water molecules.

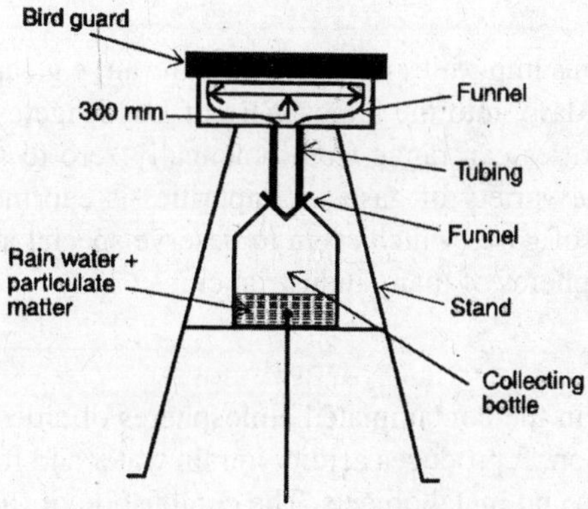

Fig. 5.1 A Typical Dust-Fall Gauge

The number of nuclei in the atmosphere usually exceeds the number of dust particles by a factor of several thousands. This has been attributed to the fact that the dust particles being larger, are subjected to considerable sedimentation, while the nuclei remain suspended because of convection currents and Brownian movement. However, it is probably also true that compared to dust particles, a larger number of nuclei is produced by many dispersion processes.

Biological Aerosols

Aerosols of biological origin are probably not important in direct chemical reaction that may occur in the atmosphere. However, the study of aerobiology has provided information that may be important as it applies to the transport of other materials in the atmosphere.

Biological aerosols have been found even at great distances from their sources. Living spores of various fungi have been collected by an aeroplane above the Caribbean sea, 600 miles from their nearest source, while all organs have been identified at least 1,500 miles from their probable origin. In spite of the usually low concentrations at the source, marine bacteria have been collected 80 miles inland from the nearest sea coast.

Marine bacteria are removed from the sea only when the surface is stirred sufficiently to produce spray. Since, on an average, the number of marine bacteria seldom exceeds 500 per milliliter of sea water, the population of marine bacteria in the air must be sparse everywhere, except, perhaps, at times when the sea is rough or in the vicinity of coastal breakers.

Occasionally, sea water becomes highly contaminated with micro-organisms that are carried into the atmosphere, e.g., dinoflagellate gymonodium was present in quantities sufficient to cause the sea to appear red. Ocean spray, under these conditions, produces severe respiratory irritation among persons who come in contact with the spray.

Micro organisms are reported to exist at various levels in the air, up to a height of 20,000 ft. Spore-forming bacteria were predominant and 29 bacteria were identified. The ratio of dust particles to micro-organisms (bacteria and molds) was found to be about 100:1.

Many observers have reported great irregularities in concentrations at different levels of the atmosphere, often finding heavier concentrations at higher altitudes than at lower levels. There are several recorded instances of such biologic stratification, e.g., spera ceilings are often marked by a cloud layer or a visible haze.

Gaseous Impurities

A large number of gaseous impurities is emitted into the air, e.g., approximately 700 tonnes of volatiles are emitted daily into the atmosphere of Los Angeles from automobiles. The concentrations of impurities can range from practically zero to about 100 percent at the source. Furthermore, the variety of gaseous impurities is enormous. However, there are a few gases and classes of gases which seem to deserve special attention because of their prevalence in the atmospheres of many industrial cities.

Sulphur Dioxide

Sulphur dioxide occurs in the contaminated atmospheres of cities at concentrations of up to several parts per million. It produces acidity in rain water and fogs and is a major source of corrosion of buildings and metal objects. The combustion of fuels, smelting operations, refineries, and chemical plants are the chief sources of sulphur dioxide in industrial cities. A power station burning 5,000 tonnes of coal per day may discharge 500 tonnes of sulphur dioxide into the air. The generalized emission factors for sulphur dioxide from different fuels and operations are given in Table 5.5.

Hydrogen Sulphide

Hydrogen sulphide is usually an important contributor to air pollution problems only under rather localized conditions. This probably results in part from the fact that hydrogen sulphide is easily burned to form sulphur dioxide. Thus, it is not generally released into the atmosphere following combustion. However, because of its great toxicity, it is a hazard in the oil– refining and rubber industry, in tanneries and other industries where animal matter is handled, as well as at plants manufacturing sulphur dyes, and artificial silk by the viscose process. Even when present in the air in concentrations below the level of physiological significance, it discolors lead particles.

Table 5.5
Generalized emission factors for sulphur dioxide from selected fuels and operations (modified after NAPCA publication*)

Source	*SO_2 emission factor*
Combustion of coal	(38 times per cent 5 by weight) 0.4536 kg SO_2/1000 kg coal.
Combustion of fuel oil	(158.8 times per cent 0.5 by weight), 0.899 kg SO_2/10,000 litre oil
Open burning dumps and municipal incinerators	0.544–0.907 kg SO_2/1000 kg refuse
Sulphuric acid manufacture	9.07–31.75 kg/1000 kg 100 percent acid
Copper smelting (Primary)	635.04 kg SO_2/1000 kg concentrated ore
Lead smelting (Primary)	299.376 kg SO_2/1000 kg concentrated ore
Lead smelting (Secondary cupola)	29.83 kg SO_2/1000 kg metal charged
Zinc smelting (Primary)	490.424 kg SO_2/1000 kg concentrated ore
Kraft mill recovery furnace	1.088–6.078 kg SO_2/1000 kg air–dried pulp
Sulphite mill recovery furnace (assuming 90 percent recovery)	18.144 kg SO_2/1000 kg air–dried pulp

*National Air Pollution Control Administration, "Control techniques for sulphur oxide air pollutants", NAPCA Publications No. AP-52. US Government Printing Office, Washington DC, 1969.

Oxides of Nitrogen

Oxides of nitrogen are produced by the combustion of organic matter and are, thus, introduced into the atmosphere from automobile exhausts, furnace stacks, incinerators, and many other similar sources. The oxide of nitrogen may be forced from nitrogen compounds in the organic material, but they are also formed by nitrogen fixation. Concentrations as high as 0.5 ppm have been found in the Los Angeles atmosphere and as high as 0.8 ppm in Baltimore. The oxides include nitric oxide (NO), nitrogen dioxide (NO_2), nitrogen pentoxide (N_2O_5) and the hydrated nitrogen pentoxide, nitric acid (HNO_3). Nitrogen dioxide is in equilibrium with its dimer, nitrogen tetroxide.

Nitrogen dioxide has received considerable attention as an air pollutant because it is considered a hazard in numerous industries. Its insidious nature as a poison was emphasized by the Cleveland Clinic Fire (USA) which occurred in May, 1929. Many deaths occurred following that fire as a result of the inhalation of the nitrogen dioxide produced from burning X–ray film.

Ammonia

Ammonia is another nitrogen compound which is frequently present in the air. It has been found in the atmospheres of Los Angeles, and of Charleston, USA, at concentrations as great as 0.2 ppm, and in the atmosphere of other cities at lower concentrations. The relatively high concentrations at Charleston has been attributed to the fact that ammonia is a by product and raw material in the extensive organic-chemical industry of the area.

Ammonia is a product of many combustion processes, including domestic incineration and the operation of automobiles. It is also discharged from certain refinery operations and is always detectable in the air near stockyards.

Hydrogen Fluoride

Fluorides, in general, including both hydrogen fluoride and various solid fluorides dispersed as aerosols, have received considerable attention because relatively small amounts produce flurosis in cattle. The contaminated atmospheres of cities generally contain lower concentrations of fluorides than most of other commonly determined contaminants. The maximum concentration found in most cities is about 0.025 ppm. The highest maximum concentration reported has been 0.08 ppm in an industrial area of Baltimore, U.S.A.

Fluorides are emitted into the atmosphere by aluminium plants, steel plants, and phosphate-fertilizer plants. Fluorides in the atmosphere have also been attributed to the burning of coal. Hydrogen fluoride itself is used in the chemical industry and in refining processes.

Hydrocarbons

Recently, hydrocarbons have received considerable attention as air pollutants because they may participate in reactions, in the atmosphere, which produce objectionable intermediate compounds and products. Such intermediates and products may cause irritation and plant damage resulting from contaminated city air. The concentrations of hydrocarbons in the atmospheres of most cities have not been measured. This is probably largely due to the difficulty of making such determinations/The concentration of hydrocarbons in Los Angeles smog has been estimated to be about 2 ppm, of which about 1.6 ppm is paraffin and 0.4 ppm is olefins. Nearly 700–1,000 tonnes of volatile hydrocarbons are emitted daily into the Los Angeles atmosphere from automobile exhaust. Hydrocarbons are also emitted into the atmosphere from automobiles by oil refineries and by the evaporation of gasoline at service stations.

Local high concentrations of hydrocarbons in the air are common in garages, service stations, dry-cleaning establishments, oil refineries, and many other industries. In general, aliphatic hydrocarbons are not considered to be hazardous if the concentration is less than 20 percent of the lower inflammable limit, although such a high concentration (2,000 ppm) in the case of gasoline may produce unpleasant effects on the human system. Benzene and other aromatic hydrocarbons are used extensively for solvent extraction purposes. They often occur locally in the air at relatively high concentrations where they can be quite a health hazard. The concentration of aromatic hydrocarbons in city air is probably generally less than 0.1 ppm although some aromatic hydrocarbons are present in automobile-exhaust gases.

Aldehydes and Ketones

Aldehydes and ketones are introduced into city air from automobile exhaust gases, incinerator smoke and stack gases from the combustion of various organic substances. Aldehydes and ketones are evidently also produced by the oxidation of hydrocarbons after they are admitted into the atmosphere. Such oxidations are discussed later in this section.

Concentrations of aldehydes and ketones have been determined in the air of several cities in the USA. The maximum concentrations ranged from 0.12 ppm (Baltimore) to 1.0 ppm (Los Angeles). The variations may represent differences in analytics techniques rather than significant difference in concentrations. Studies at the Stanford Research Institute revealed that replacement of the usual sodium bisulfite absorption train by an efficient cold–trap system greatly increased the amount of aldehydes and ketones collected from a given volume of Los Angeles air. In the Los Angeles atmosphere, at least, less than half of these substances are formaldehyde, the remainder being ketones and higher aldehydes.

Organic Acids

Most of the processes which emit aldehydes and ketones into the atmosphere also emit organic acids. The present of formic acid in Los Angeles smog has also been reported. The Los Angeles County Air Pollution Control District has reported acids varying from 2–12 carbon atoms in chain length, some of which contained hydroxyl and carboxyl groups.

Organic Halides

Organic halides have been identified in Los Angeles smog by several workers, and they are probably present in the air of other cities also. The concentrations are probably generally below 0 1 ppm. Organic halides have been the subject of considerable speculation as possible eye irritants to contaminated city air. Some of these compounds produce eye irritation at very low concentrations. The threshold lachry-matery concentrations for cyanogen chloride, chloroacetophenone, and bromobenzyl cyanide are 0.05 and 0.02 ppm, respectively. Unfortunately, the individual compounds are very difficult to identify at such low concentrations.

Carbon Monoxide

Carbon monoxide is commonly found in city air at concentration of up to about 55 ppm. Concentrations much higher than this occasionally occur in the open atmosphere or locally in garages, tunnels, behind automobiles, etc. Carbon monoxide is produced by the incomplete combustion of organic material, and automobiles are notorious for their production of this gas.

The effect of air pollutants on materials is given in Table 5.6.

Table 5.6
Air pollution effects on materials

Pollutant	*Type of effect*	*Materials affected*
Ammonia	Deterioration associated with SO_2 and moisture	Damage to varnish and paint surfaces, discolours fabrics
Biological aerosols		
Saprophytic bacteria	Deterioration of surfaces and food spoilage	All material surfaces in contact with air, most unprotected food
Fungi	Deterioration of surfaces	Electronic circuits, leather
Carbon dioxide	Deterioration caused by combination of CO_2 and moisture to form carbonic acid	Building stone
Chlorine	Corrosion and discolouration	Metals, paints, textiles
Chromium	Corrosion in the form of chromic acid discolouration	Metals, paints/building materials, paper, textiles
Hydrochloride acid	Corrosion	Most metals and alloys
Hydrogen fluoride	Etching	Glass and metals
Hydrogen sulphide	Discolouration and tarnishing	Paint (especially lead based), copper, zinc.
Iron	Stain in the form of iron oxide, soiling	Paint and other materials, textiles
Manganese	Soilant, especially near ferro-manganese plant	Most materials, textiles
Nitrogen oxides	Cause dyes to fade & whites to turn yellow	Textile
Odour–producing pollutants	Odours that cling to skin, hair, clothing (especially bad near soap plant)	Requires more frequent laundering and drycleaning of clothes
Ozone–organics oxidants	Deterioration, fading of dyes, cracking	Textiles, rubber
Particulates	Abrasion and corrosion when combined with gaseous pollutants	Most metals, paint, textiles
Phosphorus	Corrosion in the form of phosphoric acid	Most materials
Sulphur oxides	Corrosion	Steel, zinc, electrical equipment, limestone, roofing state, mortar, statues, tiles, leather, book bindings
	Electrochemical deterioration	Iron, aluminium, copper, silver, building materials, leather, paper, textiles.

Meteorological Aspects of Air Pollution

Movement of Air Masses

There are three basic geographical factors associated with the measurement and extent of concentration of pollutants and they are:

1. The distribution of population and industries

2. The climate of an area and prevailing winds
3. The nature of the surface terrain.

The atmosphere around traffic junctions of urban centres receives the maximum input of lead, the distribution of which in various directions is a result of several meteorological parameters, local turbulence and aerosol removal processes like sedimentation and coagulation, etc. Six traffic corners of Ahmedabad city were studied and the lead levels determined are 0.59–13.34 mg/m^3 with mean S.D. of 3.9 ± 2.3 mg/m^3 in summer and of 8.6 ±3.3 mg/m^3 in winter. The seasonal dependence of air concentrations, as a function of traffic density, is given in Table 5.7.

Table 5.7

Seasonal dependence of air concentration as a function of traffic density

Season	*Cone, range (mg/m^3)*	*Mean ± S.D.*	*Correlation coefficient*	*Regression equation*
Summer	0.59–11.38	3.9 + 2.3	0.05	$Y = 3.47 + 0.00013X$
Winter	2.34–13.34	8.6 ± 3.3	8.60	$Y = 0.6 + .0027X$

where X = Traffic density (No. per hour)
Y = air–lead conc. (gm/meter^3)

Turbulence

In windy weather, the smoke emerging from chimneys does not flow smoothly but can be seen to emerge in an eddy-like turbulent motion. When the wind velocity is high, the degree of turbulent motion is also high and this not only causes pollutants to great heights but also to be carried away to great distances horizontally, as shown in Fig. 5.2. The dependence of atmospheric concentration of SO_2 and NO_2 on the prevalent wind speed and direction is given in Table 5.8.

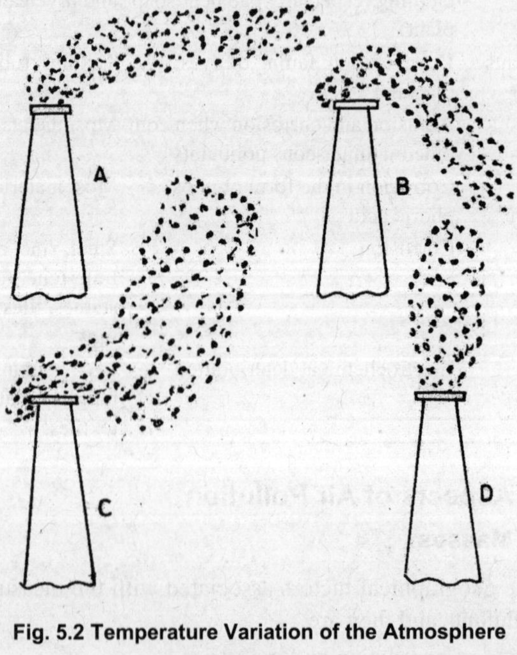

Fig. 5.2 Temperature Variation of the Atmosphere

Table 5.8
Dependence of the atmosphere concentrations of SO_2 and NO_2 on prevalent wind speed and directions

Hours of day	*Wind speed km/h*	*Concentration, g/m³*		*Hours of day*	*Wind speed km/h*	*Concentration, g/m³*	
		SO_2	*NO_2*			*SO_2*	*NO_2*
6	—	—	—	18	4	115	12
7	—	—	—	19	8	268	13
8	—	70	32	20	0	320	28
9	—	—	—	21	0	500	45
10	7	3.3	10	22	—	—	—
11	15.5	3.3	4	23	—	—	—
12	14.5	10	4	0	9	60	30
13	21	19	9	1	—	—	—
14	20	200	11	2	—	—	—
15	30	320	7	3	—	—	—
16	46	145	6	4	0	75	13
17	25	120	11	5	—	—	—

Rainfall

When a process of condensation takes place resulting in rain, atmospheric smoke particles get attached to falling raindrops and are washed away, thereby, cleansing the atmosphere. This is also the case with gaseous pollutants such as sulphur dioxide. In this way, both solubles and pollutants are cleansed from the atmosphere by rain fall. The average concentrations and the rates of deposition of various constituents in rain water and of S02 in air are given in Table 5.9.

Table 5.9
Observed average concentration and the rates of deposition of various constituents in rain water and of SO_2 in air

Constituent	*Arithmetic mean concentration*	*Deposition on land (kg/hectares) during monsoon*
PH	4.8	—
SO_2 (rain)	1.57 (mg/1)	31.4 or 15.7 as S
SO_2 (air)	10.6 (g/m3)	13.2 as S
SO_3	8.0 (mg/1)	160 or 53.3 as S
CI	6.7 (mg/1)	134
NH_4	1.22 (mg/1)	24.4 or 19.0 as N_2
NO_2	0.59 (mg/1)	11.8 or 2.7 as N_2

Effect of Air Pollution

Air pollution, as it is related to health, is basically an ecological problem. It is a problem faced not only by human beings but also by other forms of animal as wells as plant life. Most air pollutants, like other forms of matter, in time, appear in water, or soils, and eventually in human food.

There is a dearth of understanding about the effects of air pollution on health. There is strong evidence to prove that air pollution accompanied by prolonged stagnation, contributes and aggravates respiratory ailments such as chronic bronchitis, pulmonary emphysema, bronchial asthma, lung cancer, and pulmonary edema.

Air pollution also has considerable economic and aesthetic effects upon non–living materials such as stone, metals, mortar, wood, paint, electrical writing, rubber, paper, leather, textile materials and foods.

Materials, for example, may be damaged directly by an air pollutant in an abrasive action, which is more physical than chemical or the damage may be due to a direct chemical attack such as tarnishing of silver and etching of a metallic surface by an acid mist. The effect may be an indirect chemical attack, such as an absorption of sulphur oxides by leather which, if followed by moisturisation, produces sulphuric acid that destroys the leather. Electrochemical corrosion of ferrous metals occurs when a layer of water, containing air pollutants, provides electrical conductivity that destroys the protective film of oxygen on metal surfaces. The effect of air pollutants on human beings is summarized in Tables 5.10 and 5.11.

Table 5.10

Effects of gaseous pollutants

Pollutants	*Effects*
Sulphur Dioxide (SO_2)	Breathing rate increases while breathing itself becomes less deep and a general feeling of air starvation is experienced-some even show signs of Bronchial spasms and asthmatics are badly affected. Any SO_2 which oxidizes to SO_3 may dissolve in body fluids to form H_2SO_4, a very strong and corrosive acid.
Carbon monoxide (CO)	CO combines with the hemoglobin in the blood to form carboxyl hemoglobin and when about half of the hemoglobin of the blood is used up, death ensues as the carboxyl hemoglobin is useless for respiratory purposes. Persons poisoned by carbon monoxide exhibit a characteristic bright pink colour of the flesh due to the presence of carboxyl hemoglobin in the blood.
Oxides of nitrogen (NOx)	Prolonged exposure of human beings to even low concentrations of oxides of nitrogen, can cause a chronic irritation of the respiratory tract, headache, loss of appetite and corrosion of teeth. Nitric oxide reacts with air to form brown nitrogen dioxide which is very poisonous.
Ozone (O_3)	In high concentrations, ozone exhibits a noticeably blue colour and an odour not unlike chlorine. It is poisonous in comparatively low concentrations and can cause irritation and a total ozone concentration of 26g/m_3 may lead to asthma attacks.

Table 5.11
Effects of non-biological air pollutants on man

Pollutant	*Source*	*Effects*
Aldehyde (formaldehyde and acrolein)	Autoexhaust, waste incineration, fuel combustion, photo-chemical reactions	Odours irritant to eye, skin and respiratory system.
Ammonia	Chemical industries, coke ovens, refineries, stocks yards and fuel incineration.	Corrosive to mucous membranes, damaging to eyes and respiratory tract.
Arsenic	Metal smelters, arsenical pesticides and herbicides	If inhaled, ingested or absorbed through skin, it causes dermatibis, mild bronchitis and nasal irritation, suspected carcinogen.
Asbestos	Asbestos factory or mine construction sites	Pulmonary fibrosis, pleural calcification, lung cancer.
Barium	Industries, mining, refining, barium based chemicals, smoke suppressant, additives in diesel fuels	Affects heart muscles, gastrointestinal tract and central nervous system and respiratory tract.
Beryllium	Industrial usage, production of fluorescent lamps, motor fuels	Pulmonary damage and damage to skin membranes from handling and mucous soluble salts of beryllium.
Boron	Industry producing boron, petroleum fuel, or additives, present in coal	Toxic through ingestion of inhalation, as dust causes irritation and inflammation; boron hydrides can cause damage to central nervous system which may result in death.
Cadmium	Metal industries engaged in extraction, refining, machining, electroplating and welding materials. Byproduct of refining lead, zinc and copper. Pesticides, fertilizer, cadmium, nickel batteries, reactor poison in nuclear fission plants, used in production of tetraethyl lead gasoline.	Chronic and acute poisoning. Inhalation of fumes and vapours, causes damage to kidney, emphysema, bronchitis, cancer, gastric and intestinal disorders, diseases of heart, liver and brain.
Chlorine	Process industries using chlorine, accidental breakage during storage and transportation.	Irritates eye, nose and throat. Large doses damage lungs, producing edema, pneumonitis, emphysema and bronchitis.
Chromium	Metallurgical and chemical industries, products employing chromate compounds, cement, asbestos.	Irritative, corrosive and toxic to body tissues. Believed to cause carcinogenic action. Develops dermatitis and ulcers of the skin and perforation of nasal septum.
Ethylene	Motor vehicle emissions, chemical industries, incineration of agricultural wastes, emitted by growing plants.	Eye irritation as a result of photochemical reaction with nitrogen oxide and ozone.

(*Contd..*)

Pollutant	*Source*	*Effects*
Hydrochloric acid	Byproduct from chlorination of organic compounds, burning of chlorinated plastics and paper, combustion of gasoline containing ethylene chloride.	Coughing and choking from inhalation, inflammation and ulceration of upper respiratory tract, clouding of the cornea.
Hydrogen sulphide	Biological decay of protein material in stagnant water, kraft paper mills, industrial waste disposal ponds, sewage treatment plant, refineries, coke ovens.	Headaches, conjunctivitis, sleeplessness, and pain in eyes. In high concentrations, can lead to blockage of O_2 transfer, it acts as a cell poison and damages nerve tissues.
Iron	Iron and steel plants, fly ash from combustion of coal and fuel oil, municipal waste incineration, use of welding rods.	Benign pneumoconiosis and siderosis (iron pigmentation of the lungs). Iron oxides act as a vehicle for transporting carcinogens and sulphur dioxide deep into the lungs.
Lead	Automobile emissions, lead smelters, combustion of coal and fuel oil, lead arsenate pesticides.	Absorbed through gastro-intestinal and respiratory tract and deposited in mucous membrane of nose, throat and in the lungs.
Manganese	Blast furnaces producing ferromanganese compounds, organic manganese fuel additives, use of welding rods, incineration of manganese containing products.	Manganese poisoning of central nervous system, manganic pneumonia caused by absorption, inhalation, ingestion or through skin.
Mercury	Mining and refining of mercury, use of mercury in laboratories. Pesticides containing mercury.	Vapours inhaled may cause intoxication or protoplasmic poisoning.
Nickel	Metallurgical plants using nickel,. engines burning fuels containing nickel additives, burning coal and oil, nickel plating facilities, incineration of nickel products.	May cause cancer of lungs and sinus, other respiratory disorders, dermatitis.
Phosphorous	Plants producing phosphate fertilizers, phosphoric acid, phosphorous pentoxide. Emission from vehicles and aeroplanes using phosphorous as corrosion inhibitors in fuel.	Skin irritation to systematic poisoning. High concentrations affect nervous system.
Radioactive substances	Direct contamination by radioactive gases or suspended dust from natural or artificial sources. Indirect contamination when radio–nuclides are ingested from food chain as a result of contact with contaminated ground, water, plants or animals.	Somatic effects such as leukemia and other types of cancer, cataracts and reduction in life expectancy. Genetic effects include mutation in human gametes that show up only in future generations.

Pollutant	*Source*	*Effects*
Selenium	Combustion of industrial and residual fuels, refinery waste gases and fumes, incineration of waste including paper products.	Irritation to eyes, nose, throat, respiratory tract, and gastrointestinal tract, chronic intoxication from industrial toxicants. Effects on kidney, liver and lungs.
Vanadium	Vanadium refining industries, alloy industries, power plants and utilities using vanadium-rich residual oil.	Physiological effect of varying severity on the gastrointestinal and respiratory tracts. Inhibition of chloesterol synthesis. Chronic exposure related to heart disease and cancer.
Zinc	Zinc refineries, manufacture of brass, zinc-galvanizing process.	Fumes have a corrosive effect on the skin which irritate and damage the mucous membrane.

Photochemical Reactions in the Atmosphere

The thousands of substances produced as waste products by human activity mix with the natural components of the atmosphere and may undergo oxidation and petrochemical reactions to produce unstable intermediates and primary and secondary products during their residence. Among the more reactive pollutants are sulphur dioxide, oxides of nitrogen, hydrocarbons and other organic substances. The products include free radicals, ozone, aldehydes, organic acids and peroxides or ozonides of hydrocarbons including nitrated and sulphonated derivatives.

Atmospheric chemical reactions usually require more activation energy than can be supplied by molecular collisions due to ambient air temperature. The necessary activation energy for most atmospheric reactions is supplied by solar radiations.

The elementary Nature of Photochemical Reactions

A photochemical reaction begins with the act of absorption of radiation. By the Stark–Einstein law of photochemical equivalence, this is a quantum process involving one photon per absorbing molecule. The number of absorbing molecules is, therefore, equal to the number of photons absorbed.

The immediate result of the absorption of a photon is an excited state of the absorbing molecule, which has excess absorbed energy. As most vibrations and rotational spectra lie in the infrared and most electronic spectra in the visible and ultraviolet region, it is the latter region, *i.e.*, the ultraviolet region which is of photochemical importance.

The electronically excited molecules produced by absorption may undergo any of the following changes:

1. The may dissociate
2. They may react with other molecules on collision
3. They may internally rearrange or polymerize
4. They may lose their excitation energy by fluorescence or deactivation and thereby return to their original state.

Any of these possibilities except the last one serves as an initial chemical step or primary process in a photochemical reaction. The three steps involved in an overall photochemical reaction are:

1. Absorption of radiation
2. Primary reactions
3. Secondary reactions

Radiation

The temperature variation with altitude is shown in Fig. 5.3. Sunlight in the wavelength range below 2900 Å is removed effectively by the stratosphere ozone layer before reaching the lower atmosphere. It is in the ultraviolet region with a wavelength of 3,000–5000 Å, that the radiation is of any use in photochemical reactions. The ultraviolet light available in the troposphere contains sufficient energy to break carbon-carbon and nitrogen-oxygen bonds by primary photochemical reactions.

Absorption

Light absorption by pollutant molecules may lead to the formation of an excited state in which the excited molecules interact. Alternatively, excited molecules may transfer their energy to other molecules or atoms or may lose their energy by emission of light as fluorescence.

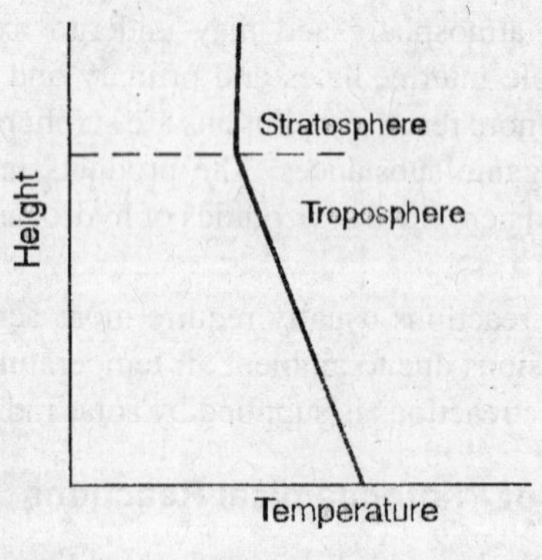

Fig. 5.3

The absorbers of solar radiation include the following components: NO_2, SO_2, aldehydes, nitrogen and nitric acid, hydrogen peroxide, ketones, organic peroxides and many other organic compounds and aerosols such as metal oxides.

Primary Reactions

The most important primary photochemical reaction is the dissociation of nitrogen dioxide into nitric oxide and atomic oxygen:

$$NO_2 + hv \rightarrow NO + O \tag{5.1}$$

Nitric oxide in the atmosphere is oxidized relatively slowly by oxygen or very rapidly by ozone to form nitrogen dioxide. Consequently, the above reactions form a reacting chain which may be broken only by the complete conversion of NO, to nitric acid by hydration and catalytic oxidation in the presence of fog droplets and aerosols. The sequence of read ions may be postulated as follows:

$$2NO + O_2 \rightarrow 2NO_2 \tag{5.1.1}$$

$$NO + O_3 \rightarrow NO_2 + O_2 \tag{5.1.2}$$

$$2NO_2 + O_3 \rightarrow N_2O5 + O2 \quad (5.1.3)$$

$$4NO_2 + 2H_2O + O_2 \rightarrow 4HNO_3 \quad (5.1.4)$$

Nitric acid and nitrous acid may absorb light and be dissociated photochemicaliy to NO_2 and NO as follows:

$$HNO_3 + hv \rightarrow NO_2 + HO^\circ \quad (5.2.1)$$

$$HNO_2 + hv \rightarrow NO + HO^\circ \quad (5.2.2)$$

$$HNO_2 + hv \rightarrow NO_2 + H^\circ \quad (5.2.3)$$

Formation of Free Radicals. The formation of free radicals from the photo–dissociation of aldehydes and other compounds which absorb solar radiation could lead to eye irritation, plant damage and photochemical smog. The following reactions indicate possible modes of formation of free radicals.

$$\underset{\displaystyle \text{H}}{\text{R—}\underset{|}{\text{C}}} = O + hv \longrightarrow R^\circ + HCO \quad (5.3.1)$$

$$\begin{matrix} R \\ & \searrow \\ & & CO + hv \longrightarrow R^\circ + R^\circ C \\ & \nearrow \\ R \end{matrix} \quad (5.3.2)$$

$$RONO + hv \rightarrow RO^\circ + NO^\circ \quad (5.3.3)$$

R may be an alkyl or an aryl group or hydrogen.

The above reactions denote primary photo-dissociation processes but secondary reactions involving free radicals may also take place.

Secondary Reactions

In most case, the direct effect of light ceases with the photochemical primary process. Secondary reactions are thermal and arc independent of the means by which the readmits concerned are produced. The following example illustrates the formation of free radicals by the reaction of ozone with olefins or reaction of free radicals with oxygen, ozone. NO, and other organic substances.

$$RCH = CHR + O_2 \rightarrow 2RCHO + O_2 \quad (5.4)$$

$$R^\circ + O_2 \rightarrow ROO^\circ \quad (5.5)$$

$$ROO^\circ + NO \rightarrow ROONO \quad (5.6)$$

The alkyl and aryl radicals unite with oxygen to form peroxyl, a radical, which in turn reacts with oxygen to give O, and with NO, giving peroxyacyl nitrate (PAN), formaldehyde (an irritant) and polymcric compounds (which reduce visibility). The formation of PAN takes place as follows:

$$R\overset{\displaystyle O}{\overset{\|}{C}}OO^\circ + NO_2 \longrightarrow R\overset{\displaystyle O}{\overset{\|}{C}}OONO_2\,(PAN) \quad (5.7)$$

Peroxyl acetyl nitrate (PAN) belongs lo a family of compounds which includes peroxy acetyl nitrate, peroxy propionyl nitrate, etc.

Chain Termination. A chain is terminated by any one of the following:

1. Interaction of two free radicals to form a stable end product.

$$ROO^\circ + RO^\circ \rightarrow ROR + O_2 \tag{5.8}$$

2. Reaction of a free radical with NO or NO_2

$$ROO^\circ + NO \rightarrow ROONO_2. \tag{5.9}$$

3. Formation of an absorbed layer or polymer complex by impingement of the free radical on the surface of the aerosol particle.

Photo Oxidation of Sulphur Dioxide

SO_2 in the presence of oxygen is slowly photolyzed, when exposed to solar radiation, yielding SO_3, and in the presence of water, to HS_2O_4.

$$SO_2 + hv \rightarrow SO_2^\circ \text{ (excited)} \tag{5.10}$$

$$SO_2^\circ + O_2 \rightarrow SO_4^\circ \tag{5.11}$$

$$SO_4^\circ + O_2 \rightarrow SO_3 + O_3 \tag{5.12}$$

$$H_2O + SO_3 \rightarrow H_2SO_4 \tag{5.13}$$

The rate of photo–oxidation of SO_2 and formation of H_2SO_4 aerosol is greatly enhanced by the presence of olefin and the oxides of nitrogen.

Los Angeles Smog

Studies made in the Los Angeles area of the United States reveal an interesting sequence of concentration levels of various atmospheric pollutants during photo-oxidation reactions that accompany photochemical smog episodes. It is initiated by the photo-dissociation of nitrogen dioxide and subsequent oxidation reactions involving unsaturated hydrocarbons, other organic compounds and free radicals to form ozone and organic peroxides. The phenomenon occurs during warm, sunny days with gentle winds and low level inversion. Visibility is reduced markedly. Eye irritation, plant damage, a characteristic odour and accelerated cracking of rubber goods are obvious results.

An important feature of photochemical smog is the production of aerosols that markedly reduce visibility. Aerosols of similar composition are formed by the irradiation of olefins or gasoline in the presence of NO_2. It has been experimentally confirmed that the presence of unusually high ozone in the atmosphere is due to solar irradiation. Also, ozone is produced during photosensitized reactions; it is destroyed or removed by dark reactions, such as oxidation of NO to NO_2, the formation of PAN and production of ozonides and peroxides of hydrocarbons.

Chemical Reactions in a Contaminated Atmosphere

A variety of chemical reactions occurs in the contaminated atmosphere of cities. The products of such reactions have been blamed for many of the unpleasant properties attributed to polluted atmospheres. For example, it has been suggested that the products of the oxidation of hydrocarbons in the presence of nitrogen dioxide and sunlight are responsible for eye irritation, decrease of visibility, plant damage, and cracking of rubber goods.

The substances which can react chemically in the atmosphere fall into two groups: major natural constituents of the atmosphere, which are present in high concentrations, and contaminants, usually present at low concentrations. These groups differ in concentration by a factor of 10^4 to 10^6. This large difference in concentration is convenient for purposes of classification of reactions and calls for careful interpretation of the kinetic and photochemical data available, *e.g.*, when nitrogen dioxide is irradiated by near ultraviolet radiation, molecular oxygen and nitric oxide and formed by the following reactions:

$$NO_2 + h\nu \rightarrow NO + O \tag{5.14}$$

$$NO_2 + Oh \rightarrow NO + O_2 \tag{5.15}$$

However, in an atmosphere containing a fraction of a part per million of nitrogen dioxide and about 21 percent of oxygen, the following reaction (where M is any molecule) will be faster:

$$O + O_2 + M \rightarrow O_3 + M \tag{5.16}$$

when a reaction of the following type occurs:

$$nA + mB \rightarrow \text{products} \tag{5.17}$$

and this reaction obeys the following rate law:

$$-d(A)/dt = k(A)^n(B)^m \tag{5.18}$$

where $-d(A)/dt$ = rate of consumption of A

(A) and (B) = concentrations of A and B, respectively

k = a constant (5.19)

If $n + m$ is 2 or larger, *i.e.*, if the reaction is kinetically of second or higher order, relatively small decreases in the concentration of A and B would greatly decrease the rate of reaction. The rates of most gas–phase reactions are studied with reactions present at partial pressures between 1 mm of mercury and 1 atm. If a reaction is of a second or higher order, then, a conveniently measured rate, under these conditions, would imply a completely negligible rate if the reactants were present at fractions of a part for million. The well-known reaction of nitric oxide with oxygen to form nitrogen dioxide illustrates this effect. The equation is

$$2NO + O_2 \rightarrow 2NO_2 \tag{5.19.1}$$

This reaction follows the rate law:

$$-d(NO)/dt = k\,(NO)_2(O_2) \tag{5.19.2}$$

Since the concentration of oxygen in air is essentially constant, the reaction is kinetically of second order in the atmosphere and the time required for one-half of the nitric oxide to disappear is given by the equation:

$$t_{0.5} = \frac{1}{k(O_2)(NO)_{initial}} \tag{5.20}$$

When the concentration of nitric oxide is 10,000 ppm (1 per cent), the half-life is about 36 hr but when the concentration of nitric oxide is 0.1 ppm, the half-life is about 1,000 hr.

The half-life for a first-order reaction does not change with concentration of the reactant. In this case, the reaction occurs in the atmosphere at a conveniently measurable rate if the energy of activation is below about 25 kcal.

The velocity constant, k, for a reaction is usually a function of temperature. The relationship between velocity constant and temperature can generally be indicated by an equation of the form:

$$k = Ae^{-E/RT} \tag{5.21}$$

where A = a constant having the same dimensions as k

E = activation energy for the reaction

R = gas constant

T = absolute temperature.

Values for A and E for a number of reactions which may occur in contaminated atmospheres are presented in Table 5.12.

Table 5.12

Some constants for atmospheric reaction

Reactions	*A*	*E, kcal*
$2NO + O_2 \rightarrow 2NO_2$	8.0×10^9	0 or negative
$NO + O_2 \rightarrow NO_2 + O_2$	8.0×10^{11}	2.5
$2NO_2 + O_3 \rightarrow N_2O_5 + O_2$	5.9×10^{12}	7.0
$N_2 + H_2C \rightarrow CH_2$ + products	3.5×10^5	0.0
$O_3 + H_2C(CH_2)_2\,CH \rightarrow$ Products	5.6×10^6	0.0
$O_3 + HC = CH \rightarrow$ Products	3.0×10^7	4.8
$CH_3 + CH_3 \rightarrow C_2H_6$	4.5×10^{12}	0.0
$CH_3 + NO \rightarrow$ Products	8.0×10^{11}	0.0
$CH_3 + O_2 \rightarrow CH_3O_2$	10^{10}	0.0

All values have the dimensions cm^3 $mole^1$ s^1 except for the reaction of nitric oxide with oxygen which is third–order and has the dimensions cm^6 $mole^{-2}$ s^{-1}.

Photochemically active radiation in sunlight, near the earth's surface, varies in wavelength from about 2,900–7,000 Å. Substances which absorb radiation in this region can serve as primary photochemical reactants for photosensitizers, which function by transferring the absorbed energy to potentially reactant molecules. If a substance is present in small concentrations, it must have a high specific absorption in the 2,900–7000 Å wavelength region if it is to initiate photochemical reactions of any importance. If a substance is present in large concentrations, it can absorb relatively weakly and still initiate reactions of considerable importance to the properties of polluted atmospheres. Many reactions can be postulated which might occur among the constituents of contaminated atmospheres.

If the kinetics of a postulated reaction has been studied, the extent to which the reaction would occur can usually be predicted. If the reaction has not been investigated, considerable information regarding the possibility that the reaction would occur to an appreciable extent can often be obtained by thermodynamic considerations. The free energies and heats of formation of a large number of substances are known or can be estimated. These values can be used to calculated the change in free energies and heat content accompanying postulated reactions. The free energies and heats of formation of a number of substançes which may occur in contaminated atmospheres are shown in Table 5.13.

Table 5.13

Some heat and free energies of formation

(Values in kcal at 25°C. All substances listed in gaseous state)

Substance	*H°, kcal*	*F°, kcal*
$O(3P_2)$	59.1	55.02
$O(D_2)$	104.3	—
$O_2(1+)$	37.40	—
O_2	34.50	39.40
$H(2S\frac{1}{2})$	51.9	48.35
HO	–5.93	–4.80
H_2O	–57.8	–34.64
H_2O_3	–33.60	–24.73
S	66.3	56.60
S_2	–5.3	–H
SO_2	–70.90	–71.74
SO_2	–93.90	–88.0
$N(3S\frac{1}{2})$	85.10	81.00
N_2O	19.65	24.9.3
NO	21.60	20.66
NO_2	8.00	12.27
N_2O_4	3.06	23.44
N_2O_5	–0.60	26.44
CH_4	–18.24	–12.20
C_2H_4	11.00	—
C_4H_6	–20.96	–10.70
HCHO	–28.70	24.90
HCO_2H	88.65	–85.1
CO	–26.84	–33.01
CO_2	–04.95	–34.0

A number of reactions which might produce oxygen in the atmosphere is shown in Table 5.14. Oxygen atoms reacting with molecular oxygen produce ozone. Table 5.14 also shows the maximum wavelengths which would supply the energy required by the endothermic reactions It was assumed in calculating these wavelengths that each reaction as written absorbs one quantum of the radiation.

Table 5.14

Some reactions and their energy deficiencies

Reaction	*H.kcal*	*Have lengths*
$O_2 \rightarrow O + O$	+ 118.2	2.420
$O + O_2 + M \rightarrow O_3 + M$	– 24.6	Dark

(Contd..)

Reaction	*H.kcal*	*Have lengths*
$SO_2 + O_2 \rightarrow SO_2 + O$	+46.1	6,197
$H_2S + O_2 \rightarrow H_2O + S + O$	+72.4	3,919
$O_2 \rightarrow O_2$	+.37.4	7,638
$NO + O_2 \rightarrow NO_2 + O$	+45.5	6,279
$NO_2 + O_2 \rightarrow NO + O_3$	+ 48.1	5,940
$CH_4 + O_2 \rightarrow CH_3OH.+ O$	+28.9	9,885
$C_{2H}6 + O_2 \rightarrow C_2H_4 + H_2O + O$	+33.3	8,579
$HCHO + O_2 \rightarrow HCO_2H + O$	–0.8	Dark
$CO + O_2 \rightarrow CO_2 + O$	–8.5	Dark

The thermal reaction of oxygen to form ozone can be used to illustrate the application of such data. Table 5.13 shows that this reaction would occur with an increase in free energy of 39.4 kcal/mole. The equilibrium constant AT for the reaction can be calculated from the equation

$$F = RT \ln K \tag{5.22}$$

K is found to be about 10^{-29}. Then,

$$(O_3)/(O_2)^{3/2} = 10^{-29} \tag{5.23}$$

where (O_3) and (O_2) are the concentrations of ozone and oxygen expressed in atmospheres. Substituting 0.2 for (O_2), the equilibrium concentration of ozone from the thermal reaction is found to be about 10^{-30} atm or 10^{-24} ppm. Thus, the thermal reaction would produce a negligible concentration of ozone in the atmosphere.

With the exception of the decomposition of oxygen, all the reactions listed in Table 10.12, from an energetic standpoint alone, proceed towards the right with the light available at the earth's surface. Some could even go in the dark, though this does not mean that they actually do. First, the energy required for the initial intermolecular process (the activation energy) is not taken into account. Second, in the case of those reactions requiring light, the ability of one of the reactants to absorb solar radiation is not indicated in Table 5.14. The list could be expanded indefinitely.

Reactions of Oxides of Nitrogen

Oxides of nitrogen undoubtedly undergo many reactions in the atmosphere, both in sunlight and in the dark. It is also, possible that they act as photosensitizers. Thus, they probably play an important role in the chemistry of contaminated atmosphere.

For nitric oxide at 1 ppm, tire half life is 100 hrs, and at 0.1 ppm, the half life 1,000 hrs. After a few days, there would be considerable amounts of both nitric oxide and nitrogen dioxide. Given this situation, the following reaction is known to be very rapid:

$$NO + NO_2 + H_2O \rightarrow 2HNO_2$$

If tire concentrations of nitric oxide and nitrogen dioxide are equal, and about 2 percent of water vapour is present, at equilibrium, the concentration of nitrous acid would be 19 percent of the concentration of nitric oxide. The following reactions attain equilibrium, almost instantly, even at 0.1 ppm:

$$2NO_2 \rightarrow N_2O_4 \quad (5.24)$$

$$NO + NO_2 \rightarrow N_2O_2 \quad (5.25)$$

However, at these low concentrations, the equilibrium lies far to the left. Nitrogen dioxide reacts with water vapour and oxygen to give nitric acid vapour

$$H_2O + 2NO_2 + \tfrac{1}{2}O_2 \rightarrow HNO_3 \quad (5.26)$$

At equilibrium, about 90 percent of the nitrogen oxides would be present in the form of nitric acid. The rate of reaction is much slower than the gas–phase reaction:

$$H_2O + 3NO_2 \rightarrow 2HN_3 + NO \quad (5.27)$$

Nitrogen dioxide reacts rapidly with moist solid sodium chloride to produce nitrosyl chloride:

$$2NO_2 + NaCl \rightarrow NOCl + NaNO_3 \quad (5.28)$$

Nitric acid reacts with ammonia and amines to form the corresponding nitrates. Nitric oxide reacts rapidly with organic free radials to stop free radial chain reactions, while, nitrogen dioxide reacts rapidly with organic free radials to produce stable nitroparaffins. However, in the dark and at room temperature, nitric oxide, nitrogen dioxide, and nitric acid vapour do not react rapidly with hydrocarbon vapours at concentrations usually existing in the contaminated atmospheres of cities.

Such reactions are termed 'dark reactions', i.e., reactions which occur even in the absence of light. However, numerous photochemical reactions involving oxides of nitrogen may occur in contaminated atmospheres. Nitric oxide absorbs visible and near–ultraviolet light so weakly that it is unlikely that this absorption is responsible for any appreciable chemical reaction in a contaminated atmosphere. The absorption spectrum of nitric acid vapour is not very well known. There may be moderated or weak absorption in the near-ultraviolet region, and such radiation decomposes liquid nitric acid. However, this decomposition may result from absorption by nitrogen dioxide, in which case, the following reaction may occur:

$$HNO_3 + hv \rightarrow HO + NO_2 \quad (5.29)$$

Nitrosyl chloride, which might be formed in the atmosphere by reaction (5.28), absorbs near ultraviolet radiation very strongly to form nitric oxide and chlorine:

$$NOCl + hv \rightarrow NO + Cl \quad (5.30)$$

Nitrogen dioxide absorbs strongly in the visible and near ultraviolet regions. Its photochemistry has been thoroughly investigated. The photolysis of nitrogen dioxide to form nitric oxide and oxygen atoms and the combination of the oxygen atoms with molecular oxygen to form ozone were discussed previously (Eqs. 5.14 and 5.16). However, the nitric acid and ozone formed according to 5.14 and 5.16, respectively, would react very rapidly to form nitrogen dioxide and oxygen. Thus, a low, steady–state concentration of ozone would quickly attained. For 1 ppm of nitrogen dioxide in sunlight, the steady state ozone concentration would be 0.1 ppm, and for 0.1 ppm of nitrogen dioxide, the steady-state ozone concentration would be about 0.03 ppm. Thus, these reactions cannot explain the ozone content of the atmospheres of some cities, where the concentration of ozone is often several tenths of a ppm. This result has been qualitatively confirmed at Stanford Research Institute by irradiating mixtures of nitrogen dioxide and air, and measuring the ozone produced.

Reactions of Sulphur Dioxide

Sulphur dioxide absorbs solar radiation between 2,900 and about 4,000 Å, with the maximum absorption probably occurring between 2,900 and 3,000 Å. It reacts very slowly with oxygen in sunlight to form sulphur trioxide

$$2SO_2 + O_2 + hv \rightarrow 2SO_3 \qquad (5.31)$$

This reaction is first order with respect to sulphur dioxide and the reaction amounts to about 0.1 to 0.2 percent per hour in air in intense natural sunlight. It is also known that nitrogen dioxide in concentrations of 5 to 20 percent of the sulphur dioxide concentration had no significant effect on the reaction rate. Sodium nuclei and a variation of the relative humidity in the range 30 to 90 percent also had no effect on the reaction rate. It is of interest to speculative the effect of chlorine on the reaction of sulphur dioxide with oxygen. Chlorine absorbs sunlight strongly, with a maximum absorption coefficient at about 3,400 Å. It is a powerful photoactivator. Apparently, the primary effect of light is to decompose the molecular chlorine:

$$Cl_2 + hv \rightarrow Cl + Cl \qquad (5.32)$$

When an oxidizable substance is exposed to radiation in the presence of chlorine and oxygen, a sensitized oxidation almost always occurs. Chlorine is probably formed in the atmosphere by the reaction of nitrogen dioxide with salt (Eqs. 10.28 and 10.30) and by the reaction of ozone with salt.

$$2H^+ + 2Cl^- + O_3 = O_2 + H_2O + Cl_2 \qquad (5.33)$$

However, the concentration of salt in the air of most cities seldom exceeds about 0.1 mg/ cu m, and it is doubtful whether enough chlorine would ever be produced to appreciably affect the oxidation of sulphur dioxide.

The rate of reaction of sulphur dioxide with ozone, even when both are present at relatively high concentrations, is also very slow. When the concentration of ozone is about 1 percent, the concentration of sulphur dioxide is 1 to 10 percent, and the concentration of water vapour is 0 to 1 percent, i.e., less than 0.1 percent of the sulphur dioxide reached during 24 hrs.

Reaction of Ozone with Unsaturated Hydrocarbons

Fairly rapid reaction occurs between ozone and various olefins at concentrations at which they may occur in contaminated atmospheres. The reaction mechanisms are not precisely known, and a variety of products is obtained. However, the initial rates follow a second order rate law:

$$-d(O_3)/dt = k(O_3)\ (\text{Olefin}) \qquad (5.34)$$

The final products include formaldehyde, higher aldehydes, and polymers of unknown composition. The reactions maybe tentatively summarized.

$$O_3 + \text{Olefin} \rightarrow \text{Olefin} - O_3 \text{ complex} \qquad (5.35)$$

Olefin-O, complex = decomposition fragments, including free radials.

At high concentrations of reactants, a visible aerosol forms at concentrations which would probably exist in the smog laden air of cities, no aerosol has been experimentally demonstrated.

The reaction of ozone with acetylene has also been investigated. This reaction also follows a second order rate law, but the velocity constant k is very small. The rates of reaction of ozone with benzene and with paraffin hydrocarbons are so small that they could not be determined by the methods employed in these investigations.

Initial second–order constants and half–life for the reaction of ozone with various substances are shown in Table 5.15.

Table 5.15

Rate constant and half–life of initial rate of reaction of ozone with various substances

Substance reacting with ozone	*Half-life if reactant and ozone are 0.2 ppm min. are l ppm min.*	*Half-life if reactant and ozone*	*Rate constant ppm^{-1} min^{-1} at 25°C*
Ethylene	1.000	220	0.0045
1–Hexane	330	66	0.0150
Cyclohexane	37	12	0.0870
Gasoline	250	76	0.0130
Acetylene	500,000	24,000	0.00010
Nitric oxide	0.16	0.03	32,00000
Nitrogen dioxide	65.00	13.00	0.07700

It has been noted that the reaction of nitric oxide with ozone is 2,000 times faster than those of 1–hexane and ozone. Nitrogen dioxide reacts with ozone about five times faster than 1 –hexane. Thus, these last two reactions would proceed at the same rate if, for example, the concentrations of nitrogen dioxide and 1–hexane were 0.2 and 1 ppm, respectively.

Photochemical Reaction of Aldehydes, Ketones and Olefins

Simple aldehydes and ketones absorb radiation which begins between 3,000 and 4,000 Å and extends towards shorter wavelengths, usually terminating between 2,300 and 2,500 Å. The absorption coefficients in the solar region are relatively low. The absorption regions for diketones are displaced toward larger wavelengths to an extent which depends upon the proximity of the groups written the molecule. Thus, glyoxcal and diacetyl absorb up to about 5,000 Å.

The most important primary photochemical reactions of aldehydes and ketones are to break the molecule into free radicals. For example, acetaldehyde decomposes into methyl and fromyl radicals.

$$CH_3CHO + h\nu \rightarrow CH_3^0 + HCO^\circ \tag{5.36}$$

Acetone decomposes into methyl and acetyl radicals:

$$(CH_3)_2CO + h\nu \rightarrow CH_3^0 + CH_3CO^\circ \tag{5.37}$$

The free acetyl radical slowly decomposes into free radicals and carbon monoxide:

$$CH_3CO^\circ \rightarrow CH_3^0 + CO \tag{5.38}$$

The free radical HCO is remarkably stable. However, it does very slowly decompose:

$$HCO^{\circ} \rightarrow H + CO \tag{5.39}$$

$$H + O_2 \rightarrow HO_2 \tag{5.40}$$

It might react directly with oxygen:

$$HCO + O_2 \rightarrow HO_2 + CO \tag{5.41}$$

Reactions of free radicals such as those formed by the photolysis of aldehydes and ketones are discussed in the next articles. However, it may be pointed out here that large numbers of secondary reactions follow the primary photolysis. Most of the studies of the reaction products have been made in the absence of air. Under these conditions, formaldehyde undergoes a chain reaction giving, among other products, carbon monoxide, carbon dioxide, and water. Among the products of the photochemical decomposition of acetaldehyde in the absence of air, are methane, carbon dioxide, glyoxal, diacetyl, formaldehyde and an unidentified material of high molecular weight. Acetone forms carbon monoxide, methane, ethane, diacetyl and material of high molecular weight. In the presence of air, the radicals tend to react rapidly with oxygen. Thus, somewhat different compounds are produced. In absence of air acetone appears to give among other products, acetic acid and dimethyl peroxide. Acetaldehyde apparently gives diacetyl peroxide as a major product. Irradiation with sunlight of mixtures of diacetyl and air has been found to produce ozone, although not enough to account for the ozone concentrations, sometimes, found in contaminated atmospheres. The reactions involved are not precisely known, but the following presumptions are not unreasonable:

$$CH_3COCOCH_3 \rightarrow 2CH3CO \tag{5.42}$$

$$CH_3CO + O_2 \rightarrow CH_3COO_2 \tag{5.43}$$

$$CH_3COO_2 + O_2 \rightarrow CH_3COO + O_3 \tag{5.44}$$

Mono–olefins do not absorb radiation in the low atmosphere. However, conjugated diolefins absorb near–ultraviolet radiation fairly strongly to produce electronically excited molecules which react with oxygen.

$$\text{Diolefin} + hv = \text{excited diolefin}$$

$$\text{Excited diolefin} + O_2 = \text{free radical } HO_2$$

Oxygen absorbs weakly the many atmospheric bands in the visible region to produce excited oxygen molecules;

$$O_2 \xrightarrow{hv} O + O \tag{5.45}$$

By analogy to reaction 5.45, one could write down

$$O_2 + RH \rightarrow R + HO_2 \tag{5.46}$$

There appears to be no data for or against these reactions.

Reactions of Organic Free Radicals in the Atmosphere

A number of reactions which may occur in contaminated atmospheres yield organic free radicals as products. Others produce atoms or inorganic free radicals which, in some cases, would attack any organic molecule, saturated, unsaturated, or aromatic, to produce organic free radicals. The following are expected rapid reactions of inorganic free radicals to form organic free radicals:

$$O^\circ + RH \rightarrow OH^\circ + R \quad (5.47)$$

$$OH^\circ + RH \rightarrow H_2O + R^\circ \quad (5.48)$$

$$Cl^\circ + RH \rightarrow HC1 + R^\circ \quad (5.49)$$

$$H^\circ + RH \rightarrow H_2 + R^\circ \quad (5.50)$$

$$H_2O + RH \rightarrow H_2O_2 + R' \text{ or } 2OH + R \quad (5.51)$$

Reaction 5.38 is known to be very fast, but the products are uncertain and vary with the nature of the reactants. The other cases may vary with reactant also, for example, oxygen atoms may simply add to an olefin, hydroxyl atoms may split out an alcohol instead of water, etc. The point to emphasize here is that virtually every photochemical reaction expected to occur in contaminated air may result in the production of an organic free radical.

Many organic free radicals, such as those produced by extracting a hydrogen atom from a hydrocarbon molecule, react rapidly with oxygen to form peroxy free radicals:

$$R + O_2 \rightarrow RO_2 \quad (5.52)$$

The peroxy free radicals can react, in turn, with other organic substances to form organic peroxides and new free radicals:

$$RO_2 + R'H \rightarrow RO_2H + R' \quad (5.53)$$

Other reactions expected of organic free radicals include polymerization of olefins:

$$R' + R - CH = CH_2 \rightarrow R - CH(R') - CH_2 \quad (5.46)$$

Such oxidations and polymerizations are chain reactions, new radicals being generated by reaction (5.52) and (5.53) to maintain the chain.

In the literature, there is some speculation, but no proof, concerning the production of ozone from peroxy free radicals according to the reaction:

$$RO_2 + O_2 \rightarrow RO + O_3 \quad (5.55)$$

Equation 5.38 shows a special case of this reaction. If reaction (8.55) has any tendency to go, atmosphere conditions (with large amounts of oxygen and, thus, relatively small competition from reaction 5.52) are highly favourable.

Chain reactions involving free radicals terminate when the chain–maintaining radicals react with some substance without forming free radicals. Terminating steps for free radical chains in contaminated atmospheres include:

$$R + NO \rightarrow \text{unknown products} \quad (5.56)$$

$$R + NO_2 \rightarrow RNO_2 \quad (5.57)$$

$$R + R' \rightarrow RR' \quad (5.58)$$

Absorption and destruction of the radicals occur on surfaces, probably including the surface of particulate matter in the atmosphere. Also, one would expect that organic free radicals, would be absorbed and destroyed on the surfaces of most systems used for sampling and analysis of the atmosphere.

Reactions Involving Particulate Material

Reactions involving particulate material suspended in the atmosphere are of, at least, three types. One type consists of heterogenous gas-phase reactions, *i.e.*, reactions which occur, at least, in part on the surface of particles. The particles may absorb reactant gases and catalyze the reaction, e.g., the decomposition of ozone is catalyzed by a solid surface. Particles absorb and destroy free radicals, thereby, decreasing the rate of free radical chain reactions. The absorption of gas on solid surfaces might change the absorption spectrum of the gas for sunlight, e.g., oxygen absorbed on carbon particles might absorb sunlight much more strongly than would free oxygen.

The reactions just described produce relatively little change in the particulate material. A sound type of reaction involves both the gases and the particles and produces gross chemical changes in the latter. For example, the rate of oxidation of gaseous sulphur dioxide by oxygen or ozone is very slow. However, contaminated atmospheres may contain relatively large amounts of essentially aqueous droplets. Such droplets would dissolve sulphur dioxide from the atmosphere. The sulphurous acid, thus formed, would quickly be oxidized to sulphuric acid. Such droplets have been found to contain nitrates, sulfates, and organic material. Thus, throughout the lower atmosphere, reactions typical of aqueous solutions may occur inside such droplets. Reactions of ozone or nitrogen dioxide with salt particles (reactions 5.10 and 5.13) and of ammonia with sulphuric acid droplets are other examples of such reactions. A third type involves reactions between suspended particle, e.g., reactions between sulphuric acid droplets and limestone dust. Actual contact between the particles is necessary for such reactions to occur. Since the rate of agglomeration in city air is very slow as was pointed out earlier, these reactions would usually be slow except near the sources.

Though at present relatively little is known concerning reactions involving dusts and aerosols, they should not be over-looked as possible chemical or photochemical reactants or catalysts.

Lapse Rate and Inversion

Troposphere: In this region, which is nearest the surface, the temperature decreases fairly steadily from the ground temperature to a temperature to –50 to –80°C, at a rate of about 6.5° C/km, which is referred to as the lapse rate of the troposphere (Figs. 5.4,5.5). The air in the troposphere is well-mixed by convection currents and contains approximately 90 percent of the total mass of atmosphere. This layer contains most of the atmosphere's water, cloud and particulate matter. The height of this region is 15–18 km at the equator and only 8 km at the poles. The temperature curve changes slope rather suddenly in a narrow transitional layer known as the tropopause. The temperature at the tropopause is the least at the equator.

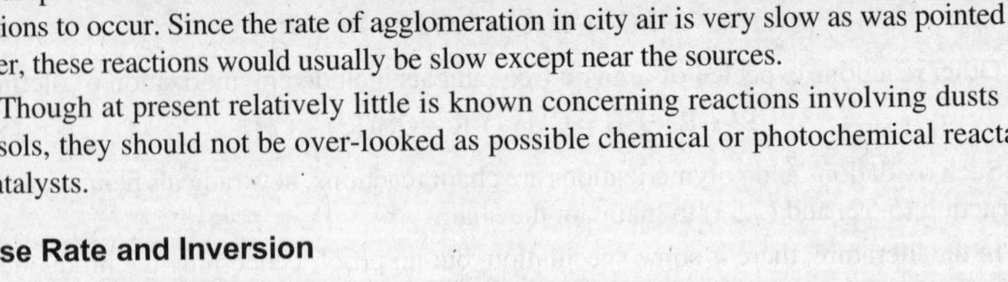

Fig. 5.4 Lapse rates on Temperature Profile

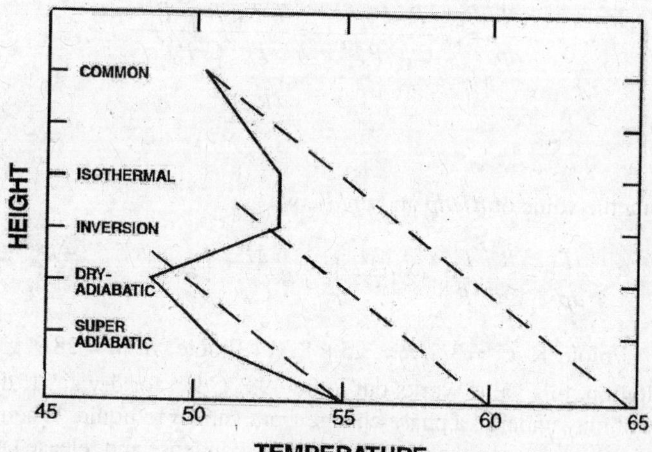

Fig 5.5

Stratosphere: Above the tropopause, the temperature curve shows a warming trend with increasing height. The warmth is due to the absorption of solar ultraviolet radiation by ozone, whose concentration in the stratosphere is in the range of 1–5 ppm by volume. The air is very dry and clouds and convection currents from the troposphere usually do not penetrate easily into it. Some transport of air masses, however, does take place between the two regions and their composition is very similar.

Stratopause: This extends to about 50 km in height and is the warm region in the atmosphere. It reflects sound waves from earth back to the surface.

Mesopause: It is the region with the coldest temperature in the atmosphere; i.e., of the range of–100°C.

Lapse Rate

The change of temperature with height in the troposphere is called the lapse rate. As we go higher in the atmosphere, the height or weight of air above decreases and so does the pressure. Any gas, free to expand, will tend to move from the region of high pressure to tire region of low pressure. As it does so, it expands and, if there is no interchange of heat with the surroundings, the gas will become cooler. This is called adiabatic cooling. This adiabatic lapse rate can be obtained by considering the pressure-volume-temperature relationship, the adiabatic expansion and the change of pressure with height.

1. Equation of state $PV = nRT$. (5.59)

2. Change of pressure with height $dp/dh = -g\dfrac{nM}{V}$ (5.60)

3. Law of adiabatic expansion P γ = constant or $T/T_0 = (P/P_0)^{R/C_p}$

Now, adiabatic lapse rate = $dT/dh \;=\; dT/dp.dp/dh \;= -g\dfrac{nm}{V}\left(\dfrac{dT}{dp}\right)$ (5 61)

dT/dp can be obtained as

$$\frac{dT}{dp} = T_0 \frac{R}{C_p} \frac{P^{R/C_p - 1}}{P_0^{R/C_p}} = \frac{T_0 T_R}{T} \frac{R}{C} \frac{P}{P_0^{RC_p P}}$$

$$= \frac{R}{C_p} \frac{T}{P} \qquad (5.62)$$

Substituting the value of dT/dp and dp/dh, we get

$$\frac{dT}{dp} = \frac{R}{C_p} \cdot \frac{T}{P}\left(-gn\frac{M}{V}\right) = -g\frac{M}{C_p} \quad \left(\text{as } n\frac{RT}{PV} = 1\right) \qquad (5.63)$$

($R = 8.314$ J/mole°K, $C_p = 3.5$, $R = 3.5 \times 8.314$ J/mole °*K*, $M = 28.9$, $g = 9.8\text{m/s}^2$)

On substitution, this value works out to be –9.8°C/km for dry air. If the air is moist, the water present may undergo a phase change from vapour to liquid. When a moist parcel of air rises, expands and cools, the water vapour can condense and release latent heat. Thus the actual moist adiabatic lapse rate is less than the dry rate and depends on humidity. It is in the range of –6 to 7°C/km with higher values occurring at greater heights where the water content is less. This is shown in Fig. 5.6.

On a clear summer day, rapid heating of the earth by the sun warms the air near the surface to the point where the lapse rate is super adiabatic. Under these conditions, the atmosphere is said to be in unstable equilibrium and marked vertical mixing of air results. This is the condition in which pollutants are rapidly dispersed.

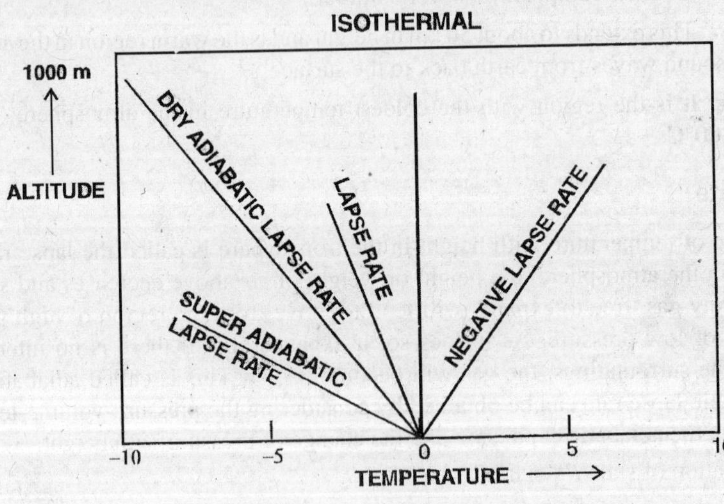

Fig. 5.6 Position of Lapse Rate under different atmospheric conditions

The opposite condition is the negative lapse rate or temperature inversion. In this case, the temperature increases as we go higher. This condition is most undesirable for the dispersion of pollutants.

Inversion

Inversion takes place in the atmosphere due to two reasons: 1. Radiation inversion 2. Subsidence inversion.

Radiation Inversion. The air near the surface cools during night by long wave radiation. Thus, the temperature is lower near the ground than at a height. This is called radiation inversion. When the sun rises and heats air near the ground, the inversion disappears. This is shown in Fig. 5.6.

Subsidence Inversion. This kind of inversion results when the upper layer of air descends (subsides) during a developing anticyclone (high pressure centres). The subsiding air warms as it contracts but the warming will be greater at the upper part than at the lower part near the ground.

Why Inversion is Important. When inversion develops, the atmosphere is said to be stable. The dense cold air lies at the bottom and has no natural tendency to rise. If a hot plume is omitted from a chimney, it will rise to some height, cooling as it goes up, but soon the temperature of the plume will stabilise at the temperature of the surrounding air and there will, then, be no driving force for the air to go higher. The pollutants will, thus, concentrate in the atmosphere instead of being dispersed, and this will increase the concentration and will be very harmful to mankind.

In the case of high level inversion, the lower inversion layer will form a lid for pollutants, which will cause them to accumulate and, thus, raise the concentration.

Many of the episodes of air pollution which have taken place in the world are due to inversion. Details of the famous London smog of 1952 that killed 4000 people and lasted for 5 days are given in Table 5.16. In towns, which are situated in valleys, this kind of phenòmenon, where the dense air, filled with pollutants, slips down to the valleys and forms a lake of polluted air, is a very harmful situation.

Table 5.16

Mortality increase in the London smog of 1952

Cause	*Seasonal norm*	*No. of deaths in the week after smog*	*Relative increase*
Bronchitis	75	704	9.4
Coronary disease	122	281	2.3
Myocardial degeneration	84	244	2.9
Pneumonia	37	168	4.5
Vascular lesions of CNS	98	128	1.3
Respiratory tuberculosis	17	77	4.5
Cancer of lung	36	69	1.9
Other respiratory diseases	8	52	6.5
Other causes	410	761	1.9
All causes	887	2,484	2.8

The problem of air pollution takes a serious dimension when climatic conditions are adverse to its effective dispersion. Obviously, in India, climatic conditions are favourable to dispersion in most of regions and lor almost 90 percent of the time. The possibility of inversion is also much less than in cold countries but the meteorological conditions, especially the direction, could be better utilized for pollutant dispersion, which is not the case at present. However, the atmosphere can not be used indefinitely for dumping pollutants. One of the unfavourable factors is the absence of high grade coal. The Indian coal available for combustion/gasification consists of a fairly large amount of ash moisture as will as volatile matters. The equipment used for combustion, both for power generation as well as in process industry, is not based on modern technology, resulting in poor combustion efficiency and, thus, a higher percentage of carbon mono–oxide in the effluent. In this regard, a special mention could be made of fluidized bed combustion which has a higher combustion efficiency than other conventional equipments.

Chimney Design Requirement

The chimney is an essential part of any furnace, boiler, thermal power plant, etc. It is normally used to create as natural draft and provide the air necessary for combustion. But chimneys could also be used as an efficient channel for proper dispersal of gaseous pollutant. The selection of the height of the chimney used is fairly important especially when it is located in a thickly populated area or is close to the same. Keeping the meteorological conditions, especially direction and velocity of wind, in mind, the dispersal of gaseous pollutants could be carried out in such a way that the population around the factoiy is not affected. The different aspects of the designs of chimneys have been briefly described in this chapter.

Regarding the stack design, on the basis of observation of past design, several factors that can be used as aids in future stack design or to predict pollutant concentrations to be expected from pollutant stacks have been determined. Generally, under the same meteorological conditions, ground–level pollutant concentration at a given point, down wind from a stack, is reduced as the stack height is increased. This is due to the fact that pollutants emitted from the stack are allowed more time to diffuse in the atmosphere before reaching the ground.

The effective stack height (H') is the physical height of the stack (H) plus the height differential due to the exit velocity (hv)oi the stack gases and the buoyancy (h_1,) of the stack gases, shown in Fig. 5.7.

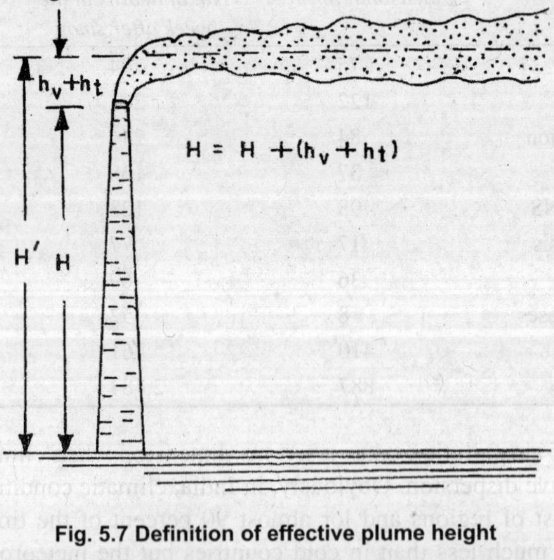

Fig. 5.7 Definition of effective plume height

It is obvious that some of the gases from a chimney will eventually reach the ground by diffusion whatever be the height of discharge or density of the gases. This type of diffusion is known as eddy diffusion, and is far faster than the classical kinetic diffusion. The mechanism is clearly visible in flat country by observation of smoke from chimneys which are tall enough for the plume to be undisturbed by down draughts into the lee of buildings or by turbulence generated by the ground contours.

It is now possible to calculate with sufficient accuracy the amount of dilution of the gases reaching the ground from a free-flowing plume at a particular height, and, therefore, the maximum time–mean ground-level concentration of any noxious constituent. This is important to the chemical engineer concern with the specification for the design of a plant for purification including dust and fume removal of waste games. The facts to be considered are:

1. Wind directions and velocities. (10 year averages can be obtained from the nearest meteorological station or from the meteorological department.)
2. The frequency of radiation type atmospheric temperature inversions likely to extend up to heights above 35 m.
3. Character of the surrounding district in terms of background air pollution.
4. The velocity of discharge from the chimney and the use of a multiple flued chimney for a plant with an output varying with the season, etc.
5. The aerodynamic effects caused by adjacent buildings, including existing or proposed 'high–rise' offices or dwellings within 10 chimney heights of the chimney, and the effects of high ground heights which should be considered in terms of the height of the base level of the chimney.
6. The thermal rise of a hot discharge by virtue of the temperature of the gases.
7. The calculated time–mean ground level concentration of noxious pollutants and dust–fall on 'sensitive' areas downwind, taking into account their height above chimney base level.
8. The persistence of visibility of the plume.

Aerodynamic Effects

A chimney is less effective for dispersion of an emission if the gases and fine dust do not flow smoothly away. In order to prevent down draughts, a chimney should be at least $2\frac{1}{2}$ times the height of the adjacent building. This well known rule has been substantiated in wind tunnels and by experimentation. An adjacent building can be defined, with some factor of safety, as one which is distant from the chimney by less than $3\frac{1}{2}$ times the cross wind width of the building. The longitudinal axis of the building should be at right angles to the most frequent wind. Large emissions such as those from power station type boilers should have chimneys which are $1\frac{1}{2}$, times the height of high rise buildings, lying within a circle of radius equal to 10 building heights.

Wind–tunnel tests have also been used for the design of a root with a necessarily short stack to ensure the smooth flow of flue gases from the top of a large block of offices and to prevent them from being drawn down on to balconies and into top windows.

Velocity of Discharge

Figure 5.8 shows the downdraught on the lee side of a chimney. The phenomenon is known as downwash. It is obvious that it reduces the effective height of the stack.

Downwash is overcome by discharge of the flue gases at a velocity greater than $1\frac{1}{2}$ times that of the wind passing over the chimney top. Since the highest frequently occurring wind is 10 m/s, the minimum velocity from ordinary industrial chimneys of up to 4 m diameter should be 15 m/s. Appreciably higher velocities are necessary from the multi–flue chimneys of about 20 m diameter of large power stations; these velocities are determined by wind– tunnel experiments which, nevertheless, tend to exaggerate the effect.

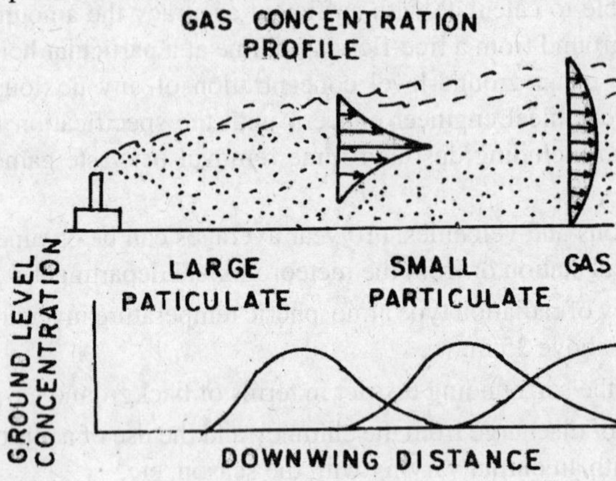

Fig. 5.8 Comparison of gaseous and particulate plumes at s given wind speed

Another objection to low effluent velocities is that wind can, then, eddy down inside a chimney to a depth of several diameters, thereby, cooling the walls of even an insulated chimney to below the dew point of the walls of the bases. Particles adhere to the dew and later strip off after they have built up to a thickness of a few mm; they, then fall near the chimney in the form of 'blobs' from dusty flue gases and as acid smuts from oil-fired furnaces.

The problem of downwash and air ingress has been overcome by the addition of a nozzle to the chimney mouth. The design of the nozzle should facilitate minimum pressure drop. It is essential that the flue gas should not leave the internal surface of the nozzle at any point. Since the addition of the nozzle increases the velocity head press are within the chimney mouth, it is necessary to line the inside of a concrete or brick stack with an impervious material, resistant to sulphuric acid in order to prevent a corrosive attack of the structure.

Temperature Inversions in the Atmosphere

Normally, the temperature of the air falls with increase in height and warm flue gases rise and are gradually cooled by mixing with the air. On clear nights, however, the temperature of the ground falls more quickly by radiation than does that of the air above, and there develops a boundary layer above, where the temperature of the air again increases with height. More than one inversion layer can develop. The mixture of air and flue gas from *C*, though still warm, cannot rise in the warmer air at the inversion boundary and, therefore,, accumulates below it (see Fig. 5.2). The flue gases from A issuing above the inversion, flow smoothly away and, because of the temperature gradient, cannot diffuse down to the ground through the inversion layer. If the volume of flue gases is very large and the chimney reaches nearly up to the inversion boundary, they may penetrate it, as proved by observation from a loft.

Accumulation of flue gases below an inversion boundary can become most unpleasant and even dangerous in a steep–sided valley as proved by disasters at Donera (U.S.A.) and the Meuse Valley (Belgium). When there is a development of water mist (fog), its mixture with smoke is called 'smog'. The SO_2 in the flue gases dissolves in the water droplets and is quickly oxidized to form dilute sulphuric acid, H_2SQ_4; this hinders evaporation of the water and stabilizes the fog.

Inversions frequently develop upwards from the ground to a height of about 40 m, and infrequently up to 100 m as during the London smog of 1952. It is highly desirable that, factory chimneys, with their large volumes of flue gas, compared with that from houses, be, atleast, 40 m high. At this height, turbulence and down–draughts from buildings do not disturb the flow of gases from most factories. Immediately after the London smog, the 1952 UK Government Committee on Air Pollution recommended a height for factory chimneys of 120 ft. (37 m), with discretion for small emissions. The complaints from certain small fertilizer factories ceased when the chimneys were raised to 37 m as reported in the United Kingdom.

Importance of Ground–Level Concentrations

The principle to be followed in deciding the height of a new chimney is that the estimated concentration of pollutants reaching the ground, when added to the background concentration, derived from other sources (both near and distant), should be sufficiently low so that appreciable damage to property and the health of people, animals and vegetation, is avoided. In an industrial country, however, there must be some compromise.

Concentrations of pollutants are expressed as micrograms per cubic meter (ng/nv) at atmospheric temperature; 10° C is usually taken.

$$1\text{ppm} = \frac{\text{Mol. wt. of pollutant}}{2.32} \text{g/m}^3 \text{ at } 10°\text{C}$$

A reason for expression as mass/volume is that living things breathe air by volume but are affected by the mass of pollutants absorbed. 10°C is not suitable for tropical countries as the temperature is generally higher

Thermal Rise of a Hot Gas Plume

Provided the chimney is of sufficient height to avoid a down draught, most theoretical and empirical equations reduce to

$$h = a\, Q_4\, v^{-1} \text{ metres}$$

where QH is the heat content in MW of the effluent above ambient temperature, usually taken as 10°C, v the wind speed in m/s at chimney height, and a is related to the height of emission and, therefore, takes some account of the turbulence of the air above the chimney. Empirical measurements indicate that $h - Q.25$.

For chimney heights he above 100 m

$$a = 475 + \text{Q}.61(h_c - 100)$$

For he between 47 and 100 m

$$a = 470 + 0.67 + 5.7 \times 10^{-3} h_c - 47$$

Hence, the effective height of the plume Hp above a point of interest is $Hp = h_c + h - hp$, where hp is the height of the point if interest above the chimney base level. This applies to buildings and gently sloping ground. For hills, where the wind is diverted upwards, hp is to be taken as about half the elevation above chimney base. Maps to the scale of 1: 25000 should be used ($2^{1/2}$″/mile, not 1″/mile/scale) and heights being converted to meters. Various types of smoke plumes are shown Fig. 5.9 with an accompanying temperature profile that corresponds to conditions normally present when these plumes occur. Figure 5.9 indicates that, with a very stable atmosphere the gas effluent from the stack should form a fanning plume. In the morning, with the warming of the ground surface, the atmospheric stability becomes unstable, and as this unstable layer of air reaches the farming plume, the highly concentrated pollutants are forced to the ground by the turbulence, creating a variable plume when winds are light to moderate.

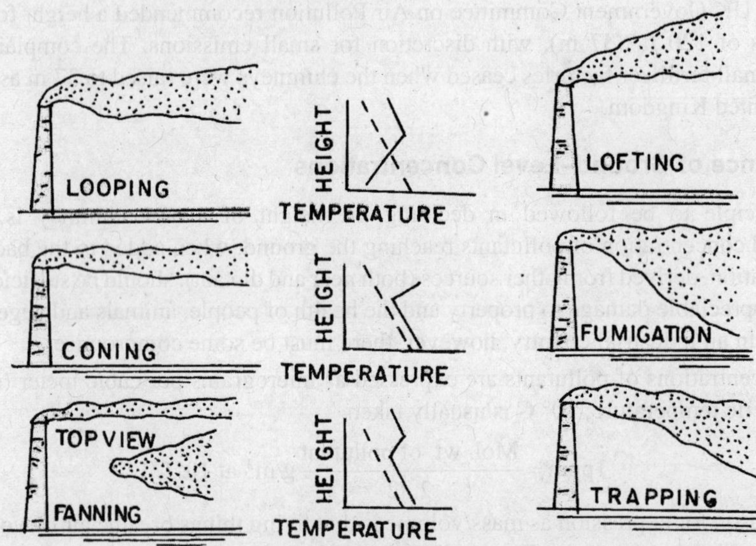

Fig. 5.9 Atmospheric stability on the behaviour of air pollution

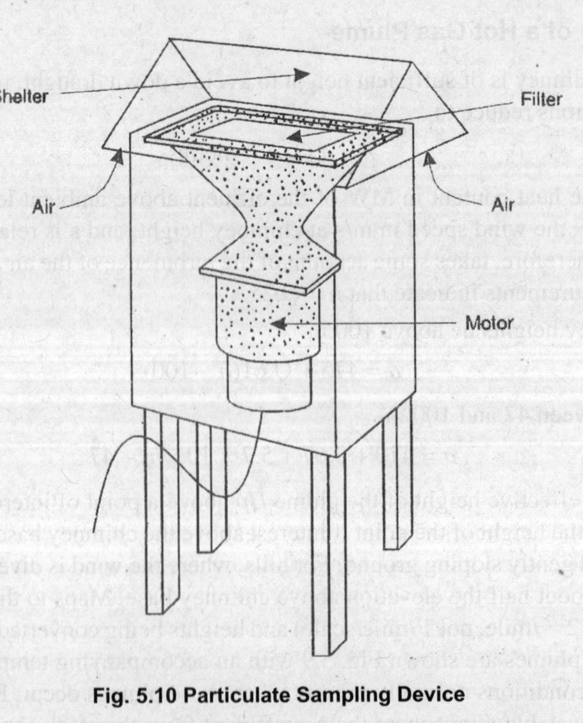

Fig. 5.10 Particulate Sampling Device

When an inversion occurs in an otherwise stable atmosphere with light winds aloft and moderate below, a trapping plume may be observed. A clear hot day accompanied by light winds may produce a looping plume. With moderate to strong winds and turbulence more mechanical than thermal, a coning plume may be expected. Towards sunset on a fair day, with considerable turbulence aloft and little turbulence below, a plume may become lofting as the adiabatic lapse rate changes to inversion conditions.

Air Pollution Problems in Industry

Industries are considered to be one of the potential known sources that release toxic gases, fumes, vapours and particulate matter into the immediate work environment and the general living environment, which causes deterioration in the quality of air that we breathe and ultimately affects our health. Let us examine today the environmental pollution problem posed to the living environment of Greater Bombay which is blessed with 60 percent of the total industries of Maharashtra State. According to one emission inventory estimate, a refinery of capacity 3.7 million tonnes of crude oil p ;r annum pollutes the environment by throwing 52.8 tonnes of sulphur dioxide, 4.6 tonnes of nitrogen oxides, 28.5 tonnes of hydrocarbons, 0.7 tonnes of particulated matter and 76.5 tonnes of carbon monoxide into the atmosphere everyday. Likewise, a fertilizer plant manufacturing 140 tonnes of sulphuric acid can emit 20.9 kg of sulphur dioxide per tonne of acid produced.

A factory manufacturing lubricating oils was found to emit about 22 tonnes of sulphur dioxide, a by–product of fuel oil combustion and the burning of hydrogen sulphide in the flare. An olefin plant consuming 200 metric tonnes of naphtha per day for reducing 6 metric tonnes of toluene, one metric tonne of acetylene, 15 metric tonnes of propylene, 55 metric tonnes of ethylene, and 15 metric tonnes of benzene per day, was estimated to release 5.28 metric tonnes of sulphur dioxide, 4 metric tonnes of oxides of nitrogen and 2 metric tonnes of hydrocarbons per day into the atmosphere.

A group of 155 cotton and textile mills of Bombay are capable of emitting 74 tonnes of sulphur dioxide, 12.2 tonnes of nitrogen oxides, 3.7 tonnes of particulate matter, 10 tonnes of cotton fluff and 40 tonnes of kerosene vapour into the living environment every day. It is estimated that a total of 10,000 tonnes of pollutant are thrown into the Bombay environment per day. Undoubtedly such emission inventories may not reflect the exact degree of emissions, but they definitely indicate the pollution potential that exists if it is not arrested or minimized by adopting suitable control technology.

Although enough information on the total pollutants emitted by various industries in the country is not available, according to one estimate 2.548 million tonnes of carbon mono oxide, 5.475 million tonnes of sulphur dioxide, 1.858 million tonnes of nitrogen oxide, and0.26 million tonnes of hydrogen sulphide are thrown into the atmosphere in India annually. There have been a few studies conducted by the National Environmental Engineering Research Institute, Nagpur, Society of Clean Environment, and other such organizations to identify and quantify the levels of harmful pollutants in some localities. For instance, it is known that Chembur–Bombay region is highly polluted because of indiscriminate discharge of pollutants into the atmosphere. Table 5.17 provides some of the data available on some of the important industrial cities in India, indicating average as well as the maximum concentration for sulphur dioxide, nitrogen oxides, hydrogen sulphide and particulate matter. Some of the results of sulphur dioxide measurement in the different localities of Greater Bombay are presented in Table 5 .18. The high incidence of asthma, bronchitis, coughs, breathlessness, sneezing and nasal blockage in the area are: found to be associated with the high levels of sulphur dioxide prevailing in the atmosphere surrounding the Chembur area. It is interesting to note that concentrations of

Table 5.17
Important air pollutants in some Indian cities

City	Sulphur dioxide in parts per million		Nitrogen oxides in parts per million		Hydrogen sulphide in parts per million		Particulates, micrograms/ cubic meter	
	Av.	Max.	Av.	Max.	Av.	Max.	Av.	Max.
Ahmedabad	.004	.0105	.005	.0109	—	—	341.91	504.7
Calcutta	.0148	.0664	.017	.0556	—	—	349.72	663.4
Delhi	.022	.133	.0085	.019	.002	.001	630.79	996.8
Hyderabad	.0031	.09	.0037	.0096	—	—	130.20	219.9
Jaipur	.0019	.005	.0033	.0067	—	—	439.00	1114.0
Kanpur	.0300	.0600	.0042	.0120	—	—	59.06	1567.4
Madras	.0014	.0180	.0139	.0600	.004	.016	59.8	103.3
Nagpur Centre 1	.0037	.0119	.128	.0283	—	—	334.86	671.9
Nagpur Centre 2	.0046	.0136	.0136	.034	—	—	269.6	420.7

Table 5.18
Monthly average of SO_2 concentration (ppb)* around Greater Bombay

Location	*Jan.*	*Feb.*	*March*	*April*	*May*	*June*	*July*	*Aug.*	*Sept.*	*Oct.*	*Nov.*	*Dec.*
BARC (mod. labs.)	—	—	—	—	10	13	13	10	10	0	10	10
BARC (mod. labs.)	*1970-71 values in par an thesis*					62	52	41	26	17	24	17
BARC (mod. labs.)	21(13)	13(12)	1(13)	23(13)	23(4)	18	13	15	10	·8	8	11
Bandra	(10)	(10)	(7)	(7)	(3)	—	—		—	—	—	10
Collector's col. (Chembur)	18(20)	18(18)	18(16)	16(15)	39(19)	46	33	55	45	22	19	17
Chinchpokli	—	—	(37)	(18)	(17)	—	—	—	—	—	—	—
Deonar	(11)	(8)	(10)	(8)	(5)	—	—	—	—	2	2	9
Ghatkopar	(3)	(3)	(4)	(6)	(1)	—	—	—	—	9	8	8
Koliwada	—	—	—	—	—	—	—	—	—	3	3	4
Mahul (Bahrinagar)	(15;	(8)	(7)	(7)	(5)	—	—	—	—	25	25	17
Matunga	(18)	(9)	(7)	(9)	(10)	—	—	—	—	18	18	17
Parel	(17)	(15)	(15)	(6)	(5)	—	—	—	—	13	21	21
Sion	—	(13)	(12)	(6)	(3)	—	—	—	—	—	—	—
Worli	(16)	(9)	(7)	(7)	(3)	—	—	—	—	31	31	12

* lppb SO_2 = 2.85 $\mu g/m^3$ at STP

pollutants vary widely during the day. Diurnal and seasonal variations of atmospheric sulphur dioxide, total oxidants (including ozone) and nitrogen dioxide at the BARC side were studied in 1972, as four hourly average concentrations. The results are presented in Table 5.19. The observed inverse correlation between S02 and oxidant concentrations suggests their destructive interactions in the atmosphere. Besides this, there are other concentrated pockets of industries around big cities, e.g., Calcutta, Madras, Delhi. Ahmedabad, Bangalore and Kanpur which may also be undergoing similar ecological changes, the effects of which are yet to be assessed.

Because of the paucity of adequate data on the degree on air pollution that prevails in and around the industrial cities, its effects on the health of the community and the ecological system, in general, can only be speculated but the deteriorating trend of the environment of such cities cannot be denied. This fact has been demonstrated by the heavily industrialized and developed countries. To cite, the Environmental Protection Agency (EPA) of USA has estimated that air pollution takes an actual toll of 6.10 billion dollar's because of sickness, loss of working time, medical bills and premature death. Damage to crops and vegetation is estimated at another 100 billion dollars; damage to variety of materials at 4.7 billion dollars and damage to residential property at 5.2 billion dollars annually.

The pollution levels of some toxic chemicals in the work environment of a few typical industries as revealed by the studies conducted by the Central and the Regional Labour Institutes are presented in Table 5.20. A critical examination of the data would definitely convince one that the prevalence of toxic chemicals, at levels higher than their permissible standards, requires immediate attention to prevent adverse effects to health. The pollution problem of the immediate work environment may be further aggravated by the growth of industries and by the introduction of new hazardous chemicals with inherent moderate to high toxicity to which a large number of workers would be exposed. Some data on the extent of increase of typical industries and the workers along with the possible environmental pollutants are presented in Table 5.21. The data show that, within a period of 4 years, the number of workers exposed to several pollutants in industries such as chemicals, plastics and petroleum, cotton and textiles and sugar, increased substantially. For instance, in the cotton and textile industry, where pollution of work environment by cotton dust, in levels more than 0.2 mg/m^3 can cause byssinosys, the work force increased from 9,34,000 to 10,42,000. In the sugar industry, where the exposure to bagasse dust can result in Bagassis a lung disease, the workers strength increased from 1,19,000 to 1,30,000. The chemical industry wherein a large number of toxic chemicals with cyanogenic, carcinogenic, mutagenic and other health impairing properties are used, also witnessed an increase in the strength of workers from 2,69,000 to 11,000. This indicates that the problem of air pollution in the work environment of industries has a greater possibility of causing adverse effects to the health of workers in comparison to the general living environment, where the pollutants get diluted several folds before reaching localities. This matter has a tendency to remain stored in the cells of the body. Some data on the levels of toxic chemicals prevailing in different industries and their effects on the health of workers has been given in Table 5.22.

Industry wise, the manufacture of caustic soda, using mercury as a cathode, posses an environmental pollution problem due to the escape of metallic mercury vapours and chlorine from different streams, joints, etc. Exposure to mercury vapours for prolonged periods has been found to cause the manifestation of the signs and symptoms of nervousness, tremors, loss of teeth, stomatitis, kidney damage, etc. The vapours of this metal being colourless and odourless, are hard to detect. 80 percent of the vapour inhaled are absorbed and the presence of mercury can be estimated in the body fluids. This matter has a tendency to remain stored in tire cells of the body. Some of the results reported are given in table 5.22. The in table 5.22. The pollution effects of lead and its compounds also require attention. Lead compounds are present either in the form of dust or gases or vapour and if absorbed in the v body, it may lead to anaemia, renal colic, gingivitis, bonearrow, etc. Zinc and lead smelters, storage battery manufacture, printing presses, and refineries while soldering, and blinding of lead tetraethyl with gasoline are some examples of plants which emit these toxicants.

It is true that rapid industrialization in the country poses problems of air pollution and consequently adversely affects health but this growth cannot be stunted or dwarfed as it helps provide minimum requirements of employment, basic needs of clothing, food and shelter in a developing country. It is, therefore, a great challenge for industries to realize their social obligation towards the society by minimizing pollution at work and the general living environment. For this, feasible and economically viable equipment and techniques for controlling pollution, irrespective of its location, must be provided. Pollution caused by sulphur dioxide in sulphuric acid plants can be reduced from 2,000–5,000 ppm to 500 ppm by using the Double Catalyst Double Absorption (DCDA) technique. Likewise, fluorine evolved in the manufacture of phosphoric acid and phosphate fertilizers can be successfully absorbed by using a properly designed plant, thus, abating air pollution. Industries may have to spend 1–2 percent of their total outlay incorporating control devices for air pollution abatement.

Table 5.19(a)

Four–hourly monthly–average concentrations of SO, (μg/m³) for the year 1972

Month	*Hours* 0600 to 1000	1000 to 1400	1400 to 1800	*Day time mean*	*Hours* 1800 to 2200	2200 to 0200	0200 to 0600	*Night time mean*	*Daily mean*
January	23	13	16	17	19	35	19	24	21
February	16	10	24	17	32	28	14	25	21
March	—	20	50	35	—	—	—	—	—
April	19	32	17	23	25	14	25	21	22
May	17	20	20	19	29	18	14	20	20
June	20	20	41	27	52	40	29	40	34
July	81	72	63	72	78	65	92	78	75
August	73	59	73	68	96	84	78	86	77
September	34	11	24	23	24	25	18	22	23
October	—	—	—	—	—	—	—	—	—
November	51	38	48	46	19	17	21	19	33
December	31	19	49	33	25	34	36	32	32
Yearly Av.	37	29	39	35	40	36	35	37	36

Table 5.19(b)

Four-hourly monthly-average concentrations of total oxidants (as ozone), μg/m³

Month	*Hours* 0600 to 1000	1000 to 1400	1400 to 1800	*Day time mean*	*Hours* 1800 to 2200	2200 to 0200	0200 to 0600	*Night time mean*	*Daily mean*
January	41	40	16	32	24	15	22	20	26
February	43	31	16	30	12	18	17	16	23

(Contd...)

Month	Hours 0600 to 1000	1000 to 1400	1400 to 1800	Day time mean	Hours 1800 to 2200	2200 to 0200	0200 to 0600	Night time mean	Daily mean
March	0	23	2	8	2	0	0	1	4
April	11	14	2	9	7	4	5	5	7
May	6	10	2	6	7	5	4	5	6
June	10	13	5	9	3	3	5	4	6
July	6	10	3	6	2	3	3	3	5
August	8	15	6	10	3	3	2	3	6
September	21	26	9	19	10	13	20	14	16
October	—	—	—	—	—	—	—		
November	47	27	21	22	32	26	16	23	27
December	34	34	6	25	5	8	16	10	17
Yearly Av.	21	22	8	17	9	8	11	9	13

Table 5.19(c)

Four-hourly monthly-average concentrations of nitrogen dioxide(mg/m^3)

Month	Hours 0600 to 1000	1000 to 1400	1400 to 1800	Day time mean	Hours 1800 to 2200	2200 to 0200	0200 to 0600	Night time means	Daily mean
January	12	11	12	12	8	10	4	1	10
February	6	6	6	6	5	7	7	6	6
March	2	6	7	5	4	8	16	9	7
April	7	8	5	7	10	4	6	7	7
May	8	7	6	7	6	7	6	6	7
June	13	9	9	10	8	6	8	7	9
July	16	19	19	18	14	11	13	13	15
August	14	13	13	13	16	14	13	14	14
September	13	9	11	11	10	10	10	10	11
October	—	—	—	—	—	—	—	—	—
November	15	19	9	14	5	9	10	8	11
December	15	20	15	17	12	12	21	15	16

Table 5.20

Pollutant levels in some industrial work environment

Industry	*Pollutant*	*Pollutant levels***	*Permissible standards*
Sulphuric acid plant	Sulphur dioxide	12.2–35.0 ppm	10 ppm
Steel plant	Dust containing free Silica (foundry)	3–1075 mppcf	5 mppcf
	Refractory Dust	2–17 mppcf	20 mppcf
	Carbon monoxide (blast furnace)	20–200 ppm	100 ppm

Industry	*Pollutant*	*Pollutant levels***	*Permissible standards*
	Aromatic hydrocarbons (benzene)	20–50 ppm	35 ppm
A chemical factory manufacturing sodium carbonate and ammonium chloride	Ammonia	34–107 ppm	50 ppm
		40–172 ppm	
		204–430 ppm	
		75–1240 ppm	
		187–860 ppm	
Chemical works	Oxides of nitrogen (Nitric acid plant)	1 1–31ppm	5 ppm
	Chromic acid mist (Chromic acid plant)	0.5–2.1 mg/m^3	0.1 mg/m^3
	Bauxite dust	1–198 mppcf	50 mppcf
Blending of pesticides	Soapstone dust	33–134 mppcf	20 mppcf
	DDT	15.3–17.8 mg/m^3	1.0 mg/m^3
	BHC	25.2–29.8 mg/m^3	0.5 mg/m^3
Engineering industry (tool room)	Isophrone	296 mg/m^3	55 mg/m^3
Pharmaceutical laboratory	Talc dust	60–90 mppcf	20 mppcf
	MIBK	408–792 mg/m^3	410 mg/m^3
Pharmaceutical works	Ethyl alcohol	482–7812 mg/m^3	1900 mg/m^3
	Iron compound dust	0.67–5.58 mg/m^3	1 mg/m^3
Heavy engg. factory manufacturing electrical equipment	Alumina dust	15.0–32.4 mppcf	30 mppcf
	Silicone	37.1–4156.6 mppcf	30 mppcf
	Coal dust	28.0–35.3 mppcf	
	Iron dust	17.9–51.5 mppcf	30 mppcf
	Sand bearing free silica	23.5–101 mppcf	6 mppcf
	Asbestos	847.2–1517.9 fibres/cc	5 fibres/cc
	Oil mist	4–158 mg/m^3	5 mg/m^3
	Noise	97–120 db	85 db.

** Range of means and minimum and maximum values.

Standard for Air Pollution control in India

The ambient air-quality standards have been prescribed for sulphur dioxide, suspended particulate matter, nitrogen oxides and carbon monoxide. These standards have been prescribed especially for

1. Industrial and mixed–used areas
2. Residential and rural areas
3. Sensitive areas

Their values are as follows:

Area category	*Concentration micrograms per metre cube*			
	SPM	SO_2	CO	NOx
Industrial and mixed–use	500	120	5000	120
Residential and rural	200	80	2000	80
Sensitive	100	30	1000	30

It is clear from the above that the tolerance limits are relatively higher for industrial and mixed-used areas, while they are lowest for sensitive areas. It is also recognized that the emission standards should be finalized for industrial environments. It is expected that emission standards, especially for cotton mills, cement plant, asbestos, etc., will be finalized soon.

Environment degradation through motor vehicles

With growing number of automobiles and diesel vehicles, especially in cities, air and noise pollution is increasing day by day. In one of the studies, conducted at Agra, to find out the contribution of vehicles to sulphur dioxide at Agra, it was concluded that the contribution was not so significant as to require any immediate control.

However, pollution control from vehicles is briefly mentioned here.

The annual pollutant load of the world atmosphere exceeds 100 million tonnes. Estimates indicate that blame is to be almost equally shared between automobiles and all other sources put together. Automobiles have received most publicity since they form the single largest class of defaulters. It has been a popular concept that air pollution due to automotive emissions is a problem of developed nations only, and developing countries like India need not be concerned about it. The basis for this notion is obviously the meager population of automobiles in India as compared to developed nations. There are factors other than population, which contribute equally significantly towards enhancement of the problem.

The total number of automobiles on the road in India, when presented as vehicle area density, i.e., number of vehicles per square km area on an overall nationwide basis, works out to a very unimpressive figure. The factor which is of immense importance is that these vehicles are concentrated in just a very few metropolitan cities. The vehicle area density related to these localized zones is an alarming figure. Such computation for Bombay indicates that the magnitude of the problem in Bombay is no less serious than in the most polluted cities of the world like Los Angeles and Tokyo. The overall pollution hazard is further magnified due to the fact that these cities, like Bombay, have undergone phenomenal growth in the last one decade. Industrial concentration in and around the city has imposed exponential demands on transport systems, resulting in a large increase in the number of automobiles. To add to the problems, the extra kilometer age of load provided to accommodate this increasing traffic is in no way proportional. Traffic jams have become a matter of everyday life. Most city roads have a large number of traffic junctions wherein the vehicles have to decelerate, idle and accelerate. It being a technical fact that cruising is the best mode of driving, which gives the best fuel efficiency and minimum concentrations of toxicants in the exhaust in any other mode, both the fuel economy and emission performance of engines deteriorate considerably. Conditions of the roads is also an important contributory factor to the problem of air pollution by vehicle emissions. Cruising is almost impossible on roads in Bombay, Calcutta, Varanasi, etc.

The condition of the vehicle in general and the condition of the engine in particular are very important factors from the point of view of emission performance. A poorly maintained machine emits as much as ten times more pollutants as compared with an ideally maintained machine. The current maintenance practices belong to the breakdown class rather than the preventive class, which has its own repercussions. Besides these aspects, factors like overloading and overspeeding, which are not uncommon in the city, escalate the problem to a great extent. The problems of air pollution caused by vehicle emissions, therefore, work out to be of too serious a nature to be projected by considering merely area densities.

Table 5.21

Growth of some industries and corresponding increase in number of workers occupationally exposed to potential pollutants

Industry	*No. of factories*		*No. of workers ('000)*			*Increase (+) or decrease (-) of workers*	*Potential pollutants*
	1971	*1973*	*1971*	*1973*	*1974*	*from 1971–74*	
Sugar	233	242	119	123	130	+11,000	Bagasse, sulphur dioxide, noise
Colton and textiles	5,236	5,525	934	1,018	1,042	+98,000	Cotton dust, acids, alkalies,solvents, dyes, noise
Paper, pulp and board	343	451	60	79	83	+23,000	Organic dust, bleaching agents
Leather and leather fur	580	601	44	42	44	No change	Organic dust, wetting solvlents, corrosive liquids
Rubber, plastics, coal, and petroleum products	1,745	2.151	107	120	128	+21,000	Resins, vinyl-chloride, antioxidants, and solvents
Chemicals and chemical products	2,709	3.124	269	292	311	+42,000	Aromatic nitro and amino compounds, mineral acid and acid gases, pesticide solvents
Asbestos	107	117	12	11	—	—	Asbestos fibre
Iron and steel	273	368	114	122	—	—	Sand dust, heat, noise, carbon monoxide, aromatic hydrocarbons
Foundries	2,052	2,376	115	185	188	+33,000	Silica dust, heat, metal oxides, carbon monoxide
Food products	29,548	29,384	676	739	787	+11,000	Bacteria, spores, grain dust.
Glass	396	459	53	58	61	—	Sand dust, heat, lead
Cement	180	194	37	40	40	+3,000	Cement dust, heat
Dry and wet batteries	54	84	14	17—		—	Lead dust and fumes, acid fumes and gases

Table 5.22

Environmental pollution and its impact on health of working population in some industries

mppcf (million particles per cubic feet of air), mg/m^3 (milligram per cubic metre of air) ppm (parts per million)

Type of Industry	*Polluting chemical*	*Level of pollutant*	*Permissible standard*	*Workers examined*	*Workers affected*	*Affections*	*Cause*
1	2	3	4	5	6	7	8
Dichromate manufacture	Dust and mist bearing hexavalent	—	—	631	50.7	Skin, ulcers, nasal, perforations	Inhaling dust and mist containing hexavalent chromium and skin contact with chrome liquids
Chromic ore mining	Dust bearing quartz and chromium	—	—	99 including 9 women workers	32	X-ray ground and glass 1 and ground glass 2 making	Inhalation of dust containing chromium and free silica
Magnetite	Quartz dust	—	—	59 including 50 women workers	15.3	Ground glass 1 and ground glass 2 making	Inhalation of dust containing free silica
Storage battery	Lead dust	6.7-25.7 mg/m^2 Range of means	0.15 mg/m^3	492	10.6	Load line on gums and fumes (66 cases) Pollar lead (126 cases) Constipation (126 cases) Muscle pain (6 cases) Vertigo (13 cases) Diarrhoea (52 cases) Tremor (2 cases)	Inhalation of dust containing free silica
Mica processing	Mica dust	3-133 mppcf	50 mppcf	61	36	Lung X-ray ground glass 1 and 22.9 and ground glass 2 44.3 markings	Inhalation of dust containing mica
Hand drilling in mica mining	Dust bearing free silica	—	—	62	27.4	Silicosis	Inhalation of dust containing free silica

1	*2*	*3*	*4*	*5*	*6*	*7*	*8*
Metal grinding	Dust bearing free silica	13-145 mppcf	25 mppcf	44	33.6	Silicosis	Exposure to dust containing free silica
Refractories	Dust bearing free silica	—	—	327	21	Silicosis silica	Inhalation of dust containing
Viscose rayon	Carbon ci	2.2-58.1 ppm	20 ppm	270	27.2	Psychic(36)	Intake of gases in the body through inhalation
	sulphide. sulphurdioxide	1.6-90.8 ppm	10 ppm		10.0	Neurological signs 4.4 ocular signs and symptoms Silicosis	
Lead and zinc mining	Dust bearing free silica	1-44 mppcf	2- mppcf	171	30.4	Silicosis	Inhalation of dust containing free silica
Coal mine	Coal dust	2-132 mppcf	50 mppcf	950		Pneumoconiosis (118 cases) Bron- chial-spasm (9 cases') Emphysema (26 cases) Cough (289 cases) Breathlessness on exertion (161 cases)	Exposure to coal
erro manganese	Manganese	4.0-88.0 mg/m^3	5 mg/m^1	179	35	Manganese poisoning (62 cases) Pneumonitis (34 cases) Pigmentation (110 cases) Metallic taste (55 cases) Bron- Bronchitis, Lassitude (22 cases) Paraesthesia (14 cases) Somnolescence (8 cases)	Inhalation of manganese dust and fumes
Leather tanning	Tail pit liquid	0.84 mg/lit	—	5	100	All fatal	Inhaling lethal concentration

(*Contd...*)

Table 5.22 (Contd...)

1	*2*	*3*	*4*	*5*	*6*	*7*	*8*
	hydrogen sulphide gas						of hydrogen sulphide
DDT manufacture	DDT, Chlorine and Benzene			76		Respiratory ailments, stomatitis, anorexia	Inhalation of pollutants
Nitric acid manufacture	Noise			85	18.7	Mild to moderate hearing loss (6 cases) marked hearing loss (9 cases)	Exposure to noise
Pesticide formulation	Parathion			57	74 65 44 26	Excessive pair Headache Giddiness Blurred vision (8 cases)	Parathion absorption through inhalation or skin contact
P.C. meters pairing	Metallic mercury vapours	0.1-0.50 mg/m^3	0.05 mg/m^3	24	25	Mercury poisoning (8 cases) Mercury intoxication (17 cases)	Mercury absorption through respiratory system
Foundry	Dust bearing free silica	13-195 mppcf	3-4 mppcf	864	16.8	Chest pain, Inhalation of foundry dust lowered pulmonary function (47 cases) X-ray abnormalities (25 cases) Adventurous lung sound (22 cases) Blood pressure abnormality (20 cases)	

1	2	3	4	5	6	7	8
Leather industry	Biological	2-10 mppcf and above	—	396	23.4	Chronic bronchitis	Long term exposure to dust
Leather tanning and manufacture	Tanning agents Solvents Wetting agents Sodium sulphide	—	—	2010	3.2 5.4	Dermatitis (64 cases) Other skin diseases (129 cases)	Skin contact with chemicals
Pesticide formulation	BHC	0.32-1.02 mg/m^3	0.5 mg/m^3	32	40.6	Skin and eye irritation, Constipation	Inhalation of BHC vapours
	Copper chloride [3]	8.0-44.7 mg/m	1 mg/m^3'	2	100	Metal fume fever, Chronical headache, Tightness of the chest, choking	Absorption of copper oxychloride through inhalation
Chlorakali plant	Metallic mercury	0.02-0.18 mg/m^3	0.15 mg/m^3	81	25	Gingivitis Stomatitis, Less teeth, Anorexia, Tremors, Loss of mercury, Insomnia, Nervousness, Irritability	Inhalation of vapour of mercury and possible absorption through skin
Metal reed	Lead fumes	0.003-1.324 mg/m^3	0.15 mg/m^3	49	8	High lead content in urine	Absorption of lead through inhalation
Engineering Industry (welding with low hydrogen electrode)	Iron oxide fumes Fluoride Oxides of nitrogen Manganese	15.06 mg/m^3 4.76 mg/m^3 0.82 ppm 0.85 mg/m^3	5 mg/m^3 2.5 mg/m^3 5.0 ppm 5 mg/m^3	10 welders	100 40 50	Eye irritation (10 cases) Erytheme of exposed parts (4 cases) Excessive irri-	Inhalation of pollutants and exposure to radiations

(Contd...)

Table 5.22 (Contd...)

1	*2*	*3*	*4*	*5*	*6*	*7*	*8*
						tation and dryness of throat (5 cases)	
	Ozone Carbonmon-oxide	0.07 ppm 200 ppm	0.1 ppm 50 ppm		50 40	Metal fume fever (5 cases), X-ray abnormalities (4 cases)	
Cotton and textile mills	Cotton dust	0.53-7.85 mg/m^3 0.59-7.6 mg/m^3 0.74-3.0 mg/m^3	0.2 mg/m^3 0.2 mg/m^3 0.2 mg/m^3	432 311 156	16 26 3	Byssinosis Byssinosis dust Byssinosis	Chronic exposure to cotton
Welding shops	Nitrogen oxides, Ozone Fluoride Manganese Iron oxide	2.5-15.4 mg/m^3 0.06-0.46 mg/m^3 0.74-2.31 mg/m^3 0.18-1.74 mg/m^3 0.27-1.53 mg/m^3	9 mg/m^3 0.2 mg/m^3 5 mg/m^3 5 mg/m^3 5 mg/m^3	60	11.6 15.0 5.0 20.1	Increase in B.P. to 240/90 Systolic press 140 mm/Hg Diastolic press 90 mm/Hg Metal fume fever	Exposure to gases and metallic fumes
Heavy organic chemicals	Chlorinated vapours	0.06-23.33 mg/m^3	3 mg/m^3	55	90.0	Weakness (55 cases), Chest pain (24 cases), stomach pain (35 cases) Urinary infection (8 cases), Headache (25 cases) Skin itching (22 cases), Giddiness (8 cases), Difficulty in breathing (2 cases)	Absorption of vapours of nitro compounds through halation and skin contact
Viscous rayon plant	Carbon di sulphide	3.5-79,0 mg/m^3	60 mg/m^3	120	—	Chest pain and Exposure to carbon disulphi- sleepness (20 de and hydro- gen sulphide	

1	2	3	4	5	6	7 •	8
	Hydrogen sulphide	0.6-18 5 mg/m^3	15 mg/m^3			cases), Sore eyes (11 cases), Eye irritation (3 cases), Keratoconjunctivitis (3 cases), Serum cholesterol above 250 mg (16 cases).	

Awareness of the probable hazards of automotive emission was created not very long ago. The main emittants referred to in this context are unburnt hydrocarbons, carbon monoxide, oxides of nitrogen, smoke and other particulates, and oxides of sulphur. There are two main sources of unburnt hydrocarbons, i.e., evaporated fuel from carburetors and fuel tanks, and those emitted through the exhaust. The problem of unburnt hydrocarbons is of the greatest concern for two-stroke engines which are used in scooters and three wheelers whose population is increasing exponentially. Besides being toxic, unburnt hydrocarbons also mean loss of fuel efficiency. Evaluation of engines is in progress and devices like thermal reactors are being designed for them. With the use of thermal reactors, it is estimated that unburnt hydrocarbon level of two–stroke engines will be brought down from 10000 ppm to about 800 ppm.

Carbon monoxide is a problem confined to gasoline engines, both two-stroke and four-stroke. The causes and remedial measures for abatement of carbon-monoxide are similar to those of unburnt hydrocarbons.

Oxides of nitrogen have become a major concern from the point of view of health hazards caused by vehicles emissions. Both gasoline and diesel vehicles share the blame equally. This class of toxicants is known as vicious, since they do not warn the human body of impending damage and the damage is of a permanent nature. One of the most effective methods for the control of oxides of nitrogen is exhaust gas recirculation. A certain amount of exhaust gas is recirculated through the engine. Formation of oxides of nitrogen is a temperature–sensitive phenomenon. The presence of exhaust gases in the cylinder effectively brings down the maximum temperature of the cycle and, hence, the levels of oxides of nitrogen formed. It has been experimentally proved that by recirculation of about 20 percent exhaust gases, as much as 60–80 percent reduction in exhaust oxides of nitrogen levels can be achieved. It has also been proved that this recirculation does not appreciably affect either the power capacity, or the fuel economy of the engine. The effect of exhaust gas recirculation being through the process of temperature control of the cycle, further experiments were conducted to study the effect of the temperature of exhaust gas recirculation on oxides of nitrogen control. The exhaust gases to be circulated were cooled to pre-decided temperatures prior to entry into the engine. The aim of this exercise was to explore the possibility of either a higher percentage of reduction in oxides of nitrogen levels or reduction of the quantity of exhaust gas recirculation for achieving a given reduction. The investigations were carried out on both types of engines, i.e., gasoline and diesel.

An extremely important aspect is the pollution problem caused by smoke emissions from diesel engines. The current level of prices, government policies and the fact that diesel engines are inherently more fuel efficient that gasoline engines has, of late, sparked off a trend of dieselization. Right from light passenger vehicles up to heavy load carriers, diesel engine application is almost replacing its counterpart. As regards emission problems, diesel engines are more noisy and smoky. The smoke in the diesel engine exhaust is not just unburnt carbon particles but contains semiburnt and unburnt hydrocarbons, some of which are proved carcinogens. In addition to being a traffic hazard by reducing visibility, smoke contains extremely hazardous constituents. Here, too, the conditions of the engine, the quality of the fuel and the driving pattern have a lot to contribute to his problem. Overloading and overspeeding increase the magnitude of the problem considerably.

The various other methods available for oxides-of-nitrogen control include water injection, blended fuels and duel fuel operation. Each of these has its own merits and demerits. Cost and simplicity wise, however, exhaust has recirculation is preferred to all other methods.

Air Monitoring

It is essential to have baseline data with regard to air pollution, especially in big industrial towns. The harmful effects of pollution can be envisaged only if adequate data are available, with a well selected number of sampling stations, duration of sampling and monitoring methods. It is also preferable to conduct both biological monitoring as well as physico-chemical monitoring with the end objective being to develop a well integrated approach for air pollution monitoring and eventually for its effective control.

The end objectives of air pollution monitoring may be summarized under three broad headings:

1. Physico-chemical monitoring of air.
2. Biological monitoring and effect of pollutants on vegetation, farm animals and human systems.
3. Correlation between physico-chemical monitoring and biological monitoring. The details of each are given below.

Physico–Chemical Monitoring

1. A suitable number of study and sampling sites should be selected within city limits and in the suburban areas, and their micro-meteorology should be studied.
2. An inventory of the pollution sources and of their emissions should be made.
3. Characterization of pollutants, both gaseous and particulates, should be determined.
4. Periodic determination of concentration of air pollutants at each side should be carried out.
5. Concentrations of pollutants such as CO, nitrogen oxides, hydrocarbons, SO_2, HF, O_3, pb, etc. should be determined in the air sample.

Biological Monitoring

Effect of Pollutants on Vegetation

1. Plants growing at each site should be listed substrata wise–bark, soil, wall, etc.
2. A complete inventory of plants present at each side should be prepared.
3. Study of growth behaviour and fertility of plants at each site, should be conducted.
4. The branching pattern, canopy–size and canopy– geometry of each tree–species should be carefully scrutinized and photographed with specific conditions.
5. Symptom studies and analysis of tree leave's should be carried out.
6. Microscopic investigation of cryptograms and other plant samples to decipher external and internal changes, should be made.
7. Productivity pattern through determination of phytomass values of plants of known ages should be assessed.
8. Concentrations of chlorophyll, proteins, sugars, calorific energy and pollutants such as SO_2, fluoride, Pb etc., in plant and soil samples, should be determined.
9. pH and buffer capacity of leaves, bark and soil–extracts, should be determined.
10. Fumigation studies with selected plants and pollutants should be undertaken under known ecological conditions to obtain a prior evidence for the cause–effect relationship.

Effect on Farm Animals

1. Symptoms of acute and chronic fluorine poisoning should be investigated.
2. Symptoms of acute and chronic lead poisoning should be investigated.
3. Urine samples should be analysed for fluorides and lead.

Effect on Human Systems

1. Effect of gaseous pollutants
2. Effect of particulate pollutants
3. Air pollution as a casual factor in chronic diseases, e.g., tuberculosis, eosinophil, pneumoconiosis, fluorosis, etc.

Correlation of Physico-Chemical Monitoring and Biological Monitoring

1. Study of the relationship between the pollutant level in the air and as in detected plants.
2. The entire city limit, including the suburban areas, should be delineated into different pollution zones based on pollutant data in air, soil and plant samples.
3. Selection of plants for creating shelter belts in highly polluted cities.
4. Determination of Ascorbic acid and protein content of pollution tolerant plants to assess their limit of toleration.

Based on these investigations, the conclusions could include:

1. Preparation of a pollution map for cities, clearly indicating heavily polluted, moderately polluted and clean areas, i.e., practically pollution-free areas.
2. Indication for location of industrial areas.
3. Guidelines for dispersal of industry.
4. Suggestion of suitable control measures to those industries which are found to be heavy polluters.
5. Suitable guidelines for development of housing complexes and planned development of the town.
6. Recommendations for the height of chimneys.
7. Recommendations for sites available for landfill incinerators.

The advantages and disadvantages of various collecting devices are given in Table 5.23. Various equipment and techniques used for sampling are given in Table 5.24.

Table 5.23
Advantages and disadvantages of particulate collection devices

Collector	*Advantages*	*Disadvantages*
Gravitational	Low pressure loss, simplicity design and maintenance.	Much space required. Low collection efficiency.
Cyclone	Simplicity of design and maintenance, little floor space required, dry continuous disposal of collected dusts.	Much head room required. Low collection efficiency of small particles. Sensitive to

Collector	*Advantages*	*Disadvantages*
	Low to moderate pressure loss. Handles high dust loadings. Temperature independent.	variable dust loadings and flow rates. Tends to clog up.
Wet collectors	Simultaneous gas absorption and particle removal. Ability to cool and clean high temperature, moisture laden gases. Corrosive gases and mists can be recovered and neutralized. Reduced dust explosion risk. Efficiency can be varied.	Corrosion and allied problems Added cost of wastewater treatment and reclamation. Low efficiency on sub-micron particles, contamination of effluent steam by liquid entrainment. Freezing problems in cold weather. Reduction in buoyancy and plumerise, water vapour contributes to visible plume under some atmospheric conditions.
Electrostatic precipitator	99% efficiency obtainable. Very small particles can be collected. Particles may be collected wet or dry. Pressure drops and power requirements are small compared to other high efficiency collectors. Maintenance is nominal unless corrosive or adhesive materials are handled. Few moving parts. Can be operated at high temperature (550–850°F).	Relatively high initial cost. Precipitators are sensitive to variable dust loadings or flow rates. Resistivity causes some material to be economically uncollectable. Precautions are required to safeguard personnel from high voltage. Collection efficiencies can deteriorate gradually and imperceptibly.
Fabric filtration	Dry collection possible. Decrease of performance is noticeable. Collection of small particles possible. High efficiencies possible.	Sensitivity to filtering velocity. High temperature gases must be cooled to 200° F to 550°F. Affected by relative humidity (condensation). Susceptibility of fabric to chemical attack.
After burner, direct flame	High removal efficiency of submicron odour causing particulate matter. Simultaneous disposal of combustible gaseous and particulate matter. Direct disposal of non toxic gases and wastes to the atmosphere after combustion. Possible heat recovery. Relatively small space requirement. Simple construction. Low maintenance.	High operational cost. Fire hazard. Removes only combustibles.
After burner, catalytic	Same as direct flame after burner. Compared to direct flame, reduced fuel requirements, reduced temperature, insulation requirements and fire hazard.	High initial cost. Catalysts subject to poisoning. Catalysts require reactivation.

Table 5.24

Particulate Sampling Equipment

Sampling device	*Collection techniques*	*Settleable collected*	*Method of analysis*
1	*2*	*3*	*4*
Dust fall bucket	Gravity: 30 days	Setteable particulates	Gravimetric
High volume sampler	Filtration: 24 hrs	Suspended particulates (also organic, inorganic and radioactive compounds)	–do–
Paper tape sampler	Filtration: 2 hrs	Suspended particulates (fine soiling matter)	Transmission meter, density meter which measures amount of light absorbed by a sample spot on the table.
Dweham sampler restored	Inertial (impaction)	Pollen spores	Count
Sticky tape	Inertial (impaction)	Total particulates	Grubber particles comparator
Anderson sampler	Inertital (impaction)	Bacteria–particulates	Count
Cascade sampler	Inertial (impaction)	Total particulates	Microscopic airing
Greenberg-Smith	Inertial (impingement)	Total particulates	Gravimetric
Midget Impinger	Inertial (impingement)	Total particulates	Gravimetric
Cyclone sampler	Inertial (centrifugal separation)	Particulates of 5 microns in diameter	Gravimetric
Electrostatic precipitator	Precipitation	Radioactive particulates	Type study-not quantity
Thermal precipitator	Precipitation	Total particulates	Gravimetric

Atmospheric Sampling and Analysis

Atmospheric sampling deals with the pollutants within the total air mass surrounding the earth.

The purpose of atmospheric sampling is to develop air quality criteria, which are the basis for setting air quality standards. Atmospheric sampling measures pollution, provides control data, and renders background information for use in trend evolution and source detection.

Sampling Procedures

The complete sampling procedure is based on the pollutant sampled, the techniques used in collecting the pollutant, the device chosen, and the method of analysis. Atmospheric sampling is related to analysis in that a volume of air, for example, is collected. This volume of air is analysed to determine quantity of air pollutant collected, which is measured in microgram (mg). The pollution concentration in the air sample is, then, expressed in micrograms per cubic meter (pg/m^3).

Pollutants are classified as particulates or gaseous, collecting devices or techniques are varied.

Collection Techniques

Collection techniques are determined by particulate involved. Figure 5 .11 indicates these particulate sampling devices and a summary of the samples of particulates is listed in Table 5.24.

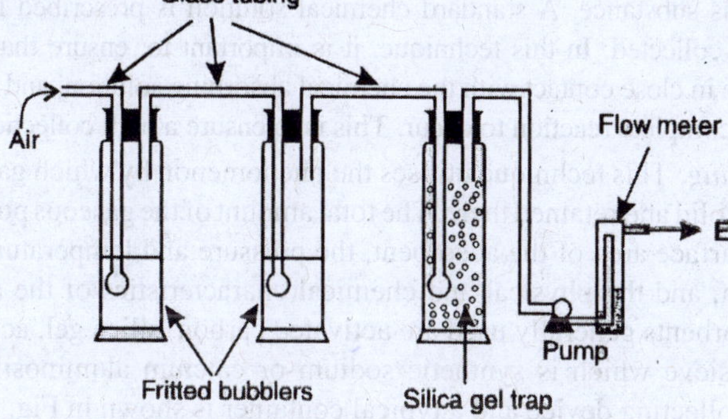

Fig. 5.11 Dust Fall Sampling Device

Gravity Technique: The gravity technique is used to collect settleable particulates that settle out of the atmosphere as a result of the force of gravitational pull. Devices that use this technique are referred to as dust fall sampling instruments. Dust fall sampling (as shown in Fig. 5.11) may be done with a dustfall brush or cellophane tape coated with a material that captures dust or its sticky surface, but is most often done with a dust fall bucket. Dust is rinsed from the bucket, evaporated to dryness, and, then, weighed in milligrams. The amount of air sampled is based on the measurement of the area of the bucket. The standard collection period is 30 days. The results are reported in milligrams per square cm per 30 days (mg./cm^2/month).

Filtration Technique: This technique is used to collect suspended particulates that do not settle out of the air. Particulates are removed from air sample by a suction apparatus, e.g., vacuum pump and are deposited on a porous filter. The high–volume sampler is most frequently used when sampling for suspended particulates.

The paper tape sample is another filtration instrument used for suspended particulates. It is most suitably adopted to collect fine or soiling materials.

In the inertial technique, total particulates are collected. In this technique, a polluted air stream containing particulates is drawn into a sampler where obstacles are placed across the path of the airstream. The obstacle causes the airstream to change direction but particles continue to travel in the initial direction and collide with the obstacle. If the obstacle has an adhesive surface, the particulates are impacted on it. If the obstacle is immersed in a fluid, the particulates are collected by impingement in the liquid.

Precipitation Techniques: These techniques are divided into thermal and electrostatic precipitation. Thermal precipitation uses a heated wire to drive radioactive particulates by thermal convection and molecular bombardment out of gaseous stream into a cold collecting surface. Particles 0.01m to 10m adhere best to a collecting surface.

Electrostatic precipitation uses an electrical charge to force radioactive particulates to migrate out of the air stream onto a collecting surface. It is most effective for particles 0.01μ to 10μ, that can be impressed by an electric charge.

Collection Techniques and Sampling devices for Gaseous Pollutants

The four basic techniques for collecting gaseous pollutants are absorption, adsorption, condensation (freeze out), and grab sampling.

Absorption Sampling: It is the process by which a gaseous containment in air is removed by bringing the contaminant into close contact with a liquid chemical with which it reacts to form a non-gaseous substance. A standard chemical solution is prescribed for each gaseous contaminant to be collected. In this technique, it is important to. ensure that all the gaseous contaminants come in close contact with the chemical absorbing solution, and are retained long enough to allow a complete reaction to occur. This is to ensure a high collection efficiency.

Adsorption Sampling: This technique utilises the phenomenon by which gases are attracted to the surface of a solid and retained there. The total amount of the gaseous pollutant adsorbed is related to the surface area of the adsorbent, the pressure and temperature maintained in the sampling train, and the physical and chemical characteristics of the adsoilbent used. The different adsorbents generally used are activated carbon, silica gel, activated alumina, and a molecular sieve which is synthetic sodium or calcium aluminosilicate. Fig. 5.11 shows a sample collecting device and a typical container is shown in Fig. 5.12.

Freeze Out or Condensation Sampling: This method is used to collect hydrocarbons, radioactive gases and insoluble or non-reactive vapours. Air pollutants, existing as gases, can be trapped or removed by the freeze out or condensation method; trapping implies collecting a pollutant, and removal implies freeing unwanted gas contaminants from the gas stream. The mechanics of the freeze out condensation process is as follows: Air is drawn through collection chambers at a progressively lower temperature; if the chamber temperature is equal to or less than the boiling point of the gas, the gas will change into a liquid. This liquid or condensate is collected in the chamber where the phase change from gas to liquid occurs. Sampling trains, using the free-out principle, have the ability to collect several gases at the same time when several collection chambers are provided. A typical freeze-out sampling train is given in Fig. 5.13.

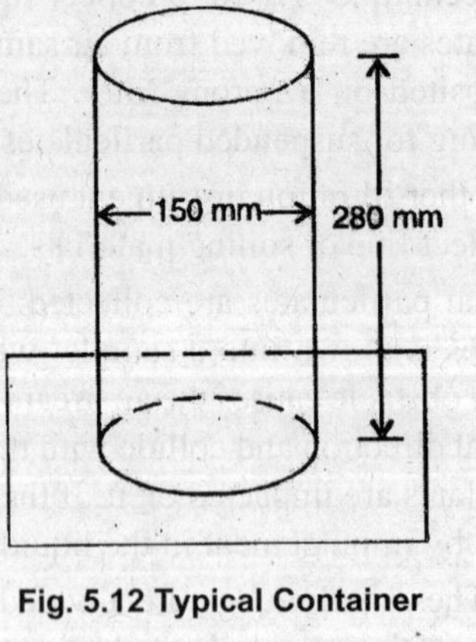

Fig. 5.12 Typical Container

Grab Sampling: This is another technique for collecting gaseous pollutant samples. A grab sample is taken out at a particular time, within an interval of a few seconds to a minute. The pollutant–absorbing solution is placed in the sampling apparatus, and the sample collected is allowed to come to equilibrium with the absorbing solution available. A deflated plastic bag evacuated flask (Fig. 5.14), gas/displacement collector or liquid/displacement collector (Fig. 5,15 and Fig. 5.16) are used

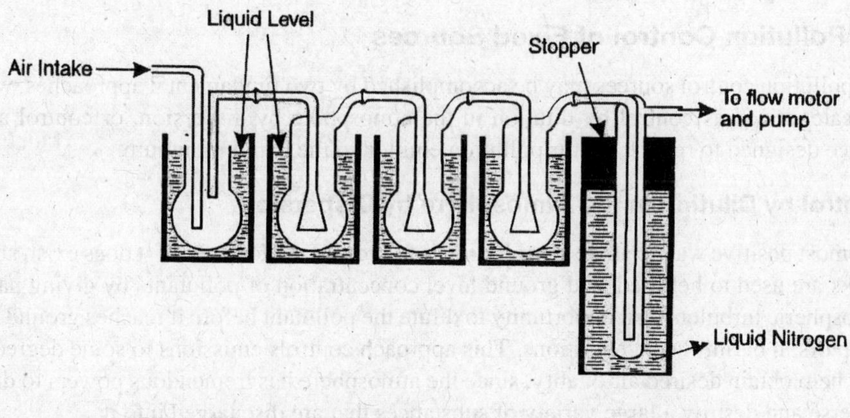

Fig. 5.13 Freeze–out Equipment for Atmospheric Samples

Sampling devices, collection techniques, pollutants to be collected and methods of analysis for gaseous sampling are summarized in Table 5.24.

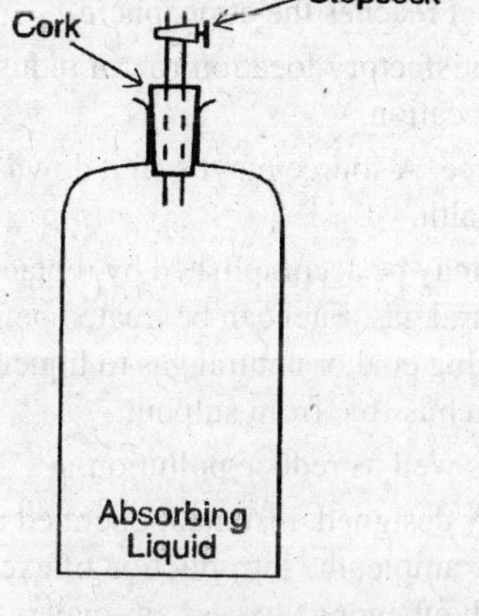

Fig. 5.14 Deflated Plastic Bag Evacuated Flask

Fig. 5.15 Gas Displacement Collector

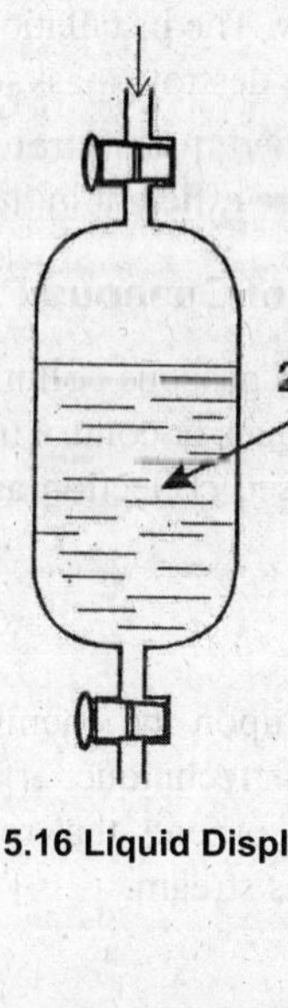

Fig. 5.16 Liquid Displacement Collector

Air Pollution Control of Fixed Sources

Air pollution control sources may be accomplished by two fundamental approaches, which are categorized as control by dilution in the atmosphere by dispersion, or control at the source designed to reduce the air pollution emitted to the bared minimum.

Control by Dilution in the Atmosphere by Dispersion

The most positive way to abate air pollution is to prevent it. However, if it does exist, smoke stacks are used to help reduced ground level concentration of pollutants by giving natural atmospheric turbulence an opportunity to dilute the pollutant before it reaches ground level receptors in harmful concentrations. This approach controls emissions to some degree and may help obtain desired air quality, since the atmosphere has tremendous powers to dilute, disperse and destroy a large variety of substances that are discharged into it.

Control at Source

Control at source may be accomplished by controlling the pollutant from coming into existence or by destroying, altering or trapping it before it reaches the atmosphere.

Source Relocation: It is possible to determine a more satisfactory location for an industry that is causing unacceptable air pollution in its present location.

Source Shutdown: It is another method of control at source. A source maybe shut down for a period of time if air pollution levels threaten public health.

Fuel or Energy substitution: Fuel or energy substitution may be accomplished by replacing soft coal with hard coal, residual oil, distillate oil or natural gas. Fuel can be treated before combustion by desulfurising coal and fuel oil or by refining coal or natural gas to liquefied natural gas (LNG) or to liquid petroleum gas (LPG) which is free from sulphur.

Process Changes: When used, it will conserve energy as well as reduce pollution.

Good Operating Practices: Equipments must be properly designed, installed, operated and maintained to minimize the emission of pollutants; for example, the introduction of excess liquid sulphur in the burner at a sulphuric acid plant, without enough excess air, may result in undue emission of sulphur dioxides.

Air Pollution Control Devices or Techniques: The installation and operation of air pollution control devices or techniques are designed to destroy, mask, counteract or collect pollutants.

Control devices are generally designed to control either gaseous pollutants or particulate pollutants, since a few devices are efficient in the control of both.

Devices and Techniques for Control of Gaseous Pollutants

The techniques and devices used to control a gaseous pollutant depend on the properties of the specific gas to be controlled. The techniques or control methods are generally classified as absorption, adsorption, combustion, closed collection and recovery system as well as masking and contraction.

Gas Absorption

The efficiency of gas absorption depends upon the chemical reactivity of the pollutant gas in the liquid phase. In the gas absorption technique, effluent gases are passed through absorbers (scrubbers), containing liquid absorbents that remove, treat, or modify one or more of the offending constituents in the gas stream.

Gas Adsorption

In this process, gases react with a solid adsorbent, which takes place when the molecules or atoms adsorbed are concentrated only at the interface of the solid. Gas adsorption is based on the principle of passing effluent gas through solid absorbers, contained in an adsorption collecting device.

Adsorption may be physical or chemical in nature. Solid adsorbents of the industrial type are generally capable of adsorbing both organic and inorganic gases. However, their preferential adsorption characteristics and other physical properties make each one more or less specific for a particular application. As an example, activated alumina, silica gel–6, and their molecular sieves (synthetic, silicate or zeolite) will adsorb water preferentially from a gas phase mixture of water vapour and an organic contaminant. Alumina and silica gel are used industrially to dry gases. Bauxite is used in the treatment of petroleum fractions and drying of gases. Activated carbon is most often used for removal of organic solvent vapours.

Combustion

Many organic compounds released from manufacturing operations can be converted to innocuous carbon dioxide and water by combustion. To obtain complete combustion, the proper proportion of oxygen, the right temperature and turbulence must be provided at the right time. Combustion may be categorized as furnace combustion, flare combustion, or catalytic combustion.

Other Controls of Gaseous Pollutants

In case of petroleum storage tanks, there are condense hydrocarbon vapours in a floating roof tank to prevent loss to the atmosphere. This is referred to as a closed collection and recovery system.

Devices and Techniques for Control of Particulate Pollutants

Particulate material, found in ambient air, originates from both stationary and mobile sources. An estimate of particulate emissions into US atmosphere for 1969 has been broken down as follows:

Particulates (Million of tonnes)	*Source*
14.4	Industrial processes
7.2	Fuel combustion in stationary sources (mostly power generation)
0.8	Transportation or mobile sources
1.4	Solid waste disposal
11.4	Miscellaneous
35.2	Total

To exercise control at source or to reduce the effects of particulate pollution, the following techniques can be used:

1. Gas–cleaning devices for removal of particulates
2. Source relocation
3. Fuel substitution
4. Process changes
5. Good operating practices
6. Source shutdown
7. Dispersion

Criteria for Selection

The selection of a specific type of collector or cleaning device involves the following considerations:

(*i*) Particulate characteristics,

(*ii*) Process factors,

(*iii*) Economic factors and

(*iv*) Collection efficiency.

Types of Gas Changing Devices

Terminology and classification of these devices are: mechanical devices, wet collectors, filter systems, electrostatic precipitators, and after burners.

Mechanical Devices: These are settling chambers and cyclones.

Wet Collectors: These can be classified according to the method of particle collection, as liquid carriage or particle conditioning. Liquid carriage consists of a moving body of liquid carrying trapped dust particles to a location outside the collector. Separation of particles from the gas stream occurs when the particles are made to strike a liquid surface within the collector. The liquid serves to prevent particle retrainment and to carry the particles to some place of ultimate disposal. Particle conditioning consists of increasing the effective size of small particles so that collection can be better accomplished by other collection mechanisms. The increase in size may be accomplished by condensation of water upon particles by causing the water temperature to pass through its dew point.

Filter Systems: They consist of a woven or filter fabric through which dust laden gases are forced. The particles are collected on the fabric fiber.

Electrostatic Precipitators: These utilise an extremely high voltage electric current to separate dust, fumes or mist from a gas stream. Four basic steps are involved: electrically charging the particles by ionization, transporting the charged particles to a collecting surface by the force exerted upon them in the electric field, neutralising the electrically charged particles precipitated on the collecting surface, and remaining the precipitated particles from the collecting surface. Removal of particles is performed by rapping or by washing.

After Burners: (direct flame or catalytic) are considered mostly as a control device for gaseous pollutants.

Advantages and disadvantages of particulate collection devices are listed in Table 5.23. Selection of these devices depends upon the degree of control designed and the economics involved.

Techniques for air pollution control are briefly compared in Table 5.25 and different processes available for sulphur dioxide removal are given in Table 5.26. Both the tables are considered useful for selection of pollution control devices.

Table 5.25

Techniques for controlling air pollution

Type of controlling equipments	*Principles*	*Operating conditions*	*Application*	
			Industrial	*Contaminant*
Cyclone separator	A cyclone collector is a structure without moving parts in which the velocity of an inlet gas stream is transformed into a confined vortex from which centrifugal forces tend to drive the suspended particles to the wall of the cyclone body	Cyclones as a class of equipment provide the lowest collection efficiency of particulate matters.	Rock products, Iron and steel plants	Cement, phosphate, bauxite dust
		Ranges of efficiency vary with the size of particles. In general, efficiency will increase with increase in dust particle size, gas inlet body, velocity, cyclone or cone length.	Mining and metallurgical industries	Metal
Electrostatic precipitator	Particles in the gas/air stream are electrically charged as they enter a highly ionised zone and are separated from the gas flow with the help of electrostatic forces in a powerful electric field.	The operation of a precipitator is governed largely by the magnitude of the charge, the electric field, and the extent of re–entrainment of collected dust. Electrostatic precipitators can be used for separation of particles which have a gas temperature as high as 500°C and there is no limit of the collecting efficiency which can be achieved if consideration is not given to plant size and investment cost. The size of particles which can be collected can vary between 0.1 and 100μ.	Utilities and power plants	Coal oil
			Pulp and paper industries, Rock products	Soda Cement, Phosphate, Alumina
			Iron and steel industries Mining and Metallurgical	Bauxite, Silica Phosphate, Sulphate
			Chemical industries	Sulphuric acid
Mechanical collectors	This category includes devices which collect particulate matter by gravity or centrifugal force but which do hot depend upon a vortex, as in the case of cyclones.	Not efficient for fine particulate matters	Utilities and power plants	Coal oil
			Rock products	Cement, phosphate, Alumina, Bauxite

(*Contd...*)

Type of controlling equipments	*Principles*	*Operating conditions*	*Application*	
			Industrial	*Contaminant*
	These devices include setting chambers, buffer chambers, etc.			
Fabric filters	The most commonly used type of bag consists of cylindrical bags which are hung in a framework equipped with an automatic shaking device for cleaning of the bags. The bags are connected to a dust hopper where also the inlet of the dusty air is located. The pass fly dust is collected on the inside of the same.	Filter media can only be used in the temperature range within which they are stable. Also the air/gas should be dry as otherwise there is risk of condensation inside the filter which can cause clogging.	Rock products Pigment Miscellaneous	Cement, Phosphate, Bauxite, Lead, Chromium dust Flour dust Dust
Wet scrubbing	Wet scrubbing of flue gas with lime or lime stone absorbs considerable amount of SO_2. Aqueous solutions of ammonia, potassium carbonate, hydroxide or poly phosphate, or aqueous slurry of MnO_2, MgO_2 can also be used. Resulting by products can be used as useful chemicals and fertilizers.	Wet processes cannot be used at temperatures where the liquid would either freeze, boil or evaporate too rapidly.	Chemical industries Mining and metallurgical	SO_2, NH_3, etc. Metal fumes, SO_2, etc.

Table 5.26

A comparison of sulphur dioxide removal processes

	Low temperature (20°C–100°C)	*Intermediate temperature (100°C – 160°C)*	*High temperatures*
Absorption of SO_2 on carbon	primarily physical, especially at room temperature	primarily chemical.	virtually 100% chemical above 250°C
Efficiency of chemi–	probably now dissociative	limited to active surface sites corn–	enhanced by presence of sulp hur surface conformed during

	Low temperature (20°C–100°C)	*Intermediate temperature (100°C – 160°C)*	*High temperatures*
sorption of SO_2 on carbon	limited to active surface sites com posed primarily of free carbon radicals usually involves less than surface enhanced by presence of H_2O, O_2 especially both together.	posed primarily of free carbon radicals enhanced by presence of H_2O, O_2 especially both together.	reaction. new sites constantly produced by decomposition of bed.
Regeneration techniques	water wash (H_2SO_4) produced ammonia –water wash $(NH_4)^2$ SO_4 produced	heating to 250–350°C (SO_2 produced)	heating (oxides of sulphur bearing gas) free sulphur produced
Advantage of process	negligible sorbent-catalyst decomposition and loss pretreatment of gases not usually necessary little chance of spontaneous ignition within system products potentially markstable	pretreatment of gases not usually necessary	high efficiency (especially near 800°C) spontaneous desorption products precooling of gas not necessary
Disadvantages of process	only small factions of carbon surface actually used optimum conditions for adsorption do not necessarily correspond lo those for regeneration diffusional resistance and limited solutbilities in liquid phase of liquid stream, regeneration is employed precooling of gas stream necessary.	only small fractions of carbon surface actually used regeneration problems; loss of carbon during process; possible explosive fires. desorbed SO_2 is usually treated in sulphuric acid plant	products objection regeneration produces severe loss of carbon; possible explosion; fires

Pollution Tolerant Plants

Certain trees, shrubs and weeds can tolerate pollution upto some extent. A list of such pollution tolerant plants is given below:

Pollution Tolerant Plants

Trees

1.	Bcr (Rhamiiacoae)	Zizyphus mauritiana L
2.	Chatian (Apocynaceae)	A Schalarbris R. Br.
3.	Chaitan (Apocynaceae)	Alstonia macrophylla wall
4.	Junglejalebi (paplionaceae)	Pithecolabium dule (Koxb) benth
5.	Maharuk (Simaroubaceae)	Ailanthus excelsa Roxb
6.	Neem (Miliaceae)	Axadirachitalndica A Juss
7.	Palas (Ulmaceae) ButaeMonasperraa	Lain, Kunze
8.	Papri (Ulmaceae)	Integrifolia Planch
9.	Peepal (Moraceae)	Ficus religiosa
10.	Sham (Mimosaceae)	Propsopis Juliflora Dc.
11.	Shisham (Papilionaceae)	Dalbergia Sissoo Roxb
12.	Tendu (Ebenacaceae Diosphyros)	Melanoxyloiv Roxb
	Shrubs	
13.	Behaya (Convolvulaceac)	Ipomoea Fistulosa Mart Ex Choisy
14.	Chandani (Apocynaceae)	Tebernacemontana cornariaR Br.
	Weeds	
15.	Bhatkaiya (Solanceae)	Solanuin xaiithocarpum Schard & Wendl
16.	Litjira(Amaranthaceae)	Achyranthes asperia L.
17.	Sliialkanta (Papaveraceae)	Argemone Mexicana

6

Noise Pollution and its Control

The term noise may be defined as unwanted sound. A given sound may be music to one person's ears but noise to another's, pleasant when soft but noisy when loud, acceptable for a short time but non–acceptable when prolonged, intriguing when rhythmic but noisy when randomly repeated, reasonable when you make it but noisy when someone else makes it. Of all the attributes that distinguish wanted and unwanted sound, the one considered most significant is loudness. There is ample evidence that prolonged exposure to loud sound is harmful in various ways—the louder a sound is, the more likely it is to be considered noise. Awareness of these problems has increased in recent years and any comprehensive discussion of the environmental problems must now include a study of noise, along with the more traditional problems such as air pollution, water pollution and solid waste disposal.

Unfortunately, noise pollution has not been given enough importance in this country. Besides, there is no statutory standard for this purpose in India. The instruments required for measurement of sound level have not yet been fully developed in this country and, hence, are not easily available for measurement of sound level. However, there is an urgent necessity to scientifically monitor sound levels in large cities, in the engineering industry and in large as well as medium chemical, metallurgical and other industries.

Excessive noise could adversely affect productivity which is already low in India in comparison with advanced countries. The elimination of noise should also help prevent accidents. It is also known that noise has a delayed impact resulting in loss of hearing. Therefore, it is essential to take suitable precautions, especially when children or young persons are involved. Suitable introductory material along with pollution abatement techniques are given in this chapter.

Sound is a form of energy and requires a medium which may be a gas, liquid or solid for its propagation. Any vibrating surface such as a loudspeaker diaphragm which moves to and fro, generates sound. As the diaphragm moves forward it compresses the portion of the gas nearest it. Because of the forces developed by this compression, portions of the gas farther away are progressively set in motion as the inertia of the air molecules is overcome. When the diaphragm reverses its direction of motion, it produces a rarefaction of the gas near it, and a movement of the air particles farther away occurs progressively in the opposite direction. Every small volume containing molecules, wherever located, oscillating forward and backward, under the influence of the diaphragm, will cause molecules further away to oscillate at the same frequency.

The inertia of the particles and the poor elasticity of the gas cause the disturbance (the pressure—variation the sound energy) to travel at the relatively slow speed of around 340 ms^{-1}. The extent of the disturbance depends upon the initial intensity, the dissipative losses in the gas, the presence of wind, turbulence, temperature gradients and on the boundary surfaces.

Frequency

If the pressure varies regularly and repeatedly (that is, if they are cyclic), then the time between successive high pressures (or low pressures) is called the period. The frequency is the reciprocal of the period and is the rate of repetition (of the cycles) of a periodic phenomenon. For the human listener, sound, in the detectable frequency domain, includes frequencies between 2 and 20,000 Hz (Hertz = the unit of frequency, previously called cycles per second). The value quoted are the typical frequency limit of the ear. However, the lowest frequency, that has a pitch–like quality, is about 20 Hz and the upper frequency, audible to the average adult, is about 12,000 Hz. This range of frequencies is called a frequency band which has a bandwidth of 11,980 Hz.

A frequency band (often just called "band", frequency being implied) defines a range of frequencies between the specified or implied limits. The centre frequency (of a frequency band) is the frequency corresponding to the mid-point between the upper and the lower frequency limits. For a linear scale (uniform), the centre frequency of the band 500 to 1000 Hz is 750 Hz since equal scale divisions correspond directly to equal frequency divisions. However, in acoustics (and many other subjects), a logarithmic scale is far more common. The frequency band 707 to 1414 Hz has a centre frequency of 1000 Hz (and not the average frequency of 1060 Hz). Frequencies, that are in octave apart, sound similar and one of the frequencies is double of the other. Thus, the band 707 to 1414 Hz is an octave band (often shortened to oct. band) centered on 1000 Hz, the bandwidth of which is 707 Hz. The term octave-band centre-frequency (often corrected to oct. centre frequency or even centre frequency f_0) is frequently used to completely specify the band.

The preferred octave-band centre-frequencies are 31, 63, 125, 500, 1000, 2000, 4000, 8000, and 16000 Hz. The octave bands may be further divided is equal parts, Europe, a three part division is normally used and each part is called a third octave band.

Intensity

The intensity, *I*, of a sound can be determined with precision and is related to the amount of sound energy received per sec. from the source of sound. Human ears can perceive a vast range of intensities from around 1×10^{-12} Wm^{-2} to around 1000 Wm^{-2}. The intensity level in decibel, written as L_I in dB/ten times the log of the intensity ratio,

$$L_I\ 10\log_{10}\left(\frac{1}{I_0}\right),\ dB\ re\ I_0$$

where I is the measured intensity in Wm^{-2} (watts per square meter) and I_0 is the reference intensity usually 10^{-12} Wm^{-2}.

One important result of working in intensity levels is that if the intensity of the source is doubled, then, because of mathematical compression, there is only an increase of 3 dB in the intensity level.

Unfortunately, there are practical difficulties in accurately measuring intensity. However, it is relatively easy to measure the consequence of the energy passage, the pressure, variation. Since the intensity is directly proportional to the square of the pressure the Sound Pressure Level (SPL) in dB defined by

$$SPL = 20\log_{10}\left(\frac{P}{P_0}\right) dB$$

(An increase of 20 dB in, sound pressure level, corresponds to the sound pressure increasing by a factor of 10).
where P is the measured pressure in Nm^{-2}. P_0 is the reference pressure, usually equal to 2×10^{-5} Nm^{-2}. This value is used since it is the nearest whole number corresponding to the reference intensity.

Band Pressure Level

The term Band Pressure Level in dB combines both the energy and frequency band concepts.

Filters and Analysers

An acoustical filter will ideally allow all those frequencies, in the input signal, within the range of the filter, to pass unhindered, and, at the same time completely attenuate (block) all those frequencies that are outside the range. However, in practice, frequencies, lying just outside the range, are only partially attenuated. Two of the common types of analysis in a filter are:

1. Those having constant bandwidth, where the filter bandwidth is constant, the bandwidth is, often, very narrow. This permits detailed analysis of the sound (or signal). This type of analogies can be important where harmonic distortion is to be investigated or when analysis is made of the vibrational response of an excited mechanical or electrical construction containing a number of very lightly damped resonances.
2. Those having a constant percentage Bandwidth when the width (range) of the analysing filter, the filter bandwidth, is a constant percentage of the band centre frequency independent of the value of this frequency.

This type of analyser is often used in loudness (or noise) summation techniques. An example of the type of instrument that uses this type of filter is the continuous band analyser which uses either whole or third octaveband filters. For example, the fifth filter in an oct. band-set whose centre frequency is 500 Hz allows all frequencies in the range of 553 to 707 Hz to pass, whilst the next filter, centre frequency 1000 Hz passes frequencies from 707 to 1414 Hz.

Loudness (An Observer's Auditory Impression of the 'Strength' of the Sound)

The loudness of a multi–frequency (normal) sound is not linearly related to its intensity. Human beings perceive sounds that have the same intensity but different frequencies as different loudness since the ear is a non-uniform transducer whose sensitivity varies from ear to ear. Those impulses are transmitted to the brain where they are analyzed, thus, introducing another variable—our personality factor. For example, a sound can be sweet and enjoyable to one person, whilst to another person standing alongside him, it may seem an altogether intolerable noise.

Noise Pollution Sources		
Busy Urban Street	—	110 Jet aircraft at 1000 ft
	—	100 Buses at 60 ft
	—	80 Power mover at 80 ft
	—	70 Automobiles at 50 ft; air conditioner at 20 ft
300 ft from Heavy Traffic	—	60 Power station at 50 ft
Commercial Area		
Quiet suburb (day time)	—	50
Quiet suburb (night time)	—	40
Quiet rural (night time)	—	40
A	—	Weighted sound level in dB(A)

Fig. 6.1 Typical source of community noise

130	—	Fire arms, Fire works and toy guns (132—167 peak level)
120	—	Oxygen torch; construction machinery; snowmobiles; rock–n–roll band
110	—	Rivering machine; chainsaw
100	—	Textile machinery
90	—	Farm machinery
80	—	Average factory
70	—	Noisy office
A	—	Weighted sound level in dB(A)

Fig. 6.2 Typical occupational and recreational noise sources

Loudness Level

Loudness level of a sound of any nature is measured by the SPL of a standard pure tone of specified frequency which is assessed, as the model value of the judgement of normal observers, as being equally loud.

Loudness Evaluation

The three procedures, namely Stevens, dB(A) and Leg, commonly used, have some common factors, e.g., they produce eventually a single number for the overall loudness, they weigh certain frequencies or values at the expense of others and the procedures can all be carried out automatically with the necessary instrumentation.

Weighting (Frequency): This is where more account is taken of some frequencies than of others.

In acoustics where the SPL is a logarithmic number, the weighting factors are, thus, normally also logarithmic, and the weighting is accomplished by addition.

Stevens Procedures: The octave BPL's are measured and converted using a standard table. Then, a loudness value, in sounds, is calculated using the empirical formula:

$$L = 0.7\ S_{max} + 0.3_{Sone}$$

where S_{max} is the maximum octave band loudness index and S is the arithmetic sum of all the loudness indices.

Frequency Hz	*i*	*Sound pressure level L_i*	*Octave hand loudness index S_j*
63	1	55	1.1
125	2	65	3.7
250	3	66	5.0
500	4	63.5	5.3
1000	5	65	6.5
2000	6	59.5	5.6
4000	7	51	4.0
8000	8	45	3.4
			34.6

dB(A) The octave BPL values are measured and, then, the appropriate A-weighted correction is added to obtain the A-weighted BPL. The arithmetic sum of all the F values is, then, reconverted.

Leg Equivalent continuous sound pressure level, Leg, is based on the equal energy hypothesis, *i.e.*, equal amounts of energy with certain limitations cause the same effect. It is expressed as

$$\text{Intensity} \times \text{Time} = \text{Constant}$$

$$I \times t = 2I \times \tfrac{1}{2}t$$

or, in terms of intensity level,

$$L_I \text{ for } t \text{ hours} = L_I + 3 \text{ for } \tfrac{1}{2}\ t \text{ hours}$$

International Standards

Composite Noise Rating: Composite noise rating, CNR, is obtained by adding to the value of the loudness level in PNdB. For example, in a given class of flight operation, a correction may be obtained from a table which distinguishes between day and night, percentage runway utilization and the number of movements of aircraft.

Traffic Noise Index *TNI*:

$$\text{TNI} = L_{90} + 4(L_{10} - L_{90}) - 30$$

where L_{90} is the level exceeded for 90 percent of the time, L_{10} is the level exceeded for 10 percent of the time.

Noise Pollution Level LNP:

$$\text{LNP} = L_{eq} + 2.56\sigma\ \text{dB(NP)}$$

in which L_{eq} = energy equivalent sound level of a sufficiently long *A*-weighted sample of noise in dB(A)

σ = standard deviation of the sample in dB(A)

Note that the units are expressed as dB(NP). Should the probability distribution of the instantaneous levels be close to a Gaussian distribution, then, the L_{10}, L_{60} and L_{90} levels can be used in the equation. This leads to the following equation:

$$\text{LNP} = L_{eq} + (L_{10} - L_{90})dB(A)$$

$$\text{LNP} = L_{50} + (L_{10} - L_{90})(L_{10} - L_{90})^2/(dBA)$$

Storindex Q (Germany): $Q = \frac{1}{13.3}\log_{10}\frac{1}{T}10^{12.2Q(t)}\,dt$

where $Q(t)$ is the sound pressure level in dB(A) or in PNdB.

Average Peak Noise Level: For most purposes, it is convenient to define the average peak noise level of a number of aircraft as the logarithmic average of the individual noise levels.

$$\text{Average peak noise level} = 10\log_{10}\frac{1}{N}\int_{1}^{N}10^{L/10}dB$$

$$\text{Equivalent noise level } L_{eq}\text{: } L_{eq} = 10\log_{10}\left(\frac{1}{(t_2 - t_1)}\int_{t_1}^{t_2}10^{L/10}dt\right)dB$$

L = Sound pressure level

Traffic Noise Levels: The Wilson report, which does not actually define an index, implies that certain indoor levels in dBA should not be exceeded for more than 10 percent of the time. However, recent Swedish work by Fog el al casts doubt on the appropriateness of this measure since it was found to have a lower degree of correlation than other levels, particularly the energy mean level in dBA. This is, of course, the same as the BIS specification for aircraft noise except that dBA replaces PNdB.

Effect of Noise

On Physical Health

Acute Effects: These effects depend upon pressure and frequency.

At very high levels, e.g., 150 dB, immediate permanent hearing damage can be caused.

At lower levels 100+ dB, nausea, loss of physical control and physiological changes, caused by stress, are noticed. These effects cease with the noise, although, in some cases, after a time delay.

Chronic Effects: The principal chronic effect is that of noise induced hearing-loss. For this, there is one rule: 'a person, exposed to high noise levels, goes deaf more quickly than he would otherwise have done'. This effect depends upon the pressure, frequency, and time of exposure, becoming more rapid as the pressure rises, and, generally, more damaging with high frequencies. The loss starts, in the frequency range, around 4000 Hz, irrespective of the frequency of the source, causing the damage, and is more marked with impulsive noises.

There are two components to the hearing loss: the temporary and permanent threshold shifts. Table 6.1 shows expected percentage risk as a function of continuous sound level at work in dBA and years of exposure. Table 6.2 shows the influence of noise on speech perception.

Table 6.1
Percentage risk of developing a hearing handicap

Age, years	20	25	30	35	40	45	50	55	60	65
Exposure, years (re age 20)	0	5	10	15	20	25	30	35	40	45
80 total	0.7	1.0	1.3	2.0	3.1	4.9	7.7	13.5	24.0	40
due to noise	no increase in risk at this level of exposure									
85 total	0.7	2.0	3.9	6.0	8.1	11.0	14.2	21.5	32.0	46.0
due to noise	0.0	1.0	2.6	4.0	5.0	6.1	6.5	8.0	8.0	8.5
90	0.7	4.0	7.9	12.0	15.0	18.3	23.3	31.0	42.05	4.5
	0.0	3.0	6.6	10.0	11.9	13.4	15.6	17.5	18.01	4.5
95	0.7	6.7	13.6	20.2	24.5	29.0	34.4	41.8	52.0	64.0
	0.0	5.7	12.3	18.2	21.4	42.1	26.7	28.3	28.0	24.0
100	0.7	10.0	22.0	32.0	39.0	43.0	48.5	55.0	64.0	75.0
	0.0	9.0	20.7	30.0	35.9	38.1	40.8	42.5	40.0	35.0
105	0.7	14.2	33.0	46.0	53.0	59.0	65.5	71.0	78.0	84.5
	0.0	13.2	31.7	44.0	49.9	54.1	1 57.8	57.5	54.0	44.0
110	0.7	20.0	47.5	63.0	71.5	78.0	81.5	85.0	88.0	91.5
	0.0	19.0	46.2	61.0	68.4	73.1	73.8	71.5	64.0	51.5
115	0.7	27.0	62.5	81.0	87.0	91.0	92.0	93.0	94.0	95.0
	0.0	26.0	61.2	79.0	79.0	83.9	86.1	94.3	89.5	55.0

Table 6.2
Influence of the noise on speech perception

Speed interference levels (in dB re 0.002 microban) which barely permit reliable conversion at the distance and voice levels indicated

Distance, ft, between source and listener	*Normal voice level dB*	*Raised voice level dB*
0.5	71	77
1	65	71
2	59	65
3	55	61
4	53	50
5	51	57
6	49	55
12	43	49

The acceptable noise levels for outdoor and indoor noise are given in the following table:

Table 6.3
Acceptable outdoor noise level in residential areas

Location	*Noise level dB(A)*
Rural	25–35
Suburban	30–40
Residential (urban)	35–45
Urban (residential and business)	40–50
City	45–55
Industrial area	50–60

Acceptable indoor noise levels for various types of buildings

Location	*Noise level dB(A)*
Radio and TV studios	25–30
Music rooms	30–35
Hospitals, class rooms, and auditoriums	35–40
Apartments, hotels, homes, conference rooms, small offices	35–40
Court rooms, private offices, libraries	40–45
Large public offices, banks, stores, etc.	45–50
Restaurants	50–55

Mental Health

There is very little specific evidence of the onset of mental or nervous illness caused by noise. There are some temporary effects such as lack of concentration and, at high levels, mental disorientation. There is also a real risk of the aggravation of an existing condition.

Communications

Noise interferes with communications based upon sound when the frequency of the interfering noise coincides, approximately, with that of the desired sound.

Working Efficiency

Loud continuous noise interferes with working efficiency and causes the incidents of errors to rise.

Industrial Accidents

In so far as noise interferes with sound communication, it may mask warning signals, and, thereby, increasing, at the same time, the incidence of errors which may make accidents more likely.

Personal Comfort

The effect depends upon the pressure and frequency and on the time of exposure. At levels well below those which cause rapid hearing damage, noise becomes intrusive, interferes with speech communication and with peaceful enjoyment of leisure. The last three effects are essentially a nuisance. If is difficult to assess, varies very much from individual to individual and becomes tolerable with continuous exposure. Total and impulsive characteristics and intermittence modify individual reactions.

The National Environment Policy Act of 1969 has required, since January 1, 1970, that federal agencies consider noise as an influence on the quality of environment. This has been implemented in the form of environmental impact statements required on all federal actions significantly affecting the human environment. In April 1972, the Federal Highway Administration (FHWA) issued the Policy and Procedure Memorandum (PPM) 00.5 which compatible with different land uses. Some details of standards in Tables 6.4 –6.7.

Table 6.4
Permissible time limit with noise level

Noise level dB(A)	*Time, hrs.*
90	8
93	4
96	2
99	1
150	Rupture of membrane

Noise Threshold Limit Values

The American National Standard Specification for sound level meters, SI(197) Type 52A, is given in Table 6.5.

Table 6.5

Duration per day, h.	*Sound level dBA*
16	80
8	85
4	90
2	95
1	100
1/2	105
1/4	110
1/8	115

When the daily noise exposure is composed of two or more periods of noise exposure of different levels, their combined effect should be considered, rather than the individual effect of each. If the sum of the following fractions:

$$\frac{C_1}{T_1}+\frac{C_2}{T_2}+\cdots+\frac{C_n}{T_n}$$

exceeds unit, then the mixed exposure should be considered to exceed the threshold limit value. C_1 indicates the total duration of exposure at a specific noise level, and T_1 indicates the total duration of exposure permitted at that level.

Example 6.1. In a work area, the noise levels are read as 95 clB (A) for two hours a day, 90 dB(A) for four hours a day, and 80 dB(A) for the remaining two hours a day.

The problems is to find the permissible durations for each noise level. The permissible exposures are:

95 dB(A) = 2 hrs. 90dB(A) = 4hrs

80 dB(A) = 16 hrs

2. When we add the ratios

Noise levels (dBA)	95	90	80
Measured (hrs)	2	4	2
Permissible (hrs)	2	4	16

$$\frac{2}{2}+\frac{4}{4}+\frac{2}{16}=1+1+\frac{1}{8}=\frac{17}{8}=1\frac{7}{8}$$

This exceeds the permissible limit of 1.

Example. 6.2. Noise in an area measures 90 dB(A) for one hour, 90 dB(A) for two hours and 70 dB(A) 2 hrs.

Noise levels (dBA)	90	90	70
Measured (hrs)	1	2	2
Permissible (hrs)	2	4	any period of time

$$\frac{1}{2}+\frac{2}{4}+0=\frac{1}{2}=\frac{1}{2}=1$$

or, the noise exposure is within limits.

Impulsive or Impact Noise

It is recommended that exposure to impulsive or impact noise should not exceed the limits listed in Table 6.6. No exposures, in excess of 140 decibels, peak sound pressure level, are permitted. Impact noise includes those variations in noise levels that involve maxima at intervals of greater than one per second. Where the intervals are less than one second, it should be considered continuous.

Table 6.6
Threshold limit values of impulsive or impact noise

Sounded level dB *	*Permitted number of impulses or impact* per day
140	100
130	1,000
120	10,000

* Decibles peak sound pressure level.

Levels at which a hearing conservation programme should be introduced where ear protection is used.

Corrections for sound pressure levels at work places are given in Table 6.8. Suggested noise criteria for steady background noise for different indoor functional activity are given in Table 6.9.

Maximum allowable levels of ultrasound

Frequency based cycles/s	*With ear plugs (decibels)*	*With ear muffs (fluid seal type) decibels*
37.5–150	110	120
150–300	110	115
300–600	110	118
600–1200	110	125
1200–2400	110	122
2400–4800	110	125

Table 6.7
Maximum allowable sound pressure levels at the workplace in the vicinity of ultrasound sources

Geometric frequency means by third octave bands (in Hz)	12500	16000	2000
Sound pressure level (in dB)	75	85	110

Table 6.8
Corrections for sound pressure levels at work places in the vicinity of ultrasound sources

Total ultrasound exposure duration (hrs)	*Correction (dB)*	*Total ultrasound exposure duration (min.)*	*Correction (dB)*
1–4	+6	5–15	+18
1/4–1	+12	1–5	+24

The duration of ultrasound must be calculated or based on technical documentation.

Monitoring

A long-term programme should be drawn up involving workers' participation to keep noise and vibration risks under control.

Table 6.9
Recommended category classification and suggested noise criteria for steady background noise as heard in various indoor functional activity

Type of space (and acoustical requirements)	*PNC curve*	Approximate L_A *dB (A)*
Concert halls, opera houses and recital halls (for listening to joint musical sound)	Not to exceed 15	26
Broadcast and recording studios (distance microphone pickup used)	10–20	20–30
Large auditoriums, drama theatres and churches (for very good listening conditions)	Not to exceed 20	Not to exceed 30
Broadcast, television, and recording studios (close microphone pickup used only)	Not to exceed 25	Not to exceed 34
Small auditoriums, small theatres, small churches, music rehearsal rooms, large meeting and conference rooms, (for very good listening) or executive offices and conference rooms for 50 people (not amplification)	Not to exceed 35	Not to exceed 42
Bedrooms, sleeping quarters, hospitals, residences, motels., etc., (for sleeping, resting, relaxing)	25–40	37–47

(*Contd...*)

(*Contd...*)

Private or semiprivate offices, small conference rooms, class rooms, libraries, etc. (for good listening conditions)	30–40	38–47
Living rooms and drawing rooms in dwellings (for conversing or listening to radio and TV)	30–40	38–47
Large offices, reception areas, retail shops and stores, restaurants, etc. (for moderately good listening conditions)	35–45	42–52
Lobbies, laboratory work spaces, drafting, and engineering rooms, general recreator areas (for fair listening)	40–50	47–56
High maintenance shops, office and computer equipment rooms, kitchens and laundries (for moderately fair listening conditions)	45–55	52–67
Shops, garages, power plant control rooms, etc., (for just acceptable speech and telephone communication) levels above NC or PNC-60 are not recommended for any office or communication	50–60	56–66
For work spaces where speech or telephone communication is not required, but where there must be no risk of hearing damage.	60–75	66–80

PNC Curve–Preferred Noise Criteria Curve

The aims of this programme should be

1. To ensure that the protective action which has been taken remains effective
2. To ensure that the levels, as measured previously, remain unchanged or fall.
3. To ensure that any change made in manufacturing processes will not lead to the emergence of new risks.
4. To promote the study and implementation of more efficient preventive measures and
5. To ensure that the health of the workers is effectively protected.

Environmental Monitoring

1. Measurements made in places of work should be repeated at suitable intervals, and a record of the readings obtained should be maintained in an appropriate manner.
2. Measurements made at places of work should be repeated whenever there is a change in premises, equipments or production which might affect noise and vibration. Likewise, they should repeated with a view to assessing the effectiveness of the preventive action being taken.
    (*a*) An inspection programme should be drawn up by the enterprise to ascertain whether technical preventive measures taken remain effective.
    (*b*) This inspection programme should comprise regular periodical inspections and special checks whenever necessary.

(*c*) Special attention should be paid to the use of an inspection check list to reduce noise or vibration, or both, as well as to personal protective equipment and its use.

Health Monitoring

1. Statistics should be derived from the data obtained by medical examinations, so as to ascertain whether the preventive action taken has proved satisfactory.
2. The medical records should also be used for research purposes, and for epidemiological studies intended to help in defining more precisely maximum permissible levels as well as to collect data on individual sensitivity.

Comparison of Findings

1. The data provided by noise and vibration measurements in places of work should be correlated with the outcome of medical examinations to ascertain how effective preventive action has been and what groups of workers are most at risk.
2. Within the programme of an occupational health service, technical and medical dose response records, when properly maintained, should form an important part of an epidemiological long–term follow–up of working conditions.
3. The data available within the undertakings should as far as possible be made available for research purposes for the assessment of the noise and vibration hazards and their prevention.
4. Scientific research institutes in individual countries should undertake, in close cooperation with each other, more intensive research on the biological effects of noise and vibration, and epidemiological studies should be carried out.

Noise Measuring Equipment

Sound Level Meter

This is used for the evaluation of sound pressures either on a linear or weighted scale. It normally indicates the RMS value of the sound, but can be calibrated to read the peak level.

The dynamic characteristics of the meters generally available are:

1. Slow, with a rise time of 500 ms.
2. Fast, with a rise time of 700 ms.
3. Impulse, with a rise time of 35 ms.
4. Impulse hold with a rise lime of 3 5 ms and a slow fall.
5. Peak, and Peak hold, as impulse and impulse and impulse hold, but measuring peak, not RMS level.

There are two grades of sound level meters:

1. IEC 123 3/4 with limited accuracy, particularly at high and low frequencies, but cheap ana robust. Useful for rough survey, to be followed by more accurate measurement, if necessary.
2. IEC 179 3/4 with a high degree of accuracy, are expensive and delicate. Used when accuracy is essential.

Octave Band Analyser

This is used in conjunction with, or as an integral part of the sound level meter, to determine the average sound pressure of the standard octave bands. It is a sufficiently accurate guide to the frequency content of a noise to determine treatment to reduce it, for the selection of ear protectors (defenders) or for identifying the source of a noise. If more accurate information is required, 1/3 octave band analysers are available.

Magnetic Tape Recorder

A high quality record is fed directly from a microphone or through a sound level meter. It is used to record the actual noise for storage or for better evaluation. The recorder needs to be run at fast speed to preserve frequency content and, therefore, is also expensive on tape, which also needs to be of good quality.

Cassette Recorder

This instrument is cheaper and of a lower quality than the above mentioned one, and is used for storage of noise or for rough evaluation.

It is used for digital recording of sound pressure levels for computer evaluation. This system gives no record of the actual noise but the data on the tape can be stored. The equipment is expensive but it can use cheap tape run at low speed as quality is not important.

Pen Recorder

This recorder can be fed directly, or from sound level meters, etc. or from magnetic tape recording on one of two systems:

(*a*) A continuous record of the sound pressure level against time is given which can be used for storage, or to obtain approximate statistical levels by inspection. The movement of the pen can be sampled during the writing operation to give a statistical breakdown of the sound pressure–level distribution (see mechanical statistical analysers infra). Either the dynamic range of the instrument or the accuracy will be limited, depending on the price.

(*b*) A discontinuous record in the form of instantaneous sound pressure levels, sampled from the incoming noise. Statistical levels can be found on inspection, but the dynamic range of the device is limited and normally only one level can be found with any degree of accuracy.

Statistical Analyser

Mechanical: It is used in conjunction with the pen recorder (qv) to give any statistical level or an L_{eq}.

Electronic: It can be fed directly, through a sound level meter or from a magnetic tape recording, to give any desired statistical analysis, within the limits of the equipment. It can be set up to work unattended but will provide a single analysis. It can also be coupled up to a print out to give a permanent record. Accuracy would normally comply with IEC 179 and dynamic range can be 60 dB or more.

Digital Tape Processor: This is fed from digital tape recordings (qv) to provide any statistical analysis or an Leq. This system can give high accuracy and good dynamic range, but it is expensive. The processing time can be much shorter than the recording time.

Noise Average Meter

It is fed directly or from magnetic tape recordings to give an L_{eq} as a continuous digital display, or as a print out. Dosemeters work on the same principle, but record the information as a percentage of a present dose, rather than as a L_{eq}. It normally complies with IEC 179.

Noise Analyser

This is fed directly or from magnetic tape recordings and consists essentially of a sound level meter (IEC 179) feeding both a statistical analyser and a noise average meter. It can be coupled to give an analogue or digital recording of the processed data, with both periodic and cumulative evaluations for print out. It gives also a digital display, and normally complies with IEC 179.

Noise Control

Noise Control on Blower

The blower was set to operate at the specified maximum pressure and, using a suitable Impulse Precision Sound Level Meter, sound levels were measured and analysed. Three locations, spaced 0.6 meters (m) apart, were chosen for measurement in each direction. Noise levels were also measured at a few representative locations around the blower, in an area situated 5 to 50 m away, from the blower. This latter area is referred to as the general working area.

The principal sources of noise were identified as being due to the inlet and outlet air streams and the vibrations of the blower casing and mounting. Four designs of silencers were fabricated to muffle the air noise. Their impact on environmental noise distribution was assessed by repeated measurements at the same chosen locations. The procedures chosen were aimed at inlet streamlining, reducing the exhaust pressure and velocity, changing the direction of air flow and accomplishing multiple reflection.

Based on the results obtained, a new facility was developed to earn' out large scale testing of blowers from a distance.

Efficacy of Silencers

With the use of silencers on either the air inlet or outlet side, only marginal reduction can be accomplished. However, when both the inlet and outlet sides arc fitted with silencers, noise hazards cease to exist in the general working area and are confined to an area within about 5 m from the blower.

A comparison of the relative effectiveness of silencers càn also be had from Table 6.3. Type *P*, although lined with substantial absorptive material all around, gave nominal reduction and was loo short to be effective for sound waves of 500 Hz (wave length 0.60 m). The type *Q* which did not use absorptive material, but served only as an expansion chamber was better than the type *P*. The many directional changes which air had to undergo in passing through it made this type very effective. The type *S* was also very effective because of its length which gave an opportunity for multiple impingement of sound waves over the absorptive lining. The final choice between types *R* and *S* would have to depend upon the cost of fabrication and their resistance to air flow.

Vibration Isolation and Suppression: After the installation of the type *S* silencers on the inlet and outlet sides, it was found that air noise at the entry to the inlet and exist of the outlet was as low as 93 to 94 dB(A) while noise levels at another location still ranged between 99–108 dB(A) and progressively increased to 112 dB(A) at locations 1 and the centre of the blower. It was apparent that in this condition, noise due to the vibrations of the pump casing and mountings was more dominant than air noise. Vibration reduction was sought to be accomplished at the proposed new test facility.

Mew Facility for Testing

The well–known principles of process segregation, isolation of personnel, the rate of absorptive materials, silencers resilient mounts should be considered. It is hoped that with the use of this facility, testing can be carried out without any noise hazards and without unduly disturbing the calm of the neighbourhood even at night.

Control of undesirable noise, which is as important as the control of air or water pollution. can be accomplished by a number of methods. A brief chart of noise control techniques is given below.

Chart of noise control techniques

Control at the source

- (*i*) Reduction of the amplitude of the exciting forces
  - (*a*) Reduction of impacts of impulsive forces
  - (*b*) Balancing of moving mass
  - (*c*) Balancing of by magnetic forces
  - (*d*) Use of dynamic compensation
  - (*e*) Reducing frictional forces
  - (*f*) Vibration isolation
- (*ii*) Reduction of the response of various components to the exciting forces
  - (*a*) Alteration of the natural frequency of the resonant element
  - (*b*) Increasing the energy dissipation
- (*iii*) Changes in operating procedure
  - (*a*) Siting
  - (*b*) Building layout
  - (*c*) Path deflection
  - (*d*) Providing enclosures
  - (*d*) Absorption
  - (*f*) Impeding the sound discontinuities between source and receiver

Control of the Transmission path

- (*i*) Siting
- (*ii*) Building layout
- (*iii*) Path Deflection
- (*iv*) Enclosures
- (*v*) Absorption
- (*vi*) Impedance mismatch

Control at the Receiver

- (*i*) Use of personal protective equipment
- (*ii*) Education and publications
- (*iii*) Exposure control

Noise Pollution Control in India

In India, at present, there is no separate regulation for noise control. However, it is expected that suitable parameters, i. e., noise level and frequency, will be prescribed both for ambient conditions as well as industrial environment, particularly engineering as well as fabrication industries. Noise pollution from vehicles is important, particularly in metropolitan areas. Noise directly affects the senses and, consequently, the quality of the urban environment, more than any other nuisance, stemming from technical progress. Urban noise is an erratic combination of 'peak noise' and background noise of a lower intensity ranging from about 50 to 70 dB(A), for which motor vehicles are regarded as one of the major contributors. This is in spite of the significant progress achieved in the last decades in silencing exhausts and reducing mechanical noise, in developed countries. Noise disturbs sleep and may be a cause of stress.

The noise-control levels enforced in Europe, Japan and the USA generally result in a minimum of exhaust pipe noise, achieved by means of advanced silencers, using gas expansion and noise frequency interference techniques. It may be difficult, technically, to further reduce this source of noise. Conversely, exploration of ways and means to reduce the following acoustic energy emissions and radiations which are unrelated to exhaust should continue:

— Fan aerodynamic noise, particularly from air-cooled engines,

— Mechanical noise from engine cylinder block and crank case, gear box transmission and alternators,

— Rolling noise from tyres in contact with the road.

Diesel–equipped vehicles are noisy due to the nature of the engine combustion under very high compression. Public transport and heavy commercial vehicles require special consideration. Particular attention to their proper maintenance and periodic inspection, including their silencing devices, should be paid.

7

Treatment, Utilisation and Disposal of Sewage

In developing countries, the organic load of river system is a major problem. In India, the contribution of local bodies, e.g., Nagar Mahapalika, Nagar Palika, Town Area, etc., through sewage is about 90 percent, while 3 percent is contributed by small-scale and 7 per cent by medium and large-scale industries. Unfortunately, control of pollution due to sewage cannot be self supporting, e.g., it is not economically viable. However, considering the social responsibility and other indirect advantages of pollution control, it is essential to have pollution control for sewage. Even in developed countries, pollution control measures are slower in case of domestic effluent than in that of trade effluent. With the establishment of the River Ganga Authority, pollution control, due to sewage, is receiving greater attention. It is expected that even those local bodies, which are not contributing directly to the pollution of rivers Ganga and Yamuna, will go in for pollution control in the near future. Pollution control for sewage has been described in this chapter, with Kanpur, one of the largest industrialized cities of North India, as a typical example.

The people of Kanpur generate 1800 cubic meters, *i.e.*, approximately 900 tonnes of refuse and 1700 cubic meters of night soil, every day. Only about 25 percent of the refuse is transported by the Municipality and removed, the remaining 75 percent is carried away in open drains, creating a great health hazard.

As a result of excessive discharge of untreated sewage, sullage and effluents, the river Ganga, noted for its high natural self-purification capability has become extremely polluted at Kanpur and its water is unfit for use. At present, all 17 aquaducts in Kanpur are discharging sewage/sullage into the river Ganga as many sewers are undersized, silted and damaged. The drains also discharge effluents from various industrial units. The volume and BOD load transported dally by the waste out falls are nearly 225 million litres and 75 tonnes, respectively. The sewage contributes about 50-55 percent of the total load on the stream[7].

As the sullage drains from Kanpur start pouring into the river Ganga, the quality of water steadily deteriorates. At various ghats, viz., Bhaironghat, Sarsaiya ghat, etc., the quality of water ranges between class 'C' and 'E', *i.e.*, it is unfit for any beneficial use (Table 7.1).

In view of the deteriorating situation and the significant contribution of organic load, estimated to be about 50–55 percent, through sewage, it is considered essential to suitably treat sewage before introduction into the river Ganga.

Table 7.1
Standards for polluted waters

Class	*Use*	*Standard*
A	Drinking water after chlorination	Without filtration B. Coli 50 per 100 ml
B	Bathing, recreation and shell fish culture	No visible sewage matter B. Coli 100 per 100 ml
C	Fishing	Dissolved oxygen content to be 3 and preferably 5 ppm, C02 40 and preferably 20 ppm
D	Rough industrial use and irrigation	Absence of nuisance, odours and unsightly suspended floating matters. Dissolved oxygen should be present.

Disposal of Sewage

The following methods are considered to be of potential importance in sewage treatment.

Broad Irrigation

In this method, sewage is disposed off on land. The land area acts as a crude filter and stabilizes sewage by aerobic filtration. The sewage is usually given primary treatment before disposal. This method is similar to intermittent sand filtration.

Sewage Farming

In this method, the water and fertilizing elements, viz., nitrogen, phosphorous and potash are utilized to raise crops. It has the special advantage of fertilizing the land and also being beneficial from the economic point of view.

Dilution

In this method, the sewage is discharged into large bodies of water such as rivers, lakes or the sea. The sewage is treated to ensure that the condition of the receiving water stream does not deteriorate to the extent of impairing its normal utility. A comparison of the two main systems of disposal, i.e., the broad irrigation and dilution methods is given in Table 7.2. In Kanpur, the latter method is mainly used for sewage disposal. Its working is considered satisfactory during the rainy season when the dilution factor is extremely high, but not suitable for the period November through June when the volume of flow is low.

Table 7.2
Comparison of the two methods of sewage disposal : Dilution and Broad Irrigation

S.No.	*Disposal on land*	*By dilution*
1.	For land disposal, large areas with preferably sandy type of soils are required.	Large volume of clean water (i.e., having low or no initial B.O.D.) with high D.O. contents are necessary.
2.	All the land required may not be available at one place and more number of disposal points may be required.	Similarly, large volumes of water may not be available throughout the year, summer being the most critical season when the volume of water and the available D.O. both are less.
3.	The cost of land might be prohibitive but by adopting sewage farming, some	Low cost operation and no return is possible.

(*Contd. ...*)

(*Contd. ...*)

	return can be obtained, for which good management is also required.	
4.	It requires either preliminary or primary treatment of sewage.	Dilution may usually need either full or, atleast, partial treatmt.it. This involves extra cost and operational troubles. But when treatment is not required, it offers the most simple solution to the sewage disposal problem.
5.	It saves the inland streams from getting polluted by the sewage and returns to the land the fertilizing elements present in the sewage.	It causes stream pollution and unavoidable health hazards. Towns situated downstream, therefore, cannot use the water in the stream for their water supply purpose without adequate treatment. The pollution also travels long distances downstream and the stream may lose its utility for different human activities over a considerable distance.
6.	It requires high head pumping, the operational cost of which is, therefore, high.	It usually requires no or low head pumping because streams pass through the lowest contours and valleys.

Treatment of Sewage

The general operations in a sewage treatment plant and the units employed for the purpose are given in Table 7.3. The main features are as follows:

Primary Treatment

The primary treatment consists of physical separation of floating and suspended (settleable) solids from the sewage. Screens, grit chambers, detritus tanks, skimming tanks and settling tanks are used for this purpose.

Table 7.3
Sewage treatment pliant operation

SI. No.	*Type of treatment*	*Operation*	*Unit employed*
1.	Preliminary	Removal of (*i*) lighter floating materials, e.g., leaves of trees, pieces of rags, wood charcoal. (*ii*) Fats and grease.	(*i*) Screens of different designs. (*ii*) Skimming tanks.
2.	Preliminary	Removal of heavier suspended inorganic material, e.g., grit sand.	Detritus tanks Grit chambers
3.	Primary	Removal of larger suspended (organic) solids.	Settling tanks
4.	Secondary	Removal of fine suspended and dissolved organic material by means of biological flocculation and precipitation and then by settling out.	(*i*) a. Intermittent sand filters. b. Trickling filters. (*ii*) Activated sludge treatment plant and secondary settling tanks.
5.	Final	Removal of harmful bacteria and other organisms.	Chlorinator

Note:

Operation no. 5 is practiced only under special circumstances, i.e., where the sewage is disposed off by dilution and the out fall is very near to water intake of some other town.

Secondary Treatment

The secondary treatment includes flocculation and precipitation of the remaining material in the sewage with the help of biological agencies, and their physical separation in secondary settling tanks. A layout for a typical sewage treatment is shown in Fig. 7.1. Figure 7.2 shows schematic diagram for bio-gas production from sewage.

For simplicity and economy of operation, the treatment processes are usually carried out in the sequence indicated in Table 7.3. The efficiencies normally encountered in practice, in the various units of a treatment plant, are given in Table 7.4.

The by-products of the treatment process are screenings, grit and sludges of different kinds, of which the first two can be easily disposed off by burial or burning. Sludge contains unstable volatile organic materials and may be treated by the method of digestion, in which gases are produced with high calorific values which can be successfully utilized for heating or power generation. The solid material left, behind, i.e., the digested sludge, contains good manorial elements and is useful as a manure or soil buildings.

Table 7.4
Relative efficiencies of sewage treatment plant units

Sl. No.	*Treatment process unit*	*% Removal*		
		Suspended solids	*5 Day 20C BOD*	*Bacteria*
1.	Fine screens	2–20	5–10	10–20
2.	Chlorination of the settled sewage	—	15–30	90–95
3.	Plain settling tanks	40–70	25–40	25–75
4.	Chemical precipitation	70–90	50–85	40–80
5.	High rate trickling filters preceded and followed by plain sedimentation	65–92	65–95	80–95
6.	Low rate trickling filters preceded and followed by plain sedimentation	70–92	80–95	90–95
7.	High rate activated sludge treatment preceded and followed by plain sedimentation	65–95	65–95	80–95
8.	Conventional activated sludge treatment preceded and followed by plain sedimentation	85 90	75–95	90–98
9.	Intermittent sand filtration	85–95	90–95	95–98
10.	Chlorination of biologically treated sewage		—	98–99

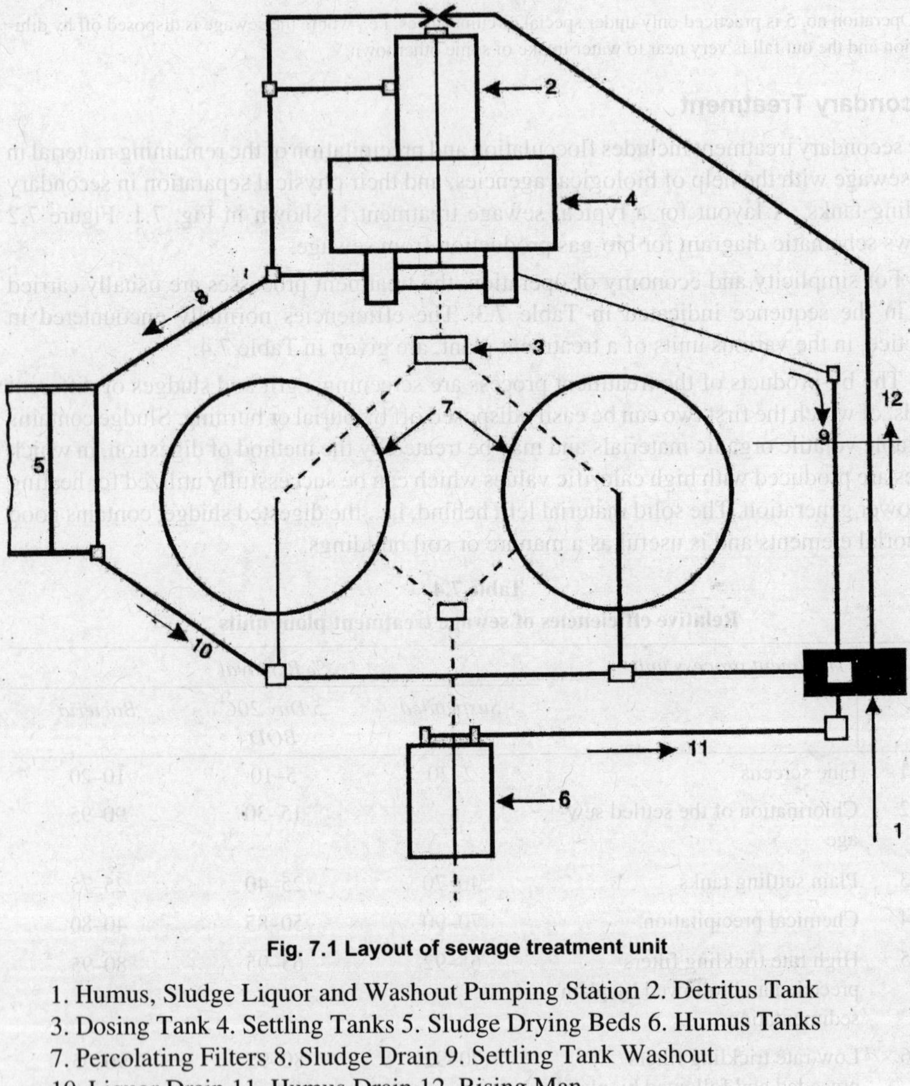

Fig. 7.1 Layout of sewage treatment unit

1. Humus, Sludge Liquor and Washout Pumping Station 2. Detritus Tank 3. Dosing Tank 4. Settling Tanks 5. Sludge Drying Beds 6. Humus Tanks 7. Percolating Filters 8. Sludge Drain 9. Settling Tank Washout 10. Liquor Drain 11. Humus Drain 12. Rising Man.

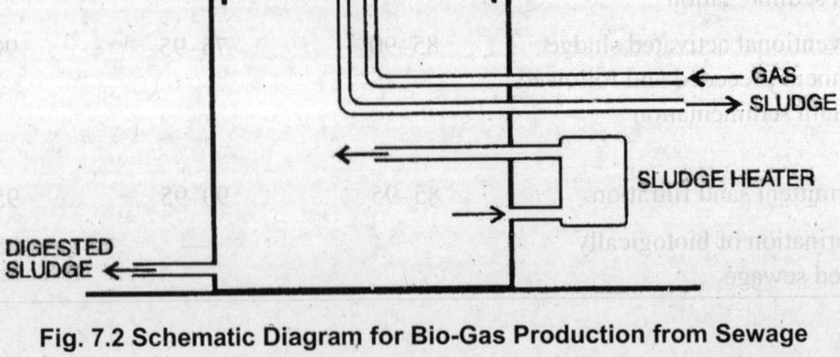

Fig. 7.2 Schematic Diagram for Bio-Gas Production from Sewage

Sludge Digestion

The process of sludge digestion is the liquefaction of organic material by anaerobic bacteria which produce an alkaline reaction. When sludge is first placed in a tank, acid digestion with the production of noxious gases results, but eventually alkaline digestion prevails and, once established, the alkaline condition remains for an indefinite period of time. The gases given off by the sludge during digestion are mainly methane with some CO_2 and smaller quantities of other gases.[6] Digestion takes place in three stages :

1. A short period of rapid digestion, during which the pH value of the sludge decreases.
2. An extended period of slow digestion during which the pH value rises slowly with low gas production.
3. During the third stage, it attains a pH of 7.0 and gas production is maximum.

Two-stage digestion is usually preferred because it simplifies gas collection and assists the removal of supernatant water. A major part of the gas is produced in primary tanks, which is collected for utilization. Supernatant water is removed from secondary tanks. Primary tanks have to be treated for this purpose but there is no need to heat the secondary tanks.[2]

Table 7.5
Different types of tanks and their special features

	Types of tanks	*Special features*
1.	Septic tanks	*i.* Large, in size about 300′ × 100′ × 6′. *ii.* Whole of organic matter, i.e., sludge can be digested producing gas and soluble materials.
2.	Imhoff tank	*i.* Sedimentation and sludge digestion are effected in upper and lower compartments of the tank, respectively. *ii.* Popular in the US A and Europe.
3.	Travis hydrolytic tank	*i.* Complete settlement of colloids. . *ii.* A circular tank with a central monhole containing penstocks of drawing of sludge and three angular rings, the outer being divided into four portions.
4.	Field house tank	Circular in shape with central conical bottomed tank and an outer ring with several hopper bottoms and a common periph eral weir.
5.	Dibdin state beds	Depth 3 feet with horizontal layer of state.
6.	Contact beds	Filled with sewage, retained for some time, then drained off with gravity to take up oxygen from air that has moved in on the outflow of the liquid.

In primary digestion tanks at a temperature of 32°C, about 40.8 percent digestion of volatile solids takes place, giving 0.96 cubic metre gas/kg of solids destroyed or 29.25 per , head of population per day. However, this depends mainly on the animal and vegetable oil content of the sludge, The digestion period depends on the temperature and can be reduced to 15 days at 52° C. At all temperatures, the total amount of gas produced during digestion remains the same.

Digestion tanks : As the gas is collected in the tanks, it is desirable to use floating covers which rise and fall with the level of the sludge as the tanks are filled and emptied.

For the sake of economy of cost and to reduce heat losses, digestion tanks should be deep and circular. Different types of tanks with their special features are given in Table 7.5[4]

Feeding method: To prevent several risks, e.g., the production of an explosive mixture of gas and air inside the tank and the sucking in of air by negative pressure, the following methods should be adopted.

In the feeding method, sludge is delivered into the tank, causing digested sludge to pass over an adjustable weir, such as a telescopic weir, and on to secondary digestion or disposal. By adopting this method, the sludge can be maintained within safe limits. In case there are many tanks, the sludge should be fed to them in equal quantities, preferably once a day, when the primary sedimentation tanks are sludged.

Seeding and Mixing : Raw sludge is mixed with about 20 percent of actively digested sludge before it is passed into the primary tank. For stirring, mechanical stirrers can be used.

Heating methods : Any of the following methods, singly or in convenient combinations, can be used to heat the digestion tanks:

1. By circulating hot water through fixed coils of pipes of about 4 cm diameter, located near the walls of the tank.
2. By rotating coils or grids of pipes in which hot water is circulated. The pipes serve the double purpose of heating and stirring the sludge.
3. By drawing sludge from the primary tank, heating it in a heat exchanger and passing it back into the digestion tank.
4. By heating alkaline supernatant water drawn off from the secondary tank and returning it into the primary tank.
5. By injecting steam into the bottom of the tank.

Sludge control: The sludge is pumped (usually daily) into the digester and passes into the tank through the recirculation return part at the bottom of the sludge heater chamber, which is specially designed, so that the direction and velocity, at which the sludge enters the digester, give a rotatory motion to the tank contents. The sludge feed displaces an equal volume of digested sludge, which passes through the sludge draw-off pipe, from the central discharge point, at the bottom of the cone, to the sludge draw-off chamber. It, then, passes over an adjustable weir penstock into the discharge chamber before being delivered to the secondary digester or sludge drying beds. By adjustment of the weir-penstock, the sludge level in the tank can be controlled.

Removal of supernatant water : The secondary digestion tanks serve the purpose of completing digestion to an economic limit, and providing quiescent conditions to permit separation of supernatant water.

The common arrangement for the removal of supernatant water is the installation of several small-diameter valves, connected at various levels in the tank. The operation is to open a valve at a time, to find where the supernatant water is, then, to draw it off until sludge appears. The percentage of dewatering varies between 10-50 percent, depending upon the nature of the sludge.

Sludge Gas arid its Utilization

Sludge gas consists of about 67 percent methane, 33 percent CO_2 and small quantities of other gases. As methane has about 8000 kcal/m^3 calorific value, the calorific value of sludge gas can be taken to be approximately 5334 kcal/m^3. The sludge gas occupies

0.95 m^3/kg at normal day temperature and atmospheric pressure. The weight of sludge gas produced is about the same as in the digestion process.[5]

On the basis of the amount of sewage discharged from Kanpur city, it is estimated that about 2.5×10^4 cubic metre gas could be generated per day with 1.6×10^8 kcal calorific value. As reported by the Indian Oil Corporation, the consumption of Indane gas at Kanpur is about 50,000 cylinders per month, each containing 15 kg of LPG. The total consumption works out 750,000 kg of LPG per month, having a calorific value of5,370 kcal/kg. On the basis of this calorific value of Indane gas, the total calories consumed in the city of Kanpur, at present, is approximately 1.33×10^8kcal.

The main use of sludge gas, apart from heating the digestion tanks, is for power. The power generated is sufficient to pump the entire sewage. At activated sludge works, the power can be used for aeration purposes. Elsewhere, it finds use in recirculation pumping in the alternating double filtration scheme. It has also been used for driving road vehicles. For this purpose, the gas has to be purified, particularly its C02 content. After which it is compressed and stored in high-pressure cylinders. It can also be used for cooking purposes.

Dried digested sludge can be used as a fetilizer as it contains 0.8-3.5 percent nitrogen, 1.6 percent phosphorous, and 0.35 percent potash on the basis of the dry weight of solids. It may also be used for land filling, dumped in large bodies of water, or incinerated to produce heat and power.

Conclusion

The population of Kanpur is about 17 lakhs and the total sewage discharged from the city is 3500 m^3/day (3000 tonnes/day). The sewage of the city is discharged into the river Ganga through sewers, without any treatment, producing about 45 tonnes of organic load on the stream, which is about 50–55 percent of the total organic load. By the digestion of sludge at Kanpur, about $2.5 \times 103m^3$ gas would be produced per day, which is sufficient to generate 1.6×10^8 kcal per day. A comparison of this value to that produced by Indane gas at Kanpur shows that the gas produced from sludge would provide almost equal calories to the city of Kanpur as supplied by Indane gas.

References

1. Buswell, M. A., *The Chemistry of Water and Sewage Treatment*, Chemical Catalogue Co., New York, 1928, p. 268.
2. Escritt, L.B., *Sewage and Sewerage Disposal*, Contractors Record Ltd., London, 1962, p. 327–28.
3. Escritt, L.B. *Sewerage and Sewage Disposal*, II, Facdonald & Evancs Ltd., London, 1972, p. 324–364.
4. Fuller, George W. and James R. Mo Clintock, *Solving Sewerage Problems*, McGraw- Hill Book Co. Inc, New York, 1926, p. 294.
5. Kshirsagar, S. R., *Sewerage and Sewage Treatment*, Roorkee Pusblishing House, 1968, p. 160–169.
6. Metcalf, Leonard and Harrison P. Eddy, Sewerage and Sewage Disposal, McGraw-Hill Book Co. Inc., New York, 1930, p. 236.
7. The Citizen 17 (4–5), June-July, 1982.

8

Solid Waste Disposal

Before undertaking solid waste management, it is essential to have some knowledge about the solid waste materials that are normally encountered. Generally, solid waste materials are classified into two broad categories :

1. Household solid waste, and
2. Commercial waste.

Generally, household solid materials are collected locally and the amount depends upon the size and consumption habits of the population. It is disposed off on either public property or private contractors' sites. Commercial wastes are generated by commercial establishments but are usually disposed off by public facilities. Industrial wastes are those generated by manufacturing firms. A detailed classification is given in Table 8.1.

The detailed statistics for the generation and disposal of wastes are not available for developing countries. The typical analyses of some of the waste materials discharged at Kanpur, Calcutta and Nagpur are given in Table 8.2. Another study carried out by Bhide et al, on refuse in Indian cities, is tabulated in Table 8.3. In this case, the classification has been done on the basis of population. The effect of population on the composition of solid wastes is obvious; for example, paper, rubber and leather, plastics, metals and glass increase with the increased population of the city. The total compostable matter also increases with the size of tire city. A similar study carried out in Nigeria, another developing country, by Oluwande is given in Table 8.4. The figures available from the United States indicate that 10 lb of waste per capita per day is generated. But only 5.12 ib per day per capita is collected. It is common practice for each household in the US to bum a large proportion of its rubbi sh in a back-yard incinerator. Mainly food scraps, bottles and unburnable articles are collected. This is, of course, socially undesirable.

In the United States, the growth rate between 1922 and 1965 was about 1.2 percent but a growth rate of 1.4 percent was expected for the period 1965 to 1980. The selected components of solid wastes, by weight, for some of the important countries/cities, are given in Table 8.5. A clear scrutiny of the composition, both in developing and developed nations, clearly indicates that the percentage of paper, rubber, leather, plastics, metals and glass increases considerably with increasing industrialization due to wide application of these materials in day-to-day life. Table 8.6 shows the various biological processes used for the conversion of solid waste.

Table 8.1
Characteristics of refuse materials

Name	*Content*	*Source*
Garbage	Wastes from the preparation, cooking and serving of food; Rubbish, Market refuse; waste from the handling, storage, and sale of produce and meats; Combustible (Primarily organic): paper, cardboard, cartons, wood, boxes, excelsior, plastics, rags, cloth, bedding, leather, rubber, grass, leaves, yard, trimming Noncombustible (Primarily inorganic): Metals, tin cans, metal foils, dirt, crockery glass, bottles, other mineral refuse	Households, institutions and commercial concern such as hotels, stores, restaurants, markets, etc.
Ashes	Residue from fires used for cooking and for heating buildings, cinders	
Bulky wastes	Large auto parts, tyres, stoves, refrigerators, other large appliances, furniture, large crates, trees, branches, palm fronds, stumps, flotage	
Street refuse	Street sweepings, dirt, leaves, catch basin, dirt, contents of litter receptacles	Streets, sidewalks, alloys, vacant lots, etc.
Dead animals	Small animals : cats, dogs, poultry etc.; Large animals : horses, cows, etc.	
Abandoned vehicles	Automobiles, trucks	
Construction and demolition wastes	Lumber, roofing and sheathing scraps, rubble, broken concrete, plaster, etc. Conduits, pipes. wires, insulation, etc.	
Industrial wastes	Solid wastes resulting from industrial processes and manufacturing operations, such as : food-processing wastes, boiler house cylinders, wood, plastic and metal scraps and shavings, etc.	factories, power, plants, etc.
Special wastes	Hazardous wastes; pathological wastes, explosives, radioactive materials, security wastes, confidential documents negotiable papers, etc.	Households, hospitals, institutions, stores, industry etc.
Animal and agricultural wastes	Manures, crop residues	Farms, feed lots
Sewage treatment residues	Coarse screenings, grit, septic tank sludge, dewatered sludge	Sewage treatment plants septic tanks

Table 8.2

Characteristics of city refuse from residential areas

Parameters	*Kanpur*	*Calcutta*	*Nagpur*
Glass	0.5–1.5%	1.04%	0.1–1.5%
Metal	0.5–1.2%	0.92%	—
Coal	5.7–8.0%	6.7%	—
Ash and earth	57–64%	58.9%'	—
Stone	7.9–11.1%	10.2%	—
Bones	0.09–0.36%	0.25%	—
Wood	1.3–1.9%	1.75%	—
Hay, straw and leaves	6.6–8.8%	8.98%	2.5–10.4%
Rags	2.4–6.4%	4.4%	3.1–7.6%
Paper	2.7-5.1%	3.5%	2.0–6.8%
Leather	0.45–1.9%	1.3%	—
Plastics	0.15-0.45%	0.3%	0.05–11.3%
Vegetables	1.2–3.4%	2.2%	0.6–13.1%
Compostable matter	15.4–23.9%	19.7%	15.3–36.5%
Organic matter	19.8–23.3% .	21.8%	25.1–42.6%
pH	8.0–8.8	7.3	7.7–8.4
Moisture	15.5–33.1%	41.1%	8.8–33.5%
Carbon	11.5–13.5%	19.5%	—
Nitrogen	0.44–0.56%	0.55%	0.51–0.74%
Potassium as K_2O	0.26–0.45%	0.40%	0.49–0.80%
Phosphorous as P_2O_5	0.50–0.67%	0.57%	0.49–0.94%
C/N Ratios	22.2–27.7%	37.4%	
Total refuse			
Collection/day	450 tons		
Refuse/capita/day	0.3 Kg	0.57 kg	

Abatement

There are two methods, commonly used, for solid waste:

1. Landfill technique
2. Incinerators.

Solid waste management in some US cities is given in Table 8.7.

Sanitary Landfill

The landfill technique is, often, confused with the 'open dump'. This is especially true in developing countries. There are five principles which should be strictly adhered to :

1. Solid waste must be deposited in a controlled manner.
2. Solid wastes are spread in thin layers.
3. Ground cover of not less than six inches is applied daily.
4. No open burning.
5. All the factors which are likely to allow deposited wastes to contribute to water pollution must be eliminated.

Table 8.3(a)
Physical characteristics of city refuse in Indian cities

Category	*Population*	*No. of cities studies*	*Paper*	*Rubber and leather*	*Plastics*	*Metals*	*Glass*	*Ash and fine earth*	*Total compostable matter*	*Miscellaneous*
I	2 lakh	9	3.09	0.487	0.57	0.512	0.29	46.6	33.41	15.041
II	2-5 lakh	15	4.76	0.631	0.59	0.387	0.34	34.97	39.76	19.562
III	5-20 lakh	7	3.80	0.620	0.81	0.638	0.44	41.81	40.15	11.732
IV	20 lakh	2	7.07	0.866	0.86	1.031	0.76	31.74	41.69	15.983
Cities in developed countries	—	—	40-55	2-4	2-4	6-10	6-10		5-20	10-40

Table 8.3(b)
Chemical characteristics of city refuse in Indian cities

Category	*Moisture*	*pH*	*Organic matter*	*Carbon*	*Nitrogen*	*Phosphorous as P_2O_5*	*Potash as K_2O*	*C/N ratio*	*HCV (Calorific value, BTU/lb)*
I	22.116	8.18	22.02	12.255	0.602	0.706	0.705	20.35	1442.21
II	25.05	8.16	22.51	12.506	0.611	0.715	0.739	20.468	1574.80
III	22.45	8.34	21.51	11.95	0.557	0.6768	0.722	21.454	1560.00
IV	31.18	7.68	27.57	15.316	0.584	0.590	0.678	22.226	2056.58

Note : All values, are calculated on dry weight basis, except moisture, and given in percentage, except, pH, C/N and calorific value.

Table 8.3 (c)
Quantities of refuse in kg/head/day collected at Salmonella during Jan. - Dec.1962

Day	*Monday*	*Tuesday*	*Wednesday*	*Thursday*	*Friday*	*Saturday*	*Sunday*
Quantity	0.35	0.26	0.25	0.25	0.26	0.27	0.23

Table 8.4
Composition of refuse from Ibarapa division

Components	*Mean% by weight*		*App.% in Britain**
	Ibarapa staff houses	*Local community*	
Leaves	28.1	49.9	—
Paper	8.1	0.7	39
Garbage	43.0	4.4	25
Tin	3.7	0.0	10
Glass	4.3 ‘	0.0	10
Rags	2.0	0.5	2
Dust and ashes	10.0	44.5	26
Density, kg/m^3	274.0	211.0	—
Moisture content	57.6%	43.1%	—

*Lloydd, D.O. "Refuse Disposal" *Insst. of Pub. Hlth.Engrs. J.*,(March 1973)

Table 8.5
Selected components of solid waste, by weight, 1900–1965

Component	1900			1965		
	New York	*London*	*Berlin*	*US*	*UK*	*W. Germany*
Ash	80.5	84.0	53.0	10.00	30–40.0	30.0
Paper	5.5	4.3	4.3	42.0	25–30.0	18.7

Table 8.6
Biological processes used for the conversion of solid wastes

Process.	*Conversion product*	*Preprocessing required*	*Comment*
Composting	Humus-like material	Shredding, air separation	Lack of markets is primary shortcoming; technically proved in full scale applications.
Anaerobic digestion	Methane gas	Shredding, air separation	Technology on laboratory scale only.
Biological conversion to protein	Protein, alcohol	Shredding, air separation	Technology on laboratory scale only.
Biological fermentation	Glucose furfural	Shredding, air separation	Used in conjunction with the hydrolytic process.

Table 8.7
Solid waste management in some US cities (1966)

City	*Daily waste output, tonnes*	*Landfill sites*		*Incinerator*	
		No.	*Total disposal area, acres*	*No.*	*Operating capacity tonnes/day*
New York city	20,200	9	3,088	8	9,500
Philadelphia	5,100	6	35	8	3,150
Atlanta	1,570	8	10	3	1,180
Pittsburgh	4,000	3	360	1	100

Note: The above table indicates the relative position.

In the US, on the basis of the national survey conducted in 1968, it was concluded that 94 percent of sites are unacceptable and represent disease potential, threat of pollution, and land blight.

A high degree of opposition and resentment often accompanies announced plans for a sanitary landfill. This is especially true when some or all of the waste destined for the site is generated in an adjoining, usually large city. Only in those cases where there has been a definite plan of action, involving planned solid waste management, has there been any real success in the establishment of sanitary landfills.

Planned management with respect to sanitary landfills begins with the analysis of solid conditions, surrounding a proposed site. A ravine or man-made gravel pit is generally sought as a sanitary landfill site. Soil conditions, surrounding the site, are significant to the ultimate success of the landfill. Fine-grained soils are more useful in containing unwanted gas and water movements outside the landfill area. The type of soil will also ultimately determine how the landfill will be utilised once completed.

Within the landfill itself, unwarranted gas and water movements can adversely affect its utility. The production of gases (usually either methane or carbon dioxide), within a landfill, is a function of matter placed there for disposal. Control of these gases can usually be maintained by ensuring that soil, immediately surrounding the landfill, is not porous. Except for the case, with which it disperses itself away from the landfill, containment of water within the landfill presents much the same problems as gas. In order to avert water pollution, the lowest level of the landfill should be no less than ten feet above the expected level of the high water table. In addition, proper surface drainage should be established and maintained in order to prevent waters from washing through the rubbish and re-entering the existing water routes.

This cursory probe, into the considerations of sanitary landfill preparation and management, should serve to alert the reader to the magnitude of the work to be done, especially when it is observed that 94-percent of land disposal sites, in use today, fail to meet one or more of the standards for sanitary landfill.

The next decade will no doubt witness the continued upgrading of our seemingly ubiquitous open dumps and landfills to confirm to sanitary landfill specifications. Stronger local laws, regulating landfill operations, as well as stringent air and water pollution laws, will serve to make these operations more efficient. These actions while generally beneficial to overall land management, are particularly critical in urban areas. As urban expansion continues to move outward from the central city, land suitable for sanitary landfill becomes increasingly scarce and, sometimes, inaccessible. Technological benefits such as those occurring from more efficient handling of solid wastes, can offset this disadvantage to some degree. Establishment of central collection or transfer stations will enable cities to ultimately transport solid wastes to more distant disposal sites more efficiently. Depending on tire degree of density, surrounding the urban area, it is not improbable that the 1980s will see the use of rail transportation as a means of moving solid wastes to distant sanitary landfill sites. Several feasibility studies have already been undertaken to determine the possibility of using rail transportation by some of the big US cities, e.g., Chicago, Denver, and Los Angeles. To date, however no major city has embarked on a plan of action involving rail transportation. Although the day-to-day costs of operating a sanitary landfill vary from one location to another, they are generally acknowledged to be greater than incineration. However, in terms of final costs to the community, they are probably no more, and, perhaps, even less, because planned sanitary landfill, conceived and administered with modern solid waste management, can provide the community with an annuity in the form of future land sites.

Ultimately, our land will have to accept virtually all solid wastes generated by man. Whether intermediate steps of incineration or compaction are employed, the final disposition of our wastes remains unchanged. What is altered, however, is the efficiency with which the land can be managed through the utilisation of a solid waste management plan.

The current state of the art, then, calls for appraising the current condition of landfill operations, recognizing what needs to be done to conform to sanitary landfill standards and taking steps to improve techniques through implementation of solid waste management programmes at the community level. Important factors that must be considered in the design and operation of sanitary landfills are shown in Table 8.8.

Table 8.8
Important factors that must be constructed in the design and operation of sanitary landfills

Design	Paved all weather access roads to landfill site; temporary roads to unloading areas.
Cell design and construction	Will vary depending on whether gas is to be removed; each day's wastes should form one cell; maximum depth of 10 ft, cover at end of day with 6 inch of earth; grave! gas vent should be installed every 60 to 2000 ft.
Cover material	Maximize use of on site earth materials. Approximately, 1/yd^2 of solid wastes, mix with sealents to control surface infiltration.
Drainage	Install drainage ditches to divert surface water runoff; maintain 1 to 2 per cent grade on finished fill to prevent ponding.
Equipment requirements	Vary with size to landfill.
Fire prevention	Water on site; if nonpotable, outlets must be marked clearly, proper cell separation prevents continuous burn through if combustion occurs.
Ground water protection	Divert any underground springs; if required, install sealants for leachate control, install wells for gas and ground water monitoring.
Land area	Areas should be large enough to hold all community wastes for a minimum of 1 year but preferably for 5 to 10 years.
Landfilling method	Selection of method will vary with terrain and available cover.
Litter control	Use moveable fences at unloading areas; grews should pick up litter at least, once per month or as required.
Operation plan	With or without the co disposal of treatment plant sludges, and the recovery of gas.
Spread and compaction	Spread and compact waste in layers less than 2 ft thick.
Unloading area	Keep small, generally under 100 ft on a side; operate separate unloading areas for automobiles and commercial trucks.
Operation communications	Telephone for emergencies.
Days and hours of operation	Usual practice is 5 to 6 days/week and 8 to 10 h / day.
Employee facilities	Rest rooms and drinking water should be provided.
Equipment maintenance	A covered shed should be provided for field maintenance of equipment.
Operational T records	Tonnage, transactions, and billing if a disposal fee is charged.
Salvage	No damaging, salvage occur away from the unloading area, no salvage storage onsite.
Scales	

Incineration

Incineration of solid wastes serves the function of reducing the volume of these wastes from their row or collected states to more management levels, thus obtaining lower transportation costs to the ultimate disposal site, and accommodating the wastes of a greater number of people for a given acreage available for landfill. The two main disadvantages of the technique are that both capital and operating costs are high and equipment is expensive. There is a considerable cost to the quality of the air. Table 8.9 show you various compaction equipments used for volume reduction. Imported design factors in the selection of conventional compaction equipment are given in Table 8.10.

Table 8.9
Compaction equipment used for volume reduction

Location of operation	*Type of compactor*	*Remarks*
Solid Waste generation points	Stationery/ residential	
	Vertical	Vertical compaction ram, may be mechanically or hydraulically operated, usually hand-fed, wastes compacted into corrugated box containers or paper or plastic bags, used in medium and high–rise apartments.
	Rotary	Ram mechanism used to compact wastes into paper or plastic bags on rotating platform; platform rotates as containers are filled, used to medium-and high-rise apartments.
	Bag or extruder	Compactor can be chute-fed, either vertical or horizontal rams, single or continuous multistage, single bags must be replaced .and continuous bags must be tied off and replaced; used in medium and high-rise apartments.
	Undercounter	Small compactors used in individual residences and apartment units, wastes compacted into special paper bags. After wastes are dropped through a panel door into bag and door is closed, they are sprayed for odour control and button is pushed to activate compaction mechanism.
	Stationary/commercial	Compactor with vertical or horizontal ram, waste compressed into steel container, compressed waste are manually tied and removed; used in low medium-and high-rise apartments, commercial and industrial facilities.
Collection	Stationery/packer	Collection vehicles equipped with compaction mechanisms.
Transfer and/ or processing station	Stationary/transfer trailer	Transport trailer usually enclosed, equipped with self-contained compaction mechanism.
	Stationary	Wastes are compacted into large containers.
	Low pressure	Wastes are compacted into dense bales or other forms.
	High pressure	
Disposal site	Movable wheeled or tracked equipment	Specially designed equipment to achieve maximum compaction wastes
	Stationery/track mounted	High pressure moveable stationary compactors used for volume reduction at disposal sites.

Table 8.10

Important design factors in the selection of conventional compaction equipment

Factor	*Value*		*Remarks*
	Unit	*Range*	
Size of loading chamber	yd^3	1–11	Fixed and maximum size of wastes that can be placed in the unit.
Cycle	see	20–60	The time required for the face of the compaction ram, starting in the fully retracted position to pack wastes in the loading chamber, into the receiving container and return to the starting position.
Machine volume displacement	yd^3/h	30–1500	The volume of wastes that can be displaced by the ram in 1 hr.
Compaction pressure	lb/in^2	15–50	The pressure on the face of the ram.
Ram penetration	in	4–26	The distance that the compaction ram penetrates into the receiving container during the compaction cycle. The further the distance, the less chance there is for wastes to fall back into the charging chamber and the greater the degree of compaction that can be achieved.
Compaction ratio		2:1–8: 1	The initial volume divided by the final volume after compaction. Ratio varies significantly with waste composition.
Physical dimensions variable of unit		Variable	Affects the design of service areas in new buildings and provision of service to existing facilities.

Incineration has had a cyclical existence. First used in 1885, incinerators rose and fell in popularity, so that by 1952, over one-third of the cities, operating incinerators, had phased them out. One of the main problems was that incineration furnaces were modified from the existing manufacturer's design, rather than being specifically designed for solid wastes. However, since 1950 there has been a resurgence of the trend towards incineration. Table 8.11 shows the growth in number and capacity of operating incinerators in the United States. Table 8.12 shows the principal components in the design of large municipal incinerators. Comparative air pollution control data.

Table 8.ll

Operating incinerators and rated capacity in the United States, 1950–1966

Year	*Number of installations*	*Tonnes rate capacity*	*Capacity/ installation*
1950	90	22,932	255
1960	205	57,044	278
1966	254	74,578	294

Table 8.12
Principal components in the design of large municipal incinerators

Component	*Purpose/Description*
Scale	Required to maintain accurate records of the amount of wastes processed.
Storage pits	Design of pits depends on furnace capacity, storage requirements (approximately 1 day capacity), collection schedules, and truck-discharge methods.
Cranes	Used to transfer wastes from storage pit to charging hoppers to mix and redistribute wastes in storage pit.
Changing hoppers	Constructed of metal or concrete; used to introduce wastes to furnace grates.
Furnace grates	Used to move wastes through furnace. Travelling, reciprocating, rocker arm and barrel grates have been used successfully. Burning rate of 60 to 65 lb/ft /hr has been adopted as a generally allowable standard for mass firing.
Combustion chamber	Water-walled and refractory chambers are used.
Heat-recovery system	Types of systems vary. Typically, two boiler sections are used: convection and economiser.
Auxiliary heat	Need depends on moisture content of wastes as delivered.
Air pollution control facilities	Used to control particulate emissions.
Auxiliary facilities and equipment	Normally includes residue handling facilities, air supply and exhaust fans, incinerator stacks control building, etc.

Table 8.13
Comparative air pollution control data for municipal incinerators

Collector	*Relative capital cost factor FOB*	*Relative space percentage*	*Collection efficiency percentage*	*Water to collector, gal/ min /1000ft^3 min.*	*Pressure drop of water*	*Relative operating cost factor*
Setting chamber	N.A.	60	0–30	2–3	0.5–1	0.25
Multicyclone	1	20	30–80	None	3–4	1.0
Cyclones 60 in dia.	1.5	30	30–70	None	1–2	0.5
Scrubber	3	30	80 96	4-8	6–8	2.5
Electrostatic precipitator	6	100	90–97	None	0.5–1	0.75
Fabric filter	6	100	97–99.9	None	5–7	2.5

Two types of incinerators are generally used for unsorted wastes. The batch-type plant is manually stoked and has a relatively small rated capacity. The operation is intermittent (hence the name "batch") so there is a lack of uniform burning temperature. This promotes inadequate combustion and, thus, an attendant heavy output of particulate matter, less than optimal volume reduction and an unstable residue often containing putrescibles. These units are generally unsuitable for large urban centers, although they are used in the smaller, surrounding communities. The continuous feed plant has larger storage bins, automatic feed hoppers, and a variety of types of moving gates and ash removal systems. The unit maintains a uniform combustion temperature range, can be fitted with pollution control devices, albeit at a higher cost, and generally yields a stable residue. The reason incineration is experiencing rapid growth is the volume reduction that van be achieved in a well designed and operated incinerator with controlled furnace temperature in the range 1,400-1,800 F. A ton of refuse, at the generating source, occupies 13.3 cubic yards—a density of 150 lb/cubic yard. After substantial compaction in the collection vehicle, and further compaction in a sanitary landfill, it will occupy 2.22 cubic yards and its density will be 900 lb/cubic yard. However, if the refuse is incinerated and, then, landfilled after one year, the original ton will only take up 194 cubic yards of space and have a bulk density of 2,700 lb/cubic yard. With land growing increasingly more scarce, more expensive and available only at longer distances from the collection points, the value of incineration is that it cuts the land requirement to one-third of that required if the refuse were to be landfilled. Moreover, a stable residue cuts drastically, or eliminates entirely, the need to import cover material to the landfill site.

Public acceptance of incineration is retarded by the existence of a substantial number of old and inefficient (mainly batch-type) units which frequently operate substantially below their rated capacities, are visibly dirty in particulate emission, and can not be economically modified to meet emission standards. A well-run, modem, large-capacity incinerator is not a major source of air pollutants. In an ordinary ton of mixed refuse, for example, sulphur constitutes as little as one-tenth of one percent.

In a study of major atmospheric contaminants in several large US cities, it was found that particulates emitted from incinerators accounted for 18.2 percent of total particulates from all sources. However, two devices, the wet-scrubber and electrostatic precipitator, can effect removal of between 90–99 percent of incinerator pollutants, and even at 90 percent efficiency, the result of fitting these devices would be to cut total emission of particulates by 13.9 percent. Marginal costs of efficiency of a precipitator from 90– 99 percent can increase the cost of the unit by 50 percent. Scrubbers, although less expensive, have a high water consumption, emit unsightly vapour plumes, and create unwanted pressure drop in the furnace. Most European installations (which, as a rule, are quite clean in emissions), and most planned modifications to existing domestic units are expected to use precipitators. Other types of pollution control equipment, such as subsidence chambers, baffling systems, centrifugal collectors, and cloth filters have either low efficiencies or high space requirements that render them impractical for use on incinerators.

Development of incinerators in the immediate future will probably tend to have large units of water-cooled steel walls, rather than the refractory-lined design. The reason for this is that precipitators and other pollution control devices require cooler raw temperatures while permitting higher burning temperatures. When higher furnace temperatures are achieved in refractory-lined units, melting glass adheres to the walls and forms a bond stronger than that holding the fire-brick together, and serious damage can occur. Another advantage of the water-cooled units is that the waste heat of combustion can be utilised. Recent installations have used the recovered waste heat for steam generation that is used for space or district heating, electricity, and desalinaiion of sea water. While these installations are still a rarity in the United States, they are almost standard in large European units, and there exists a wealth of technology to make such installations an expected near-term reality in this country. Mixed refuse has a thermal value of between 3,500 and 5,500 BTU/lb., or about 37 percent that of high-grade coal; and the trend is towards higher heat values for refuse waste heat recovery especially if OBWs are shredded prior to incineration. The situation in Europe may now be quite different. Natural gas production in the Netherlands has surpassed its peak output and the general attitude is in favour of conserving it. In the remainder of Europe too, efforts to conserve energy are widespread. In Britain, a pilot plant is in operation in which refuse is shredded, mixed with coal and used as a fuel for power generation. As for European practice, Rogus has said, "There are some indications that this trend (towards waste-heat recovery) may not continue should the natural gas resources recently opened in the Netherlands be made economically available in Central Europe. Thus, waste heat recovery modification should be weighed against alternate energy sources and their effect on the environment. A considerable recovery of non-ferrous metals is possible from municipal incinerators but this may only be significant in developed countries. The operation of incinerators can be integrated with sewage processing. At Avonmouth, near Bristol, all of the electrical machinery in the incinerator is powered by generators which run mainly on methane from sludge digesters.

A major problem for water-cooled installations is the increasing proportion of polyvinyl chloride (PVC) in the refuse 'mix'. Today, PVC accounts for between 25 and 35 percent of total plastics, and about 2 percent of all unsorted refuse. The heat value of PVC is about one–half that of other plastics (which have a heat value approximating fuel oil) and when incinerated, PVC forms hydrogen chloride gas, a toxic emittant, and one that can rapidly corrode metal walls. The rapid growth of plastics could lead to a dangerous concentration of 5-6 percent PVC of total mixed refuse, at which time the PVC would have to be removed prior to incineration, thus increasing the already high costs of incineration.

These are two technological innovations in the art of incineration, both of which have to be evaluated beyond their initial promise, before they can be put into production. As with some projects in the past, whose expectations fell with production, a great deal of caution should be exercised in their evaluation as alleviants to the solid waste situation.

The first unit, the CPU-400, is an outgrowth of aerospace technology. It is designed as a turboelectric generator plant using solid wastes as fuel. Unsorted wastes are passed through a shredder, dried by the hot gases, discharged from the combustor, and injected into the combustor at high pressure. Then, the wastes are "fluidised" as they pass through the chamber. The plan is that the hot gases produced will drive a gas turbine which will drive an electrostatic precipitator, and the hot gases will be expelled at atmospheric pressure. The unit is currently in the development stage.

The second unit, the Melt Zit slag-tap process, derives from blast furnace technology. The idea is to melt everything, as the glass component of solid wastes becomes liquid at 1,800° F, and while most of the ash becomes molten at 2,350° F. The resulting magma can either be molded into large blocks, or run into water to produce a coarse type of sand suitable for road or concrete aggregate. In Germany, the Volkswagen Works operates a slag-tap plant, but there are no estimates on when this process will become commercially feasible here.

"Of the more than 12,000 governmentally controlled land disposal sites in the United States, 94 percent are unacceptable and do not meet even the minimum standards for sanitary landfills." This refers to open dumps. In urban areas, other factors, such as housing and crime, can magnify the role of solid wastes in contributing to urban decay. The open dump in an abandoned quarry is quite different from its counterpart in an abandoned urban building. A short drive through a central city ghetto area will confirm this contrast.

Composting

Another method for disposal of solid waste is composing. Composting is a biological process where fresh organic wastes are transformed by decomposition into a stable humus like substance.

For many centuries, farmers and gardeners throughout the world have been practicing composting by placing vegetable manures and animal manures in piles or pits for decomposition prior to use. Conditions are quite different today. The processing of organic wastes, unlike the backyard compost pile, is accomplished in a mechanised process, resulting in an organic manure which can be used agriculturally. As with the backyard compost pile, the micro-organisms, which effect the decomposition, are ingredients to the wastes themselves, but when there is a variety of domestic wastes granulation of the dry waste is necessary along with a thorough mixing to ensure homogeneity and definite control of moisture content as well as complete aeration of the material being treated. Under these conditions, the wastes decompose rapidly at decomposition temperatures which are lethal to pathogenic organisms.

A completely automatic system involves several steps. The crude refuse is dumped into a container on to a belt conveyor, and then iron or metallic particles are removed by a magnetic separator. There is also a means for extracting magnetic metal materials which will not decompose. The degradation of the material actually occurs in a rotating cylinder similar to a rotator}' drier. This cylinder contains as much as 5 day's supply of refuse, depending upon the degree of treatment required, and these wastes are delivered to the cylinder in a moistureed condition. This cylinder rotates slowly on large 'tyres', much like a cement kiln, and the wastes move from one end towards the other. They are thoroughly mixed and granulated by abrasion. Air is added at low pressure and in controlled amounts throughout the length of the cylinder. In this manner, an environment is created where the action of aerobic micro-organisms ensures a rapid decomposition of the wastes under inoffensive conditions. Normal operating temperatures up to 140° F are spontaneously developed. The final process material is, then, delivered on to a conveyor belt and through a screen where the compost is separated from more durable matter, and delivered into a storage container, where splinters of glass from bottles, etc. are extracted. From 100 tonnes of crude refuse, it is possible to extract between 60 and 70 tonnes of compost.

India has made remarkable and speedy progress in organizing many compost plants. Four plants have already gone into production, while 21 other plants are at various stages of completion/implementation. The Ahmedabad plant was commissioned in 1975, the Baroda plant in 1977, while the Bangalore and Calcutta plants were recently commissioned. The plant at Bombay has the largest capacity, viz., 300 TPD. The minimum plant capacity is 100 TPD.

In India, mechanical compost plants were encouraged by the Government of India as a national programme. Under this scheme, substantial incentives are also offered to municipal corporations for generating infrastructure facilities to ensure supplies of refuse to compost plants.

The know-how and equipment required for the establishing of compost plant is indigenously available. In fact, Indian Engineering firms are coming out with many innovative and practical suggestions and are offering equipments with know-how at competitive prices. Indian know-how is now offered to other needy countries by the National Research Development Corporation—a Government Company.

There is another interesting and useful area where compost is used—the Indian Agricultural Research Institute, Pusa, New Delhi, has developed strains of blue green algae for use in rich fields for direct nitrogen fixation. An appropriate technology is being developed in India to produce blue green algae coated granulated compost.

The importance attached to and the momentum that composting has attained is clearly reflected by studying the list of installed and proposed units as given in Table 8.14. Important design consideration for anerobic composting processes and for anaerobic digestion are given in Tables 8.15 and 8.16.

Table 8.14
Municipal solid waste composting plants in India, August 1978

Location of plant	*Implanting agency*	*Capacity TDP*	*Estimated capital cost Indian ₹ in millions*	*Process Status*
Ahmedabad	Gujarat Agro-Industries Corpn. Limited	150	6.00	In Production
Baroda	Municipal Corpn., Baroda	150	7.00	In Production
Calcutta	West Bengal Agro Industries Corpn. Ltd.	150	6.30	In Production
Bangalore	Karnataka Compost Development Corpn. Ltd.	200	8.90	In Production
Madras	Municipal Corpn., Madras	150	7.00	Under Implementation
	Kanpur Municipal Corpn., Kanpur	200	9.30	
	Lucknow Uttar Pradesh Jal Nigam		4.97	
Allahabad	Uttar Pradesh Jal Nigam		4.97	
Varanasi	Uttar Pradesh Jal Nigam		4.97	
Jaipur	Rajasthan State Agro Industries Corpn. Ltd.	150	4.50	Turn-key order placed, expected to go into production in Dec.. '78
Bombay Co. Pvt. Ltd.	Bombay Organic Manures	300	12.10	Under Implementation
Amritsar	Punjab Water Supply & Sewerage Board, Chandigarh	200	6.60	
Ludhiana	Punjab Water Supply & Sewerage Board, Chandigarh	200	6.60	
Jalandhar	Punjab Water Supply & Sewerage Board, Chandigarh	150	6.60	
Delhi	Municipal Corpn., Delhi	150	7.95	Turn-key order placed, expected to go into production in May 1979
Jodhpur	Rajasthan State Agro Industries	125	2.92	Turn-key order placed, expected to go into production in Feb. 1979
Agra	Uttar Pradesh Jal Nigam	100	6.29	Under Implementation
Poona	Maharashtra Agro Industries Development Corpn. Ltd. & Municipal Corpn., Poona	150	6.50	
Nagpur	Maharashtra Agro Industries Development Corpn. Ltd. & Municipal Corpn., Nagpur	200	8.25	
New Delhi	New Delhi Municipal Corpn., New Delhi	200	5.30	
Solapur	Solapur Municipal Corpn., Solapur	150	4.50	
Cochin	Cochin Kerala Agro Industries Corpn.	150	6.25	
Gauhati	Municipal Corpn., Gauhati	125	4.50	
Hyderabad	Municipal Corpn., Hyderabad	200	4.19	
Vijayawada	Municipal Corpn., Vijaywada	140	4.59	

Table 8.15
Important design considerations for aerobic composing processes

Item	*Comment*
Particle size	For optimum results, solid wastes should be ground finely (1 to 3 in.).
Seeding and mixing	Composing time can be reduced by seeding with partially decomposed solid waste to the extent of about 1 to 5 per cent by weight. Sewage sludge can also be added to prepare solid waste. Where sludge is added the final moisture content is the controlling variable.
Mixing/turning	To prevent drying, caking and air channeling, material in the process of being composed should be mixed or turned. This will depend on the type of composing operations.
Air requirements	Air with at least 50 per cent of the initial oxygen concentration remaining should reach all parts of the composing material for optimum results, especially in mechanical systems.
Total oxygen requirements	The theoretical quantity of oxygen required can be estimated. The actual quantity of air that must be supplied will vary depending on the operation.
Maximum rate of oxygen consumption	The rate can be estimated using the relationship WO2 = 0.07 x 10^{-61}T, where, WO2 is equal to the rate of oxygen consumption in mg O2/h/g of initial volatile matter and T is equal to the temperature in °C.
Moisture content	Mcisture content should be in the range between 50 and 60 per cent during the composing process. The optimum value appears to be about 55 per cent.
Temperature	The optimum temperature for biological stabilization is between 45 and 55°C. For best results, it has been found that the temperature should be maintained between 50 and 55°C for the first few days and between 55 to 60°C for the remainder of the active comporting period. If temperatures are allowed to go beyond 60°C, biological activity can be reduced significantly.
Heat evolution	Heat released during the composing process is equal to the difference in the energy content of the material at the beginning and at the end of the composing process.
Carbon-nitrogen ratio	It has been found that initial carbon-nitrogen ratios (by weight) between 35 and 50 are optimum for aerobic composting. At lower ratios, nitrogen is in excess and will be given off as ammonia. Biological activity is also impeded at lower ratios. At higher ratios nitrogen may be a limiting nutrient. After composing, the carbon-nitrogen ratio for most municipal solid-wastes will usually fall between 10 and 20.
pH	The pH should be prevented from rising above about 8.5 to minimise the loss of nitrogen in the form of ammonia as a gas.
Degree of decomposition	The degree of composition can be estimated by, measuring the reduction in the organic matter, present using the COD (Chemical Oxygen Demand) test.
Respiratory quotient, RQ	$RQ = \frac{\text{Volume of } CO_2 \text{ evolved}}{\text{Volume of } O_2 \text{ consumption}}$ RQ can be used as a measure of the degree of decomposition. When

	RQ = 1, the total oxygen has been used for oxidation of carbon. When RQ > 1, more CO_2 is being formed than O_2 is being supplied, which is indicative of anaerobic decomposition. When RQ < 1, only part of the oxygen is being used to oxidise carbon. Low RQ values are characteristics of aerobic processes.
Control of pathogens	If properly conducted, it is possible to kill all the pathogens, weeds, and seeds during the composting process. To do this, the temperature must be maintained between 60 and 70°C for 24 hrs.

Table 8.16
Important design considerations for anaerobic digestion

Item	*Comment*
Size of material shredded	Wastes to be digested should be of a size that will not interfere with the functioning of pumping and mixing operations.
Mixing equipment	To achieve optimum results and to avoid scum buildup, mechanical mixing is recommended.
Percentage of solid wastes mixed with sludge	Although amounts of waste varying from 50–90 per cent have been used, 60 per cent appears to be a reasonable compromise.
Hydraulic and mean cell residence time = 8 hrs.	Washout time is in the range of 3 to 4 days. Use 7 to 10 days for design or base design on results of pilot plant studies.
Loading rate	0.04 to 0.10 lb/ft^3/day. Not well defined at present time. Significantly higher rates have been reported.
Temperature	Between 55 and 60°C.
Destruction of volatile solid wastes	Varies from about 60–80 per cent; can be used for estimating purposes.
Total solids destroyed	Varies from 40 to 60 per cent, depending on the amount of inert material present originally
Gas production	8 to 12 ft^3/lb of volatile solids destroyed (CH_4 = 60 per cent, CO_2 = 40 per cent).

9

Environmental Pollution Monitoring and Control in Tannery

The increasing demands of the world market for semi-finished and finished Indian leather (Kips) has encouraged the growth of a large number of tanneries in India, especially in the last few years. According to the recent statistics published by Labour Bureau, Shimla (India), there are about 660 registered leather industries in India under the Factories Act.

Tannery effluents, being voluminous and highly persuasible in nature, when discharged untreated, damage the normal life of the receiving stream. Since streams are no longer just a means of waste conveyance but are more important for other applications, e.g., power generation, drinking, bathing, fishing, irrigation and recreation, an industry should, therefore, have a moral and legal responsibility to avoid any contribution to their pollution.

It has always been a practice to discharge effluents into natural streams but now natural streams at various places, have already reached a point of saturation where they cannot receive any more effluents. However, industries continue to discharge them without any real concern, due partly to non-availability of necessary information regarding total pollution load, assimilation capacity, harmful effects of pollutants on health of the river, etc. This is especially true in the case of tanneries because their contribution to the organic load is significant. In this chapter, the position of the tanning industry, tanning operations, chemicals used, identification of pollutants in tanneries, harmful effects of important pollutants, desired limits, monitoring of pollutants and, finally, pollution abatement have been briefly discussed.

Tanning of Leather

Leather is nothing but a fibrous protein, called collagen, with minor amounts of lipids, albumins, globulins and carbohydrates. In preparing leather (tanned), the processes involved are used to remove the undesired non-fibrous protein constituents of the hide, followed by the tanning of the collagen, via different tans, e.g., vegetable tan, chrome tan or syntans, etc., and finishing operations. In the removal of undesirable constituents, the processes used are named curing, fleshing, washing, soaking, dehairing, lime splitting, bating and degreasing. The finishing operation includes bleaching, stuffing and fat liquoring and colouring. In India, tanning is mainly either through vegetable tans (oak or Quebracho bark extracts), or chrome tan (basic chrome sulphate).

Chemicals Used in the Tanning Industry

The chemicals which are commonly used in the different stages of the tanning operations and their annual consumption are given in Table 9.1.

Table 9.1
Chemicals used in tanning operations

Process chemicals	*lb used*	*BOD* ppm	*ppm in* waste
Sodium chloride	1,368,000	0	684
Lime	2,410,000	0	1235
Sodium sulphide	981,000	40	490
Sulphuric acid	350,000	0	175
Soda ash	161,000	0	80
$(NH_4)_2SO_4$ (Oropon)	144,000	0	72
Calcium formate	88,000	12	44
Lactic acid (30%)	77,000	32	38
Sodium formate	56,000	2	28
Sterizol	42,000	0	20
Ammonium chloride	20,000	0	10
Chemicals absorbed by hide			
Tanolim R (16% chromium)	1,670,000	0	6261
Tamol L	729,000	0	36
D.I. oil	37,000	83	2
Other oils	650,000	80	33
Quebracho	146,000	5	7
Soyarich flour	100,000	0	5
Tanbark-H	88,000	11	4
Gamtade	156,000	4	8
Titanium dioxide	88,000	0	4
Maraten B	136,000	—	7
Methocel	20,000	6	1
Oratan TV	30,000	5	2
Semisot glue	37,000	—	2
Upper tan'	28,000	—	1

On the basis of processes and chemicals, used during the tanning operations, the following are considered pollutants:

1. Sulphides
2. Chlorides
3. Chromium (Hexavalent)
4. Insecticides
5. Arsenic
6. High pH and high BOD
7. Suspended and dissolved solids.

However, this list does not include noise, thermal and air pollution. This problem will also be of concern to the leather industry once suitable provisions are made for this purpose. It is interesting to note that the total contribution from tanneries to BOD load on the river Ganga at Kanpur is 20% while the total volume of effluents is about 1 %.

Desired Limits of Pollutants

Due to wide variations in the process of tanning, which depend upon the type of leather required and the process chemicals used, a large fluctuation in the strength and characteristics of the effluents from tannery to tannery has been recorded. However, different agencies in India have instituted limits for the disposal of tannery effluents in order to protect the natural water resources (Table 9.2.).

Table 9.2
Standards for disposal of tannery effluents

Characteristics	*UP. Jal Pradushan Nivaran Tatha Niyantran Board No. 133 ARN 1976*			*BIS : 2490 (Part III) 1974*	
	Into inland surface water	*Into public sewers*	*On land for irrigation*	*Chrome tanning*	*Vegetable tanning*
Colour and Odour	should be absent as far as possible			Absent	
BOD, 5 days, 20°C mg/1 max.	30	500[a]	500	30	30[b]
COD. mg/1 max.	250	—	—	—	—
pH	5.5–9.0	5.5–9.0	5.5–9.0	5.5–9.0	5.5–9.0
Suspended solids mg/1 max.	100	600[c]	—	—	100
Total dissolved solids (inorganic) mg/1 max.	—	2100[d]	2100	—	—
Sulphides, mg/1 max.	2.0	—	—	—	—
Chlorides, mg/1 max.	—	600	600	1000	1000
Chlorides (hexavalent) mg/1 max.	0.1	2	—	0.1	—
Ammonical nitrogen mg/1 max.	50	50	—	—	—

[a] Subject to relaxation or tightening by the local authority.

[b] For existing vegetable tanneries, relaxation up to a value of 100 may be granted.

[c] Relaxable to 750 by the local authority.

[d] These requirements shall apply only when, after treatment, the sewage is disposed of on land for irrigation.

Origin and Characteristics of the Effluents

Hides received in tanneries are usually in a wet salted or dry salted conditions to avoid biodegradation through proteolytic enzyme actions.

Washing and Soaking

Hairdirt, salts, insecticides, blood and non-ferrous protein of the salted hides are removed and the moisture lost during preservation and storage is restored. Consequently, the effluents are voluminous and consist of a high percentage of solids, BOD, and volatile solids, the pH usually being 7.8.

Unhairing

Unhairing is accomplished by the use of lime with or without sodium sulphide. Thus, the effluent contains hair, high pH and high percentage or sulphide.

Liming

Here splitting of skin into two layers is brought about by the use of lime and sodium sulphide. Therefore, the waste contains a high percentage of solids and the pH and BOD is low compared to other process waters.

Deliming and Bating

After the operation, deliming and bating are done to reduce the swelling, peptize the fibres and remove the protein degradation products, thus, making the skin ready for tanning. As ammonium salts are used for bating and protein degradation, products are squeezed, effluents of this process contain high BOD and volatile solids.

Vegetable Tanning

Effluents produced in this process, although being very minimal in volume, constitute the strongest liquor. Bark extracts, used in the process, contain high amounts of biodegradable as well as non-biodegradable (tanning, etc.) compounds. Therefore, the effluent colour remains dark brown, and the odour is highly offensive and acidic in nature.

Pickling

This process is necessary before chrome tanning to prevent the chances of chrome salt precipitation during tanning. As the baled skins are treated with salts and acids, effluents of this process contain very high solid concentration and low pH 3.0.

Chrome Tanning

During chrome tanning, only 68-74% of tan (chromic sulphate) is utilized by the skins. Consequently, a large amount of chrome sulphate drains out to the effluent, making the effluent colour green, while the pH lies in the range of 2.6-2.8.

Colouring and Finishing

Unused dye and fat emulsions constitute the major part of the effluent of this process.

A typical effluent analysis of different operation in tanneries is given in Table 9.3. The characteristics of the waste from different tanning processes as are given in Table 9.4.

Polluting Effects of Waste Water

Serious pollution has been caused in many parts of the world by the discharges of waste water from tanneries into natural streams. The liquors contain a high proportion

Table 9.3

Characteristics of wastes from various operations

Parameter	*Sections*						
	Soaking	*Liming*	*Deliming*	*Vegetable tanning*	*Pickling*	*Chrome tanning*	*Colouring and finishing*
PH	7.5-8.0	10.0-12.5	3.0-9.0	5.0-6.8	2.9-4.0	2.6-32	7.4
Total solids, mg/1	8000-28000	16000-45000	1200-12000	8000-50000	16000-45000	24000-12000	2300
Suspended solids, mg/1	2500-4000	4500-6500	200-1200	5000-20000	600-6000	300-1000	800
Chlorides, mg/1	15000-20000	—	—	—	-	-	94
BOD (5 days at 20°C), mg/1	1100-2500	6000-9000	1000-2000	6000-12000	600-22000	800-1200	1800

of biologically oxidizable materials in solution and also large quantities of putrescible suspended matter which may form the bulk of sludge on the bed of a river, and particularly in hot weather, may deoxygenate the water and decompose, emitting foul-smelling gases. Vegetable tanning liquors are dark in colour and may discolour river water for a long distance from the point of discharge. This discolouration is accentuated when the water contains iron, with which tanning liquors interact to form black compounds. Some tanning liquors contain toxic substances, e.g., arsenic, sulphides, chromium, etc. Lime, when present in high concentrations, may block sewers by forming loose deposits or adherent calcium carbonate scale. The presence of toxic substances, solvents and insecticides may inhibit biological processes. Tanning wastes, when discharged untreated, adversely affect aquatic life, particularly fish and algae, apart from becoming unfit for irrigation and human consumption. The work carried out on distribution of chromium in fresh water fish clearly confirms that the distribution of chromium in different parts is not even. Similar work carried out in the USA corroborates this finding.

Table 9.4
Characteristics of wastes from various operations

Parameters	*Type of tanning*		
	Vegetable tanning	*Combined tanning*	*Finishing unit*
PH	5.5–11.5	7.5–10.0	5.8
Total dissolved solids, mg/1	1680–26520	9000–20000	4400
Suspended solids, mg/l	160–6200	1250–6000	800
Chloride (as CI), mg/1	600–7100	1900–26200	600
Sulphate, mg/1	80–2020	–	2040
Chromium Hexavalent, mg/1	Nil	–	–
BOD(5 days at 20°C), mg/1	400–1200	2000–3000	900
COD, mg/1	1000–10300	5100–7200	2760

Spores of the 'Bacillus Anthracis', the organism which causes anthrax in animals and man, may be present in the waste. The spores are very resistant and may live for a long period and for this reason disposal of untreated tannery wastes for irrigation on land may be dangerous.

Harmful effects of some of the pollutants present in the tannery wastes are given in Table 9.5.

Table 9.5
Harmful effects of pollutants present in tannery effluents

Pollutants	*Harmful effects*	*Remarks*
Chromium	(*i*) Corrosive effects in the intestinaltract and nephteritis.	By large dosage of chromates
	(*ii*) Toxic dose for man	0.5 g of $K_2Cr_2Q_7$
	(*iii*) Destruction of fish	

(*Contd*....)

(*Contd. ...*)

	(*a*) Lethal limit for stickle	102 mg/1 $Cr_2(SO_4)^3$
	(*b*) Toxic in 30 minutes for gold fish	52 mg/1 Cr_2O_3
	(*c*) Toxic value for browntrout	5.2 mg/1 of $K_2Cr_2O_7$
	(*iv*) Accumulation in algae by factors	100–500 or more
	(*a*) Impairement of photosynthesis activities of algae	10–20% reduction by 5 days
	(*Macrocystis pyrifera*) at conc-1 mg/1	20-30% reduction by 7–9 days
	(*v*) Destruction of micro-organisms	
	(*a*) Toxic threshold for *Daphnia magna*	0.10 mg/1
	(*b*) Thieshold effect in protozoa	0.21 mg/1 $K_2Cr_2O_7$
	(*c*) Threshold effect on *E.coli*	0.7 mg/1 $K_2Cr_2O_7$
Sulphides	Fatal to sensitive fish (trout) even in neutral or alkaine water.	0.5-1.0 mg/1
Suspended matter	(*i*) Destruction of fish food, bottom fauna, and spawning grounds of fishes	Through bottom deposition
	(*ii*) Choking sewers	Through $CaCO_3$ deposition on walls
	(*iii*) Impairment of fertility of farm soil.	By application for irrigational purposes.
Organics	(*i*) Imposition of high and lasting oxygen demand	By biodegradation of protein and tanning.
	(*ii*) Anthrax and dermatitis	Streams containing tannery effluents
pH	(*i*) Fish are either killed or seriously handicapped.	pH drop from 5.0 or rise above 9.0.
	(*ii*) Destruction of fish food	By acidic discharge
	(*iii*) Corrosive to concrete structures (sewers)	pH below 6.0
Ammonia (Ammoniacal nitrogen)	(*i*) Chronic acidosis and tissue changes	Ingestion 0.5% ammonia for 17 days.
	(*ii*) Retards hemoglobin activity, thus, suffocates the fish	1 mg/1
	(*iii*) Complete disappearance of algae (Aphanizomenon)	0.4 to 0.5 mg/1
	(*iv*) Toxicity threshold for organism of B-Saprobic & Oiigosaprobic zone toxicity threshold for L-meso saprobic zone. Toxicity threshold for polysaprobic zone.	0.3 to 0.4 mg/l as free NH_3 0.3–4.3 mg/13.2-220 freeNH_3

Method of Pollution Abatement

One difficulty in designing standardized methods of treatment of tannery wastes is that they include liquors of a widely differing character, the relative volumes of which differ from one tannery to another. There are treatments commonly given to effluents:

1. Physical Treatment
   (*a*) Screening
   (*b*) Grit chamber separation
   (*c*) Grease trap
   (*d*) Plain sedimentation
2. Chemical Treatment
   (*a*) Neutralization
   (*b*) Coagulation
   (*c*)Flocculation
3. Biological Treatment
   (*a*) Anaerobic treatment in
      (*i*) High rate anaerobic digester
      (*ii*) Anaerobic lagoons
   (*b*) Aerobic treatment in
      (*i*) Oxidation ponds
      (*ii*) Activated (sludge
      (*iii*) Trickling filters
      (*iv*) Aerated lagoons
      (*v*) Oxidation ditches.

Some of these have been briefly described below.

Screening and Sedimentation

It is desirable to pass the tannery wastes through screens to remove flesh, hair and other large solids. It has been found that a considerable reduction in the suspended solids of the tannery waste can be achieved by sedimentation, as given in table 9.6.

Table 9.6
Field and laboratory observations on settlement of vegetable tannery effluents

Characteristics	*Raw effluents*	*Settled effluents*	
		Fill and draw tank	*Laboratory (16 hours)*
pH value	8.6	8.8	8.75
Alkalinity (as $CaCO_3$), mg/1	4500	4200	4350
Chlorides (as Cl), mg/1	4600	3900	4300
Suspended solids, mg/1	4600	1460	2040
Chemical oxygen demand, rng/1	10300	8260	8900
BOD (5 days at 20°C), mg/1	4200	2600	3000

If, another experiment, liquors, from different operations, were mixed, treated with sulphuric acid to maintain pH 5.5 and retained overnight in a sedimentation tank. It was found that although the concentration of suspended solids was reduced by more than 50%, the BOD was reduced by only 9%. Results are given in Table 9.7.

Table 9.7
Average results of treatment of mixtures of tannery wastes by sedimentation after addition of sulphuric acid to pH 5.5

Parameters covered	*Before treatment*	*After treatment*	*Reduction (Percent)*
pH value	5.8	5.0	—
Total solids	2163 mg/l	2058 mg/l	14.9
Total volatile solids	984 mg/l	877 mg/l	10.9
Suspended solids	249 mg/l	110 mg/l	56.1
Biochemical oxygen demand in 5 days at 20°C	377 mg/l	343 mg/l	9.2
Total alkalinity (as CaO)	237 mg/l	184 mg/l	24.1

Chemical Treatment

Considerable reduction in BOD of the tannery waste is achieved by sedimentation after addition of lime. Particulars of the results of tannery waste treated by lime are given in Table 9.8.

Table 9.8
Particulars of treatment of tannery effluents by sedimentation after addition of time

Type of leather manufactured	*No. of tanneries*	*Period of retention sedimentation tanks (hrs.)*		*Average reduction per cent)*		
		Range	*Average*	*Setteable solids*	*Suspended solids*	*BOD*
Heavy leather (mostly vegetable tanning)	21	4–133	39	96	92	73
Light leather (mostly chrome tanning)	10	1.3–20	10	93	87	70

Aerobic and Anaerobic Biological Treatment

It has been found that considerable reduction in the tannery waste can be achieved by adopting aerobic and anaerobic biological treatment. The efficiency of different treatment techniques are given in Table 9.9.

Electrolytic Processes for Tannery Wastes Containing Chrome

Tannery wastes containing chromium are toxic for the micro-organisms and, hence, cannot be suitably treated by aerobic or anaerobic biological processes. For this purpose, the electrolytic process has been tried and has worked out satisfactorily. In this process, the waste is passed through sand beds to remove suspended particles like flesh, hair, etc. After adjusting pH to 3.5, the liquor is passed through an "Electrolyzing Column". A current of 4 amperes at 11 volts is maintained between the electrodes. The dissolved organics are oxidized by the nascent oxygen produced, and suspended solids float out with the evolving hydrogen bubbles. The electrolyzed liquor, after sand bed Alteration, can be recycled for tanning purposes. The solid materials involved in a typical tannery and their environmentally sound utilization practices are given in Table 9.10. The practice suggested

Table 9.9

Efficiency of different treatment techniques

Treatment technique	*Separating conditions*	*Efficiency*	*Remarks*
1. Physical treatment screening	The liquid waste from a tanning industry, which may contain impurities such, as hair, dirt, dung, fleshing, etc., are screened.	In screening treatment, the coarser impurities are removed like hair and fleshing, etc.	
Equalization and sedimentation	The discharge of waste from the tanning industry is not uniform and it fluctuates with wide variations, with both acidic and alkaline characteristics prevailing. Hence, to even out the flow and to allow for mixing the acid and alkaline waste for neutralization, and equalization tank of one day's capacity may be provided. The equalization tank provides for settling also.	Simple sedimentation of waste brings about 70-80% reduction in suspended solids and 20-30% reduction in BOD.	
Removal of hydrogen sulphide	The evolution of hydrogen sulphide can be reduced to a considerable extent, if the sulphide content of the lime liquor is reduced by diffused aeration in the presence of a catalyst such as magnous salt. Precipitation with iron salts or blowing flue gas may also reduce sulphide content.	In this process hydrogen sulphide gas is reduced to a considerable extent.	
2. Chemical treatment	Tannery waste can be treated with chemical coagulants such as alum, carbon dioxide, sulphuric acid, ferric chloride and lime.	Considerable reduction in suspended solids and BOD.	This process involves high cost and disposal of the resulting chemical sludge also poses a problem.

(Contd....)

(Table 9.9) *Contd. ...*

Treatment technique	*Separating conditions*	*Efficiency*	*Remarks*
3. Biological treatment (a) Anaerobic treatment (i) Anaerobic digestion	Degradation of organic matter brought about by the action of micro-organisms in the absence of air and free oxygen, under controlled lab conditions.	Anaerobic digestion of the vegetable tan liquor indicated a BOD reduction of 93%. But this was reported at a low loading of 0.8 kg/m^3 of volatile solids, Detention period is high.	Bulk of the BOD of the tannery waste cane be removed by anaerobic process and the rest of the BOD in further aerobic treatment.
(ii)Anaerobic lagoon	The Anaerobic lagoon method of treatment employs the principles of anaerobic digestion with no gas collection. The capacity of the lagoon will be about 15 to 20 days storage : the depth will be 3 m. These lagoons can be operated at high loading, varying from 250 kg/hec/ day to 100 kg/hec/day.	BOD reduction of tannery waste is 70–80%.0nce the lagoon stabilizes and methane fermentation sets in, it becomes self-sustaining. Studies have indicated that the BOD of the settled tannery waste came down from 1500 mg/1 to 190 mg/1.	This process involves low capital and running cost.
(b) Aerobic treatment (i) Oxidation pond	This is an earthen shallow pond utilizing sun light and aerobes for treating organic wastes. The depth of the pond varies from 1.0 to 1.5 m and BOD loading is 250 kg/hec/day while detention period is 40 days.	The BOD of the settled and diluted waste mixed with sewage in the ratio of 3:1 came down to 218 mg/1 from 802 mg/1.	
(ii) Activated sludge process	In this process, organically polluted waste water is made to come in contact with aerobic micro-organisms present in the form of a flocculent biological mass, termed as activated sludge. Through differenced air system or other methods,	Studies have indicated that a mixed liquor suspended solid (MLSS) concentration of 3000 to 4000 mg/1, the BOD of the pretreated effluent came down to 34 mg/1 from 988 mg/1 within 24 hours of aeration. Generally a BOD	

Treatment technique	*Separating conditions*	*Efficiency*	*Remarks*
	the activated sludge is made to come in intimate contact with the liquid part.	removal of 85 to 95% can be expected from this system.	
(iii) Trickling filtration	The trickling filter is an aerobic biological treatment process. It is a porous bed made of solid particles of stone or synthetic material, usually PVC, on the surface of which a fixed growth of microorganism is contained. A microbial film develops on the surface of the bed media and removes the organic materials from waste water. As this is an aerobic biological system, oxygen is required for rapid metabolism of the removed organic matter. The large surface area of the filter media permits a rapid transfer of oxygen by simple diffusion from the void space into the liquid layer.	BOD of pretreated vegetable tannery effluent came down from 900 mg/1 to 158 mg/1. Settling the filtered effluent brought down the BOD to 56 mg/1. In case of chrome tanning waste, the BOD was brought down to 129 mg/1 from 800 mg/1 and further reduction in BOD was obtained at a value of 56 mg/1, after settling the effluent from trickling filtration.	
Aerated lagoon	The aerated lagoon consists of an earthen tank with 2.4 to 3.0 metres depth. The aeration is accomplished either with diffused air or surface aerators. Detention time of the aerated lagoon varies from 3 to 5 days.	A BOD removal of 70 to 90% can be achieved with this system.	
Oxidation ditch	This is an extended aeration system with low organic loadings and high mixed liquor suspended solids concentration of the order of 4000 mg/1.	A BOD removal of 95 to 98 % can be expected out of this system.	

will not only eliminate associated health hazards but will also provide variable materials in some cases.

Electrolytic Processes for Tannery Wastes Containing Chrome

Tannery wastes containing chromium are toxic for the micro-organisms and, hence, cannot be suitably treated by aerobic or anaerobic biological processes. For this purpose, the electrolytic process has been tried and has worked out satisfactorily. In this process, the waste is passed through sand beds to remove suspended particles like flesh, hair, etc. After adjusting pH to 3.5, the liquor is passed through an "Electrolyzing Column". A current of 4 amperes at 11 volts is maintained between the electrodes. The dissolved organics are oxidized by the nascent oxygen produced, and suspended solids float out with the evolving hydrogen bubbles. The electrolyzed liquor, after sand bed Alteration, can be recycled for tanning purposes. The solid materials involved in a typical tannery and their environmentally sound utilization practices are given in Table 9.10. The practice suggested will not only eliminate associated health hazards but will also provide variable materials in some cases.

Table 9.10

Environmentally sound practices of solid waste disposal in a tannery

Solid waste	*Environmentally sound utilisation practice*
Green fleshing	Drying and immediate disposal for glue manufacture, etc.
Hair	Washing, drying and utilization for carpet, drugget industry , etc.
Lime sludge	Utilization for building-construction, soil conditioning, etc.
Limed fleshings and trimmings	Utilization for glue and gelatin manufacture, etc.
Vegetable tan bark	Used as fuel
Vegetable tan sludge	Used as fertilizer, soil conditioner
Vegetable and chrome tanned shavings	Used in manufacture of leather boards, etc., incineration along with sludges.
Effluent sludges:	
Vegetable tanning sludges	Dewatering and incineration with other solid wastes
Chrome tanning sludges	Disposed of on land or into sea in consultation with local authority.

Screening, sedimentation, neutralization and anaerobic and aerobic biological processes for the treatment of tannery waste are well-established. As pointed out earlier, the characteristics of effluents vary widely from tannery to tannery. Hence, a certain amount of design calculation and modifications of process parameters are necessary in each case.

There are a few small tanneries, for whom it is not easy to go in for pollution abatement. In such cases, it is advisable to have common arrangements for abatement, whereby the cost-benefits may be divided in proportion to the amount of effluents discharged.

Regarding chrome tanning, it may be pointed out that chromium is non-renewable material. The importance of recycling is obvious for two important reasons. Firstly, some of the heavy metals, e.g., cadmium, lead, arsenic and chromium, which are dumped into natural streams, are serious pollutants. Secondly, the resources of such non-renewable materials are in limited supply. For example, the world's known reserves of chromium are about 775 million metric tonnes, of which about 1.86 million metric tonnes are mined annually at present. Thus, be the current rate of use, known reserves would last about 420 years. Under the assumption of constant use, the linear depletion of chromium reserves would be expected. The actual world consumption of chromium is increasing, however, at the rate of 2.5 percent annually. If the growth rate continues to increase at this rate, it will deplete the resource, not in 420 years but in just 95 years. If it is assumed that reserves yet undiscovered could increase the present known reserves by a factor of five, thus, extending the lifetime of the reserves only from 95 to 154 years. Even if it were possible from 1970 onwards to recycle 100 percent of the chromium so that none of the initial reserves were lost the demand would exceed the supply in 235 years. Chromium is definitely one of the most serious pollutants known. Most of the natural streams do not have any further assimilation capacity and, hence, cannot be used for the disposal of such materials any longer.

The natural stream has all along been used as an open dump of effluents. The irreversible change in the eco-system, due to an over-discharge of effluents is responsible for this alarming situation. It is, therefore, equally essential to consider the assimilation capacity visa-vis the total pollution load while deciding the degree of treatment for effluents.

10

Pesticides - Pollution and Abatement

The use of insecticides in the field of agriculture has proved very useful in protecting crops from pests and, thereby, significantly improving the yield. Besides agriculture, the role of insecticides in protecting human life by controlling the spread of epidemics and providing human life hygienic environment is also well-known. The most familiar example is that of DDT (Dichlorodiphenyltrichloroethane), the use of which has saved millions of human fives by successfully checking malaria. On the agricultural side too, the crop yield has been considerably increased by the use of DDT Hence, its popularity. Paul H Muller, the inventor of DDT was awarded the Nobel Prize in 1948 for his invention.

The extensive use of insecticides became a cause of concern, however, when some of their harmful side-effects were observed. On both the fronts, i.e., that of agriculture and human health, on the basis of quantitative results, it became evident that in the long range, the use of insecticides is not in the overall interest of man.

Rachel Carson alerted the nation against the use of pesticides in her book Silent Spring.

Chemical pesticides are primarily classified by referring to the type of pest they control, and, thus, we speak of acaricides, fungicides, insecticides, nematicides, rodenticides and weed killers or herbicides. Some chemicals fall into more than one of these categories: parathion, for example, while being an insecticide, is also a nematicide and an acaricide.

Insecticides are commonly classified as organo-phosphates and organo-chlorines. A great variety of them is in use, either singly or in combination, under different technical and trade names. They have their specific applications and characteristic harmful effects from the point of view of pollution. About 50,000 pesticide formulations are currently available for use on a, world-wide scale. The harmful environmental effects of insecticides are outline in the following paragraphs.

In general, every chemical pesticide is a poison to some living thing and no poison has yet been discovered that .will affect only one kind of insect or weed. If analysed, it is found that the results are good on a short term basis but in the long run, the results are disappointing. An example of the use of DDT over a long period of time would serve as a good illustration. In 1949, the experiments on the use of DDT were carried out on cotton fields. Initially, the yield increased from 440 Ibs/acre. to 648 lbs/acre After 3 years it was found that the DDT was no longer effective in controlling the pests; the first pests were killed but DDT resistant strains had risen. Afterwards, it was found that six types of pests had appeared, and ultimately after 5 years, it was observed that the yield of cotton reduced to 1/3' of the original.

From the preceding example, it is evident that the overall effect is not beneficial, even from the point of view of yield. Here, another important point to be noted is that while attempting to kill one species of pest, other species are also killed and some of them may be natural predators to the very species we want to kill. It is reported that in practically every spray operation, thousands of non-target insects are also killed. Further, many new insect species develop which are resistant to the insecticides.

The killing of 'non-target' species disturbs the balance in the natural cycle and the evolution of new species necessitates more severe environmental control measures.

As far as human beings are concerned, the harmful effects of insecticides have been a cause of concern. The people working on farms, involved in the handling, etc., are expose directly and are likely to become victims of the toxic effects of insecticides which may be lethal. Organophosphates decompose more rapidly than the organochlorines but some of them have a toxic strength which is 300 times higher. Organophosphates build up residues on foliage after application. In one case, 90 peach pickers were poisoned while working in orchards, subjected to heavy spraying of parathion, over a period of several months. The toxic effect of some of the insecticides are given in Table 10.1.

Table 10.1
Toxicity ratings of some common organic phosphorous insecticides

Common or trade name	*Oral LD_{50} (rates, mg. kg)*
Malathion	1500
Methyl parathion	25
Parathion	10
Chlorthion	1500
Nilate or Ethion	200
Guthion	1500
Phostex	1200
Trithion	100
Dibrom	430
Dementon or Systox	10
Di-Syston	10
Phosdrin	12

Note: Data on oral toxicity to rates. LD_{50} values represent the amount of insecticide per unit of body weight required to cause the death of 50% of group of test animals.

Persistence of insecticides in the environment after application is not desirable from environmental considerations. In general, the organochlorines persist longer in the environment than the organophosphorous-based insecticides. Data regarding persistence of organochlorines in the soil are given in Table 10.2.

Table 10.2
Approximate persistence of chlorinated hydrocarbon insecticides in soil

Name	*Duration of persistence*
Toxaphene	> 6 yr
Heptachlor	> 9 yr
Aldrin Dieldrin	> 9 yr
DDT	> 10 yr
Hexachlorocyclohexane	> 10 yr
Chlordane	> 12 yr

The persistence of insecticides in any environment is harmful. Besides, they, sometimes, undergo metabolic and other degradation processes and, thereby, produce more harmful products than the parent substance.

The harmful effects of the presence in DDT, the most evidently used insecticide at one time in the environment, have been reported from different parts of the world. The presence of DDT in water, air and soil results in its presence in various species who live in those surroundings. DDI 's concentration builds up in the body and accumulates in the fat. Further, as it goes up the food chain, it concentrates more and more, and the effect is cumulative.

The quantity or extent to, which it gets accumulated in the body, varies with the kind of species. Table 10.3 illustrates this aspect.

Table 10.3

Accumulation of DDT in various species exposed to the same environment

Species	*Level of accumulation*
Plankton	250 times the applied concern
Frogs	2000 times the applied concern
Sunfish	12000 times the applied concern
Crabs	80000 times the applied concern

In the human body also, the presence of DDT has been detected. In some cases, the level has exceeded the normal limit and people are facing its harmful consequences. It is found that most of Americans have 8-10 ppm DDT in their body. In this connection, it must be noted that prior to the use of DDT, it was never detected in the human body. With its increased use, its concentration in the body has also increased.

The studies carried out to determine the DDT concentration in the human body are reported in Table 10.4.

Table 10.4

DDT concentration in the human body of the people of different countries

Population	*Year*	*No. of samples*	*Concentration of DDT & toxic breakdown products in body fat (ppm)*
Alaska(Eskimos)	1960	20	3.0
Canada	1959–60	62	4.9
England	1961	131	2.2
England	1964	100	3.9
France	1963	10	5.2
Germany	1958–59	60	2.3
Hungary	1965	48	12.4
India (Delhi)	1966	67	26.0
Israel	1963–64	254	19.2
US (Kentucky)	1947	10	—
US (all states)	1964	64	7.6

The most common way it reaches the human body is through food items, i.e., through DDT affected vegetables, fish, milk, etc. There have been reports that even breast fed babies get 70% more than the accepted amount of DDT. Like human beings, other species are also affected adversely in various ways, e.g., thinning of egg shells, etc., Therefore, precautions have to be taken for the presence of pesticide residues on foods to ensure that the quantities remaining on a fruit, vegetable, grain or animal product are reduced to such levels that do not pose any health hazard to human beings.

Table 10.5 shows the tolerance for pesticides residues according to the National Food Regulation.

The adverse effects of using insecticides have become of vital concern these days, to the extent that opinions favour to limiting the use of insecticides. The harm caused by DDT has been well-established beyond all doubt and EPA of America has banned the use of DDT since 1972. In future, environmental considerations would be the guiding factor in recommending a particular insecticide for general purposes.

There is a definite trend towards finding suitable alternatives for those insecticides which have adverse effects on the environment. In general, the organophosphorous based insecticides show greater promise than organochlorine based ones. Lastly, it would be appropriate to point out that use of insecticides would have to be carried out with greater care and control, than has been common in the past.

Table 10.5

Tolerance for pesticides residue

Trade name	*Chemical name*	*Tolerance limit in ppm*	*Loads*
DDT	1,1, l-trichloro-2, 2-bis (p-chloro phenyl)-ethane	7	Apples, beets, cattle fat. peas, etc.
Dieldrin	1,2,3,4, 10-hexachloro-6, 7-epoxy-l, 4, -4a, 5, 6, 7, 8a-octahydro-1, 4-endoexo-5,	0.1	Carrots, grapes, oats, potatoes, etc.
	8-dimethanonapthaiene	0.25	Apples, cabbage, etc.
Malathion	0, 0-dimethyl 1, 5- (l, 2-dicarbobethoxyethyl)	4.0	Meat of cattle, hogs, poultry and sheep.
	phos phorodithioate.	8.0	Apples, beans, celery, peas, strawberries, etc.
Pyrethrins	Pyrethirins	1.0	Post-harvest application on apples, beans, peas, etc.
		3.0	Com, rice, wheat, etc.

Handling of Pesticides

The harmful effects of pesticides depend on the following factors:

1. Physical form of the pesticide used.
2. Purity of the active material in the pesticide.
3. Absorption rate of the pesticide in the body of human beings.
4. Detoxification and distribution of pesticides in the body.
5. Solubility of the pesticide in the body fluid

6. Environmental conditions, e.g., humidity, temperature, etc.
7. Organ of the body in which the pesticide is accumulated.
8. Degree and extent of exposure to the body.

The field application of pesticides generally involves the use of high pressure hand spray equipment, knap sack sprayer, power sprayer, compression sprayer, bucket sprayer, rocking sprayer, air blast equipment, hand duster, rotary duster, etc. During field application of pesticides, any of the following reasons may create problems for health :

1. Use of unsuitable low cost protective measures
2. Use of unsuitable method of spraying
3. Crude methods of formulation of concentrates
4. Improper maintenance and storage of pesticides, etc.

Preventive Measures

The following preventive measures should be taken at the factory level while manufacturing pesticides :

1. Special precautions must be taken during weighing and filling of pesticides in containers.
2. The storage and processing of pesticides should be done at properly ventilated places.
3. The pesticides should never be carried in open systems and the ventilation systems should be well maintained.
4. Provision should be made for special work clothes, towels, etc., and work clothes should be cleaned regularly to reduce the possibility of the absorption of pesticides.
5. Protecting equipment and masks must be provided to each worker who is working in the factory.
6. The places where the chances of contamination of atmosphere by pesticides are maximum, should be far from the main working place of the factory and should be designed in such a way that a worker takes minimum time to complete Ms job.
7. So far as the degree of pollution in different sections of the factory is concerned, an assessment of the working environment should be conducted periodically and the results should be compared with the threshold limit values. Remedies for increase in pollution levels should be determined.
8. A periodical medical examination of each worker should be conducted for medical fitness. The medical test should also be conducted to detect individual susceptibility for any early sign and symptom of early effect. The person who is susceptible to poisoning of pesticides should never be given work involving contact with pesticides.
9. Eating, drinking and smoking should be strictly forbidden in the vicinity of the storage place of the pesticides.
10. Storage rooms should be well lighted.

First Aid Treatments and Antidotes for Pesticide Poisoning

If the poison has been inhaled, as in the case of toxic fumigants, the patient should be removed to the open air and given artificial respiration.

If the poison has been spilled on the skin, it should be washed off immediately with large amounts of warm soapy water, scrubbing the skin thoroughly. Drop or particles in the eyes should be removed by flushing with large quantities of plain water.

If the poison has been swallowed, the stomach of the affected person should be emptied as soon and as completely as possible. After this has been done, a demulcent such as raw eggs, milk or a thin flour paste can be given. These serve to absorb the poison, and to soothe the irritated membranes. If the specific poison is known, the following emergency treatments could be given.

Acids

Limewater or milk of lime, milk of magnesia should be given.

Arsenic Compounds

After emptying the stomach, raw eggs, milk, lime water, flour, and water, or sweet oil should be given.

Benzene Hexachloride

Tea or coffee and gypsum salts may be given after the stomach has been emptied.

Chloroans

Same treatment as benzene hexachloride.

DDT

The same treatment as for benzene hexachloride.

Mercury Compounds

Raw egg and milk should be given immediately.

Nicotines

After emptying the stomach, stimulants such as hot tea or coffee should be given.

Parathion

After emptying the stomach, have a physician administer 1/30 to 1/60 grain of atropine sulphate at hourly intervals, until pupils dilate.

Tetraethyl Pyrophosphate

The same treatment as recommended in the case of parathion may be given. The following information will also be useful in this connection:

IS: 4015 (Part I) 1967

Provides information with regard to the first aid measures that are necessary to be taken in cases of pesticide poisoning before a physician attends the case.

IS: 4015 (Part II) 1967

Outlines the basic information intended for Ore use of physicians with regard to the symptoms, differential diagnosis and treatment in relation to poisoning due to different types of pesticides and their formulations during their use in a laboratory, field or a factory.

Pesticide Disposal

There are a number of methods available to tackle the problem of disposal of surplus pesticides but they are not always satisfactory for all types of materials. The methods, presently in practice, include thermal decomposition, chemical neutralization, burial and biological degradation.

Thermal Decomposition

This method requires exposure of the pesticide to a high temperature (900-1000 °C) for varying periods of time. This method is satisfactory enough as it degrades about 98% or even more of most of the commercial pesticidal formulations. The exposure time should be sufficient so as to ensure complete decompositions, and care must be taken to remove air pollutants before the gases are discharged into the atmosphere. A wet scrubber and filtration through a porous clay bed and carbon filter, with lagoon treatment of the waste water, are suggested. Mercury, arsenic, lead and similar toxic compounds should not be incinerated unless special residue handling and disposal facilities are available.

Chemical Neutralization

This is feasible for most of the organophosphates and carbamate insecticides, but not for the chlorinated hydrocarbons. Various chemicals used to destroy the pesticides are nitric acid, sulphuric acid, ammonium hydroxide, sodium hydroxide, chlorine compounds, peroxides or other types of active chemicals. Calcium hydrochlorite seems to have the broadest application. A strong acid or alkaline hydrolysis does not provide complete treatment.

Burial

Burial is susceptible to contamination of waters and ground waters from leaching and run off on pesticides. Careful shallow burial with 18 in. of earth for small quantities of pesticides in clay soil is generally acceptable until a better method is developed. The location should be well above ground water level, downgrade, and several hundred feet from any source of water supply and they should also be beyond the reach of children and animals. The burial of pesticides in sandy soils is not recommended as it has greater possibility of leaching into surface water or ground water.

Biological or Natural Degradation

This method is satisfactory for short lived materials while for other more persistent materials, the rate of degradation is too slow. The persistence of some pesticides in soils is given in Table 10.6. When proper facilities are available, surplus pesticides and containers should be disposed of as described above.

Table 10.6

Pesticide	*Half life (T)yr.*
Lead, Copper, Arsenic	10 to 30
Dieldrin, BHC, DDT insecticides	2 to 4
Triazine herbicides	1 to 2
Urea herbicides	0.3 to 0.8
Benzoic acid herbicides	0.2 to 1
2,4-D: 2,4,5-T Herbicides	0.1 to 0.4
Organophosphorous insecticides	0.02 to 0.2
Carbamate (Carbaryl) insecticides	0.02

Conclusion

As stated earlier, in spite of the short term advantages of pesticides, they may create serious health hazards to human beings in the long run. The fourth report of the Council of Environmental Quality of the USA, published in 1972, has virtually banned the use of DDT because this chemical, being highly persistent, enters the food chain of innumerable forms of life which results in a total dislocation of the balance of nature.

Unfortunately, the use of DDT is increasing in India, day by day. Total consumption of pesticides per year is given in Table 10.7. At present, about 4000 tonnes of DDT is manufactured in India and an equal quantity is imported, mainly for malaria control. Apparently the malaria carrying mosquito, Anopheles culcifacious, has become resistant to many kinds of insecticides.

Table 10.7
Pesticides consumption/ target from 1955–83

Year	*Consumption in M*
1955–56	2,350
1960–61	8,620
1965–66	14,630
1970–71	56,000
1976–77	65,000
1977–78	59,000
1978–79	65,000
1979–80	69,000
1980–81	73,000
1981–82	76,000
1982–83	80,000

The universe of cultivated crops often overlaps the habitats of insects responsible for transmission of human diseases. This is particularly true in the case of the mosquito population, which breeds in diverse water bodies in all types of situations. Repeated application of different pesticides ensures exposure of genera of these insects of speedy selection for resistance to the pesticides used.

Increase in malaria during the last few years has obviously made it necessary to plan for a much greater use of DDT. Attempts are being made to find alternatives to DDT like Methaxsichlor, which, unlike DDT, is quickly degradable.

An ideal pesticide is Pyrethnun which is extracted from the flowers of a plant grown widely in Kenya. Pyrethrum is most effective, and being a natural insecticide, is completely harmless to the environment. Attempts are being made to grow Pyrethrum in Kashmir and Tamil Nadu, but, as yet, the output is very limited.

Biological control is, of course, the best way of dealing with pests. This involves the use of bacteria, virus and other pathogens which attack or by the use of predators or parasites or both. A lot of work is yet to be done in this field, and according to the Indian Council of Agricultural Research, there has been considerable success in some fields. The most successful of these was the almost total eradication of the prickly pear, opuntia Spp which had, like many toxic plants, proliferated widely over the countryside in India, and was a great menace for many years. The Indian station of the Commonwealth. Institute of Biological Control situated in Bangalore is attempting to find natural enemies of a number of pests, but this work is at a very early stage.

The extensive use of pesticides could have an adverse effect on soil fertility and on crops.

The growing requirement for the use of pesticides is obvious. But the harmful effects of pesticides with higher persistence suggest the necessity for development of pesticides which are biodegradable.

11

Radioactivity in the Environment, Its Monitoring and the Evaluation of its Significance

To fully comprehend this subject, it is necessary to be familiar with some important units and physical principles, *i.e.*, basic types of radiation, basic terms, and monitoring. In the world literature, one finds many units. The older books quote the roentgen (r or R). The latest unit is gray (Gy). All these units depend directly or indirectly on the capability of radioactive materials to cause ionization in their environment. Numerically, the roentgen rad and rem are very similar. The most frequently used unit in the established literature seems to be rad. For the purpose of this discussion, it is sufficient for the reader to know that 1 Gy = 100 rads. Basic units used in radiation are given in Table 11.1.

Table 11.1
Some of the basic units used in radiation

Roentgen unit of ionizing radiation (*r*)	$= 2.58 \times 10^4$ C kg^{-1}
1 gray (gy)	= Radiations which transfer 1 joule per kg of absorbing medium. Unit of dose to human body.
1 rem (roentgen)	= Dose in rad. × R.B.E. (Relative Biological Effectiveness; for gama and *X* radiations R.B.E. = 1 approximately)
1 Curies (Ci)	$= 3.7 \times 10^{10}$ disintegrations per second of the radioactive material
1 Becquerel (Bq)	= One disintegrations per second 2.073×10^{11} Ci
1 AMU (atomic mass unit)	= 931 me V = 1/17 mass of carbon nuclide
leV	$= 1.6023 \times 10^{19}$ Joules
1 MeV	$= 10^6$ eV
1 GeV	$= 10^9$ eV

Radioactive materials are unstable and when the atoms disintegrate, ionizing particles may be given off and in some cases, ionizing electromagnetic radiation (Gamma rays) is radiated. It is ionization which causes damage to living matter. The particles and gamma rays penetrate cells to various extents depending on the energy of emission. This varies greatly for different isotopes. The latter too vary in their half life times; thus, some with a long half life will remain an environmental hazard for many years, while some only for a few minutes.

Within the living cells, ionization is, often, quickly followed by the production of free radicals which may react very rapidly with important biological molecules including genetic material. It is in fact the nucleus of the cell where the genetic material is stored which is most sensitive. It is many hundreds times more sensitive than the remainder of the cells Fig. 11.1.

DNA NUCLEUS	$\longrightarrow$	RNA	$\longrightarrow$	PROTEINS CYTOPLASM	$\longrightarrow$	LIVING PROCESSES

Fig. 11.1

Within the nucleus, the sensitive sites are the chromosomes. These are double structures composed of DNA and protein. Each is double because it consists of two sets of identical genetic material. The reason for this is to ensure that, when the cell divides, the two new cells are identical in their genetic make-up.

When cells divide during the growth of tissues, much complicated synthesis takes place including the duplication of DNA. The number of chromosomes varies from organism to organism.

It is small wonder, then, that it is in the dividing cells that radiation causes the most damage. In cells, which do not divide (more cells), the integrity of the nuclear DNA is less critical and their tissues are classed as being radio-resistant. At the opposite end of the scale, we have the reproductive organs, blood forming tissues, the digestive tract and developing embryos. All of these are fairly sensitive to radiation.

It is time now to point out that all the facts, described above, were discovered as the result of laboratory experiments, using quite high doses of radiation from x-ray machines or artificial sources of Gamma rays. The radiation, in the environment, is much lower in intensity.

A chest x-ray gives a dose of about 1000 m rad (1 m rad = rad × 10^{-3}).

Table 11.2

Source of radiation	*m rods per year*
Cosmic rays at sea level	30
Radiation from the ground	50
Radiation from within the body	20
Total	100

It is, of course, true to say that the total background radiation will vary with altitude and location. The mineral monazite, which is found in Kerala, contains the radioactive element, thorium, and its presence increases the background radiation considerably. Man-made emission from various nuclear reactors is given in Table 11.3.

Table 11.3
Emission from various nuclear reactors

Type of reactor	*Emission products*	*Emission rate Ci/year*
Boiling-water reactor	(*i*) Noble gases (short-lived + long-lived)	D-18000
	(*ii*) Liquid fission products	1–6
	(*iii*) Tritium-liquid	5–20
Pressurised-water reactor	(*i*) Noble gases (long-lived)	0–2
	(*ii*) Liquid fission products	0–11
	(*iii*) Tritium-liquid	500–1300
Heavy-water-moderated reactor	(*i*) Noble gases (short lived + long lived)	4000
	(*ii*) Fission products and Tritium-liquid	5
	(*iii*) Tritium-gas	1200
Gas-cooled graphite reactor	(*i*) Noble gases (short lived + long lived)	100–000
	(*ii*) Fission products-liquid	2–100
	(*iii* Tritium-liquid	100–500

A comparison between man-made radiation and the natural background is very interesting and this is shown in Table 11.4 which applies to the UK population average.

We can conclude from this that the medical use of radio-isotopes contributes to the average dose more than any other man-made source. A summary of exposure to organs from radio-pharmaceuticals and from typical radio-nuclides are given in Tables 11.5, 11.6. Whether the radio-isotopes are natural or man-made-their extent of danger in the environment depends on the following factors:

1. Physical properties, such as half-life ($T_{1/2}$), type of emission and energy of emission.
2. Their ability to enter the food chain.
3. Their tendency to become concentrated in animal tissues.

Table 11.4
Comparison between man made-radiation and natural background

Source of radiation	*m rads per year*
Natural background	100
Medical exposure	20
Fallout from nuclear testing	2
Peaceful uses of atomic energy	1

Table 11.5
Sources of exposure to organs from radio-pharmaceuticals

Organ scanned	*Compound used*	*Injected amount in Ci*	*Dosein m rads*	
			Organ scanned	*Whole body*
Brain	Hg-197 Chloromerdrin	0.5	50	250[a]
	Tc-99[m] Sodium pertech	5.0	30	65
Bone	Sr-85	0.1	4400	2300
	F-18	1.0	230	73
	Tc-99[m] Polyphosphate	2.0		

(*Contd. ...*)

(*Contd. ...*)

Lung	1-131 MAA	0.3	1900	24
	Tc-99^{m}MAA	1.5	290	2.6
Kidney	Hg-197 Chloromerdrin[b]	0.1	1860	50
	Tc-99^{m} DTPA			
Liver	Au-198 Colloid	0.15	4000	100
	TC-99^{m} Sulphur colloid	2.0	440	20

[a] Dose to the kidneys is much higher, approximately 9300 m rads.

[b] Doses to the kidney and whole body are approximately ten times higher from Hg-200.

Table 11. 6

Type of exposure from typical radio-nuclides in environment

Radio-nuclide	*Half-life*	*Critical organ*	*Form*	*Probable exposure*
H(T)-3	12.3 y	Total body	HTO	Water intake
Mn-54	300 d	Total body	Insol. particle	External
Fe-55	2.6 y	Lung	Insol. particle	Inhalation
Zn-65	245 d	Total body	Sol. particle	Dietary intake
Kr-85	10.8 y	Total body	Gas	Immersion
Sr-89	52 d	Bone	Sol. particle	Dietary intake
Sr-90	28 y	Bone	Sol. particle	Dietary intake
Y-91	59 d	Lung	Insol. particle	Inhalation
Zr-95	65 d	Total body	Insol. particle	External
Nb-95	35 d	Total body	Insol. particle	External
Ru-103	40 d	Total body	Insol. particle	External
Ru-106	1.0 y	Total body	Insol. particle	External
Sb-125	2.7 y	Total body	Insol. particle	External
1-131	8.1 d	Thyroid	Vapour particle	Dietary intake
Xe-133	5.3 d	Total body	Gas	Immersion
Cs-134	2.0 y	Total body	Sol. particle	Dietary intake
Cs-137	30 y	Total body	Sol. particle	Dietary intake
Ba-140	12.8 d	Total body	Insol. particle	External
Ce-144	28.4	Total body	Insol. particle	External
Pm-147	2.6 y	Lung	Insol. particle	Inhalation
Th-232	1.4×10^{10}y	Lung	Insol. particle	Inhalation
U-233	1.6×10^{5}y	Lung	Insol. particle	Inhalation
U-235	7×10^{6} y	Lung	Insol. particle	Inhalation
U-238	4.5×10^{9}y	Lung	Insol. particle	Inhalation
Pu-238	86 y	Lung	Insol. particle	Inhalation
Pu-239	2.4×10^{4} y	Lung	Insol. particle	Inhalation
Pu-240	6.6×10^{5}y	Lung	Insol. particle	Inhalation
Pu-241	13 y	Lung	Insol. particle	Inhalation

Table 11.7
Physical properties of typical radio-isotopes

Radio-isotope	*Half-life* $T_{1/2}$	*Energy of emission* E (Mev)	*Type of emission*
Tritium	5,000 y	0.02	
Carbon-14	5,500 y	0.15	
Phosphorous-32	14 days	1.7	
Iodine-131	8 days	0.8–0.08	
Stronium-90	28 y	0.5	
Cesium-137	26 y	0.5	
Plutonium-238	86 y	5.5	
Plutonium-239	24,000 y	5.1	

Some of the physical properties are listed in Table 11.7 together with the approximate energies of emission. Note here that plutonium - 238 is particularly toxic because it combines a high energy of emission with the presence of alpha particles. These particles base particularly dense trails of ionization inside living cells which might take up the isotope.

Strontium - 90 and Cesium -137 are produced from fission reactions. They occur in fallout from nuclear testing and are produced in nuclear power stations. Strontium - 90 is made even more dangerous due to its ability to behave like calcium and, thus, incorporate itself into bone. If pastures become contaminated with Strontium - 90, it soon becomes detectable in the milk of daily cattle. Iodine - 131 is another highly dangerous isotope. These three isotopes have been given in Table 11.7.

Following accidents to nuclear power stations[1] particular emphasis in Government studies is aimed at assessing safety levels. One such type of accident could be over-heating, melting and could, perhaps, cause vaporization of the fuel.

The three isotopes mentioned above have been singled out by the British Medical Research Council which has published detailed tables of dosages which can be tolerated in pasture milk and air[1]. Of course, many other radioactive materials also may be released into the environment. In an emergency, however, it has been necessary to sort out those which are likely to be particularly dangerous. If standards are, then, applied to the most dangerous ones, it can be assumed that the others are also at safe levels. In the British M.R.C. study referred to above, a dose, called the Emergency Reference Level (ERL), has been quoted. The ERL, for various parts of the body, ranges from 10 to 60 rem. If, after a nuclear accident, measurements in the area show that members of the population are likely to receive more than this dose, then counter-measures such as evacuation must take place. In the case of iodine-131, it is possible to treat affected people with tablets containing ordinary iodine. This has the effect of displacing and speeding up the excretion of the Iodine - 131 from the body.

Discharge of Radioactive Materials into the Sea

Because of the high cost of chemical reprocessing, a small amount of nuclear waste-material is customarily released into the sea in carefully controlled amounts. It should be emphasized, however, that more radioactive waste is reprocessed and concentrated in expensive containers to prevent it from reaching the open environment. Off the west coast of Britain, in the fresh sea, the following isotopes have been released over the past twenty years. The important isotopes in this discharge are :

$$^{95}Zr\ ,\ ^{95}Nb,\ ^{106}Ru,\ ^{137}Cs,\ ^{144}Ce,\ ^{238},\ ^{239},^{240}Pu.$$

The amounts of these isotopes are limited in accordance with the rules of the International Commission for Radiological Protection (ICRP). The amounts must be low enough to fulfil the following objectives:

1. Regardless of cost, the public must never be exposed to levels above the ICRP recommended limits.
2. Regardless of cost, the entire population must not receive more than 1 rem per person over 30 years.
3. Keeping cost in mind, doses should be kept as far below the mandatory limits as possible.

When this kind of material is discharged into the sea, one must be sure t hat the isotopes do not become trapped or concentrated in the sea bed. Unlike the other isotopes in the discharge, it has been found that plutonium - 239 does in fact become bound in sediment. Most of the isotope becomes bound near the point of discharge as shown in Table 11.8. As a result of this finding, it may be necessary to reduce the amount of radioactive plutonium in the discharge.

It is possible to monitor the amount of radioactive isotopes in the sea by making use of biological monitoring organisms which live attached to the sea bed for long periods in the same area. In Finland, the authorities are studying mussels (Mytilus) in order to obtain an early warning of any environmental danger from their nuclear power programme.

Table 11.8
Concentration of ^{239}Pu

Distance from out fall, km	*Water* $p^{C_2/l}$	*Sediment* $p^{C_2/g}$	*Concentration factor in sediment*
1	0.48	36	7×10^4
9	0.46	12	3×10^4
110	0.01	0.04	0.1×10^4

It is worth noting whether or not the background radiation (in the sea) is significantly affected by nuclear waste discharge. The normal level is about 350 m rads per year. In the Irish sea near the Wind scale reprocessing plant, the background is about 600 m rads per day. This sea area is one of the few places where records of fish landings are available and where the water has higher than normal levels of radioactivity. So far no effects of the radiation have been found[2]. The sensitivity of animals towards radiation varies inversely but the dose required to cause mortality is above 100 rads (1 Gy). Below this level, genetic changes can be expected. These have been detected at doses around 10 rads. Note, however, that this is far above the levels produced by pollution so far.

There is very little reliable evidence to allow definite predictions to be made regarding the possibility that man-made radiation could affect the mutation rate to any significant extent. However, there are good reasons for saying that the environmental background should be kept as low as possible. Mutations are occurring all the times at a natural rate which is partly due to radiation and partly due to other factors such as chance and chemical processes which are unrelated to radiation.

If we do anything to increase the mutation rate, it is probable that we shall increase the number of undesirable mutations faster than those which are desirable. In general, if organisms have a high rate of reproductivity and normally experience a high selective pressure from the environment, they will be less likely to suffer from an increase in the mutation rate. This is because the undesirable mutations are ruthlessly eliminated during the struggle for survival. In populations like the human race, selection is less vigorous and undesirable mutations will tend to persist and be accumulated.

Basic Types of Radiation

Alpha Particles

1. Weakly penetrating, and stopped by 80 mm of air or by thin materials.
2. Deflected by electric and magnetic fields.
3. Relatively slow moving
4. Strongly ionizing.
5. Are a doubly ionized helium nucleus.

Beta Particles

1. Can penetrate thin sheets of aluminium. Penetrating power varies with the energy of particles.
2. Strongly deflected in electric and magnetic fields.
3. Are high velocity electrons.

γ-rays

1. Can penetrate several cms of lead depending on energy of radiation
2. Undeflected in magnetic fields.
3. Are very high frequency photons.

Radioactive Decay

This is a spontaneous process arising from a nuclear instability of some sort. It is random. *i.e.*, the probability that a given nucleus will decay, in unit ti me, i s independent of when the time interval occurs and of any chemical or physical conditions.

Decay Equation

$$N = N_0^{e^{-\lambda t}}$$

where N = number of nuclei present at time, t,

N_0 = original number of nuclei

Activity γ = decay constant

$$A = \frac{n}{t}$$

where n is the of transformations in time, t.

AN (as a mean value, since die process is random), the decaying per unit time, is subject to statistical fluctuations obeying a Poisson distribution.

Half Life ($T_{1/2}$)

It is the time taken for half of the nuclei present to decay.

Basic Terms

Ionization

Energy transferred by the atomic particle to the surrounding matter brings about ionization of atoms and excitation of molecules.

Ions

Molecules with atoms which have either lost or gained an electron are called ions. (They exist in addition to free radicals.) The biological effects of radiations depend largely on the reaction of free radicals which result as secondary products in the aqueous environment in living cells.

RLE

Every time an ion is produced (or molecule excited) the energy of the particle is reduced (around 34 eV per ion pair production). The rate of loss of energy (RLE) in a given material depends upon

1. Magnitude of charge
2. Velocity of particle.

As the ionizing particle travels through matter, it loses energy and its velocity reduces until it is too slow to produce further ionizations (i.e., it is moving at roughly the same speed as the surrounding molecules). At the same time as it slows down; its RLE increases and the ionizing density, therefore, increases progressively towards the end of the track, e.g., 1 MeV electron lias an RLE 200 eVm^{-1} initially and RLE 60000 eVm^{-1} at the end.

Width indicates	12 meVparticle
Amount of energy lost on track	3 meV

proton penetration into tissue 100 keV electron

All three have the same range 140 (in tissue).

The RLE is proportional to the density for a given material, thus, the range must be inversely proportional.

Penetration

Particle Radiation. Rays of this type, given off by radioactive substances, seldom exceed a few MeV and cannot penetrate very deeply into the body. Exposure to such rays are only likely to cause skin burns which arc not usually serious except when the doses arc very high. However, they are dangerous if they are injected or inhaled, because some have extremely long half-life and vital organs can, thus, become exposed to a cancer hazard.

High Frequency Quanta or Photon (e.g., X or gamma rays): These rays give up their energy in three main ways depending on the initial energy of the quants. Unlike particles, X-ray and gamma rays can penetrate deep into the body.

(*i*) *At lowest energies.* The incident photon is totally absorbed in the production of a photo electron (There is also a recoil nucleus).

(*ii*) *At moderate energies*. The incident photon collides with an atomic electron and rebounds, when part of the photon energy is transferred to the electron, which is thus, ejected from the atom. The deflected photon suffers a wavelength shift and is less penetrating.

(*iii*) *At high engines* (*Above* 1.02 *MeV*). A photon passing close to a nucleus is transformed into two particles—an electron and a positron (pair production) - which fly apart at speed.

Neutrons: Neutrons, being unchanged, cannot ionize directly. They only interact with matter by direct collision with a nucleus.

(*i*) *Low energy neutrons*. These can be captured by a nucleus to produce an atomic transmutation.

(*ii*) *Fast neutrons*. A proton ejected from the nucleus with which a fast neutron collides. Because nuclei only occupy a minute fraction of the volume of an atom, a neutron can travel long distances before colliding with a nucleus. The stopping power of a material, against fast neutron, depends entirely on the number of nuclei in the paths and not on the size of the nuclei or the number of electrons surrounding them. The nucleus of a hydrogen atom has the same chance of stopping a neutron as the nucleus of lead weighing 200 times as much. Since 1 kg of water contains 30 times as many nuclei as 1 kg load, the water will absorb more neutrons.

Personal Monitoring

Film Badge

This consists of a sensitive 'photographic' film sandwich between a base plate and a front surface which consists of different materials of varying thickness that act as filters for the incident radiation.

Personnel Dosimeter

Two electrodes (one fixed, the other moveable) are charged to the potential. Radiation produces ions which are deposited on the electrodes. This reduces the potential, hence reduces mutual repulsion. Thus, the electrodes move and it is this movement that gives the reading of the dose received.

Maximum Permissible Doses

Basic standards have been recommended by International Commission on Radiological Protection from past experience in the use of X-rays and radium, together with information on radiation injuries to man. They may be expected to produce effects which could be detected only by statistical methods applied to large groups of people. The basic standard is an animal limits on dose, viz.,

—5 rems to the whole-body gonads and blood forming organs

—30 rems to bone, skin and thyroid

—15 rems to all other organs or parts of the body

—75 rems to hands, forearms, feet and ankles.

Because of know sensitivity of the fetus, the whole body exposure of women of reproductive age should be restricted so that they do not receive doses, at rates in excess of those specified, assuming continuous exposures throughout the year. Thus, the dose received by an embryo during the first two months of pregnancy should normally be less than 1 rem, a dose considered acceptable by the Commission. When pregnancy has been diagnosed, the exposure during the remaining seven months should not exceed a further 1 rem.

Derived Maximum Permissible Levels

For radioactivity in the body, the important parameter is the maximum permissible body burden. This is the activity in the whole body which delivers the maximum permissible dose rate appropriate to continuous occupational exposure.

The maximum permissible concentrations in air and water, if ingested or inhaled daily, will result in the body eventually acquiring the maximum permissible body burden.

For external radiation measurements (internal radiation cannot easily be measured), the annual dose limit of 5 rem year is equivalent to

(*a*) 5000 milligram for 50 weeks, *i.e.*, 100 milligram/week.

(*b*) 1000 milligram for 40 hours, *i.e.*, 2.5 milligram/hr.

The derived level equivalent to 0.3 of the annual dose limit is, then, equivalent to

$$\frac{3}{10} \times 2.5 \text{ or } 0.75 \text{ milligram/hr}.$$

References

1. Criteria for controlling radiation doses to the public after accidental escape of radioactive material. Medical Research Council. Her Majesty's Stationary Office, London, 1975.
2. Environmental Toxicology of Aquatic Radio-Nuclides. Model and Mechanisms, Miller M.W. and Standard. J.N., editors, Ann Arbor Science Publishers, 1975.

12

Pollution Control of Effluents in the Fertilizer Industry

The importance of fertilizers in developing countries where half the population is yet to be properly fed, cannot be underestimated. In spite of fertilizer production and its import, the per hectare consumption of fertilizers in India is still on the lower side, *i.e.*, 15.3kg/hect., in comparison with 355.3 kg/hect. in South Korea, 163.9 kg/hect. in France and 265 kg/hect. in West Germany. These data amply justify the increased production of fertilizers in India. However, this increases the pollution load on natural streams. Nitrogenous fertilizer effluents, particularly, are known to create problems, primarily due to the presence of ammonia. The urea produced from ammonia is the best nitrogenous fertilizer, with 48 percent nitrogen. The effluent can no longer be discharged without treatment, as was being done earlier, in rivers, seas or on the surface as it affects the availability of water for drinking purposes. Strict regulations have, therefore, been made by the State Governments through their Pollution Boards so that the effluents are treated and fall within the prescribed limits before their discharge. This chapter includes the results of two case studies, one conducted at Bombay and the other at Kanpur. It also describes action taken to meet the standards laid down by the Maharashtra/U.P. Prevention of Water Pollution Board (MPWPB/UPWPB) for effluents before they are drained in the creek/river Pandu located on the western boundary of fertilizer complex.

Kanpur Unit

The fertilizer factory situated at Kanpur has an installed capacity of 450,000 tpd of urea, using naphtha as feed stock for producing ammonia. The source of water supply for this fertilizer factory is from the adjacent lower river Ganga canal. Consumption is about 13,500 m^3/day, while approximately 5500 m^3 of effluent has to be disposed of. The main effluents generated in the factory are classified as non-nitrogenous and nitrogenous effluents. The main sources of non-nitrogenous effluents, containing non-nitrogenous substances dissolved in it are: purge from clariflocculated, regenerated waste from the DM water plant via a neutralization pit, black wash water from water treatment plant, purge from cooling tower, boilers down and steam condensate. Total non-nitrogenous effluent generated per day is approximately 2900 m^3.

The main sources of nitrogenous effluents are as follows:

Ammonia Plant

Wash water from carbon dioxide scrubber, cooler catchpot, condensate from acid gas cooler catchpot, condensate from syngas cooler catchpot, cooling water from syngas compressor gland cooling, syngas compressor knockout pots blow down, ammonia synthesis and recovery section drains and process condensate drain (during plant upset).

Urea Plant

Gland cooling water, pump drain/plant washing and crystallizer, cooling tower, purge water. Approximately 2600 m^3 of nitrogenous effluents are generated per day.

Trombay Unit

The second typical example is that of the Trombay Fertilizer Complex, which consists of an ammonia plant (350 Te/D), urea plant (300 Te/D), complex fertilizer (1100 Te/D), methanol plant (130 Te/D) and various acid plants like a nitric acid (320 Te/D), sulphuric acid plant (300 Te/D), Phosphoric acid (100 Te/P_2O_5/D) and various diversification units of other chemicals, e.g., ammonium bicarbonate, mono-, di- and tri methylamines, sodium nitrate, nitric, etc. Other ancillary facilities are steam water treatment packaging, etc.

The total liquid effluent drained into the creek ranges from 10,000 m^3—12,000 m^3 per day. This effluent is in two categories: (1) uncontaminated and (2) contaminated. The contaminated effluents comprise about 40–50 percent of the total discharge.

Uncontaminated. The sources of these effluents are mostly from the drawings of the various cooling towers and condensates or boiler blow down.

Contaminated. The sources are the complex fertilizer plant reactors and dust scrubbers, leakages and washings from the acid plant, effluents from the ammonia plant, containing particulate matter, traces of ammonia, CO_2, etc. urea plant, cooling tower, water treatment plant, condensate from methanol plant and floor washings from various plants especially urea and acid plants.

The standards for disposal of industrial effluents of different states in India and other* leading countries are given in Table 12.1. The standards prescribed in different countries are appreciably different. The necessity for consideration of total pollution load vis-a-vis assimilation capacity, total pollution load vis-a-vis dispersion of industries, substantially higher standard for industrially backward district to encourage rapid industrialization is obvious. The treated effluents from expansion plants of Trombay IV and V would amount to about 30,000 m^3/d. Thus, the total effluent discharge would amount to 40,000–45,000 m^3/d.

Requirements of State Pollution Boards

The requirements of the Madhya Pradesh Water Pollution Board are as follows :

1. The storm water, trade effluent and domestic sewage should be carried by independent drainage systems. When common drains are provided, they should be separated.
2. 'V' notches and flow indicators should be installed at the out fall points of the influents so that all discharges are measured.

BIS Standards

BIS standards for industrial effluents falling into marine coastal areas is covered under IS-1968–1976. The salient tolerance limits are:

Table 12.1(a)
Standards for the disposal of industrial effluents

S. No.	Pollutants	Effluent Board			BIS			WHO			UP. Pollution Preventive Board		
		A	B	C	A	B	C	A	B	C	A	B	C
1	2	3	4	5	6	7	8	9	10	11	12	13	14
1.	Arsenic (as As)	0.2	—	—	0.2	—	—	0.05	0.05	0.05	0.2	—	—
2.	Ammoniacal nitrogen	50	50	—	50	50	—	—	—	—	50	50	—
3.	Anionic detergents	—	—	—	—	—	—	0.2-1	0.2-1	0.2-1	—	—	—
4.	BOD, at 200 C per 5 days	30	500"	500	30	500*	500	—	—	—	30	500*	500
5.	Boron	—	2*	2	—	2*	2	—	—	—	—	2*	2
6.	Colour and odour	0	0	0	—	—	—	5-50	5.50	5-50	—	—	—
7.	COD	250	—	—	250	—	—	—	—	—	250	—	—
8.	Cyanides	0.2	2.0	—	0.2	2.0	—	0.05	0.05	0.05	0.2	2	—
9.	Cadmium	2.0	—	—	2.0	—	—	0.1	0.01	0.01	2	—	—
10.	Chromium (hexavlanent)	0.1	2.0	—	0.1	2.0	—	—	—	—	0.1	2.0	—
11.	Copper	3.0	3.0	—	3.0	3.0	—	0.05-1.5	0.5-1.5	0.5-1.5	3.0	3.0	—
12.	Chlorides	—	600*	600	—	600*	600	200-600	200-600	200-600	—	600*	600
13.	Calcium	—	—	—	—	—	—	75-200	75-200	75-200	—	—	—
14.	Fluorides	2.0	—	—	2.0	—	—	0.8-8.7	0.8-8.7	0.8-8.7	2	—	—
15.	Hardness	—	—	—	—	—	—	100-500	100-500	100-500	—	—	—
16.	Insecticides	—	—	—	—	—	—	—	—	—	0	—	—

(Contd. ...)

Table 12.1(a) (*Contd. ...*)

1	*2*	*3*	*4*	*5*	*6*	*7*	*8*	*9*	*10*	*11*	*12*	*13*	*14*
17.	Iron	—	—	—	—	—	—	0.1-1	0.1-1	0.1-1	—	—	—
18	Lead	0.1	1	—	0.1	1	—	0.1	0.1	0.1	0.1	1	—
19.	Mercury	0.01	1	—	0.01	—	—	0.001	0.001	0.001	0.01	—	—
20.	Magnesium	—	—	—	—	—	—	30-150	30-150	30-150	—	—	—
21.	Manganese	—	—	—	—	—	—	0.05-0.5	0.05-0.5	0.05-0.5	—	—	—
22.	Nickel 3	2	—	3	2	—	—	—	—	3	2	—	
23.	Nitrate	—	—	—	—	—	—	11.3-22.6	11.3-22.6	11 3-22.6	—	—	—
24.	Oil and grease	10	100	30	10	100	30	0.01-0.3	0.01-0.3	0.01-0.3	10	100	30
25.	pH	5.5-9	5.5-9	5.5-9	5.5-9	5.5-9	5.5-9	7-8.5	7-8.5	7-8.5	5.5-9	5.5-9	5 5-9
26.	Phenolic compounds	1	5		1	5		0.001-0.002	0.001-0.002	0.001-0.002	1	5	—
27.	Percent sodium	—	60	60	—	60	60	—	—	—	—	60	60
28.	Radioactive materials (*i*) Alpha emitters μ c/ml	10^{-7}	10^{-7}	10^{-9}	10^{-7}	10^{-7}	10^{-9}	3 nci/1	3 nci/1	3 nci/1	10^{-7}	10^{-7}	10^{-9}
	(*ii*) Beta emitters μ c/ml	10^{-6}	10^{-6}	10^{-6}	10^{-6}	10^{-6}	10^{-6}	30 nci/1	30 nci/1	30 nci/1	10^{-6}	10^{-6}	—
29.	Suspended solids	100	600b		100	600		5-25	5-25	5-25	100	600	—
30.	Sulphides	2	—	—	2	—	—	—	—	—	2	—	—
31.	Selenium	0.05	—	—	0.05	—	—	0.01	0.01	0.1	0.05	—	—
32.	Sulphates	—	1000*	1000	—	1000*	1000	200-400	200-400	200-400	—	100*	1000
33.	Total dissolved solids (inorg.)	—	2100*	2100	—	2100*	2100	500-1500	500-1500	—	—	2100*	2100
34.	Temperature, °C	40	45	—	40	45	—	—	—	—	40	45	—
35.	Total residual chloride	1	—	—	1	—	—	200-600	200-600	200-600	1	—	—

(*Contd. ...*)

1	2	3	4	5	6	7	8	9	10	11	12	13	14
36.	Total hardness mg/1, as $CaCO_3$	—	—	—	—	—	—	100-500	100-500	100-500	—	—	—
37.	Turbidity	—	—	—	—	—	—	5-25	5-15	5-15	—	—	—
38.	Zinc	5	15	—	5	15	—	5-15	5-15	5-15	5	15	—

A = Into Inland surface waters. B = Into Public sewers; C = On land for irrigation

[a] Subject to relaxation or tightening by the local authority

[b] Relaxable to 750 by the local authority

* Wearer requirements shall apply only where, after treatment, the sewage is disposed of on land for irrigation.

Table 12.1 (b)

Indian standards for liquid effluents as prescribed by State Boards for Prevention and Control of Water Pollution

Sl. No.	*Effluent characteristics*	*Karnataka*	*Kerala*	*Maharashtra*	*Rajasthan*	*U.P.*	*W.B.*
1	*2*	*3*	*4*	*5*	*6*	*7*	*8*
1.	Ammoniacal nitrogen, mg/1	50	50	50	—	50	50
2	Arsenic (as As), mg/1	0.2	0.2	—	—	0.2	0.2
3.	BOD, mg/1, (5 days at 20°C)	30	30	100		30-500	30
4.	Barium (as Ba) mg/1	—	—	—	0.3	—	—
5.	COD, mg/1	250	250	250		250	250
6	Chloride (as Cl), mg/l	1	1	—	—	600	—
7.	Cyanide (as CH), mg/l	0.2	—	—	—	0.2	0.2
8	Copper (as Cu), mg/l	3	—	—	—	3	3
9	Cadmium (as Cd), mg/l	2				2	2

(*Contd.* ...)

Table 12.1(a) (*Contd. …*)

1	*2*	*3*	*4*	*5*	*6*	*7*	*8*
10.	DO, mg/1	—	—	5	—	—	—
11.	Free ammonia, mg/1	1.2	1.2	—	—	—	—
12.	Fluorides (as F), mg/1	2	2	10	—	2	2
13.	Free carbon dioxide (CO_2)	—	—	90	—	—	—
14.	Hexavalent chromium (Cr^{+6})	0.1	0.1	—	—	0.1	0.1
15.	Iron (Fe) mg/1	—	—	—	0.3	—	—
16.	Lead (as Pb) mg/1	0.1	—	—	—	0.1	0.1
17.	Mercury (as Hg), mg/1	0.01	—	—	—	0.1	0.1
18.	Nitrates (NO_3) mg/1	—	—	—	50	—	—
19.	Nickel (as Ni), mg/1	3	—	—	—	3	3
20.	Oil and grease, mg/1	10	10	—	—	10-30	10
21.	Particle size of TSS, micron max.	850				850	850
22.	pH	5.5-9.0	5.5-7.0	5.5-9.0	—	5.5-9.0	5.5-9.0
23.	Phosphates (P), mg/1	1.5	5.0	—	—	—	—
24.	Phenolic compounds (C_6H_5OH), mg/1	1.0	—	—	—	1.0	1.0
25.	Residual chlorine (as Cl-), mg/1	1.0	1.0	—	—	1.0	1.0
26.	Sulphates (SO^4), mg/1	—	—	5	—	100	—
27.	Sulphides (as S), mg/1	2.0	—	—	—	2.0	2.0
28.	Selenium (as Se) mg/1	0.05	—	—	—	0.05	0.05
29.	Sodium percentage (as Na)	—	—	—	—	60.0	—
30.	TSS, mg/1	100	100	100	—	100	100
31.	TDS, mg/1	—	—	—	—	2100	—
32.	Temp., °C max.	40	40	—	—	40	40

1	2	3	4	5	6	7	8
33.	Vanadium (as V) mg/l	0.1	—	—	—	—	—
34.	Zinc (as Zn), mg/l	5	5	—	—	5	5

Table 12.1 (c)
International Standards for disposal of Industrial Effluents

S. No.	*Effluent characteristics*	*Japan*	*Switzerland*	*UK*	*USA*
1	2	*3*	*4*	*5*	*6*
1.	Ammoniacal nitrogen (as N), mg/l	—	+	—	50-110
2.	Arsenic (as As), mg/l	0.05	0.1	—	—
3.	BOD, mg/l max. (5 days at 20° C)	—	20	—	—
4.	Barium (as Ba), mg/l	—	5	—	—
5.	COD, mg/l	—	+	—	—
6.	Chlorides (as Cl), mg/l	—	+	—	—
7.	Cyanides (as CN) mg/l	—	0.1	0	—
8	Copper (as Cu), mg/l	—	0.5	10	—
9.	Cadmium (as Cd), mg/l	0.01	0.1	0	
10.	IX), mg/l	—	6	—	—
11.	Dissolved organic carbon substances (as C), mg/l	—	10-15	—	—
12.	Free ammonia, mg/l	—	—	—	75
13.	Fluorides (as F), mg/l	—	10	—	—
14.	Free carbon dioxide (as CO_2), mg/l	—	—	—	

(Contd. ...)

(*Contd. ...*)

1	2	*3*	*4*	*5*	*6*
15.	Hexavalent chromium (as Cr^{+6}), mg/1	0.05	—	—	—
16.	Iron (as Fe), mg/1	—	20	—	—
17.	Lead (as Pb), mg/1	0.1	0.5	10	—
18.	Mercury (as Hg), mg/1	0.0005	0.01	0	—
19.	Nitrates (as NO_3^-), mg/l	—	—	20	25-170
20.	Nickel (as Ni), mg/1	—	2	10	—
21.	Oil and grease, mg/1	—	20	50	—
22.	Organic nitrogen (as N)	—	20		75-125
23.	Phosphate (as P), mg/1	—	—	—	105
24.	Phenolic compounds (C_6H_4OH), mg/1	—	0.05	—	—
25.	PH	—	6.5-8.5	6-10	6-10
26.	Residual chlorine (as Cl), mg/1	—	0.05	—	—
27.	Sulphates (SO_4)	—	+	1000	—
28.	Sulphides (as S)	—	0.1	0	—
29.	Selenium (Se)	—	—	10	—
30.	TSS, mg/1, max.		20		150
31.	Temperature, °C max.		30	43.3	—
32.	Tetravalent chromium (as Cr^4), mg/1	—	0.1	—	—
33.	Trivalent chromium (as Cr^3)	-	2	—	—
34.	Zinc (as Zn), mg/1	—	2	—	—

+ Decided case by case

1. pH	5.5–9.0	
2. Oils and grease	20.0	mg/1
3. Total suspended solids, mg/l max.	100.0	
4. BOD (5 days at 20°C) mg/1 max.	100.0	
5. COD mg/1 max.	250.0	
6. Fluorides (as F) max.	15.0	
7. Ammoniacal nitrogen (N) mg/1 max.	50.0	

In addition, there are limits for many trace metals and non-metals.

Classification of Fertilizer Plants

Indian fertilizer plants can be broadly categorized as follows:

1. Ammonia and urea plants
2. Ammonia, nitric acid and ammonium nitrate plants
3. Ammonia, urea, phospheric acid and complex fertilizer plants.
4. Ammonia, urea, ammonium sulphate and sulphuric acid plants.
5. Ammonia, urea, phosphoric acid, nitric acid, sulphuric acid and complex plants.

The presence of major pollutants in liquid effluents from these plants are indicated by *x* in Table 12.2.

Table 12.2
Presence of major pollutants in liquid effluents of fertilizer plants

Pollutants	*Plant Category*				
	I	*II*	*III*	*IV*	*V*
pH	*x*	*x*	*x*	*x*	*x*
Ammoniacal nitrogen	*x*	*x*	*x*	*x*	*x*
Fluorides			*x*		*x*
Suspended solids		*x*	*x*	*x*	
Chromate from cooling tower (where ever adopted)	*x*	*x*	*x*	*x*	*x*

Typical limits for various nitrogen effluents in plants in the USA based on new technology are given in the Table 12.3.

Table 12.3
Effluent limitation parameters

Sub-category	**Effluents limitation parameters kg/100 kg of product*			*pH range*
	Ammonia (as N)	*Organic (as C)*	*Nitrate (as N)*	
Ammonia	0.055	—	—	6.0-9.0
Urea	0.0325 (non-prill)	0.12 (non-prill)		6.0-9.0
	0.0325 (prill)	0.35 (prill)	—	—
Ammonium nitrate	0.025 (solution)	—	0.0125 (solution)	6.0-9.0 6.0-9.0
	0.05 (non-solution)		0.025 (non-solution)	—

Phosphate	No discharge of process waste water pollutants.
Nitric acid	No discharge of process waste water pollutants.
Ammonium sulphate	No discharge of process waste water pollutants.
Mixed-blend fertilizers+	No discharge of process waste water pollutants.

* Values listed are the maximum/allowed average of daily average for 30 consecutive operating days, i.e., the maximum averages for 30 days. Maximum allowed single-day (average) values are equal to twice the 30-day averages.

\+ These sub-category effluent limitations are draft values only, currently under EPA

Liquid Effluent Control Measure Schemes

IRI, Kanpur

The scheme for treatment of nitrogenous effluents was introduced from the beginning in 1969 and is still in use with suitable modifications being incorporated from time to time for the improvement of effluent quality and to reduce operational problems.

Nitrogenous effluents from the ammonia and urea plants are collected through separate drainage systems into pits from which they are pumped to lagoons of about 45 acres. The material is ultimately discharged into the Pandu river but as this is a seasonal river with little flow during the dry months, the effluents are stored in the lagoons for several months every years. The areas and depths have been located so that the intense solar heat which is readily available at their location can provide the energy necessary to strip out ammonia, hydrolyse urea and evaporate water and volatiles from these liquids. As soon as the flow rate in the Pandu river increases, which happens within a week or two of the onset of the monsoon, effluents held in the lagoons are discharged in a controlled manner relative to the flow in the river.

Trombay Unit

The liquid effluent from the Trombay unit consists of fine carbon particles coming from the gas generation section in the ammonia plant, oil spillages from the compressor house, acidic effluents from the acid group of plants, fluorides and phosphates from the complex fertilizer plants and ammoniacal nitrogen from the ammonia, urea and complex fertilizer plants. After a systematic study of the quantity and quality of various effluents, it was decided to recover and reuse water whenever possible. The remaining effluent is treated before releasing it into the creek. This creek receives effluents from many other industries in the neighbourhood and the water is heavily contaminated. Several schemes as described below have already been implemented to bring the effluents to the quality mentioned above.

Domestic Sewage Separation and Treatment

Plant effluents and sewage are separated by providing a separate drainage system and collection pit. The sewage is subjected to septic tank treatment and the overflow is pumped to the municipal sewers.

Effluent Collection and Measurement

The plant effluents from ammonia, urea and methanol plants are carried in a separate pipe and measuring devices have been provided to continuously measure the effluents going in to the creek. The effluents from the complex fertilizer, sulphuric and nitric acid plants are sent through another channel which is also continuously monitored. The acidic effluents are neutralized by treating with a 10–12 per cent lime solution which is prepared in a central lime staking unit. PH meters are provided at the effluent outlet to control the pH between 5.5 and 9.4.

Ammonia Plant Effluents

The streams coming out of the ammonia plant contain carbon from its gasification section and oil from the compressor bay. In order to remove the carbon from the slurry, a considerable amount of research and development has been done on the type of filter and filter cloth. On the basis of the results obtained a continuous disc filter is suggested. This filter removes fine carbon particles from the slurry containing about 1–2 percent carbon. The filter separates the carbon cake containing 15–20 percent carbon which can easily be handled and transported. The filtrate contains less than 100 ppm of fine carbon particles and is recycled back to the plant. In addition, a pond of 2000 m* capacity has been provided with a view to storing the carbon slurry when the filter is shut down for maintenance. The cost of the entire scheme is about Rs.2 million.

Another stream from the ammonia plant contains oil coming from the compressor bay. In order to bring down the oil content, an API gravity oil separator, followed by a coke trap, has been provided. This brings down the oil content to less than 10 mg/1. Details of the arrangement are shown in Fig. 12.1.

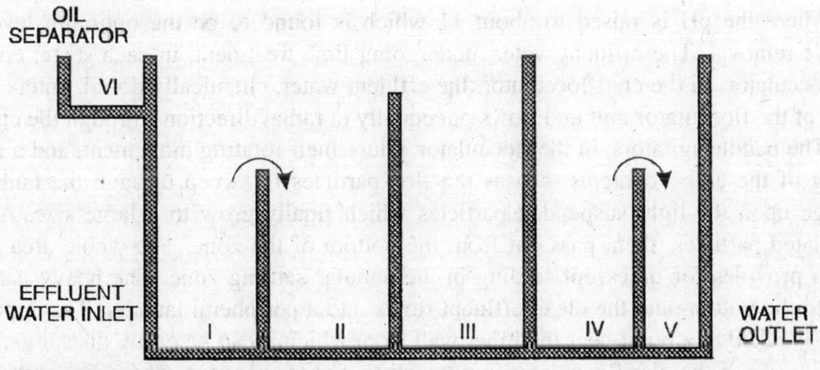

Fig. 12.1 A typical Oil Separator Pit

Phosphoric Acid Plant Effluents

With a view to neutralizing the acidic effluents and removing-the fluorides, a lime slaking unit has been installed. The lime staking plant has a capacity of 25 tpd and produces a 10 percent lime; solution. A network of distribution lines has been provided to distribute the lime solution to various acidic plants to neutralize the acidic effluents, in the neutralization pits, provided in their respective plants.

The major by-product of the phosphate acid plant is gypsum. This is generally used for the production of ammonium sulphate and also in cement manufacture. Whenever there is a slack in demand for gypsum, it is slurried with water and pumped to storage ponds, especially built for this purpose. The overflow from these ponds is sent to a naturalization tank provided, with an agitator, where a lime solution is added to neutralize and precipitate the fluoride. The cost of this system is Rs.2.5 million.

Sulphuric Acid and Nitric Acid Plant Effluents

The effluents from these plants are treated with lime for pH adjustment.

Complex Fertilizer Plant Effluents

The effluents from this plant essentially consist of fluorides, phosphates and ammoniacal nitrogen. An integrated effluent treatment plant for handling the effluents from the existing and the new complex plants is under construction. This plant consists of a lime slaking unit where lime slurry is prepared from burnt lime by using a slaker installation. From the storage bin, lime is uniformly fed to the Drum slaker, using a rotary table feeder. Water is added in the slaker in adequate quantities to make a slurry. A steam hood with a vent is provided at the discharge end of the slaker in view of the exothermic nature of the slaking reaction. The slurry produced in the slaker is passed through a classifier, to separate the coarse particles that are present in lime. At the classifier, additional water is added to obtain die desired slurry consistency. The lime slurry is stored in a tank fitted with an agitator to prevent settlement of lime particles.

The plant effluent is sent to the first reaction tank where the lime solution is added to raise the pH to 7.0–7.5. The second stage limit treatment is given in the second reaction tank where the pH is raised to about 11 which is found to be the optimum level for fluoride removal. The effluent water, undergoing lime treatment, in each stage, enters a clariflocculator. In the clariflocculator, the effluent water, chemically dosed, enters at the centre of the flocculator unit and flows out equally in radial directions through the circular tank. The paddle agitators, in the flocculator, cause their rotating movement, and a gentle stirring of the entire contents, causes the floe particles to sweep through the tank, and impinge upon the light suspended particles which finally grow to a large size. All the flocculated particles, then, pass out from the bottom of the zone. The whole area at the bottom provides for quiescent settling in the annular settling zone. The heavy particles settle to the bottom and the clean effluent flows into a peripheral launder. The deposited sludge is raked to a point near the inner wall from which it can be easily discharged. The underflow from the clariflocculator is pumped to a sludge lagoon where it is dried. The effluent is, then, further treated with acid to bring the pH to 5.5–9.0 and, then, mixed with nonfluoride effluent to bring down the fluoride level to the stipulated level.

Water Treatment Plant Effluents

The effluent from the demineralized water treatment plant, emanating from the action and anion exchanges, consists of acid and alkaline solutions. This is taken out to a separate pond and the pH is finally controlled by either addition of acid or alkali so as to meet the prescribed standards.

Problematic Areas

The main problem, in liquid effluent treatment, is the removal of ammonia. Considerable experimental work was conducted to remove ammonia by biological nitrification and a denitrification process using plant effluents. Since the results were not consistent, further review of the work in this direction elsewhere is continuing. Though air-stripping would bring down the ammonia concentration, this system is not very satisfactory due to the presence of a residential area near the factory.

However, some more likely solutions are described below:

Nitrogen Removal from Liquid Effluent

There are several methods for the treatment of waste water containing nitrogen compounds. The main techniques are:

—Chlorination treatment

—Concentration by ion exchange.

Of the four techniques mentioned above, chlorination is not adequate for treating highly concentrated waste. Concentration by ion exchange is not yet feasible

Stripping by air is one of the less expensive methods for treating highly concentrated waste, though it results in air pollution trade-off unless some recovery facilities, which are rather expensive, are installed. Stripping by steam is a potential method for relatively high concentrated waste. Stream from the top contains a high amount of ammonia and may be recycled to the process.

Biological treatment is an economically feasible way to remove nitrogen at a high rate. While several methods are under investigation for the removal of nitrogen from waste waters, biological treatment is the most promising.

Biological Treatment of Ammoniacal Nitrogen

The treatment process, as given in Figure 12.2, consists of two biological sludge systems. The waste water flows through these systems in series.

In the final settling basin, activated sludge, is separated from treated water and is recycled to the first stage.

This process essentially isolates two biological activities that can occur in conventional activated sludge treatment. The activities are nitrification and denitrification.

Nitrification is a process in which ammoniacal nitrogen is biologically oxidized to form a nitrite, which is, in turn, oxidized to form a nitrate. Oxidation to a nitrite is accomplished by Nitrosomonas while a nitrate is formed by Nitrobacter.

In the nitrification basin, there is a requirement for oxygen and inorganic carbonaceous compounds. The latter are required by nitrifying bacteria for growth. It may be possible to maintain the removal efficiency of ammoniacal nitrogen at about 95 percent under optimum environmental conditions.

Denitrification is the next unit process in the sequence. During biological denitrification, nitrates and nitrites are reduced to nitrogen gas. The ability to bring about denitrification is characteristic of a wide variety of common facultative bacteria, including the general *Pseudomonas, Achromobacter* and *Bacillus*.

Denitrification requires an organic carbon source, in the presence of organisms, in active metabolism. The absence of oxygen is also necessary in the denitrification basin. Under such anaerobic conditions, the micro-organisms can use the ionic oxygen or nitrates or nitrites to bring about the oxidation of the organic carbon source, just as oxygen is used under aerobic conditions. For the organic carbon source, which is added to the denitrification stage, methanol is usually used. Denitrification of nitrates is a two-step process:

First step: $NO_3^- + 1/3\ CH_3OH \rightarrow NO_2^- + 1/3\ CO_2 + 2/3\ H_2O$ (12.1)

Second step: $NO_2^- + 1/2\ CH_3OH \rightarrow 1/2\ N_2^- + 1/2 CO_2 + 1/2\ H_2O + 0H^-$ (12.2)

Overall $NO_3^- + 5/6\ CH_3OH \rightarrow 1/2\ N_2 + 5/6\ CO_2 + 7/6\ H_2O + OH^-$ (12.3)

It may be possible to maintain the denitrifying rate of almost 100 percent under optimum operating conditions.

At the mixed liquor outlet of the denitrification stage, flash aeration is provided. In this reaeration basin, nitrogen gas bubbles are separated from the denitrifying sludge and the organic carbon, being added excessively in the denitrification, is oxidized completely. At the end of this biological process, activated sludge settles in the clarifier and is recycled to the nitrification stage. The final effluent contains only a few ppm of ammoniacal nitrogen.

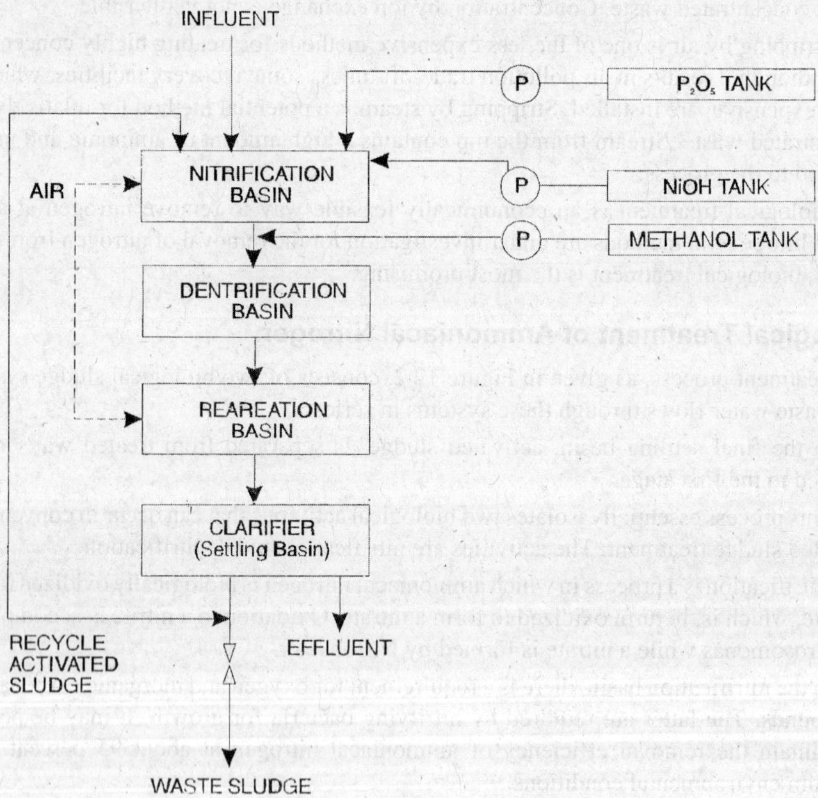

Fig. 12.2 Flow Diagram for Nitrification and Denitrification

Waste Water Recycling and Recovery System

Most of the present-day complex fertilizer plants, which discharge effluents containing phosphate, fluorine and nitrogen, are based on modern technology, which has been designed on the basis of a proper heat balance and water balances, in which most of the effluents are recycled back into the system, and the very limited quantity which does emerge is suitably treated and, then, discharged. This has become necessary with the very stringent pollution legislation, in most countries, today, which aims at reduction of the contaminants in effluents. Such reduction can only be achieved when the following requirements are fulfilled:

1. Recovery of nutrients in vapours and gases, from each process step, with subsequent recycling to the process.
2. Recycling of water used for scrubbing and cleaning. To avoid build up and process upsets, when recycling the water, a water treatment unit must be installed.

Vapours and gases are acid or alkaline and must be treated according to their nature. Acid gases, i. e., gases containing nitric acid, normally with small quantities of fluorine, can be treated with clean water. Ammoniacal gases, mainly from the neutralization and conversion section, can be absorbed in nitric acid or any other absorption media. As for vapours from the evaporators, these contain fluorine and must be treated in a fluorine scrubber before they are treated with nitric acid to absorb the ammonia.

Waste water is treated in a separate system, where P_2O_5 is removed and returned to the digestion section.

In a complex fertilizer plant, producing about 1,000 tonnes per day of NP fertilizer of the composition NP 28-14-0, the system has been designed to meet the following effluent requirements:

1. Phosphate, kg/day as P = 12
2. Nitrogen, tonne/day = 3.

Such systems are, in operation, based on modern advances and, it is claimed, that this has reduced the P_2O_5 effluent to 60 percent of the above limits, resulting in a P_2O_5,efficiency of about 99 percent, whereas the nitrogen removal has been reduced to about 50 percent of the above mentioned limits.

Choice of the Method of Treatment

The choice of the method of treatment is determined by the conditions prevailing in each situation such as (1) The character of waste (2) Circumstances pertaining to the body of the water, being used for final disposal (3) State Health Department requirement (4) The cost of the plant and its operation. In general, waste treatment and disposal practices may be classified into three categories:

1. Disposal of untreated waste by dilution
2. Primary treatment, which removes part of the suspended, floating and suitable solids.
3. Secondary treatment (complete) usually proceeds by primary treatment, designed to provide some means of satisfying the oxygen demand (reduction of BOD). In this treatment further removal (after primary treatment) of solids is with the aid of living organisms.

This treatment is also known as biological treatment.

Treatment Operations

Treatment operations are divided into three basic groups:

1. Physical
2. Chemical
3. Biological

Physical Treatment. It includes those operations which do not involve chemical changes in the waste.

Mechanical operations

1. Screening (separation of coarse, suspended and floating matter)
2. Skimming or flotation (separation of grease and oil)
3. Sedimentation (separation of finely divided suspended matter)
4. Filtration (separation of finely divided suspended matter).

Physical operations

1. Heating
2. Cooling
3. Boiling
4. Evaporation.

Chemical Treatment. The treatment involves the addition of chemicals to the waste and is concerned with chemical changes or reactions in the constituents of the waste. Topical of chemical treatment processes are:

1. Neutralization of acid or alkalies
2. Precipitation of metal hydroxide
3. Oxidation with air, ozone, chlorine and other agents

Biological Treatment. Separation of stabilization of purtrescible matter in suspension, colloidal state.

It includes

1. Aerobic biological treatment
2. Anaerobic biological treatment.

Aerobic treatment

1. Lagooning
2. Biological sludge process
3. Activated sludge process
4. Contact aerators
5. Oxidation ponds.

Anaerobic treatment

It is usually thought of as sludge digestion, but it also includes the fermentation of certain organic waste.

Sludge Treatment

1. Digestion
2. Concentration or thickening by stirring or centrifuging
3. Coagulation by heating, chemical treatment of freezing
4. Elutriation
5. Biological flotation (more or less experimental)
6. Air drying on sand beds
7. Filtration through cloth, under vacuum
8. Heat drying
9. Incineration.

Solid sludge can be disposed of without or with treatment. Sludge could be treated by the septic tank, Imhoff tank and separate sludge digester methods. Final disposal of treated sludge can be done by incineration, as land fill and as fertilizer. Similarly, liquid waste can be disposed of by an intermittent sand filter, trickling filter, contact bed, activated sludge process or chlorination methods.

Chemical Unit Process Used

Description	*Application*
Adsorption	Removal of soluble organic compounds
Coagulation	Flocculation, removal of colloidal material
Ion exchange	Removal of specific ions and compounds, removal of ionized organic and inorganic compounds
Base neutralisation acid base	pH control
Oxidation (air, Cl_3, ozone)	Disinfection
Reduction	Conversions of soluble compounds to a volatile or precipitated form for removal
Sorption	Removal of soluble organics

Biological Unit Process Used

	Description	*Application*
Aerobic	Activated sludge process, trickling filters, Lagoons	Removal of soluble or colloidal organic materials
Anaerobic	Contact process, digestion, filtration	Removal of sludge and organic waste Removal of soluble organic materials
	Imhoff tank	
Spray		Removal of soluble organic materials
Stabilization pond		Removal of soluble organic materials

Unit Operations and Process Used in Waste Treatment

Description	*Application*
Dialysis-osmosis	Recovery of process material, removal of dissolved solids
Distillation	Separation of liquid wastes for recovery
Evaporation	Sludge dewatering, removal of volatile materials and concentration of liquid wastes
Filtration	Removal of suspended solids, sludge dewatering
Filter press	Removal of suspended floating solids
Gas transfer (adsorption, aeration, stripping)	Addition or removal of gas
Screening	Removal of coarse floating or suspended material
Sedimentation	Removal of particulate matter, biological floe, chemical floe
Skimming	Removal of grease, oil
Solvent extraction	Removal of solid waste constituents, recovery of soluble process materials.

Procedure for Analysis

The various procedures used for the treatment of different salient liquid effluents are indicated below:

1. *pH*. The pH of the effluent is directly measured on pH meter.
2. *Suspended solids*. A known volume of the effluent, after proper shaking, is filtered through a gooch crucible which is already dried and weighed. The residue on the gooch crucible is dried at 110° C for 2 hours and weighed.
3. *Ammoniacal nitrogen*. Ammonium salts, when they react with formalin, produce the corresponding acid. This acid is estimated by treating against standard sodium hydroxide using Thymol Blue as indicator. From the volume of acid produced, the ammoniacal nitrogen is calculated in mg/1.
4. *Chemical Oxygen Demand (COD)*. A known volume of effluent (filtered) is refluxed with potassium dichromate and sulphuric acid, and the excess of dichroinate is titrated with ferrous ammonium sulphate. The amount of oxidizable organic matter is proportional to the potassium dichromate consumed.
5. *Fluoride*. Fluoride is separated from the other constituents of water by distillation of Fluosilicic acid from a solution of the sample in an acid with a higher boiling point. The liberated HF is absorbed in either distilled water or alkali and titrated against standard Thorium Nitrate solution with Methyl Thymol Blue as an indicator.
6. *Dissolved Oxygen (DO)*. Oxygen dissolved in water is made to react with $MnSO_4$. KIKOH solution is added followed by H_2SO_4 (conc.) Liberated Iodine is titrated against standard sodium thiosulphate solution.
7. *Biological Oxygen Demand (BOD)*. A known volume of sample is added to the dilution water to have a 2 percent strength of sample. Initial DO of this diluted sample is determined. Then, the diluted sample is incubated for 5 days at 20°C. The DO is again determined after this period. The difference between these two DO figures represents the Biochemical Oxygen Demand.

Determination of P_2O_5 has not been outlined as this is a well-known method.

With the help of modem technology which is in operation in the development various scrubbers is balanced in the heat and water balance such that most of the liquid effluents are recycled back into the system. In the urea plant, the dust which emanates from the prilling tower is scrubbed and re-used in the absorbers. Similarly, in the complex fertilizer plant, the reaction fumes and the dust containing NP are scrubbed and recycled back into the system so as to minimize liquid effluents. In the new plants being installed at Trombay and other placed in this country strict control has been exercised to ensure that effluents are kept at the minimum level consistent with available modern technological advances.

Pollution Control of Gaseous Effluents

The main gaseous levels that have to be controlled are SO_2, SO_3 + mist, NO_x, carbon monoxide, fluorine, hydrocarbons and particulate matter. Any fertilizer production unit which has ammonia, urea and comples plants, coupled with the manufacture of intermediate/raw materials required for complex fertilizers invariably results in the emission of SO_2, NO_x and dust.

The emissions of SO_2, NO_x and particulate matter, from the fertilizer plant at Bombay, before pollution control measures were adopted, were as follows:

Pollutant	*Emission in tpd*
SO_2	11.2
NO_x	7.5
Dust	5.3

Since then several antipollution measures have been implemented and the gaseous emission has been considerably reduced. The SO_2 has been cut down to 7.5 tpd. Total dust emission even after the installation of 1200 tpd complex plant is only 2.5 tpd, which is lower than the emission from the old plant. As regards the NO_x emission, this will be of the order of 3.7 tpd, even after the installation of a 750 tpd nitric acid plant.

The various sources and method of control of gaseous effluents are as follows:

Sulphur Oxides

Source 1: Sulphuric acid plants based on sulphur or sulphur based raw materials such as pyrites; ore roasters for recovery of metals as Zu, Cu, Lead, etc. The unabsorbed gases contain SO_2 and SO_3 + mist.

Source 2: Boiler houses where steam is generated by the use of fuel oil. The sulphur content in oil which may be 3 percent is converted into SO_2 and vented to the atmosphere through boiler stacks. Coals fired boilers also emit SO_2 depending on the sulphur content of the coal.

Source 3: The various furnaces or kilns based oil used for drying raw materials such as rock phosphate and granulated fertilizers, cement etc., emit SO_2.

Source 4: H_2S from ammonia plants.

The SO_2 emissions from a large single-train, 900 Te/day ammonia plant, based on the latest technology and using fuel oil as feedstock, like the plant at Nangal, Sindri modernization, Bhatinda, Panipat, etc., are as follows:

The emission from a steam generation unit using normal fuel oil would be 33 Te SO_2 per day. However, if fuel oil with a low sulphur content of 1 percent, as available in LSHS, is used, the emissions could be brought down to one third at 11 Te S02 per day.

Control of H_2S

Feed stocks generating gas for the synthesis of ammonia are based on naphtha, fuel oil or coke. Since almost all the feedstocks contain sulphur constituents, the synthesis gas, H_2S, is produced as an effluent gas. During its purification, the burning of H_2S with air gives rise to SO_2 which causes environmental pollution problem in the neighbouring areas. The quantity of H_2S depends on the type of feedstock and its origin, so that with varying amounts of sulphur in the feedstock, varying amount of H_2S is produced in various locations.

Measures. H_2S could be converted into SO_2 by controlled combustion with air and finally catalytically converted into sulphuric acid. This method is preferable in locations where a sulphuric acid plant is already installed. Alternatively, H_2S could be converted back to sulphur by the well proved 'Claus Process'. The sulphur can, then, be sold as such, thus, increasing the economy of the industry.

Control of SO_2 and SO_2 + Mist

Emissions from sulphuric acid plants could be controlled by the use of a double contact-double absorption technology for manufacture of sulphuric acid as against the conventional technology which is currently common in India. The latter is now described.

Conventional Process. In this process, the reaction of SO_2 being oxidized to SO_3 is carried out in a converter using a catalyst containing V_2O_5. The SO_2 yield is governed by thermodynamic equilibria and kinetics. Due to adiabatic conditions and the exothermic reaction heat (42342 Btu/lb mol at 77°F), the temperature of the reaction gas rises until its composition approaches the equilibrium conversion and heat must be removed if further reaction is required. Thus, at lower feed temperatures, conversions may be obtained but will be accompanied by lower reaction rates. At lower reaction rates, the catalyst requirement increases, thus, increasing pressure drop through the catalyst bed, resulting in higher operating costs. Hence, higher conversions and lower catalyst requirements, the optimum balance between which has to be ensured, are both dependent upon temperatures. The usual commercial practice is to use a feed temperature of438–446°C, in a four stage conversion, with 170-180 litres of catalyst per day, per tonne of sulphuric acid product. Below 438° C, the reaction rate slows down and is negligible around 3 99°C. Typical plant data are given below:

1. 8 percent SO_2 from sulphur burning
2. 13 percent O_2 and 79 percent N_2.
3. SO_2 conversion at four catalyst stages 72,93, 96.8 and 98 percent.

The SO_3 is, then, absorbed in 98 percent sulphuric acid.

$$SO_3 + H_2O \rightarrow H_2SO_4 + \text{Heat}$$

The overall sulphur conversion efficiency is 97 percent. Based on this, the consumption of sulphur per tonne of H_2SO_4 produced works out to be 0.336 tonne (theoretical 0.326) and, hence, die total loss in the stack would be 20 kg of SO_2 per tonne of sulphuric acid produced.

The emissions from the conventional plant stack, depending upon their performance, dependent on various factors, vary from 0.15 percent to 0.25 percent as SO_2 (v/v). The SO_3 + acid mist varies from 300–500 ppm as 100 percent H_2SO_4.

Double-Contact Double-Absorption Process (DCPA). It is similar to a conventional plant up to the conversion step. The SO_3 formed after the 2nd or 3rd stages is removed in a primary absorber and the remaining gas, now with a very high O_2/SO_2 ratio, is returned to a second converter. A heat exchanger or a series of heat exchangers reheats the gas from the absorber and cools the converted gas going into it. The second converter provides additional conversion and acid recovery in a second absorber. By this process, the effluent SO_2 content can be brought down to 500 ppm (v/v) and acid mist to 100 ppm (v/v). The sulphur efficiency is 99 percent. Since the S02 content in the gas to the 1st converter could be raised to 13 percent (conventional 8 percent), the plant capacity of the older plants on conversion could be raised by 40–50 per nt. In view of very high sulphur efficiencies, this must be considered the best solution i the problem of emission control from a sulphuric acid plant.

The fertilizer factory at Trombay has converted their 200 tonne per day sulphuric acid plant to the DCDA technology at a cost of Rs.14.0 million. The plant was commissioned in April 1977 and its capacity was raised to 300 tonne per day while emissions of SO_2 are 400–500 ppm and SO_3 + acid mist to less than 30 mg/m^3 (100 ppm).

There are various scrubbing processes which bring down the SO_2 from source 2nd & 3rd. These are detailed as follows:

Scrubbing Process for Stack Treatment. There are various developments in this field and various treatment processes have been designed to reduce the SO_2 + SO_3 emission from a sulphuric acid plant. Most of the processes comings could not be commercialized.

There are exceptions, however, and some of the successful commercial processes are described below:

Ammonia Scrubbing. In this process the stack gases are scrubbed with aqueous ammonia solution and the product, when it reacts with H_2SO_4 in another stage, yields ammonia sulphate. The reactions are:

1. $2NH_4OH + SO_2 \rightarrow (NH_4)_2SO_3 + H_2O$ (12.4)
2. $(NH_4)SO_3 + SO_2 + HO_2 \rightarrow 2NH_4HSO_2$ (12.5)
3. $2NH_4HSO_3 + H_2SO_4 \rightarrow (NH_4)_2SO_4 + 2SO_2 + 2H_2O$ (12.6)
4. $(NH_4)_2SO_3 + H_2SO_4 \rightarrow (NH_4)2SO_4 + SO_2 + H_2O$ (12.7)

Ammonium sulphate as a by-product is produced in solution which can be concentrated to recover ammonium sulphate which is sold as fertilizer. This process is being used at GSFC, Baroda, and FACT, Alwaye. Sulphur dioxide, on drying, can be recycled back to the sulphuric acid plant or sold as liquefied SO_2. The emissions can be brought down to less than 100 ppm.

Na_2CO_3 Absorption to Produce Sodium sulphite. Sulphur dioxide is absorbed in a concentrated sodium sulphate solution made alkaline by soda ash. A bleed stream is indirectly heated and crystallized. The crystals are centrifuged and dried. Alternatively, the sodium sulphite solution, after concentration, can be spray dried.

The main reactions are:

$$Na_2CO_3 + SO_2 \rightarrow Na_2SO_3 + CO_2 \quad (12.8)$$

$$Na_2CO_3 + SO_3 \rightarrow Na_2SO_4 + CO_2 \quad (12.9)$$

Such a unit is operating at Alembic Chemical Works, Baroda.

Magnesium Oxide Absorption of SO2 with SO3 Recovery. Sulphur dioxide is absorbed in a magnesium sulphite oxide slurry. The bleed stream is centrifuged. SO_2 gas is scrubbed, the gas is cooled, water condensed and the gas is recycled to the drying tower of the acid plant. The reactions are as follows:

1. $MgO + SO_2 + 6H_2O \rightarrow MgSO_3.6H_2O$ (12.10)
2. $MgO + SO_3 + 7H_2O \rightarrow MgSO_4.7H_2O$ (12.11)
3. $MgO + H2SO_4 \rightarrow MgSO_4 + H_2O$ (12.12)
4. $MgSO_3 \rightarrow MgO + SO_2$ (12.13)
5. $2MgSO_4 + C \rightarrow 2MgSO_3 + CO_2$ (12.14)

Such a process has been commercialized in Japan and is used for scrubbing boiler house effluents.

Non-Regenerative Process Using Lime. Scrubbing with lime/lime stone is one such process being used in Japan where there is a shortage of gypsum. Commonly used agents include lime stone, lime, dolomite and solid carbide wastes from acetylene plants. The reaction are:

$$CaCO_3 + SO_2 \rightarrow CaSO_3 + CO_2 \quad (12.15)$$

$$Ca(OH)_2 + SO_2 \rightarrow CaSO_3 + H_2O \quad (12.16)$$

$$CaSO_3 + \tfrac{2}{5} O_2 + 2H \rightarrow CaSO_4.2H_2O \quad (12.17)$$

This has high initial costs but low cost of products.

Monsanto Process. The process is known as Cat-Ox. Hot flue gas is taken directly from the boiler at 510° C and passed through an electrostatic precipitator, then, to a catalystic converter for conversion of SO_2 to SO_3. Subsequent absorption yields acid at 77 percent concentration. The drawbacks of this process are the high capital investment and operating costs and the product acid concentration.

Other Fixed-Bed Processes. Other processes are available such as the use of active carbon, zinc oxide and molecular sieves.

Control of Nitrogen Oxides (NO_x)

Source 1: From nitric acid plant effluent gas
Source 2 : From the oil pipe effluent of automobiles and boiler houses fired on coal.

Nitric Acid Plant. In the nitric acid plant, the main effluent is from the absorption towers of the acid plant where the tail gas contains unabsorbed NO + NO_2. Normally, the NO + NO_2 content of these gases used to be fairly high (from 2500–3000 ppm) depending on the process employed. In a nitric acid plant, with a capacity of 300 tonnes per day, N, vented per day, could be as high as the equivalent of 5–6 tonnes of nitric acid per day.

Measure. By selection of the latest technology, it has been possible to reduce the NO_x content in the stack gases to below 200 ppm by the following methods:

1. Increasing the absorption volume in the absorber. In case of medium pressure plants, this could bring down NO_x level to 5000 ppm. In the case of dual pressure processes, some designers claim to reduce it to 200 ppm level.
2. By use of a catalytic converter, to reduce the NO_x to 200 ppm level, by catalytically treating NO_x with a hydro carbon gas.
3. By use of caustic/soda as scrubbing.
4. By use of a chilled nitric acid wash.

Due to these innovations, the acid which was formerly going to waste as a pollutant could be converted into a useful product. The recovery would depend on the NO_x level that could be tolerated, in particular locations, and the regulations applicable in that area.

The emission could be reduced to the following levels for every 100-tonne-per-day capacity nitric acid plant with improved technology.

NO_x *level*	As HNO_3 *tonne*
800 ppm	0.75
500 ppm	0.44
200 ppm	0.18

This could bring down the consumption of ammonia, per tonne of nitric acid, so that nitric acid can be made more economically.

Acid Mist Removal

The sulphuric acid plant produces a fine acid mist which has to be controlled in order to avoid environmental pollution. Even with the best operational conditions, there would generally be an acid mist content in the stack gases of the order of 300–500 μg/m^3. The acid mist particles are minute in size—a bulk of them is less than 20 micron. In the Trombay DCDA plant, the mist removal is accomplished in two stages.

The first stage mist eliminator is used after intermediate absorption and the second one after the final absorption at Trombay. The acid mist content after the second brink mist eliminator can be brought down to as low as 30 micro g/m$_3$ which is almost 1/10th of original mist emissions. The mist eliminator is made of glass fiber. It is designed to remove virtually all particles above 3 microns in size and 99 percent of those which are smaller, utilizing the Brownian movement. Both increase the collection efficiency as the particle size decreases where majority of the particles are over 3 microns; the particles impinge on the fiber and are, thus, collected. The brink mist eliminator removes the submicron particles, thus, eliminating the harmful air pollutants including the plume from the stack.

Carbon Monoxide

The emissions from automobiles as well as the petrochemical industry where CO is an effluent gas, pose a hazard. Carbon could be used as a fuel gas and converted to CO_2.

Fluorine

The biggest problem from the phosphoric acid plant is the emission of fluorine. Fluorine emissions pose many problems to the health of the people as it causes bone decay and is also harmful to plant life.

Earlier, long chimneys used to be installed to disperse the fluorine but these are, often, of no use today due to nearby residential areas, as the fluorine-containing gas will settle after some time and create problems.

Measures. The fluorine is recovered as a useful hydrofluoro-silicic acid which can be used for the manufacture of cryolite and other fluorine-bearing compounds like aluminium fluorine. In India, this is of utmost importance as cryolite is presently being imported into the country for the aluminium industry. The phosphoric acid industry can bring in a good return and save foreign exchange by the manufacture of fluorine bearing compounds.

Super phosphate/Triple Superphosphate Plant

Superphosphate is made by acidification of rock phosphate with sulphuric acid. Similarly, TSP is made by acidification of rock phosphate with phosphoric acid. In both these processes, fluorine is evolved which till recently was creating a lot of pollution problems similar to those in the phosphoric acid industry.

Various processes have been developed for the recovery of this fluorine as in the phosphate industry, and hydro-fluo-silicic acid is recovered. It is possible to recover 30 to 40 percent of the total fluorine in the rock as hydro-fluo-silicic acid and this can, in turn, be converted into sodium silico fluorine or cryolite.

In India, there are two plants operating on this process and a few others are in the developing stage. Gas from the superphosphate and TSP is piped to the adjacent fluorine based industries and such units work as ancillary units and, thus, gainfully utilize the fluorine. Indian know-how is available for proper conversion of these gases to $A1F_6$ and cryolite.

Emissions. With proper controls and recovery systems, it is possible to bring down the fluorine-based gas as follows:

TSP	0.05 kg/F/tonne TSP
Single super phosphate	0.075 kg/tonne SP(0.425 kgF/tonneP_2O_5)

The existing super phosphate factories which don not recover fluorides have emissions as high as 0.6-0.7 kg/F/tonne of superphosphate.

Hydrocarbons

In ammonia synthesis, methane is the main hydrocarbon that is formed by the reaction:

$$CO + 3H_2 = CH4 + H_2O$$

In order to reduce the inerts from the synthesis loop, this has to be purged out and normally the methane is burnt in the flare header converted to CO_2. Hydrocarbon pollution, therefore, as such does not pose any significant problem. Even if ventors unburned, the amount of ammonia produced would not be more than 5 kgs per tonne (standard 4 kg/tonne).

The main source of hydrocarbon is the effluent gas from oil refining. This problem could be solved by either reducing emissions, using developed technologies or burning the hydrocarbon efficiently as is generally done. The latter solution, however, is not being heavily criticized in view of the world shortage of energy.

Particulate Matter

These are emitted from various industries but mainly from:

1. Boilers, especially powerhouse boilers based on coal
2. Boilers from sugar factories based on coal/bagasse
3. Dust from cement kilns
3. Dust from mineral grinding mills

In the fertilizer industry, the dust could emanate from:

1. granulation plants
2. urea prilling towers and
3. grinding mills for coating agent/rockphosphate.

Solution (*i*) Dust emission could be reduced by installation of good efficient cyclones or filters. In case of dust, which is hydroscopic such as that containing ammonium nitrate, cyclones followed by wet scrubbers have been successfully used.

Now cyclonic scrubbers have been installed at Trombay for washing the dust from complex fertilizer granulation plants, using a venture scrubber. The efficiency of such scrubbers, at inlet dust level of 2 mg/litre, is 97 percent.

In other industries, particulate matter can be reduced by installing efficient cyclones, electrostatic precipitators, bag filters and wet scrubbers.

Emission Standard

The BIS is considering the framing of emission standard to guide the Central and State Governments and other local bodies in establishing rules regarding air pollution.

In arriving at a decision on the tolerance limits, the local authorities should give due consideration to local conditions and, in special cases, they may relax the limits or make them more rigid. These standards, framed by the BIS, are as follows:

Sulphur Dioxide

(*a*) From sulphuric acid plants	Plants up to 200 TeD of H_2SO_4	16 kg tonne of product acid (100 percent)
	Plants above 200 TeD	12 kg/tonne of product
	New plants upto 200 TeD	12 kg/tonne of product
	New plant above 200 tonne/D	4 kg/tonne of product
(b) From refineries		3 kg SO_2/tonne of crude feed processed for existing plant

Sulphur Trioxide (SO_2) from Sulphuric Acid Plants

Existing plants	—	5 kg/tonne of product (100 percent H_2SO_4)
New Plants		
(*a*) Up to 200 Tonne/D	—	5 kg/tonne of product (100 percent H_2SO_4)
(*b*) Above 200 Tonne/D	—	5 kg/tonne of product

Nitrogen Oxides as NO_2

Existing plants	—	24 kg NO_2/tonne of HNO_3
New plants		3 kg NO_2/tonne HNO_3

Fluorine (F_2)

(*a*) *Phosphoric Acid Plants*

Existing	—	60 mg/Nm^3 of effluent gas
New	—	25 mg/Nm^3 of effluent gas

(*b*) *Single Super Phosphate Plants*

Existing	—	0.5 kg/tonne of product
New	—	0.1 kg/tonne of product

Particulate Matter

Particulate matter, when emitted through stack, shall not exceed 500 mg/Nm^3 for single super phosphate plants and shall not exceed 4 kg/ tonne of products in case of triple super phosphate plants.

In the case of nitrogenous fertilizer plants, the particulate matter in the form of dust for a urea plant, shall not exceed the following:

Existing plants	6 kg/tonne of product
New plants	2 kg/tonne of product

Ammonia

Existing units	31 kg/tonne product
New units	14 kg/tonne product

Hydrocarbons

Note more than 5 kg of CH_4 per tonne of ammonia.

Effect of Pollutants

The salient effects of some pollutants, in air, on the human system, or, otherwise, are, briefly, discussed as follows:

Sulphur Dioxide

The effect of sulphur dioxide is mostly confined to the toxicity caused By the reaction of SO_2 with moist air and the formation of acids. SO_2 is an irritant to the eyes, nose, throat and lungs, and induces reflex coughing (5 parts per million); at higher concentrations, *i.e.*, 200 parts per million, it is likely to induce rapid and severe toxic effects. WHO (1972) has recorded that SO_2 is a water soluble gas that acts as a powerful irritant to the mucous membranes of the eyes and the upper respiratory tract. It causes rapid and acute irritation of the eyes with tears and redness; its action on the upper respiratory tract causes cough, shortness of breath and spasms of the larynx.

The toxic effects of sulphur dioxide maybe summarized as follows:

1. 1 ppm for 1 hour or 0.3 ppm	Damage to green plants for 8 hours (average level)
2. 5 ppm for 1 hour (serious level)	Broncho-contriction in human beings
3. 10 ppm for 1 hour	Severe distress in human beings (emergency level).

Long Term Effects

0.01–0.2 ppm	Metal corrosion, impaired pulmonary function. Prolonged exposure to relatively low levels of SO_2 has been associated with increased cardiovasular morbidity.

Air quality standards for SO_2 in various countries are given in the Table 12.4.

Table 12.4
Air Quality Standards for SO2 in PPM

Country	*States*	*Average Time*			*Remarks*
		24 hr	*1 hr*	*Other*	
America	California	—	10	–	Emergency level
		—	5	—	Series level
		—	1	0.3 (0 hr)	Adverse level
	Colorado	0.1	0.5	—	Not to exceed more than 1 per cent of the time in any three months
	Delaware	0.8	0.21	—	95th percentile (annual basis)
	Rural	0.02	0.05	—	Geometric mean (50th percentile, annual basis)
	Residential	0.10	0.25	—	
		0.03	0.07		
	Industrial	0.15	0.35	—	
		0.06	0.12	—	
	Commercial	0.12	0.28	—	
		0.04	0.09		

(Contd. ...)

(*Contd. ...*)

	Florida Dade Country	—	—	0.1 1	←(8 hr) ←(20 min.)	
	Missouri St. Louis	0.1		0.02	←(1 yr., tentative)	
	Metropolitan area	0.5	0.1	.25	←(5 min.)	
	Montana	0.01		0.02	←(1 year)	
	New York	0.1	0.25	—		Not to exceed 1% time in a year
		0.15	0.40	—		
America	Pennisylvania	0.25	0.50	0.05	←(30 days)	Non industrial areas
	South Carolina	0.1	0.3	—		Industrial areas
	Texas	0.17	0.5			
	Industrial	0.3	—	0.5	←(30 min.)	
	Other	0.7	—	0.4	←(20 min.)	
USSR		0.058		0.19	←(20 min.)	
Polland		0.13	—	0.35	←(20 min.)	Protected area
		0.03		0.10	←(20 min.)	For specially protected area
GDR		0.15		0.20	← 30 min.)	Not to be exceeded more than once 30 min. aver, time
		0.06	—	0.19	← (30 min.)	
		0.20	—	0.30	← (30 min.)	Industrial
Canada		0.10	—	0.30	←(30 min.)	Residential
Netherlands		0.05	0.05	—		
Romania		0.09	—	0.35	←(30 min.)	
Sweden		0.10	—	0.25	←(30 min.)	
Switzerland		0.20	—	0.30	←(30 min.)	
March-Oct.		0.30		0.50	←(30 min.)	
Nov. Feb.						

Oxides of Nitrogen

Oxides of nitrogen can have biological and phytotoxic effects and they are intimately involved in the formation of photochemical smog. Nitrogen dioxide is far more toxic than nitric oxide.

The toxic action of nitrogen dioxide is primarily one of irritation of the lower respiratory tract, with pulmonary oedema developing in severe cases. In milder forms of poisoning, nausea, vomiting and vertigo, with cyanosis have been observed. Methaemoglobinaemia* may also be observed. Such severe symptoms are, however, unlikely to be caused by the concentrations normally found in polluted air. The Threshold Limit Value** (TLV) for nitrogen dioxide is a concentration of 9 mg/m^3. Damage to vegetation has been reported following a one-hour exposure to 1 mg/m^3.

* The formation of methaemoglobin in the blood, which inhibits its capacity to carry oxygen.

** The concentration which can be inhaled for an S-hour day 5-day week without Concentrations of nitrogen oxides (either as NO or NO_2) as low as 0.2 mg/m^3 can contribute to the formation of photochemical smog, a very unpleasant form of pollution, which is frequently experienced in the USA.

Fluorine

In general, available evidence suggests that damage caused by atmospheric fluorides to vegetation and animals is much more wide-spread than its ill effects on man.

The acute effects of an increasing concentration of hydrogen fluoride have been listed as follows:

2.4 mg/m^3	No immediate effects
8 mg/m^3	Many persons experience discomfort
24 mg/m^3	All persons complain and object to staying in the environment
48 mg/m^3	Brief exposures cause irritation of eyes, nose pharynx, upper chest
96 mg/m^3	Not tolerable for more than one minute, all the above effects intensified, smarting of skin.

The first sign of chronic fluorosis is mottling of the teeth. Further symptoms include pains and stiffness in the joints. Radiological examination of workers, exhibiting these symptoms, has shown evidence of bone-thickening and gasification of the ligaments (osteosclerosis). A survey of the literature, describing the exposure of workers to fluorides in industrial atmosphere, indicates that concentrations in the air were mostly less than 10 mg/m^3 (Hodge and Smith, 1970). Although there were occasional complaints of the symptoms of irritation listed above, and radiography showed evidence of mild ostesclerosis in some individuals, only a few cases of crippling fluorosis have been authenticated. These occurred in a cryolite where fluoride concentrations of 30–40 mg/m^3 were measured.

Ammonia

Due to its alkaline properties, ammonia is irritating to the mucous membranes of nose, throat, eyes and high concentrations, and to skin. Mild irritation to throat is experienced at a concentration of 35 mg/m^3 which is also the harmful effect directly. The tendency mentioned earlier, for sulphur dioxide to be oxidised in the atmosphere to an ammonium sulphate aerosol, gives rise, however, to secondary effects, which can be a considerable nuisance. Where atmospheric conditions give rise to the formation of stable fogs, the presence of ammonium sulphate increases the density, persistence and extent of the fog.

Continuous Pollutant Monitors

The key to effective environmental quality management is the ability to continuously monitor the concentrations of various pollutants, not only as they are in the ambient air but also as they leave the stack of various plants. The wet chemical methods are too time-consuming and laborious to serve the purpose. Upsets must be discovered as soon as they occur, in order to make it possible to identify the source of the problem and take immediate corrective action.

The projected system for the Trombay Fertilizer Unit will consist of these sections, viz.,

1. stack monitoring,
2. mobile ambient air monitoring using a van system
3. plant pollution monitoring device.

In the stack monitoring system continuous analyzers have been provided to monitor the SO_2 in the sulphuric acid plant stack and NO_x in the three stacks of the nitric acid plants. The SO_2 monitor is based on the pulsed fluorescence technique. Pulsating ultra-violet light of wave length 190–230 mm is focused on a fluorescent chamber containing the sample stream. The excited SO_2 molecules emit their characteristic decay radiation in the ultra-violet region which is measured by a photomultiplier tube correlated to the SO_2 concentration.

The NO_x analyzer is based on the chemiluminescence principle. The gas sample to be analyzed is blended with ozone. Nitric oxide reacts with ozone to form NO_2 and the chemiluminescence multiplier tube and converted into an NO concentration.

Mobile Air Monitoring

The mobile monitoring unit is equipped with continuous analyzers/recorders for the measurement of SO_2 and NO_x in the ambient air. The system is complete with shelter, power generation unit and Trailer so that it can operate independently at any place.

Plant Leaf as a Pollution Monitoring Device

It is possible to monitor SO_2 pollution with the help of sensitive plants, provided the pollutant concentration and plant response relationships are earlier established with tire help of fumigation experiments and physico-chemical monitoring devices. Sine plants constitute a living system, it is imperative to keep in view the different ecological parameters affecting the ambient and ground level concentration of SO_2 and its absorption by plants. As the magnitude of stress on plants by a pollutant is a function of ecological determinants, these must be considered for meaningful evaluation and precise correction of dose-response relationship. For short term monitoring measurements of photosynthetic leaf area, chlorophyll and ascorbic acid contents may be considered suitable.

Conclusion

A combination of stack monitoring, mobile air monitoring, more efficient operation of plants with proper controls, and modern technology could be a useful tool in the hands of the management and the government to control air pollution and benefit society.

13

Oil Pollution: Prevention, Control

The rapid growth of population, standard of living, resource utilization and industrialization is leading to the serious problem of environmental degradation which is a great threat to all types of animal life, vegetation and other living organisms. Industries are discharging various pollutants into the atmosphere everyday and, thus, are the major sources of these pollutional problems.

The petroleum industry is one of the major contributors of different contaminants to environment. These include gaseous pollutants, *e.g.*, hydrogen sulphide, sulphur dioxide, hydrogen vapours, carbon monoxide, smoke and water pollutants, e.g., oil water soluble organic compounds, phenolic compounds and particulate matter. The pollutants with their source of emission, harmful effects and control methods are given in Tables 13.1 (a) and (b). The tolerance limits for these contaminants, in the atmosphere, according to ISI specifications, are shown in Table 13.1(c). It is desirable that the treatment of such hazardous contaminants from the petroleum industry meets these specifications. Minimal rational standards for oil refineries are given in Table 13.1(d).

Sources

The petroleum industry may be grouped into three divisions for convenience of the study of waste water and its control methods.

1. Production
2. Refining
3. Transportation and marketing.

Production includes all probable operations, from drilling oil fields to transporting the crude to refineries. During the refining operation, the crude is converted to saleable products and marketing involves the distribution and sale of the finished petroleum products. All these activities are responsible to some extent for emission of undesirable materials into the atmosphere.

Pollutants from Refining Processes

Pollutants from the petroleum refinery are the by-products of various refining processes. These different pollutants emitted from different types of units, are shown in Table 13.2.(a) and 13.2(b). Refineries manufacture motor fuels, burning oils, lubricating oils and greases, waxes, asphalts and other by-products. Therefore, it is apparent that these wastes are produced from all these units. The wastes may be classified as free oil, emulsified oil, condensate water, acid wastes, waste caustics, alkaline water, special chemicals, waste gases, sludges and solids sanitary waste.

The characteristics of typical refinery wastes, based on the above classification, are given in Table 13.3.

Free Oil. About 0.1 to 2 percent of crude oil flows into sewers in the form of free oil from large refineries. This free oil comes from sampling taps, pump gland leaks, valve and pipeline leaks. The characteristics of oil, reaching a sewer, depend on the processing operations. The presence of light ends may even create a potential explosion hazard. Oil exists in the waste water in two fractions: one fraction is carried in suspension and the other remains in the form of oil-water emulsion.

* The world consumption of oil (excluding planned economic countries) in 1975 was about 6 million tonnes per day. Depending upon prices and rate of growth of demand, the consumption could be between 10 & 13 million tonnes per day, during the period 1985 to 2000. The proven reserves of oil in 1975 were estimated to be:

IOEC countries	*62 billion tonnes*	
North America	6	-do-
Western Europe	4	-do-
Planned Economy countries	14	-do-
Others	6	-do-
Total	92	-do-

Table 13.1 (a)
Various air pollutants from the petroleum industry

Pollutants	*Source*	*All effects*	*Control methods*
Hydrogen sulphide (H_2S)	Hydroprocessing and cracking units	Reacts to form SO_2 if burned.	(*i*) H_2S is absorbed in amine solution, which is, then, stripped off to give H_2S and converted to sulphur (*ii*) Aqueous effluents from refining process containing H_2S is steam stripped off.
Sulphur dioxide (SO_2)	Flue gases/from burning fuels containing sulphur	Irritating to eye and respiratory system	Sulphur containing oil is reacted to hydrogen at an elevated temperature and pressure in the presence of solid catalyst sulphur and is converted to H_2S.
Carbon monoxide (CO)	Stack gas from catalytic crack	Poisonous to animal life	Carbon monoxide is burnt to form harmless carbon dioxide
Smoke	Incomplete combustion in furnace and boiler	Reduces visibility	Proper control of boiler and furnace
Hydrocarbon	Evaporated from tanks	Reacts in atmosphere	Floating roofs or vapours

(*Contd. ...*)

(Contd. ...)

vapours		to form photochemical smog	recovery systems on tanks are installed
Fluid catalyst	Entrained in stack gas from catalytic cracking units		Centrifugal separation by using cyclone and electrical precipitation.

Table 13.1(b)
Water pollutants from petroleum refining

Pollutants	*Source*	*All effects*	*Control methods*
Oil	Entrained in refinery	Dirty and harmful to aquatic life	Removed by gravity separation and aeration techniques
Waste soluble or organic compounds	Dissolved in refinery waste	Many compounds toxic to aquatic life. Emits bad odours	Removal by biological treatment method.

Table 13.1 (c)
Desired limits for inland surface waters
(to be used as raw water for public water supply for bathing ghats)

Characteristics	*Tolerance limit*
pH value	6.9-9.0
Chlorides (as Cl) mg/1 max.	600
Fluorides (as F) mg/1 max.	1.5
Dissolve oxygen min.	3 mg/1 or 40% (saturation value, whichever is higher)
BOD-mg/1 max.	3
Phenolic compounds (as C_6H_5OH) mg/1 max.	0.005
Oils and greases mg/1 max.	0.1
Suspended solids	—
Tolerance limit for fish culture	
pH value	6.0 to 9.0
Free carbondioxide (CO_2) mg/1 max.	6.0
Free ammonia (as N) mg/1 max.	1.2
Dissolved oxygen, min.	40% saturation value or 3 mg/1 whichever is higher
Oil and grease mg/l max.	0.1
Suspended solids	—

Table 13.1 (d)
Minimal National Standards For Oil Refineries

Parameter	*Maximum permissible concentration in mg/l*	*Maximum permissible quantity in kg/1000 tonnes of crude processed*
Biochemical Oxygen Demand (5 days at 20°C)	15.0	10.5
Suspended Solids	20.0	14.0
Oil and grease	10.0	7.0
Sulphide	0.5	0.35
Phenol	1.0	0.7
pH shall be between 6.0 to 8.5		

Table 13.2
Various wastes generated in different units of the petroleum industry

Units	*Waste generated*
Crude and product	Oil in the form of emulsion associate with water, which is high in COD and contains less BOD.
Crude desalting	Emulsified oil, ammonia, phenol and suspended solids. These pollutants produce relatively high BOD and COD.
Crude oil fractionation	Waste water contains sulphides, oil, chlorides, mercaptans and phenol.
Thermal cracking	Various oil fractions and may be high in BOD and COD, ammonia, phenol and sulphides. Wastes may be high in alkalinity.
Catalytic cracking	Waste contains sulphides, phenol, and ammonia
Hydrocracking	Waste is high in sulphides
Reforming	Sulphides, mercaptans and oil
Polymerization	High in sulphides, mercptans and ammonia
Alkylation	Oil and sulphides
Isomerization	Low in phenolics and oxygen demand
Solvent refining	Solvents like phenol, glycol, amines having a high BOD
Dewashing	—
Hydrotreating	Major pollutants are sulphides and ammonia; phenol may also be present
Deasphalting	Sulphides, oil and ammonia
Drying and sweeting	Spent caustic, which may be phenolic or sulphide. Phenolic spent caustics contain phenol, cresol, xylenols, sulphur compounds and some neutral oils. These have high BOD and COD value.
Wax manufacture	No specific data available, may contain small particles of waste. Solvent and oil may also be present.
Grease manufacture	Soap and oil discharged through sewer system.
Lubricating and packing	High in dissolved and suspended solid sulphates, sulfonates and stable oil, oil emulation.
Blending and packing	High in emulsified oil
Hydrogen manufacture	Oil, sulphur compounds and phenols.

Emulsified Oil

This type of emulsion is not removed in tire gravity type oil separator. When it is discharged into a large stream of water, it usually breaks, as a result of dilution, and oil rises to the surface of the water. Emulsion may be formed in a sewerage system as a result of intimate contact between oil, water and emulsifying agents.

The nonseparable oil content of waste water increases in the presence of coke clay, sanitary sewage, water treating plant sludges, flocculent and fibrous solids, tars, asphalts, petroleum sludges, soaps and other numerous solvent and treating chemicals. The chemical treatment of lubricating oils, waxes and burning oils, barometric condensers and distillate

Table 13.3
Characteristics of typical refinery wastes

Source of waste	Type of unit		Waste quality									
			Acidity (ppm)	Alkalinity (ppm)	Ammonia (ppm)	BOD (ppm)	COD threshold	Odour (ppm)	Oil	pH (ppm)	Phenol (ppm)	Sulphide (ppm)
(1)	(2)	(3)	(4)	(5)	(6)	(7)	(*)	(9)	{10)	(U)	(12)	(13)
	Spent caustic		—	—	—	5,600-14,400	22,000-56,000	—	49,000-10,300	10-10.2	—	—
Slop oil treatment												
	Vacuum precoat filter		—	—	—	77-153	500-1360	—'	37-130	6.9-7.7	—	—
Water wash	Treating		—	15,313	—	7,900	86,775	—	31,600	9.79	—	—
Condenser	Combination unit		—	59.5	4.1		72.3	1.0	236	7.22	2.33	1.30
Jet vacuum pump	Lub. oil		—	520	225	425			94.3	7.03		
vacuum still												
Desalting	Desalting unit		—	739	2.0	404	865-5031	1.8	32-713	9.26	4.1	—
Low sulphur gas separator	Combination unit		—	1,518	500	408	1204	2.5	3.0	8.5	0.06	600
Vis. breaker gas gas separator	Combination unit		—	2,963	130-999	3,040	7,239	4.5	2.5	7.85	156	150
—	Light oil recovery		—	69-13175	3-8	55-9500	214-16255	3.5	6-230	5.0-9.2	0.213	5,00
Acid	Unit sewer	Alkylation unit	1105-12,325	—	1.2	31	1,251	3.7	131.5	0.6-1.9	—	—
Acid	Unit sewer	H_2SO_4 sludge conversion unit	1,140-10,050	—	2-13	10-272	910	3.5	124	1.71	—	—
Spent caustic	Alkylate waste	Chemical manufacturing	—	46,250	—	256	3,230	1.5	10	1.28	50	2

(Contd.)

(Table 13.3 *Contd.*)

(1)	*(2)*	*(3)*	*(4)*	*V)*	*(6)*	*(7)*	*(S)*	*(9)*	*(10)*	*an*	*(12)*	*(13)*
Spent caustic	—	Catalytic polymerization	—	209,330	—	8,440	50,350	—	T-12	12.9	22.2	3,060
Spent caustic	Naptha wash	Treating	—	80,020	—	51,154	144,120	—	—	13.4	23,312	—
Carbonate	Naptha wash	Fluid catalytic cracking unit	—	247,900	—	363,600	901,200	—	—	13	309,300	0-3380
Alkaline	Shutdown	Caustic methnol sweetening	—	—	—	—	371-299000	—	8.58	9.5-12.5	—	—
Special chemicals	Unit sewer	Alkalation sulfonation	18.2	150	0.2 12.6	8-1,180	2,585 51,350	—	40-7,750	7.37-9.31	—	—
Special chemicals	Unit sewer	Detergent drying	18-245		1.8	28-151	259-5382	1.2	13-1310	4.6	0.7	4
Refinery	Separator inlet	—	0-18	0.92	—	96-501	—	3.25-5.32	3,900-6,500	2.4 6.2	0.5-7.9	—

separators, desalting operations, pump gland leakage, acid sludge recovery processing, barrel and truck washing result in the direct formation of emulsions. The removal of emulsified oil, from a petrochemical refinery, is accomplished by means of coagulation and sedimentation processes. The sludge from these processes are thickened by means of vacuum their salts, mercaptans, amines, amides, phenoles, etc. The other contaminants may be ammonia, caustic soda, calcium hydroxide, etc. Refineries, processing sour crudes, usually produce condensate wastes, high in sulphides, e.g., hydrogen sulphide, ammonium sulphides and some sodium and potassium sulphides. The quantity of sulphides, in process wastes, from operating refinery units, are shown in Table 13.4.

Table 13.4
Sulphide content of process waste from various operating units

Operating units	*Flow, litre per day*	*Sulphide lb/day*
Crude oil desalter	100	532
Thermal cracking unit receiver	1,900	746
Crude oil distillation unit gasoline dehydrators	200	119
Catalytic cracking feed flashing unit	2,400	218
Potassium phosphate hydrogen sulphide scrubbing unit generator	2,600	1,047
Catalytic cracking accumulator and potassium phosphate regenerator wate	2,500	1,000 r
Total	9,700	3,662

Condensate waste, from catalytic cracking units, contains phenolic materials which may be removed by means of biological filters.

The other methods for removing hydrogen sulphide are steam stripping, use of fine gases, oxidation and burning the waste.

Acid Wastes In the petroleum industry, sulphuric acid is used as both a treating agent and catalyst. Other chemicals used as catalysts are hydrofluoric acid, phosphoric acid, aluminium chloride and zinc chloride. The source of acid bearing wastes is acid treatment of gasoline, white oils, lubricating oils and waxes.

Waste Caustics Waste of this type originates from the caustic washing of light oils to remove mercaptans, hydrogen sulphide, and other acidic material that may occur naturally in crude oil. The constituents of waste causing pollutional problems are mercaptans, thiophenol, thiocresols, phenols, cresols, disulphides, alkylsulphides.

Alkanline Waters This is generated from the washings of neutralized acid treated oils, the washing of caustic treated oils and the dehydrates of treated light oils.

Special Chemicals This includes the solvents and extraction solutions, utilized in selective solvent refining, gas purification and light oil treating.

Waste Gases The waste gases from petroleum refining are stack gases from furnaces and reactors, hydrogen sulphide and sulphur dioxide. These gases also cause water pollution problems. Hydrogen sulphide is a contaminant to other gases, i.e., methane and ethane. In removing the hydrogen sulphide from liquid and gaseous hydrocarbon streams, waste waters of highly undesirable characteristics are produced.

Sludges and Solids The sludges are fundamentally accumulated at the bottom of various crude or product storage tanks. Solids include coke, waste catalysts, filtering clays, slag and tank bottoms. It is highly objectionable to dispose of these sludges and solids into plant sewers. About 119 to 710 pounds of dry solids, per million gallons of waste, are produced in a typical refinery. The composition of sludge, withdrawn from different types of oil-water separators is presented in Tables 13.5 (a), (b), (c) and (d).

Table 13.5 (a)
Composition of sludge withdrawn from oil-water separators

	API units with removal equipment		*Air survey samples*	
	Average (% by weight)	*Range (% by weight)*	*Average (% by weight)*	*Range (% by weight)*
Water	82.4	61.2 to 98.3	66.5	8 9 to 99.5
Oil	10.9	1.1 to 20.7	15.0	0.1 to 59.0
Volcanic solids	1.4	0.5 to 2.3	5.5	0.0 to 49.4
Ash	5.3	0.4 to 15.8	13.0	0.2 to 56.2

Table 13.5(b)
Composition of oil-water separator sludges

	Average (% by weight)	*Range (% by weight)*
Oil	46.0	9.4-81.5
Volatile solids	14.7	0.0-54.3
Ash	39.3	2.3-85.3

Table 13.5 (c)
Composition of air flotation sludges

	Average	*Range*
Water removed by settling 1 hr. per cent by weight	15	2.5–42.0
Froth analysis per cent by weight:		
Oil free solids	3	1.8–5.2
Oil (by difference)	22	
Water (after settling 1 hr)	75	60.8-90.1
Ash percent by weight of solids	27	3.1-43.8

Table 13.5 (d)
Composition of tank bottom sludges

	Average (% by weight)	*Range (% by weight)*
Water	39.4	5.0-98.0
Oil	47.9	1.3–95.0
Volatile solids	4.4	0.–13.0
Ash	8.3	0.0–55.3

Marketing involves filling operations, transportation of petroleum products and their storage. During these operations, hydrocarbons which are highly undesirable, are emitted into the atmosphere.

Method of Treatment of Waste from Petroleum Refinery

The different methods of treatment of waste water from petroleum refining and petrochemical industries may be classified as follows:

1. Physical methods 2. Chemical methods 3. Biological methods

Physical Methods

Physical methods include gravity separation, air flotation, filtration, centrifugation, vacuum filtration and carbon adsorption.

Gravity separation is the first step in the treatment of refinery waste. This is accomplished on the basis of the difference in specific gravity of oil and water. The gravity chamber usually consists of a grit chamber and a main separator. Such separators are used by all types of refineries to remove free oil and oil containing waste. The skimmed oil from the separator is reprocessed and, then, recovered. The settled sludge may be dewatered and either incinerated or disposed of as land fill.

In the air flotation process, a portion of waste water feed is saturated with air at a pressure of 40 to 50 psi. The waste water is held at this pressure for a period of 1 to 5 minutes in a retention tank and, then, released at atmospheric pressure into the flotation chamber. The sudden reduction, in the pressure, results in the release of microscopic air bubbles which attach themselves to oil and suspended particles in the waste water in the flotation chamber. This results in the agglomerates, which, due to entrained air, have greatly increased their vertical-rise velocity of about 0.5 to 1.0 ft/minute. The floated material, then, rises to the surface and a layer of froth is formed which is continuously removed by special devices. A retention time of usually 10 to 30 minutes is provided in the flotation chamber. The efficiency of the dissolved flotation technique depends upon the attachment of bubbles to the suspended oil and other particles which are to be removed.

Flocculating agents are added for high efficiency of the air flotation unit. The clarified effluent from an air flotation unit may be further treated in a biological unit or may be discharged as final effluent, depending upon the BOD content and effluent requirements. The estimation of sludge production from the air flotation treatment is shown in Table 13.6.

***Table 13.6**

Estimated oily sludge production from air floatation treatment

Refinery class	*Air floatation influent TSS Orng/l)*	*Air floatation effluent TSS (mg/1)*	*TSS Removal (rng/l)*	*Flow (gal/bbl)*	*TSS Removal (lbs/mbbt)*
A	29.5	8.8	20.7	18.0	3.1
B	35.2	10.6	29.6	38.0	9.4
C	52.2	15.6	36.6	42.7	13.0
D	99.3	29.8	69.5	47.3	27.5
E	29.9	8.9	21.0	87.0	15.3
				Median	15.3

* Economics of Refinery Waste Water Treatment, American Petroleum Institute, 1973.

Chemical Methods

The chemical methods of waste-water treatment include, coagulation, precipitation, chemical oxidation, ion exchange and chemical pretreatment or sludge conditioning. These methods remove oil and solid, particularly from oil emulsions.

The delayed coking operation, in the petroleum industry, results in a substantial amount of oil-laden waste water which cannot be reused before being chemically treated. The chemical treatment of waste water from the delayed coking operation permits the reuse of oil-laden water in decoking, by reducing oil content to below 100 ppm. The chemically treated waste water from the delayed coking operation is used as a coolant in the decoking operation. Any emulsion, that may be formed when using the oil-laden water for cooling, does not interfere with the cooling of the bed and is broken when brought into contact with the hot coke.

Biological Methods

The biological waste treatment methods include

1. Activated sludge process, conventional and modified
2. Trickling filters
3. Aerated lagoons
4. Oxidation pond.

Prior to waste being treated by biological methods, it is pretreated to remove oils, suspended solids and toxic substances and to provide neutralization.

Activated Sludge Process This is considered to be the most effluent and effective biological method for the removal of organic materials. The activated sludge process operates in the efficiency range of 70 to 95 percent for BODs, 30 to 70 percent for CODs and 65 to 99 percent for phenols and cyanides. The conventional activated sludge process is most widely applied in contact stabilization and is mostly applicable when a large fraction of the organic constituents is in a suspended and colloidal form. Extended aeration is particularly adaptable to industrial applications as longer detention-periods allow micro-organisms more time to degrade the complex organics and sludge production is minimized.

Activated sludge is an aerobic biological treatment process in which, high concentrations of newly grown and recycled micro-organisms, are suspended uniformly throughout a holding tank to which raw waste-waters are added. Oxygen is introduced via mechanical aeraters, diffused air systems or by other means. The organic materials in the waste are removed from the aqueous phase by microbial growth and is stabilized by biochemical synthesis and oxidation reaction.

The activated sludge process consists of an aeration, followed by a sedimentation tank. The microbial growth of flocculants is removed in the sedimentation tank and recycled to the activated sludge tank to maintain a high concentration of active micro-organisms.

Trickling Filter. The trickling filter uses an aerobic biological treatment process. It has a porous bed, made of solid particles, of stone or synthetic material usually PVC, on the surface of which a fixed growth of micro-organism is contained. The waste is allowed to pass through the bed. A microbial film develops on the surface of the bed-media and removes the organic materials from the waste water by absorption, bioflocculation and sedimentation. As this is an aerobic biological system, oxygen is required for rapid metabolism of the removed organic matter.

The large surface area of the filter-media permits a rapid transfer of oxygen by simple diffusion from the void space into the liquid layer. The filter-media may be stone or synthetic material like polyvinyl chloride.

Trickling filter units have been used in the petroleum industry, both as complete secondary treatment, and as roughing devices to reduce the organic leaf, on subsequent activated sludge units. They have been put to extensive use to remove phenolic compounds.

Prior to the application of the trickling filter, the waste water from the petroleum industry is pretreated to remove oil and to limit concentrations of sulphides, mercaptan and phenols. Oil removal is accomplished by gravity separation and air floatation. The sulphides and mercaptans are removed by stripping.

Aerated Lagoon This also provides aerated biological treatment by mixing dilute concentrations of micro-organisms with waste water in a large, relatively deep basin. For aerobic stabilization of organic matter, oxygen is essential which is supplied by diffused aeration units. Turbulence is maintained in the basin to ensure proper distribution of oxygen and biological solids throughout the basin. The detention time in the aerated lagoon is greater than that in the activated sludge process for removal of an equivalent amount of BOD.

Oxidation Pond This method of treatment is applicable only at places where land is plentiful and cheap. Basically, the oxidation pond utilizes bacteria for aerobic stabilization of organic matter added to the pond. Bacteria consumes oxygen, supplied from atmospheric aeration at the pond surface and from oxygen production by algae in the pond. Algae produces oxygen by synthesis of cellular protoplasm, from carbon dioxide, in the presence of sunlight. As in the pond, organic loadings are low, and very little biological sludge settles down in the pond. Refinery wastes are generally treated in an oxidation pond, which is also a polishing step for the effluent from physical, chemical and other biological waste treatment processes,. Normally, pretreatmentis required to limit concentrations of sulphides, mercaptan and phenols.

Cooling Towers Cooling towers are used to biologically treat refinery effluent where cooling water supply is short. Under controlled loading conditions, cooling towers are capable of removing 99 percent phenol, 75 to 90 percent oxygen demand (COD) and 90 percent biochemical oxygen demand (BOD). The oil-bearing waste is passed through gravity separators to remove oil. The sulphides and mercaptans may be removed by treatment in a stripper.

Pollution from Oil Production and Transport

On September 25,1974, an American oil tanker, "Trans Heron" was wrecked in the Indian ocean near the Lakshadweep Islands. The oil spill on the sea engulfed Kiltan Island, and a thick oil slick, which had spread over a large area, started moving eastwards toward the Kerala coast. Sea birds started dying in the area by the thousands and there was a heavy toll of Tuna fish. Its effects on coconut trees, which are the main source of livelihood for the people of the Islands, will take years to assess. Besides this, disfiguring of the coastline and beaches will also be immense. This is apart, from the money, that will be spent to control the menace even partially.

With the growth of giant oil tankers, increased shipping of oil and other cargo, offshore drilling, etc., the problem of oil pollution has become important, especially since earlier experiences in fighting it have proved, that we are not yet fully prepared to face the problem, should it arise, on a larger scale. Developing countries like India, which have a long shoreline, and are very near shipping lanes, from major oil producing countries, must prepare themselves for any emergency of this nature. The technology and necessary equipments, personnel and agencies, finances and coordination must all be well-prepared and ready to go into action at a day's notice, as any delay in controlling oil pollution may cause incalculable harm to the biosystem and ecocycle of the area, in addition to being a great economic loss and waste of human efforts.

Oil and other hazardous materials constitute a major pollution threat to the water resources of the world. The danger exists in both land based and water based facilities. Whether the spill is large or small, whether occasional or continuous, each source must be evaluated from three stand points-the relative hazards involved, the preventive measures that should be instituted and the damage control and clean up capabilities that may be needed.

Waterborne Sources

Ships as a Source of Pollution Of particular significance is the transportation by tankers and barges, of petroleum products themselves, which now account for over 40% of the total waterborne traffic in the world. Tankers have ballast water to discharge and bilges to pump. They further face the problem of tank cleanings. Apart from the number of ships, their size has also increased manifold. In the World War II period, tankers of 16000 tonnes were common. Torrey Canyon had a capacity of 119,000 tonnes but now tankers of 312,000 tonnes are common. Larger tankers increase the hazard from any single accident.

Waste Oils There is seldom any announcement of the flow of 10 or 30 or even 300 gallons of waste oil into a nearby stream or sea. Its presence is announced only by the trail of grime and damage left behind, and even this might go unnoticed if it were not repeated so often.

Gasoline Service Stations Some 350,000,00 gallons of used motor oil must be disposed of annually by more than 210,00 gasoline filling stations in this country. Re-refining, it is not profitable, hence, it is disposed of in sewers and streams. There should be some incentive for collection and reuse of these waste oils.

Tank Cleaning Facilities Most large shipyards have facilities to clean holds, ballast tanks and engineers rooms. Some sea ports have facilities for receiving oily wastes from shipboard sources, but, generally, most ports have no such arrangement.

Oily Waste Industries Almost all major industries use water and most of them have a significant amount of oil in their wastes. Untreated oily wastes, from such sources, causes a major pollution problem.

Industrial Transfer and Storage

Pipelines In December 1962, a pipeline from a storage facility broke, releasing about 1,400,000 gallons of cutting oil, light mineral oil and xylene into the Minnesota river in the United States. Similarly, a pipeline from Barauni Oil Refinery started leaking in a big way and polluted the river Ganga.

The world now has many pipelines for transportation of oil. Many sections of this network are laid in and across navigable waterways and reservoir systems. There are enough spills from accidental punctures, and cracked wells, and enough leaks from corrosion, to required alertness and technical improvement.

Off-Shore Drilling Offshore oil and gas operations are being conducted in the Gulf of Mexico, the Southern California coastal waters, Bombay high and near Madras coast. Such operations may produce pollution of the offshore waters from blowouts of the wells, dumping of oil-based drilling muds and oil-soaked cuttings, and leakages of oil, during production, storage and transportation. A pollution threat is also posed by the pipelines, laid on the ocean floor, from offshore platforms, to storage facilities.

Prevention of Oil Pollution

Tank Vessel Design Considerations

Major design and construction changes since World War II have generally increased the potential pollution hazard, resulting from individual cases of collision and stranding. These have to be checked.

Governmental and Regulatory Body Recommendations Considerable private and public activity, following the Torrey Canyon incident, has been aimed at establishing the Marine Safety Committee.

Manoeuvreability Maoeuvreability should be very high to avoid collision and grounding in emergency conditions.

Backing Power Steam turbine propelled, single screw U. S. flag tankers with displacements ranging from 25000 to 77000 tons can be expected to stop 81/2 to 9 ship lengths from the full ahead condition. Further, periods of 51/2 to 9 minutes will be required to execute this manoeuvre, from the time the crash stop order is given. By contrast, the 144,000 dwt. combination oil/bulk vessel Cedros required 10 ship lengths and over 11 minutes to stop from an initial speed of 18 knots.

Steering and Directional Control In view of the greatly increased sizes and relatively reduced installed power of large tankers, the following suggestions are offered:

—Establishment of minimum standards of control, including the turning rate ; the turning cycles should be determined by standardized trial procedures.

—Study of Rudder design-current standard horn type rudders or conventional, closed stern, fair form rudders should be changed in order to improve characteristics at high rudder angles and at low manoeuvring speeds. The various configurations that might be improved, after study, include active rudders, biplane and triplane rudders, flapped rudders and Kort Nozzle rudders. Various bow and stern thraster systems have been developed, some well over 1000 hp in size, that can also be applied to tankers to improve the steering system.

Collision Protection A structural, shock absorbing barrier at the ship side, in way of cargo tanks should be provided. This outer space, while lost to cargo capacity, is available for clean ballast. The conventional port and starboat wing bulkheads can be located well outboard.

Mooring Gear and Ground Tackle A last resort to stop the ship, and normal tool for low speed manoeuvring, is the use of ships anchors. Hence, there should be means for more rapid release of anchor and chain. Centralized control of the mooring gears, from the bridge, is an improvement in this direction.

Cargo Contaminant in the Event of Collision and Grounding Tank compartments should be smaller and more in number. Inflammable or other types of oil booms should be carried by ships. Chemical detergents and other dispersal systems should also be carried on ships. A foamed plastic system should be available to seal off small ruptures in cargo tanks.

Radical Solutions On a global basis, serious consideration has been given to the following possibilities to limit the pollution hazard :

1. Reorganization of oil tanker operations to routes remote from populated areas or on comparatively lightly travelled ocean lines.
2. Adoption of costly navigation and/ or inertial guidance systems to insure a higher precision in the control of ship routes.
3. Use of submarine tankers, to reduce the probability of ship collisions. The hazards of grounding are, of course, increased.
4. Accelerated development of long distance oil pipelines as a substitute for tank vessels.

Off-Shore Production

Offshore oil wells and drilling operations are required to have such features as blowout preventers, storm chocks, fire preventer equipments and aids to navigation.

Control of Oil spillage

The potential of aerial photography and more especially infrared, ultraviolet and microwave imagery in surveillance and oil slick detection should be evaluated in detail.

Microwave, having all weather capabilities, should be used first, then, processed information may be used on ultraviolet and infrared photography.

FM-C W radar has a similar all weather capability, but microwaves are preferable.

Actual reconnaissance techniques are also useful for tracing surface buoys, which could be released near the oil spill, to determine the rates of surface currents. A combination of photographic, ultraviolet, infrared and microwave techniques should be used.

Prediction of Oil Slick Behaviour The behaviour and rate of movement of oil slicks on water are rather poorly understood despite the importance of deploying defensive measures. Transport and dissipation are two pertinent problems.

The direction and speed of an oil slick yields more to wind than the influence of ocean currents. This is because of the greater momentum given to the oil slick by the wind. Water currents that are near the surface, which are under the influence of wind, are expected to follow the mathematical representation of the Econ spiral. The wind created currents, thus, flow slightly to the right of the wind direction in the Northern hemisphere. Mechanically and thermally induced ocean currents, e.g., Gulf stream, which would affect the motion of an oil slick as well. As oil slick approaches a land mass, a variation in its motion is also expected.

Chemical Treatment, Absorption and Sinking Agents There are numerous compounds and materials available to collect or sink oil slicks. Four types of collecting agents have been identified and suggested for oil slick recovery. These are

1. Floating absorbents such as straw and saw dust.
2. Plastic or other polymeric material such as polyurethane foam.
3. Gelling agents.
4. Demulsifiers.

Gelling agents that can solidify petroleum materials are in developmental stage and may prove helpful in collecting spilled oil.

Numerous solid absorptions for sinking oil are also available, though the weight of material required, per unit of oil, and the attendant logistic problems present practical difficulties. Demersal fish species may be adversely affected and a resurfacing of the oil mass is also generally probable, although it is delayed and slow.

The majority opinion is against the use of these dispersants and demulsifiers, because they are toxic to aquatic life in general.

Biological Degradation of Crude Oil and Oil fraction in Oceans. Biological degradation of hydrocarbons in the ocean could be carried out using suitable species of microbiota. Although degradation will fake place in the ocean, and is, in fact, the ultimate fate of oil, the rates are very slow.

Confining Spills

The ability to confine a spill, in the area immediately surrounding the source, is principally dependent on the availability of equipment and the prevailing environmental conditions. An incident, that essentially open an entire vessel to the sea, would involve rapid spreading of oil and, therefore, the equipment must be ready for use immediately.

Floating Booms and Underwater Bubble Barriers Both these are presently suitable for relatively calm water and are subject to failure. The floating booms are, generally, superior to bubble barriers in an emergency because they are more portable and involve less erection time.

The main advantage of the bubble barrier is the unrestricted entry and exit of ship it allows while the main disadvantage is the complete less of containment in the event of air supply failure.

Burning The ability to destroy cargo on site depends largely on the nature and quantity of the cargo. If all attempts to salvage a vessel or cargo have failed and a ship has been abandoned, an attempt should be made to set the oil afire while it is still contained within the vessel. Controlled demolition techniques may be applicable to opening the vessel without allowing oil to escape while providing access to air. Mixing kerosene or other highly flammable material with crude of heavy oil cargo would greatly enhance the burning.

Skimming Mechanical devices for collecting oil from the surface of the water such as rotating cylinders and suction pumps are used.

Treatment and Disposal of Recovered Slicks

The limiting constraints in this respect are economic and environmental disposal standards.

First alum or ferric salts are added to waste-water. Lime is added when sufficient alkalinity for precipitation of the iron is not present. The waste-water is, then, gently agitated or flocculated to promote inter-particle collisions for agglomeration. The resultant suspension is, then, allowed to settle in a sedimentation basin. In some cases where oil content is high, floatation is used. This step is followed by filtration through a rapid sand filter or through a multi-media filter.

Restoration and Cleanup

Beaches Several possible approaches have been studied for restoration of oil contaminated beaches. These include:

1. Ploughing under and covering with uncontaminated sand.
2. Physical removal of contaminated material.
3. Detergent cleaning in combination with mechanical tilling.
4. Combination of the above.

In general, any procedure that applies to sand beaches can be extended to gravel or shingle beaches, but with greater difficulty.

Physical removal of the contaminated material, with appropriate earth moving or farm machinery, appears tc the best solution. When the oil is relatively unweathered and, hence, mobile addition of absorbing material such as straw, saw dust or clay can greatly assist Timing of the cleanup operation to correspond with high tides can minimize the effort.

Flowing under is unsatisfactory because wave action ultimately causes resurfacing of the oil.

Rocky Coasts, Sea Walls and Structures Detergents were used extensively in England in combination with high pressure water hosing. Burning oil from sea walls was attempted but the only apparent cleaning was achieved by spalling of the concrete surfaces Where equipments can be brought into play, steam cleaning with detergents can be effective

Waste-water loadings and waste-water of a few typical process of refinery-is given ii Table 13.7 while projected solid waste solids inventory from a typical plant is given in Table 13.8. Suggestions for source control measures to reduce air contaminants from petroleum refining are given in Table 13.9.

Table 13.7

Typical waste loadings and waste-water volumes of fundamental processes

Process	*Process capacity 1000 lb/day*	*Flow mg/d.*	*BOD lb/day*	*Phenol lb/day*	*Sulphide lb/day*
Crude oil product storage	1000	0.04	100	—	—
Crude desalting	100	0.02	200	10	200
Crude fractionation	100	5.00	20	100	100
Thermal cracking	15	0.03	15	3	15
Catalytic cracking	50	1.50	500	1,000	150
Reforming	20	0.12	Trace	14	20
Polymerization	1	0.14	3	Trace	10
Alkylation	6	0.36	6	1	60
Solvent refining	6	0.05	—	18	tract-
Dewaxing	4	0.09	2,000	6	trac
Hydrotreating	35	0.04	70	trace	7(
Desaphalting	3	—	—	—	—
Drying and sweeting	50	2.00	2,500	500	
Wax finishing	0.5	—	—	—	
Grease manufacture	0.2	—	—	—	—
Lube oil finishing	4.0	—	—	—	—
Blending and packing	100				

Table 13.8
Projected waste solids inventory from a typical unit*

Solid waste	*Dry Solids lbs/day*	*Quantity st/ wt*	*Volume*	*Characteristics*	*Remarks*
1. Gravity oil separator sludge					
(a) Oil area	95	1.2	1200	Oily sludge containing upto 10% oil and 16% solids after setting	Potential oil received
(b) New area	79	1.2	1000		
2. DAF Skimmings					
(a) Oil area	68	0.5	1700	Oil, solids and emulsion breaking chemicals	Potential oil received by chemical and heat treatment
(b) New area	197	0.5	4800		
3. Oil Sediment	1600	upto 20	Approx. 1000	Oily sediment containing clay, sand and carbonate precipitates and upto 10% oil	
4. Tank Bottoms	2500	upto 20	1500	upto 50% oil	Potential oil received if leaded and non-sludges are segregated

* Excluding Tar and CEM from the HF alkylation unti.

Table 13.9
Air pollution control measures for petroleum

Refining source	*Control method*
Storage vessels	Vapour recovery systems, floating roof tanks, pressure tanks, vapour balance, paining tanks white
Refining process gas	Ethanolamine absorption
Catalyst regenerators	Cyclones precipitation in site CO combustion, CO boiler, cyclones-water scrubber, multiple cyclones
Accumulator vents	Vapour recovery, vapour incineration
Blow down systems	Smokeless flares-gas recovery
Pumps and compressors	Mechanical seals, vapour recovery, sealing glands, oil pressure, maintenance
Vacuum jets	Vapour incineration
Equipment valves	Inspection and maintenance
Pressure relief valves	Vapour recovery, vapour incineration, ruture discs, inspection and maintenance
Effluent waste disposal	Enclosure of separatos, covering of sewer boxes and use of liquid seal, liquid on drains
Bulk loading facilities	Vapour recovery or incineration, submerged or bottom loading

14

Environmental Pollution and its Control in the Pulp and Paper Industry

There are several applications of paper. The per capita consumption of paper in some of the advanced countries as well as in India is given in Table 14.1. The increase in consumption is obvious from Table 14.2. India ranks 20th among the paper producing countries in the world There are at present 75 paper and paper board units in the private sector, with an installed capacity of 1.127 million tonnes per annum. An additional capacity of 636,000 tonnes per annum has been licensed. Moreover, letters of intents have been issued for a further capacity of 2.115 million tonnes per year. There is only one public sector unit producing newsprint in the country and it is able to meet only 20 percent of the demand. Seven public sector schemes for the establishment of total capacity of 340,000 tonnes of newsprint have been approved. There are three rayon grade pulp units and one paper grade pulp unit in the private sector. The total installed capacity of the three rayon grade pulp units till 1997–78 was 117,000 tonnes per year and during 1976–77, production was 118,000 tonnes. The export and re-export of paper are given in Table 14.3.

Table 14.1
Paper consumption in various countries

Country	*Per capita consumption kg*
USA	227.25
Canada	140.62
UK	121.00
Japan	73.43
Australia	56.24
USSR	22.00
India	1.58

The import of paper until 1976–77 is given in Table 14.4. This clearly indicates that there has been an almost exponential increase in import of paper, suggesting the necessity for further expansion of the paper industry in India. The figure for import is much higher in comparison to that for export. The projected consumption is given in Table 14.5 indicating considerable scope for further growth. With growing literacy and standard of living the paper consumption will increase, resulting in more pollution from the paper industry. Suitable measures should be taken to contain pollution while considering establishment of newer paper industries.

Table 14.2
Production of paper, paper board and pulp

Year	*Production in tonnes*	
	Paper and paper board	*Pulp*
1970–71	758,137	N.A.
1973–74	797,000	90,000
1974–75	837,000	113,000
1975–76	829,000	106,419
1976–77	911,000	118,538

N.A. Data not available

Table 14.3
Export and re-export of paper (Rs. million)

Year	*Paper and paper board*	*Articles made of paper, pulp, etc.*	*Total*
1969–70	38.4	10.4	48.8
1970–71	39.4	14.7	54.1
1971–72	14.3	15.1	29.4
1972–73	21.4	20.2	41.6
1973–74	43.2	25.9	69.1
1974–75	38.8	36.2	75.0
1975–76	16.2	38.4	54.60
1976–77	15.1	47.5	62.60

Table 14.4
Import of paper (Rs. million)

Year	*Paper, paper board manufacturers*	*Newsprint*
1960–61	121	59.5
1965–66	134	61.8
1969–70	237.4	185.7
1970–71	250.7	187.3
1971–72	349.2	275.9
1972–73	313.6	205.2
1973–74	292.4	178.1
1974–75	595.2	449.9
1975–76	576.8	383.2
1976–77	621.8	472.2

Table 14.6
Quantity of effluents discharged by paper mills

Type of mill	*Daily output. tonnes per day*	*Effluent discharged*		*BOD*		*Suspended solids*		*Population equivalent per tonne*	
		Per day ($\times 10^4$ litres)	*Per tonne of product (litres)*	*Kilograms discharged per day*	*Kilograms per tonne*	*Kilograms per tonne discharged per day*	*Kilograms per tonne*	*BOD*	*Suspended solids*
Sulphate mills									
No. 1	200	90	450000	20000	140	82100	410	2120	4500
No. 2	82	41	500000	10500	120	44200	540	1880	5950
No. 3	80	33	409000	12000	150	65700	820	2215	9040
Sulphite mill	55	12	240400	4480	82	11500	210	1200	2310
Tissue mill	20	9	454000	675	34	2290	500	275	1260
Straw mill	20	1.8	90000	3450	173	5520	275	2540	3040

Table 14.5
Projected consumption

Year	*Cultural*	*Industrial*	*Newsprint*	*Total*
1980–81	644.4	477.9	287.9	1,410.2
1985–86	747.6	565.7	335.5	1,648.8
1990–91	850.7	653.5	383.5	1,887.7

The paper industry is a highly capital-intensive industry. A new integrated pulp and paper mill of a capacity of 100 tonnes per day, producing writing and printing paper, would need an investment of Rs.700 million, including all costs, on the basis of a capital cost of Rs.20,000 per annual ton. This would take into consideration the possible escalation in costs in the coming years as it takes four to five years for a paper mill to commence production. Naturally, an investment on pollution abatement without much return has to be treated as a social obligation. The problem becomes more acute in this country when it is realized that our raw materials contain a high percentage of silica as compared to the Western World and that the quality of limestone, available in this country, near tire paper mills, is of very poor quality containing a large percentage of silica. The quantity of effluents discharged by paper mills is given in Table 14.6.

The consumption of effluents depends upon tire types of paper industry. Analyses of straw board effluent, tissue mill effluent, and sulphate mill effluent are given in Table 14.7,14.8 and 14.9. The tolerances, for water, for the pulp and paper industry, are given in Table 14.10.

Table 14.7
Analysis of strawboard effluent

Characteristic	*Analysis*			
	Spent liquor	*Washer-beater*	*effluent Machine water*	*Combined effluent*
Suspended solids, mg/1	1044–21770	3560–5700	25–1260	940–3040
PH	8–11.0	10–13.3	7.5–8.8	7.8–12.9
BOD (5 days, 20°C), mg/1	20500-75350	4630–8420	195–900	660–3655

Table 14.8
Analysis of tissue mill effluent

Characteristic	*Analysis*			
	Spent liquor	*Pulp mill effluent*	*Paper machine effluent*	*Combined effluent*
Suspended solids, mg/1	1660–22420	475–1675	555–680	240–1145
PH	10.8–12.5	8.2–8.7	8.1–8.5	8.2–9.0
BOD (5 days, 20°C), mg/1	30000–45500	550–1840	62–210	65.265

Table 14.9
Analysis of sulphate mill effluent

Characteristic	*Analysis*		
	Pulp mill effluent	*Paper machine effluent*	*Combined effluent*
Suspended solids, mg/1	290–1690	545–1050	580–2330
pH	6.3–11.0	4.5–7.6	6.9–9.8
BOD (5 days, 20°C), mg/1	105–625	120–385	155–421

Table 14.10
Tolerance for water for pulp and paper industry

Characteristic	*Tolerance*					*Method Test*	
	Ground wood paper	*Kraft paper bleached*	*Kraft paper unbleached and pulp unbleached*	*Soda and sulphite paper*	*High grade paper*	*IS: 1620-1961*	*Is: 1631-1960*
Colour (Hazen units), max	20	15	100	10	5	—	4
Turbidity (Silica! seal; unit:;), max	50	25	100	15	10	—	5
Total dissolved solids, mg/1, max.	500	300	500	300	—	—	9
Total hardness (as $CaCO_3$), max.	200	100	200	100	100	6	—
Iron (as Fe), mg/1, max	1.0	0.25	1.0	0.25	0.25	22	—
Manganese (as Mn), mg/!, max	0.5	0.1	0.5	0.05	0.05	25	—
Iron (as Fe) and Manganese (as Mn) mg/1, added together, max	1.0	0.25	—	0.25	0.25	22 & 25	—
Total residual chlorine (as Cl),	2.0	2.0		2.0	2.0	35	

Our major cellulosic raw materials for paper industry are bamboo, woods, bagasse, grasses and straws. A majority of the mills use 70–80 percent bamboo, the balance being one or more of the above mentioned raw materials. Bacteria and fungi also interact with paper making materials and eventually lead to their biodegradation. The effect of bacteria and fungi on paper making are given in Table 14.11

The analysis of some of the raw materials and used in the pulp and paper industry is given in Table 14.12.

Table 14.11
Effect of bacteria and fungi on paper making

Type of Action	*Effects Produced*
Cellulolytic	Reduction in the cellulose content of wood-chips and pulps; also loss of strength in the finish products.
Saccharoylite	Breakdown of starch additives, causing odour and loss of viscosity.
Proteolytic	Degradation of protein to aminoacids, ammonia and sulphur compounds. Leads to poor sizing and smells.
Pigmentation	Coloured stain, caused b\ fungi or bacteria which spoil product.
Sulphate reduction	Bad odour in .storage chests.
Hydroxide precipitation	Soluble salts of transition elements which oxidise to form coloured precipitates.
Proteolysis	Earlier stages of No. 3 above, which will weaken woolen drying "felts"
Slime formation	The most important aspects of the problem which may cause complete stoppage of production.
Miscellaneous	Spoilage of plastic coatings, loss of viscosity of latex additives and carboxylmethyl cellulose solutions.

Table 14.12
Analysis of cellulosic raw materials

	Ash	*Lignin*	*A-Cellulose*	*Pentosans*
Straws, grasses	6–8	17–19	33–38	27–32
Rice, straw	14–20	12–14	28–36	23-25
Depithed bagasse	2	19–21	40–43	30–32
Bamboo	2–3	22–30	50	16–21
Temperate coniferous woods	1	26–30	40–45	—
Temperate board leaved woods	1	18–25	38–49	—

The ash mainly contains silica which, as will be seen later, increases the problems of pollution.

Bamboo Dust The amount of dust produced during of bamboo is 2 to 5 percent. Utilization of this dust is a major problem because of its high silica content Laboratory experiments have been conducted, by screening it, and rejecting the fines, containing 18–20 percent silica and utilizing the accepted material, containing 6–8 percent silica along with normal chips for pulping.

The rejects containing 18–20 percent of total bamboo can be used for making, manure after composing. Processes have been patented for making soil aids from dust containing cellulose. An Australian company has developed microbes capable of composting raw dust in 6–8 weeks.

The above rejects could also be used for making cattle feed. The normal process consists in steaming the material in an autoclave, at a pressure of 10-15 atmospheres, for 2 hours, followed by treatment with ammonia.

The rejects can also be used as a fuel in boilers. However, because of the high ash content, briquettes will have to be made. The dust could also be used for making compressed boards, using synthetic resin as a binder. However, at the moment, the dust is a real problem in Indian paper mills. The chipper house is generally, full of bamboo dust, particles of which fly in the air, affecting eyes, lungs and the human respiratory system. A typical analysis of bamboo dust is : Ash 2.7--3.5 percent, SiO_2 2.6–3.7 percent, $A1_2O_3$ 0.2–0.25, CaO 0.26–0.36 percent. In the case of paper mills, using bagasse as the raw material, pith which constitutes 30 percent of bagasse, is another source of pollution, as it cannot be used for pulping purposes. Because of the high silica content, the chemical consumption is high and it chokes the wire mesh of the machine wire. A lot of it flies in the air with bagasse fibers, during depithing operation, and causes 'bagassis' to the workers in the section. It has low calorific value and, hence, cannot be used as a fuel but it could be used for making Boards using synthetic resins binder. Recently, a biological method of depithing has been developed in South Africa to counteract these difficulties (Ritter's Process). Considering that about 25–30 percent of pith is separated in the process of bagasse pulping, it is evident that proper use for this has to be found if the cost of paper making has to be reduced. It could be used for making cattle feed. While no data are available on the nutritive value of pith as cattle feed, it may be safely assumed to be similar to corn cobs which are considered in U. S. A. to have 60 percent of the feeding value of corn. Table 14.13 shows the analysis of bagasse screening along with other common roughages used in India at present.

Table 14.13
Analysis of bagasse

Roughage	*Water*	*Ash*	*Crude*	*Fiber*	*Carbohydrate*	*Fat*
Bagasse screening	6.8	5.2	1.43	42.21	43.33	9.83
Wheat straw	8.4	5.2	3.1	37.4	44.4	1.5
Oat straw	11.5	5.4	3.6	36.3	40.8	2.4
Rice straw	7.5	14.5	3.9	33.5	39.2	1.4

It could be used for making bago-molasses by mixing with molasses, salts, urea, etc. The average composition of such feed is given in Table 14.14.

Table 14.14
Composition of bago-molasses feed

Crude protein	2.71
Crude fiber	16.09
Ether extract	0.39
Total ash	16.09
Nitrogen free extract	64.45
Lime (CaO)	1.45
Phosphate (P_2O_5)	0.22
Digestible nutrients (per 100 lbs) of dry matter, crude protein	—
Starch equivalent	43.00

For the sake of comparison, food values of other agricultural products are given in Table 14.15.

Table 14.15
Starch equivalent of different feed

	Digestible protein	*Starch equivalent*
Bago-molasses	Nil	43.0
Gram husk	Nil	42.3
Wheat bhusa	Nil	22.1
Rice straw	Nil	18.6
Average mixed hay	0.5	25.0

Pith can be used as a fuel. It could be mixed with pulverized coal or bagasse and fired in coal stoker boiler furnaces. For this purpose, a sepreader stoker system has been devised in which the larger particles are burnt on a step grate, while fine pith is burnt in suspension.

Another possible field of application is in absorption of nitroglycerine for the manufacture of dynamite, because of its highly absorbent qualities. It can be used as soil conditioner. It will promote humus accumulation in soil, hold water and retain humidity, thereby, adding to the bulk. About 4–5 percent pith, added to superphosphate, would prevent its caking.

Some of the Indian Paper Mills partially use hard woods for pulping. This produces about 10–15 percent bark, depending on the age, height and species of the tree. Some of the mills also use soft woods as per their availability. Although bark could also be used for pulping with chips, it results Moreover, there is a limit up to which it could be used. It constitutes a disposal problem and the only recourse is to use it as a fuel or compost. It could be used for making particle boards. However, because of the high capital investment, the industry does not bother about small quantities, being wasted, and the barks are usually burnt.

Table 14.16
Analysis of sulphate mill effluents

	Black liquor	*Green liquor*	*White liquor*
NaOH, g/l	7.2	15–20	64–66
Na_2S, g/1	3.12	21.24	22–24
Na_2CO_3, g/1	36.57	35–60	9–12
Na_2S_4, g/1	29.45	100–110	95–102
Per cent			
Total solids	11.92	—	—
Ash	97.24	—	–
SiO_2	1.31	8–10	4-5
Na_3SO_4	—	5–7	5–7

There are two methods generally applied for pulping (a) Sulphate process (b) Sulphite process. In this country, all mills, except one, use the sulphate process because of the import of sulphur. The sulphate process utilises caustic soda, buffered with sodium sulphide as the pulping liquor and is known as white liquor. Black liquor is the waste product, obtained after pulping the raw material and contains residual caustic soda, sodium sulphide, carbonate, sulphate, silica, dissolved lignin, pentosans, etc. The whole economy of sulphate pulping depends on the recovery of pulping liquor black. There is no chemical recovery system in smaller units (say below 50 tonnes per day) since it is uneconomical and the entire black liquor his to be drained away, causing serious pollution problems, besides affecting the economy of the system. Table 14.16 gives the analysis of black liquor (liquor left after digestion of raw material), green liquor (liquor after caustic sing) and white liquor (solution used for digestion).

The black liquor, from smaller mills, could be used as a potential source for the manufacture of a variety of organic compounds since it contains lignin which is an organic polymer, mainly aromatic in nature, containing carbonyl, carboxylic, hydroxyl, methoxy groups as reactive groups. So, also there are hemicelluloses present,. which could be recovered in some form or the other. Lignin could he precipitated by passing the flue gas (carbon dioxide) to precipitate it The slimy precipitate, slow and difficult to filter, is washed with water and dried. Some of the important organic compounds that could be manufactured from lignin are vanillin and related products, organic sulphides lignin such as dimethyl sulphide (DMS). Dimethyl vanillin acid for hydroxybenzoic acid, catechols, etc. Lignin could also be used as a source o nitrogenous fertilizer. it helps in retaining moisture in soil.

In the case of mills, having a recovery system, the black liquor is concentrated to 60–65 percent in multiple effect evaporators, mixed with makeup salt cake and, then, fired in the recovery furnace. The organic to inorganic ratio, in black liquor, which is variable with Indian raw materials, as given in Table 14.17 affects the furnace operation.

Table 14.17
Composition of Black liquor

Sources of black liquor	*Ratio of organic to inorganic*
Sabai grass (soda process)	1.13
Soft woods	0.95
Bamboo	1.162
Khar	1.39
Kahi	1.32

The entire organic matter is burnt in the furnace. This is not a very satisfactory way of utilization of valuable raw material since some valuable organic compounds could be manufactured from the same. An alternative source of fuel should be used to avoid wastage.

Leakage from pumps is another source of pollution, apart from spoiling the floor of the building. However, improved types of packing are now available which avoid leakage through the glands.

The flue gases from the furnace contain soda ash and sodium sulphate particles entrained with them. Although all modern mills have electric precipitators which work at over 99 percent efficiency, the precipitators are, once in a while, thrown out of gear, causing nuisance, due to escape of soda ash in the surrounding air, which is injurious-to the health of the workers. Lime sludge or filter cake produced in the causticising plant of the recovery section is another source of pollution. About 0.6-0.8 ton of this sludge is produced for every ton of pulp manufactured and its composition is as follows:

Composition	*Percent*
SiO_2	6–8
R_2O_3	7–8
Ca as CaO	45–47
Mg as MgO	3–5

In western countries, where the quality of lime stone is better it is reburnt percent silica. Moreover, the high silica content of the raw material further aggravates the situation and the western method of disposal cannot be adopted. Several possibilities for disposal have been suggested:

1 Use raw material for nitro-lime fertilizer.

2. Use for making building material, blocks and bricks

3. Use ass agricultural lime in acidic soil.

However the problem remains unsolved on a commercial scale

The filters used in paper making (China clay, bentonite, titanium dioxide, precipitated $CaCO_3$, etc.), and the fibers, in the exit water, from the machines, are another source of pollutants in the paper mill. Different flocculants such as ferric alum, activated silica, alum, sodium aluminate have been used to reduce the total loss to less than one percent. In western countries, cationic poly-acrylamide has been used, thereby, reducing the total loss to less than 0.2 percent. The back water is treated with alum and sodium aluminate solution and settled. However, one percent solids are still present in the back water. This is treated with 2 percent bentonite slurry and, then, with one percent acrylamide solution. The water is allowed to settle and the top layer is used as fresh water.

Air pollution is caused by gases containing sulphur compounds emitted at different stages of pulping and chemical recovery. Hydrogen sulphide, methyl mercaptan and dimethyl sulphide are released at different stages, as given in Table 14.18 (pounds per ton of pulp).

Table 14.18
Gaseous effluents from pulp and paper industries

Source	*H_2S*	*CH_3SH*	*$(CH_3)_5S$*	*Particulates*	*Types of control*
Digester blow	0.1-0.7	0.9-5.3	0.9-3.8	Negligible	Untreated
Smelt tank	—	—	—	20	Uncontrolled
Lime	1	neg.	neg.	18.7	Scrubber
Recovery furnace	3.6	5	3	150	Scrubber and precipitator
Multiple effect evaporators	1.2	0.04	N.A.	neg.	Untreated
Evaporators	0-0.5	0.003-.03	neg.	neg.	Black liquor oxidation
Oxydation tower	N.A.	N.A.	0.1	neg.	Black liquor oxidation

Typical gaseous emissions, from Kraft pulping, are given in Table 14.19. The different types of controls of air pollutants of pulp industry (kraft pulp) are indicated in Table 14.20. The gaseous pollutants are controlled generally by chemical treatments. The particulate emissions from recovery furnaces are frequently controlled by an electrostatic precipitator or venturi scrubber and some reduction in odorous sulphide emission occurs in the scrubber.

Table 14.19
Typical gaseous emission ranges from Kraft pulping in parts per million

	H_2S	*CH_2SH*	*CH_2SCH_2*	*$(CH_2)_3S_2$*
Recovery furnace	0–1000	2.5–12	1–5	3–80
Flue gas electrostatic	360–1350	0–205	0	38

(*Contd. ...*)

(*Contd. ...*)

Precipitator	130–935	60–1400	125	ND
Venturi scrubber	0–300	0–117	13	109
Digester gas NO treatment	59	14,200	2,880	30
Batch	0–295	1530–36800	190–13500	53
Batch	0–137	10–52000	ND[a]	ND[a]
Black liquor oxidation without digester or evaporator gas	0	0.45	0.45	0.10
Lime kiln	0-600	0–480	0–374	0–720
Dissolving trans without control	0	0–136	0–580	0–320
Evaporators				
Direct control	0–895	0–374	0–24	0–91
Multiple effect	2000–9160	186–1860	8–42	237–179
Multiple effect	0–24150	0–36700	0–5500	0–2780
Multiple effect	(10 lb, ton)	ND[a]	ND[a]	ND[a]
Multiple effect	8700[a]		1500[b]	

[a] not determined
[b] composite analysis for all organic
[c] composite analysis for H_2S and CH_3SH

Table 14.20
Air pollution control methods in use

Source	*Methods for malodorous gases*	*Particulates*
Digester blow	Incineration Heat recovery Altalime scrubbing Chlorine-scrubbing Black liquor oxidation	
Washers	Chlorination Incineration	
Multi effect evaporator'	Black liquor oxidation Incineration Alkaline scrubbing Chlorine scrubbing	
Direct control evaporator	Secondary scrubbing Heat recovery	
Recovery furnace primary treatment	Maintain adequate secondary oxygen operate within design capacity Black liquor oxidation Tall stacks	Electrostatic precipitator venturisc rubber Tall stack
Secondary treatment	Heat recovery Secondary scrubbing	Heat recovery Secondary scrubber
Fuel condensates	Acidification air stripping and incineration oxidation by aeration	

The foul odours could be reduced by introducing black liquor oxidation prior to evaporation. In addition to minimizing the air-borne pollution, black liquor oxidation provides several other benefits:

1. Reduces corrosion problems and improves heat transfer in multiple effect evaporators.
2 Produces fuel which is less sticky and which can be fired at higher total solids concentration without trouble at the primary airports of the furnace.
3. Sodium carbonate content of green liquor is partly replaced with active sodium sulphide, reducing consumption of lime per tonne of bleached pulp produced.
4. Increases sulphidity.
5. Improves pulp yield and its bleachability and strength properties.

Fly ash, from coal fired boilers, is a source of pollution. The fly ash is carried by flue gases, and, unless electrostatic precipitators are provided, it escapes into the atmosphere.

Noise in the mill is another source of pollution. The shrill sound of blowing the digester, the kut-kut sound of chippers and the recovery-furnace sound can also be heard from a distance, particularly at night time.

15

Utilization, Treatment and Disposal of Cane Sugar Industry Effluents

Today, the sugar industry is the third largest industry in the country and ranks next only to the iron and steel, and cotton industries. The effluent from sugar industries contains a large amount of dissolved organic matter. This organic matter is readily decomposed by biological action. Consequently, discharge of these liquors to surface water causes serious damage to aquatic life. In India, there are about 314 sugar factories, of which 90 are in U.P. The statewise position, is given in Table 15.1. Of about 4.1 million tonnes of sugar produced annually, 1.1 million tonnes are produced by Uttar Pradesh, as shown in Table 15.2.

Table 15.1
Statewise sugar factories in India, 1980–81

State	*No of sugar factories*
Andhra Pradesh	33
Assam	3
Bihar	29
Goa	17
Gujarat	13
Haryana	8
Jammu and Kashmir	29
Karnataka	3
Kerala	6
Madhya Pradesh	101
Maharashtra	1
Manipur	5
Nagaland	13
Orissa	2
Punjab	3
Pondicherry	27
Rajasthan	105
Tamil Nadu	2
Total	380

Table 15.2
Statewise estimates: likely production of sugar/molasses/alcohol for the year 1979–80

State	*Sugar in million tons*	*Molasses in million tons*	*Alcohol in million litres*
Andhra Pradesh	0.250	0.100	22.000
Assam	0:080	0.00323	0.704
Bihar	0.200	0.0800	17.600
Goa	0.060	0.0024	0.528
Gujarat	0.200	0.0800	176.600
Haryana	0.104	0.0416	9.152
Karnataka	0.300	0.1400	30.320
Kerala	0.015	0.0060	1.320
Madhya Pradesh	0.040	0.0160	3.520
Maharashtra	1.320	0.5280	116.160
Nagaland	0.060	0.0024	0.528
Orissa	0.015	0.0064	1.320
Pondicherry	0.020	0.0080	1.760
Punjab	0.022	0.0128	2.816
Rajasthan	0.024	0.0096	2.112
Tamil Nadu	0.400	0.1600	35.200
Uttar Pradesh	1.100	0.4400	96.800
West Bengal	0.010	0.0040	8.800
Total	4.220	1.6443.	527.240

Source: All-India Alcohol-Based Industries Development Association.

Standards for Pollutants

The standards prescribed by the Uttar Pradesh Pollution Control Board, Bureau of Indian Standards, and some developed countries, e.g., the UK, USA, Japan and Switzerland, are given in Table 15.4. The variations in case of Biochemical Oxygen Demand, total solid and total suspended solid are especially significant. Such variations in prescribed standards. are also responsible for their being fully accepted by those who are responsible for designing suitable abatement processes. There are well established downward trends in the case of some pollutants, especially of BOD. Some industrially advanced countries, e.g., the USA, are planning to eliminate the total organic load in a reasonable period of time. There are a couple of other important reasons for the lack of keen interest in the development of suitable abatement techniques. The implementation of abatement technique generally demands investment with practically no return. Secondly, sugar factories are well spread out and the total pollution load vis-a-vis assimilation capacity does not make it absolutely essential for reduction of different pollutants to the prescribed limit. The effluents, from the sugar industry, occasionally cause serious problems due to their heavy organic load, which normally requires a lot of oxygen resulting in the exhaustation of oxygens, required for fish to survive. However, considering the great difference between the actual and prescribed values of pollutants, the implementation of a suitable abatement technique is considered essential.

Manufacturing Process

The main raw material for this industry is sugarcane. A typical flow diagram for sugar production is given in Fig. 15.1. The sugarcane is cut into pieces and crushed in a series of rollers to extract the juice in the 'mill house'. The fibrous residue of the mill house is discarded as bagasse. The cane juice from the mill house is slightly acidic. It is treated with sufficient milk of lime to adjust the pH to approximately 7.0-8.4. It is, then, heated to a temperature of 212–215°C and allowed to settle. Lime combines with pectin and other impurities and also coagulates the albuminous material present in the juice. After settling, the juice is filtered and pumped into conical tanks, through the bottom of which carbon dioxide is bubbled to precipitate the excess of lime as calcium carbonate. Any soluble calcium sucrate decomposes into black sugar. This juice, known as carbonated juice, is, then, treated with sulphur dioxide. This operation, known as sulphination, completes the neutralization of lime and the decomposition of calcium sucrate. In addition, the colour of the juice is blackened. The clarified juice is filtered to remove precipitated calcium sulphide. It is concentrated by boiling under reduced pressure in multiple effect evaporators. There, the steam produced in the first evaporator is used to boil the juice in the second. Kept at a lower pressure, the steam produced in the second is again employed to boil the juice in the third at a still lower pressure, and so on until the concentrated juice is finally passed to the vacuum pans where further evaporation reduces the water content to 60%. The 60% crystallized syrup from the vacuum pans is then are to crystallized, where compete crystallization occurs. The vacuum pans are, then, centrifuged to separate the sugar crystal from the mother liquor. The spent liquor is discarded as black strap molasses. The sugar is dried and bagged for transport.

By-Products

Of the various by-products given in Table 15.4, bagasse and molasses are the **most** important by-products of the process. The origin, importance and composition of these **are given** in Table 15.5, while standards are given in Table 15.5.

Table 15.3

By Products of Sugar Industry

(A) Bagasse (B) Molasses (C) Filter mud (D) Boiler ashes (E) Protein from cane juice (F) Cane top and leaves

(A) Bagasse Utilization

As fuel	For fiber product	Miscellaneous use
Generation of steam	Pulp and paper	Furfural
Generation of power	Paper board	Alphacellulose, Plastics
Charcoal briquettes	Fiber board	Poultry litter and mulch
Methane & producer gas	Particle board	Animal feed
		Bagasse concrete
		Soil amendment

(B) Molasses Utilization

Direct use	Distillery industry	Other fermentation industry	Miscellaneous
Export	Rum	Vinegar	Aconitic acid
Fertilizer	Ethyl alcohol	Acetic acid	Monosodium glutamate
Cattle feed	Rectified spirits	Acetone-Butanol	Dextron
	Power alcohol	Citric acid	
	Alcohol derivative	Lactic acid	
	Spent wash	Glycerin	
		Yeast	

(C) Filter Mud

Fertilizer	Waxes and Fat

(D) Boiler Ash

Foundry	Glass Product	Insulating Material

Table 15.4
Standard for the disposal of industrial effluent

Pollutant	*Effluent Board*		*BIS*		*WHO*		*UP pollutants preventing act*		*Switzerland*	*UK*	*USA*
	A	*C*	*A*	*C*	*A*	*C*	*A*	*C*			
PH	5.3-9	5.5-9	5.5-9	5.5-9	7.0-8.5	7.0-8.5	5.5-9.0	5.5-9.0	6.5-8.5	6-10	6-10
Total dissolved solid	—	2100	—	2100	500-1500	—	—	—2100	0.1	—	—
Total suspended solid	100		100	—	5-25	5-25	100	—	20	—	150
BOD (5 days at 20°C)	30	500	30	500	—	—	30	500	20	—	—
COD	250	—	250	—	—	—	250	—	+	—	—
Ammoniacal nitrogen	50	—	90	—	—	—	50	—	+	—	50-110
Oil & grease	10	30	10	30	0.01-0.3	0.01-0.3	10	30	20	50	

A Into Inland Surface Water
C On land for Irrigation
+ Decided case by case
Except for pH all other pollutants are expressed in mg/1

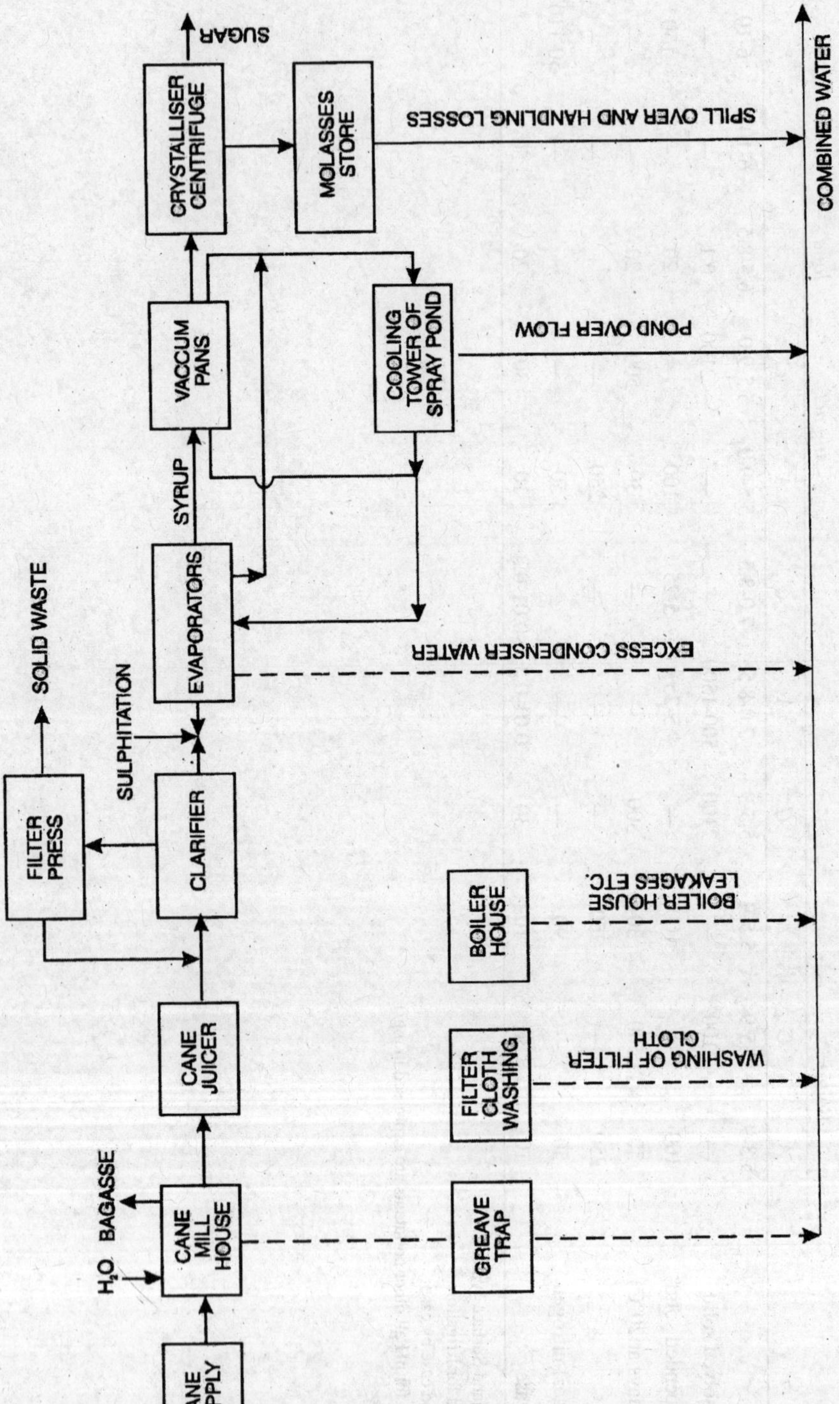

Fig. 15.1 Flow Diagram for the Sugar Manufacturing Process

Source and Characteristics of Wastes

Waste Water from Mill House

Waste water from the mill house includes water used to extract the maximum amount of juice and that used to cool the roller bearings. Such as the mill house waste.

These wastes contain high BOD due to sugar and oil from machineries.

Waste Water from Filter Clothes Washing

These clothes, used for filtering the juice, need occasional cleaning. The wash water, thus, produced, though small in volume, contains high BOD and suspended solids.

A large amount of water is required in the barometric condenser of the multiple effect evaporators and vacuum pans. The water is usually, partially or fully recirculated, after cooling through a spray pond. This cooling water gets polluted as it picks up some organic substances from the vapours of the boiling syrup in the evaporator and vacuum pans. The water from the spray pond, when it overflows, becomes a part of the waste water, usually low in BOD. But due to poor maintenance and bad operating conditions, a substantial amount of sugar may entrain in the condenser water. This polluted water, instead of being recirculated, is discarded as excess condenser water. These discharges contribute substantially to waste volume and moderately to BOD in many sugar mills.

The leakage and spillages of juice syrup and molasses in different sections and periodical washing of floors also contributes to waste water. Though these waste are small in volume and are discharged intermittently, they have a very high BOD.

The periodic blow off of the boilers produces other intermittent discharges, with high suspended solids and low BOD, usually alkaline in nature. The characteristics of wastes are given in Table 15.5.

Table 15.5
Characteristics of sugar mill waste

Characteristics	*Mill house*	*Filter cloth washing*	*Condenser water*	*Boiler house*	*Combined waste excluding condenser water*
PH	6.7	9.5	—	12	4.6–7.1
Total Solids (mg/1)	1760	6970		5130	870–3500
Total volatile solids (mg/1)		—	—	—	400–2200
Total suspended solids (mg/1)	910	4000	—	120	220–800
Total nitrogen (mg/1)	—	—	—	—	10–40
Biochemical Oxygen Demand (5 days at 20°C mg/1)	210	1765		5150	300–2000
Chemical Oxygen Demand (mg/1)	—	—	—	—	600–4380
COD BOD	—	—		—	1.3–2.0

Effect of Waste on the Receiving Stream

Organic pollutants present in the effluent, viz., sugar and other carbohydrates, when it stagnates, by the rapid consumption of oxygen, followed by anaerobic stabilization, cause bad odour, black colour and fish mortality due to formation of hydrogen sulphide.

Treatment of Sugar Industry Effluent

The various treatment processes are as follows:

1. Physical
2. Chemical
3. Biological.

The number of processes that have been adopted to treat sugar industry effluent are:

1. Prevention at source
2. Disposal on land for irrigation
3. Trickling filter and activated sludge process
4. Anaerobic treatment
5. Disposal in lagoons or stabilization ponds.

Prevention at Source

The quantity of pollutional material, being discharged into waste waters, can be reduced considerably by taking the following measures:

1. Good housekeeping, through proper operations and maintenance improves the process efficiency, thereby, reducing the total amount of pollutional material in the waste waters.
2. Efficient separation of evaporators to reduce entrainment to the minimum.
3. Routine inspection of different units, particularly pumps, conveyors, pipes and other vessels.
4. By keeping a check on the extent of entrainment of sugar syrup through the barometric condenser of the evaporators. Loading of the evaporators and vacuum pumps, when boiling at incorrect liquid level, and variation in vacuum pans, at excessive rate operation, leads to loss of sugar through condenser water.

   Improper design of these units, particularly the entrainment in separators, also results in boiling and splashing in the units. By giving proper attention to reduce this entrainment, we can reduce the effluents as well as increase efficiency.
5. Judicious use of water can reduce the waste problem, arising from floor sweeping and washing.
6. By giving a short detention time in the holding tank to the filter; cloth washing before mixing with other effluents.
7. Molasses has an extremely high BOD of the order of 90,000 mg/1, hence, proper handling and storage to avoid spillage becomes essential.
8. The material leaking from pumps and vessels in sugar factories can be collected and returned to the respective processes by making enclosures and collection pits around the pumps and vessels.

Disposal on Land for Irrigation

The effluent from cane sugar factories can be disposed off on the land as irrigation water. The process has been practiced by many factories in Uttar Pradesh and Bihar but has not gained much appreciation due to accumulation of sludge on the field, odour nuisance and large land requirement. It was observed to reduce suspended solids and BOD by 99 percent and 65 percent, respectively.

However, there are difficulties due to accumulation of sludge on field, used for disposal of unfiltered waste water from sugar factories. This difficulty can only by avoided by using only 1/3 of the available space, each year, for waste disposal, and using that section for the next two years for growing crops, grain or vegetables.

Jenson used a system for irrigation in which he used a shallow pond for removal of suspended solid resulting in very lush grasslands.

Trickling Filter and Activated Sludge Process

The treatment of sugar mill effluent, in a high rate trickling filter, reduced pollution by 70%, which could be further reduced to 95% after stabilization in a tank for 3 days. However, the process has the following limitations:

(*a*) The treatment requires large and expensive plants

(*b*) It needs skilled supervisors for handling

(*c*) It is difficult to operate in the winter season

(*d*) It requires a large quantity of water for dilution.

Anaerobic Treatment of Sugar Industry Effluent

Anaerobic treatment of sugar industry effluent is a biochemical process, caused by the facultative and anaerobic group of bacteria which, converts the organic matter into volatile acid, and methanogenic bacteria, then, converts the volatile acid to carbon-dioxide and methane.

Methanogenic bacteria are strictly anaerobic. They thrive best when pH is close to neutral but to fail to thrive at pH6.0. The bacteria are heterogenous in cellular morphology-some are rods, others cocci known as sarcinae.

The process of anaerobic digestion consists of a closed digester size, depending upon the quantity of effluent, having an inlet for the addition of waste, two outlets for methane gas and for disposal of slurry. For starting the process of digestion, the digester is seeded with 20% solution of cowdung in water for one week at 37 + 10°C. Then, the diluted effluent is added, the concentration is gradually increased. At each loading, digester is ran for sufficient time at several total displacements.

The anaerobic digestion of cane sugar industry in a closed digester for methane recovery is a promising pollution control measure as the process results in BOD up to 100 mg/*l*. The effluent from the anaerobic digester can be used for irrigations purposes.

Disposal in Lagoon or Stabilization Pond

Treatment in a lagoon or by oxidation pond had been found most feasible and economical.

Description of Plant Chakarborty et al. carried out treatment of cane sugar waste in a stabilization pond which consists of the following units:

1. *Bar screens* It is used to assess the suspended particle.
2. *Grease trap* For grease removal.
3. *Two-stage anaerobic pond*—lagoons—earthen construction
   Depth—8 ft.
   Detention time—7 days
   BOD loading—0.0145 Ib/cu. ft/day
   BOD Reduction—60%.
4. *Anerobic lagoon pond*—lagoons—earthen construction
   Depth—4ft
   Detention time—12–15 days
   BOD loading—0.0406 lb/cu. ft./day
   BOD reduction—70%
   Over all reduction—90%, *i.e.,* 100 mg/1 BOD.
5. *An algae culture tank.* An algae culture tank is for continuous seeding of the anaerobic pond content with an acclimatized culture of chlorella and scendesmus.

A model scheme of the plant based on the above working principle, installed at various places, is given in Fig. 15.2 and is discussed below. It consists of the following units.

Bar Screen These are two in number and 2 m long, 1 m wide and 1 m deep, surrounded by the strainer pit.

Grease Separator This is 15 m long, 5 m wide and 5 m deep. The grease pit is 2 in long, 2 m wide and 1 m deep.

Anaerobic and Aerobic Lagoon These are earthen lagoons, 150 m long and 50 m wide, and divided into five compartments. Of these, the first three comprise an area of 1925 m with a depth of 3.5 m, known as anaerobic ponds. The remaining two compartments, comprising an area of 6000 m and depth of 1.5 m, are called aerobic or oxidation ponds. The first compartment of this oxidation pond is provided with a crop of water hyacinth and the second with a crop of green algae (mostly chlorella and scendesmus).

Procedure The effluent from the sugar mill first goes into the bar screen where all the suspended particles are removed. It, then, goes into the grease separator where all the grease gets trapped. The strained and degreased effluent, containing suspended and dissolved inorganic and organic matter, flows to an underground anaerobic kachcha pond, where all the organic matter gets decomposed and degraded biologically and the digested effluent overflows into the first compartment of the aerobic pond. Here, all the toxic minerals and most of the phenolic and organic compounds get absorbed. The high rate of transpiration of water hyacinth helps reduce the volume of effluent. The effluent, then, goes into the last compartment where it gets oxidized by green algae.

Proposed Reduction in Values after Treatment for a Typical Sugar industry (by lagoonisig or stabilization pond)'

BOD of combined effluent = 1150 mg/1

Reduction in the Anaerobic Pond

In this pond, the BOD load of the influent is reduced by 60%.

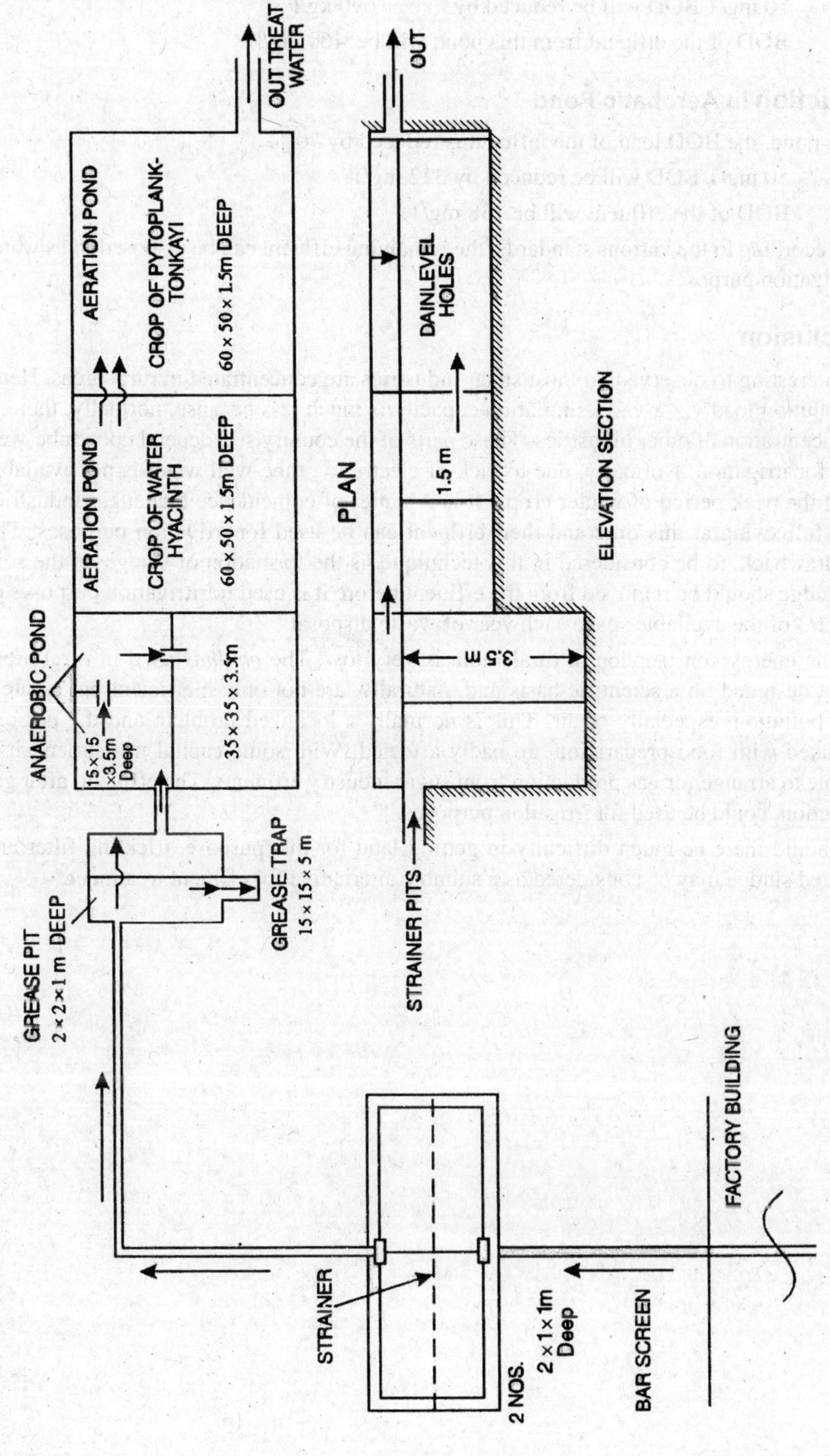

Fig. 15.2 Flow sheet for complete treatment of cane sugar effluent (a typical example)

50 mg/1 BOD will be reduced by 690 kg/l

BOD of the effluent from this pond will be 460 mg/l

Reduction in Aerobatic Pond

In this pond, the BOD load of the influent is reduced by 70%.

50 mg/1 BOD will be reduced by 322 mg/1.

BOD of the effluent will be 138 mg/1.

According to the various standards, the remaining effluent can be disposed of as water for irrigation purposes.

Conclusion

It is interesting to observe that most sugar industries are concentrated in rural areas. Here, the pollution load viz-a-viz assimilation capacity is much less because, normally, there is no concentration of other industries. These parts of the country still depend upon tube-well water for irrigation. Normally, due to lack of electricity, tube-well water is not available during the peak period of winter crops. It is a matter of coincidence that sugar industries are in full swing at this time and their effluent can be used for irrigation purposes. The only drawback, to be considered in this technique, is the formation of sludge on the soil. The sludge should be removed from the effluent before it is used for irrigation purposes or using 1/3 of the available space each year of waste disposal.

The energy consumption in rural India is very low. The *chulhas* used in rural areas are not designed on a scientific basis and, naturally, are not only inefficient but create a lot of pollution, especially of air. This is normally a localized problem and the persons associated with food preparation are badly affected. With some capital investment, it is possible to arrange for gas production from sugar industry effluents. The effluent, after gas production, could be used for irrigation purposes.

Should there be much difficulty in getting land for this purpose, trickling filter and activated sludge may be considered as a suitable alternative for effluent treatment.

16

Utilization of Distillery Effluents

Introduction

Effluent from distilleries contains a large amount of dissolved organic matter. This organic matter is readily decomposed by biological action, consequently, its discharge into surface water causes serious damage to aquatic life in the stream.

In India, there are about 140 distilleries, a State–wise position is given in Table 16.1, producing ethyl alcohol by fermentation of molasses and subsequent distillation of the fermented wash. The fermentation is carried out by yeast, which converts the sugar, present in the molasses into alcohol, while the sludge settles down at the end of the process.

Table 16.1
Statewise position of distilleries

State	*No. of distilleries*
Andhra Pradesh	16
Assam	1
Bihar	8
Goa	2
Gujarat	5
Haryana	2
Himachal Pradesh	1
Jammu and Kashmir	—
Karnataka	18
Kerala	4
Madhya Pradesh	6
Maharashtra	27
Manipur	—
Nagaland	1
Orissa	3
Punjab	2
Pondicherry	—
Rajasthan	3
Tamil Nadu	8
Uttar Pradesh	30
West Bengal	13
Total	140

After recovery of alcohol, the spent wash, left behind, is another waste product, distilleries. The spent wash is the largest effluent stream from distilleries, the volume of which varies from 14.22 times of the volume of rectified spirit produced. Spent wash is highly acidic. The characteristics of the waste are given in Table 16.2.

Table 16.2

Characteristics of spent wash from a molasses distillery

Characteristics	*Average value*
Colour	Dark brown
Odour	of molasses
pH	3.5–3.65
COD (Dicromate value), mg/1	118,000
BOD (5 days 20°C), mg/1	41,350
Solids mg/l	
i) Total	99,000
ii) Suspended	350
iii) Dissolved	9,865
iv) Volatile	62,500
Nitrogen mg/l	
i) Total	1,135
ii) Ammonia	28
Chloride, mg/l	5,500
Sulphates, mg/l	4,200
Volatile acid as acetic acid, mg/l	6,000
Total acidity (as $CaCO_3$), mg/l	16,850
Mineral acidity (as $CaCO_3$), mg/l	2,000
Potassium (K), mg/l	5,070
Sodium (Na), mg/l	1,100
Calcium (Ca), mg/l	27,000
Magnesium (Mg), mg/l	2,400
Iron (Fe), mg/l	60

Standards for Pollutants

The standards prescribed by the Uttar Pradesh Pollution, Prevention and Control Board, Bureau oi Indian Standards and some other developed countries, for example, the UK, USA, Japan and Switzerland are enumerated in Table 16.3.

As will be noticed, there are variations, especially in the case of biological oxygen demand and total suspended solids. Total solids are specially significant. Such a wide variation in prescribed standards may be responsible for lack of full acceptability by those who are responsible for designing a suitable abatement process. Why? There is a well-established downward trend in case of the pollutants, especially biological oxygen demand. Some of the industrially advanced countries, e.g., USA is planning to eliminate total organic load in couple of other important reasons, lack of hidden interest in development of suitable abatement techniques. The implementation of abatement technique generally demands investment without practically any return. Secondly, the distilleries are well spread and obviously the total pollution load vis–a–vis assimilation capacity does not make it absolutely essential for reduction of different pollutants to the prescribed limit. The effluents from§

Table 16.3
Standards for the disposal of industrial effluents

Pollutant mg/l	*Effluent board*			*BIS*			*WHO*			*UP -water pollution prevention and control act*			*Japan*	*Switzerland*	*UK*	*US*
	A	*B*	*C*	*A*	*B*	*C*	*A*	*B*	*C*	*A*	*B*	*C*				
Ammoniacal nitrogen	50	50	—	50	50	—	—	—	—	50	50	—	—	+	—	50-100
Biochemical Oxygen Demand (5 days 20°C)	30	500*	500	30	500*	500				30	500*	500		20		
Chemical Oxygen Demand	250	—	—	250	—	—	—	—	—	250	—	—	—	+	—	—
Chloride as Cl	60	600*	600*	—	600*	600	200-600	200-600	200-600	—	600*	600	—	+	—	—
Iron	—	—	—	—	—	—	0.1-1.0	0.1-1.0	0.1-1.0	—	—	—	—	20	—	—
PH	5.5-9	5.5-9	5.5-9	5.5-9	5.5-9	5.5-9	7.0-8.5	7.0-8.5	7.0-8.5	5.5-9	5.5-9	5.5-9		6.5-8.5	6-10	6-10
Sulphates	100	100b	1000	—	1000*	1000*	1000	200-400	200-400	—	1000*	1000	—	+	1000	—
Total dissolved solids	—	2100*	2100	—	2100*	2100	500- 1500	500- 1500	—	—	2100*	2100	—	0.1	—	—
Total suspended solids	100	600	—	100	600	—	5-25	5-25	5-25	100	600b	—	—	20	—	1

A Into inland surface water

B Into public sewers

C On land for irrigation

a Subject to relaxation or tightening by local authority

b Relaxation to 750 by local authority

* These requirements shall only apply where, after treatment the sewage is disposed of on land for irrigation

\+ Decide case by case

distilleries occasionally cause a serious problem due to heavy organic load which normally requires a lot of oxygen, resulting in elimination of oxygen, required for the fish to survive. However, considering such a large difference between their actual values and prescribed values, the implementation of suitable techniques is considered essential.

Pollution Abatement in Distilleries

There are several methods which could be considered for pollution abatement in distilleries. The two important methods are aerobic and anaerobic. Unfortunately, due to economic reasons, the aerobic method does not find much application, especially, when the total amount of organic load to be removed is fairly high.

Anaerobic lagooning and anaerobic digestion, which are commonly used, have been compared in Table 16.4.

Efforts have also been made for the development of a few suitable processes for the recovery of potash as well as for the manufacture of Torula yeast, and both have been briefly mentioned in Table 16.2. The possibility of using distillery effluents for irrigational purposes has also been indicated in Table 16.4.

Considering that anaerobic processes have proved economically viable, the details for the same have been given.

A critical evaluation of different techniques which could be employed for pollution control in distillery clearly indicates that practically all the methods involve a considerable amount of both capital as well as running expenditure without any equivalent return. Considering the growing concern for the development of suitable renewable resources of energy, in view of the global energy crisis, it is considered practical to opt for the generation of methane out of all biomaterial including distillery effluent. The methane gas obtained could be used either as a fuel gas or as a raw material for the petrochemical industry. Some of its characteristics are enumerated below:

Methane Gas as Fuel

1. It is a non–knocking fuel with a very high compression ratio.
2. It is a clean engine fuel.
3. It has the advantage of getting well distributed in the internal engine and shows no tendency to dilute the lubricating oil.
4. It burns with a non–luminous flame in air, forming carbon dioxide and water.
5. It emits an exhaust gas with extremely low carbon monoxide content.

Methane Gas as a Raw Material for Petrochemical Industry

1. It can be used in the production of ammonia and urea (used as fertilizers).
2. It is used in the formation of valuable derivatives, viz., methyl chloride, methyl dichloride, chloroform and carbon tetrachloride.
3. It can be used in the production of methanol.
4. It can be used in the preparation of carbon black.
5. It can be used as a source of hydrogen for synthesis gas (manufacture of petrol).

Anaerobic Treatment of Distillery Effluent

Anaerobic treatment of distillery effluent is a biochemical process, caused by the facultative and anaerobic group of bacteria which converts the organic substance into volatile acid

Table 16.4
Pollution abatement in distilleries

	Direct use for irrigation	*Anaerobic lagooning*	*Anaerobic digestion*	*Ammonification process*	*Potash recovery*	*Manufacture of Torula yeast*
1	*2*	*3*	*4*	*5*	*6*	*7*
Process	Due to high manual value of distillery waste as it contains nutrients like, K, Na, Ca, Mg and Be which can be directly used for irrigation.	Distillery waste is treated in earthen constructions of 2.2 metre deep, 5 in number for 100 days of retention time and 4 months for stabilization. Finally mixed with cooling and condenser water and disposed for irrigation.	Distillery effluent is treated in close digesters in the presence of bacteria which causes the production of methane. The slurry after treatment, is disposed in fields for irrigation.	The twice diluted waste is settled in a tank and then kept in a Pucca Pit about 2.5 metres deep. Bacterial culture from a seed tank is mixed with settled spent wash for days of retention time.	The spent wash neutralized with lime upto 7 pH is then filtered. The filtered spent wash is evaporated in multiple effect evaporators from 9%-75% solids. This thick liquor is sprayed into the top of incinerators from where it slides down and forms a substance known as spent wash coke. This then drops into the hearth of incinerators and is burnt into ash. Ash is then reached with water, filter and neutralized with H_2SO_4 and K_2SO_4 and K.	The effluent is supplied with nitrogen and phosphorus nutrients and culture is grown. A distillery producing 8000 litres of spent wash produces 8 kg of Torula yeast day

(*Contd.*)

(Table 16.4 *Contd.*)

1	*2*	*3*	*4*	*5*	*6*	*7*
BOD Reduction		80-90%	80-90%	70-80%		40-50%
Advantages	It solves the problem of high cost fertilizer.	Low capital investment.	The problems of odour nuisance and land requirement are solved.	(1) Needs short retention time. (2) Less than that is required by anaerobic lagooning. (3) Less chances of seepage as Pucca Pits are used.	(1) High grade K-salt can be recovered. (2) Fuel economy can be achieved by burning spent wash coke in waste heat boilers drying and concentrating the spent wash.	High grade protein is recovered.
Limitations	(1) Cant be employed in rainy season (2) Results in contamination of subsoil water (3) Requires large utilization of total quantity of waste.	(1) Large land requirements. (2) Odour nuisance resulting in air pollution. (3) Subsoil contamination due to seepage.	(1) Necessary technical skills are not available.	(1) Large volume of H_2O is needed for dilution. (2) Needs further treatment as it results in 70-80% BOD reduction which is far more than the recommended safe limit. (3) Needs more technical control than lagooning.	(1) Involves high consumption of steam. (2) Problems of calcium scale and corrosion of equipments are faced.	(1) High production cost. (2) Needs further treatment.

and methanogenic bacteria, and, then, converts the volatile acid into carbon dioxide and methane.

Methanogenic bacteria are strictly anaerobes. They thrive best when the pH is close to neutral but fail to thrive at pH 6. The methane bacteria are heterogenous in cellular morphology- some are rods, others cocci, and others in clusters of cocci known as sarcina. A list of methane bacteria is given in Table 16.5.

Table 16.5
List of effluent bacteria

Name of bacteria	*Nature*
Methanobacterium formicum	Mesophilic
Methanobacterium omelianskii	Mesophilic
Methanobacterium propinoxicum	Mesophilic
Methanobacterium sonngenii	Mesophilic
Methanobacterium	Mcsophilic
	Mesophilic
	Mesophilic
	Mesophilic
Methanosarcinae barkerii	Mesophilic
Metanobacterium autotropicum	Thermophilic

Mechanism of the Process

Bushwell proposed the following overall equation for conversion of organic matter in industrial waste into carbon dioxide and methane, for all three types of bacteria.

$$C_nH_nO_b + \left(n - \frac{a}{4} - \frac{b}{2}\right)H_2O = \left(\frac{n}{2} - \frac{a}{8} + \frac{b}{4}\right)CO_2 + \left(\frac{n}{2} + \frac{a}{8} - \frac{b}{4}\right)CH_4$$

For example:

Carbohydrates as in case of distillery, pulp and paper vegetable tannery effluent, straw and dry leaves, etc.

$$(C_6H_{10}O_5)_x + xH_2O \rightarrow x(C_6H_{12}O_6)$$

$$C_6H_{12}O_6 + \left(6 - \frac{12}{4} - \frac{6}{2}\right)H_2O \rightarrow \left(\frac{6}{12} - \frac{12}{8} + \frac{6}{4}\right)CO_2 + \left(\frac{6}{2} + \frac{12}{8} - \frac{6}{4}\right)CH_4$$

$$C_6H_{12}O_6 + 6H_2O \rightarrow 3CO_2\ 4 + 3CH_4$$

or 50% carbon dioxide, 50% met

Proteins, e.g., gobar, sewage, night soil and tannery effluent.

$$\underset{\text{Alanine}}{CH_3CHNH_2COOH} \xrightleftharpoons{HOH} \underset{\text{Lactic Acid}}{CH_3CH(OH)COOH}$$

$$CH_3CH(OH)COOH + \left(3 - \frac{6}{4} - \frac{3}{2}\right)H_2O \rightarrow \left(\frac{3}{2} - \frac{6}{8} + \frac{3}{4}\right)CO_2 + \left(\frac{3}{2} + \frac{6}{8} - \frac{3}{4}\right)CH_4$$

Lactic acid

$$CH_3CHOHCOOH + H_2O \rightarrow \frac{3}{2}CO_2 + \frac{3}{2}CH_4$$

or Carbon dioxide 50% Methane 50%

Fats, e.g., vegetable industry, etc.

$$\begin{matrix} CH_2OOCC_{17}H_{35} \\ | \\ CHOOCC_{17}H_{35} \\ | \\ CH_2OOCC_{17}H_{35} \end{matrix} + 3H_2O \longrightarrow \underset{\text{Stearic acid}}{3C_{17}H_{35}COOH} + \underset{\text{Glycerol}}{\begin{matrix} CH_2OH \\ | \\ CHOH \\ | \\ CH_2OH \end{matrix}}$$

$$\underset{\text{Stearic acid}}{C_{17}H_{35}COOH} + \left(18 - \frac{36}{4} - \frac{2}{2}\right)H_2O \rightarrow \left(\frac{18}{2} - \frac{36}{8} + \frac{2}{4}\right)CO_2 + \left(\frac{18}{2} - \frac{36}{8} + \frac{2}{4}\right)CH_4$$

$$C_{17}H_{35}COOH + 7H_2O \rightarrow 5CO_2 + 13CH_4$$

or Carbon dioxide 20% Methane 70%

The results obtained experimentally are in good agreement with above equation.

However, there are two available mechanisms for the digestion of organic matter. The formation of methane is completed in two steps (*i*) liquefaction or hydrolytic stage. The first step involves the conversion of organic matter, present in effluent, into fatty acid and alcohol, (*ii*) gasification stage-according to the first concept, the next step involves the formation of carbon dioxide and simultaneous reduction to methane. Carbon dioxide is actually consumed. The following general equation represents the digestion of carbohydrates, proteins and fats.

Carbohydrates

$$(C_6H_{10}O_5)_x + xH_2O \rightarrow x(C_6H_{12}O_6)$$

$$C_6H_{12}O_6 \rightarrow 2C_2H_5OH + 2CO_2$$

$$2CH_3CH_2OH \xrightleftharpoons{CO_2} 2CH_3COOH + CH_4$$

$$CH_3COOH \xrightleftharpoons{H_2O} CH_4 + CO_2$$

Proteins:

$$\begin{matrix} H \\ | \\ R\text{–}C\text{–}COOH \\ | \\ NH_2 \end{matrix} \xrightleftharpoons[\text{Decarboxylase}]{} NH_3 + \begin{matrix} H \\ | \\ R\text{–}C\text{–}COOH \\ | \\ OH \end{matrix}$$

$$\begin{matrix} H \\ | \\ R\text{–}C\text{–}COOH \\ | \\ OH \end{matrix} \xrightleftharpoons[\text{Decarboxylase}]{} \begin{matrix} H \\ | \\ R\text{–}R\text{–}H \\ | \\ OH \end{matrix} + CO_2$$

$$2RCH_2OH + CO_2 \rightarrow 2RCOOH + CH_4$$

(33–37°C) except for the other bacteria M. thermonulolropicus. Hence, a digester operating close to 35°C would be the most efficient.

Hydrogen Ion Concentration. All the methane bacteria listed in Table 16.5 are very sensitive to a pH change and are characterized by a narrow pH range, with the optimum being between 6.8 and 7.4 except the M. vaniellii which has a pH of 8.0. However, the best results are obtained at pH 7.00 as one half of the bacteria show an optimum pH 6.6 and the other half 7.4.

Nutrients Methane bacteria proliferates were in substrata that has a proper balance of elements, viz., C, H, O, N, P and S required by them. The minor nutrients are metals, viz., Ca, Mg, etc. As the distillery effluents (spent wash) contain all the nutrients, needed by them, they do not require any additional nutrient.

BOD/N ratio in organic waste should be within the range of 17:1–32:1 for satisfactory removal of BOD in aerobic biological requirements. However, such a limit of BOD/N is known in the anaerobic biological treatment process. There are some isolated instances, reported in the literature (1, 6) which shows that N-addition is beneficial in anaerobic digestion of N-deficient waste. Bushwell and Hatfield1 found ammonia nitrogen in the form of $(NH_4)2CO_2$, NH_4C1, NH_4OH as a suitable source of nitrogen for methane fermentation. Rudolf and Ambeg found that ^–addition in the form of NH_4OH or $(NH_4)_2HPO_4$ is beneficial in batch digestion of white water.

Toxic Materials The micro-organisms that help to produce biogas are easily affected by many harmful materials. The maximum allowable concentrations of such harmful materials are given in Table 16.6. These toxic materials should not either present nor should their concentration diluted with water. During anaerobic digestion, sulphate is reduced to soluble sulphides and hydrogen sulphide gas. With the presence of hydrogen sulphide gas, the activity of the methane bacteria stops. In India, where the concentration of sulphate in distillery effluent does not exceed 4000–5000 mg/1, no appreciable reduction in the efficiency of the performance of digester occurs. For guidance, it may be noted that when the concentration of dissolved sulphide exceeds 200 mg/1, the process is disrupted and ferric acetate may have to be added to precipitate the soluble sulphides.

Table 16.6
List of toxic materials with maximum allowable concentrations

Toxic materials	*Limit*
Sulphates (SO_4^{2-})	5,000 ppm
Sodium chloride (NaCl)	40,000 ppm
Copper (Cu)	100 mg/1
Chromium (Cr)	200 mg/1
Nickel (Ni)	200–500 mg/1
Cyanide	Below 25 mg/1
ABS detergent Comp.	20–40 ppm
Ammonia (NH_3)	15,000–30,000 mg/1
Sodium (Na)	3,500–5,500 mg/1
Potassium (K)	2,500–4,000 mg/1
Calcium (Ca)	2,500–4,500 mg/1
Magnesium (Mg)	1,000–1,500 mg/1

Micro-organisms Involved There are three types of methane bacteria, as listed in Table 16.5, which survive in the given range of temperature:

1. Cryophilic bacteria 0–10°C
2. Mesophilic bacteria 10–40°C
3. Thermophilic bacteria 40–60°C.

In a tropical country like India, where the sun shines for a long duration and the temperature remains between 10–40°C, mesophilic bacteria are most suitable.

Bacterial Population In the case of gobar or sewage sludge digestion, the bacteria required are present in the substrata, and they, in the presence of adequate and proper environment, multiply and achieve digestion. This period can, however, be shortened by providing an artificial culture, having large number of these bacteria. This oculum is known as seeding and can be done by an adequate amount of a well-digested sludge or other substrata.

Frequency of Feeding Bacteria work best under constant and steady feed conditions. They keep on proliferating and working as long as there is a steady supply of food. It is advantageous to feed them continuously as in continuous or semi-continuous digestion rather than on a feast and fast basis as in batch digestion for maximization of this activity.

Model Scheme

A model scheme of the plant based, on the above parameters is given in Fig. 16.1. The plant consists of a digester, carbon dioxide absorber, heating unit, condenser, carbon dioxide reservoir, diaphragm pump, methane gas holder and switch. The digester is a closed unit consisting of two inlets, one for the addition of effluent and the other for the recirculation of carbon dioxide and also two outlets, for gases formed, and disposal of the slurry formed.

The carbon dioxide absorber is a closed unit having two inlets: one for the gas produced and the other for the calcium carbonate produced by the heating unit, and two outlets— one for a methane gas holder and the other for the heating unit, which remains filled with calcium carbonate. The heating unit consists of a copper tube, having one inlet from the carbon dioxide absorber, and two outlets — one to the carbon dioxide reservoir and the other back to the carbon dioxide, and one Bunsen burner for heating the tube.

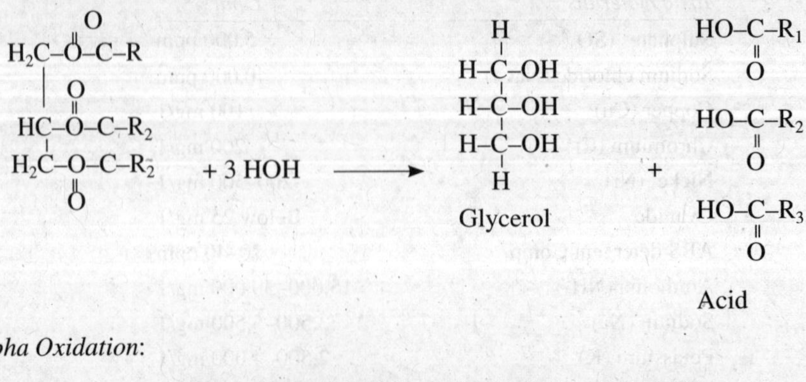

Alpha Oxidation:

$$4RCH_2\,COOH + 2HOH \rightarrow 4RCOOH + CO_2 + 3CH_4$$

Beta Oxidation:

$$2RCH_2\,CH_2\,C00H + CO_2 + 2HOH \rightarrow 2RCOOH + 2CH_3\,COOH + CH_4$$

$$CH_3COOH \rightarrow CH_4 + CO_2$$

According to the second concept, it is presumed that in the second step of gasification, each molecule of methane arises from the reduction of carbon dioxide. The tracer technique also shows that the carbon dioxide acts as hydrogen acceptor while the alcohol acts as the hydrogen donor, as in the following equation:

Ethyl alcohol		Carbon dioxide		
$2C_2H_5OH$	+ $2H_2O$	+ CO_2	$\longrightarrow$	$2CH_3COOH + 2H_2O + CH$
Hydrogen donor		Hydrogen acceptor		

Mechanism Involved:

$$2H\text{–}OH \rightleftharpoons 2H^+ + 2OH^-$$

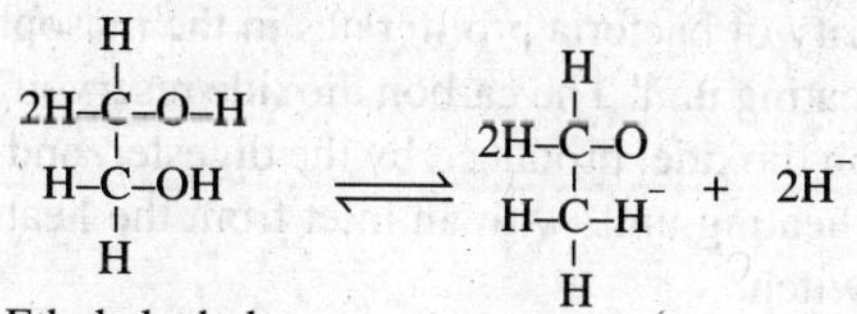

Ethyl alcohol

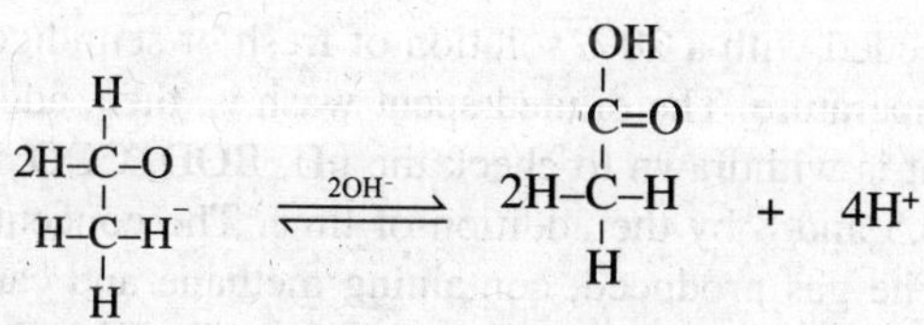

Acid acid

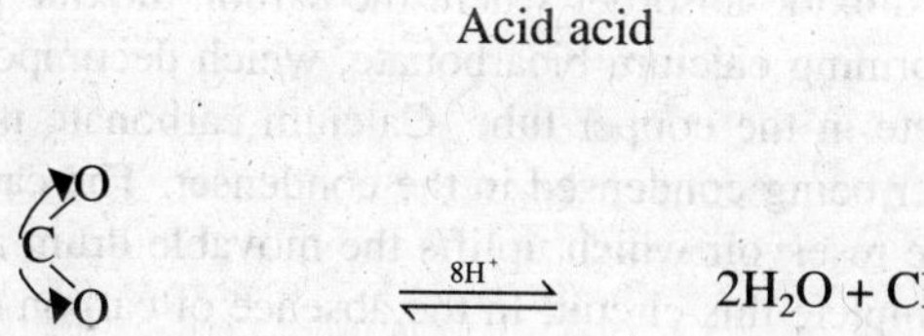

Carbon dioxide

Methods of Production of Methane

The equipment for the process of anaerobic digestion consists of a closed digester, the size of which depends upon the quantity of effluent, having one inlet for the addition of waste and two outlets, one for a methane gas holder and one for the disposal of slurry. For the start up of digestion, the digester is seeded with 20% solution of cowdung in water. For the loading, there are two methods available for methane production, viz., anaerobic digestion: (*i*) Batch Digestion—In this type of digestion, the plant is loaded periodically with waste materials and with seed materials. When gas production falls below the minimum economical rate, the plant is emptied. In order to attain continuous gas production, several such plants are operated, each being charged in succession. The advantages[2] of the system are as follows: (*i*) simple in construction (*ii*) no special mixing or loading devices are usually needed. There are, however, the following disadvantages : (*i*) Total gas available is less (*ii*) retention time is more. Preliminary batch digestion experiment was not successful in reducing BOD. Sen and Bhaskar experienced that in seeded undiluted waste, the volatile acid rose aiming to a higher value of the order of 1000 mg/1 and process failed, indicating the necessity for dilution, different dilutions and different detention time with sludge as a seed did not show any significant improvement increasing the temperature, i.e., from mesophilic (10– 40°C) to rang. The digested cowdung sludge was observed sludge for distillery waste. (*iii*) In case of continuous digestion, the digester is charged once or twice and the digested material is removed. The volume remains constant. The advantages are constant rate of gas efficient -decomposition and less retention time. But material solidifies and floats to form a crust on the liquid system, laid a special device is necessary to break the crust formed.

Parameters for Maximization Production

The rate of methane production depends upon the presence of methanogenic bacteria. The methanogenic bacteria need the following requirements to survive:

Temperature A majority of bacteria proliferates in the mesophilic range to the carbon dioxide absorber by the heating unit. The carbon dioxide reservoir is a simple arrangement for the collection of carbon dioxide, produced by the digester, and separated by the carbon dioxide absorber and the heating unit, with an inlet from the heating, and an outlet to the pump, connected to the switch.

Procedure

The digester is first seeded with a 20% solution of fresh or semidigested cowdung in tap water at 37 + 1°C temperature. The diluted spent-wash is, then, added to acclimatize the seed and some amount is withdrawn to check the pH, BOD, COD and solids. The pH is maintained between 6.5 and 8 by the addition of lime. The concentration of spent-wash is slowly increased. The gas produced, containing methane and carbon dioxide 40%, is sent into the carbon dioxide absorber where the carbon dioxide produced is absorbed in calcium carbonate forming calcium bicarbonate, which decomposes into carbon dioxide and calcium carbonate in the copper tube. Calcium carbonate is returned to the carbon dioxide absorber after being condensed in the condenser. The carbon dioxide is returned to the carbon dioxide reservoir which uplifts the movable drum and connects the system with the pump to complete this circuit. In the absence of carbon dioxide, the drum of the carbon dioxide reservoir goes down and the circuit to the pump is disconnected. Thus, the continuous separation and recirculation of carbon dioxide remains automatic.

Concentration-Incineration

Concentration-incineration as a pollution control measure is receiving more attention, especially because it aims at zero pollution. In distillery effluents, the solid content is about 10%. This effluent is concentrated in evaporators, at different stages, to about 60% solid content. This concentrated material is burnt in the boiler. Even though the basic principle is very simple and obvious, the equipment required, for concentration in the evaporators as well as combustion, is fairly expensive because of the material used in their construction. However, sufficient amounts of energy, steam and electricity are produced to meet the requirements of the distillery, the water coming out from the condenser can be reused in the fermenters and, thus, reduce the total water requirement; and potash can be used as fertilizer. Table 16.7 lists the advantages of this process. Tables 16.8 and 16.9 list the equipment and other details of this process. As can be seen from this table, approximately 4.5 crores will be required to increase concentration–incineration unit for 60 kl per day capacity distillery. This is much more than the amount required to construct a new distillery. For traditional batch fermentation of this capacity, the total capital requirement will be about Rs.2 crores, and even a continuous process with all the facilities for process control will not cost more than Rs.2.4 crores.

Table 16.7
Basis for design of concentration system

1. Distillery capacity	60,000 LPD
2. Spent wash produced	960 m^3/day
3. Sp. gr. of spent wash	1.047
4. Dissolved solid content	8.6%
5. Ash content	2.5%
6. Temperature of dilute spent wash	90°C
7. Lower calorific value of 60% conc. spent wash	1700 kcal/kg
8. Ultimate analysis of dry solids	t
(a) Moisture content	1.1
(b) Mineral matter	24.4
(c) Carbon	36.3
(d) Hydrogen	3.67
(e) Nitrogen	2.21
(f) Sulphur	—
(g) Oxygen	32.32
9. Ash analysis	
(a) SiO_2	5.04
(b) Fe_2O_3	0.62
(c) TiO_2	Nil
(d) Al_2O_3	13.2
(e) CaO	13.65
(f) MgO	4.02
(g) Sulphate	10.27
(h) Chloride	0.55
(i) Phosphate	0.80
(j) Na_2O	6.37
(k) K_2O	45.47

Performance Parameters

Neutralization System

1. Dilute Spent Wash

Concentration (%)	8.6%
Flow rate (kg/lt)	41,880
Initial pH	3.8–4.2
Final pH	8.5

2. Lime consumption

(kg/h) (80% CaO basis)	420

Evaporation System

1. Type	Quintuple effect with thermocompressor
2. Type of feed	Mixed feed (1-3-4-5-2)
3. Spent wash concentration (%)	
Inlet	8.6
Outlet	60
4. Spent wash feed rate (kg/hr)	
Inlet	41,880
Outlet	6,000
5. Steam consumption (kg/hr) at 5 bar	42,230

Incineration

1. Type of furnace	Vertical static with rotary injector
2. Thermal capacity (Kcal/hr)	1.08×10^7
3. Cone, spent wash firing rate (kg/hr)	60%, 6,000 kg/hr
4. Operating temperature/°C	
Minimum	1,100
Maximum	850
5. Fuel consumption (kg/hr)	Nil, except during start up
6. Turndown ratio	2 : 1

Waste Heat Recovery Boiler

1. Type	Membrane wall self-cleaning natural circulation boiler with economizer
2. Steam output (kg/h)	14,000
3. Steam pressure (bar abs.)	32
4. Temperature	350
5. Food water	Demineralized Deaerated at 105°C
6. Blow down (%)	3% continuous
7. Thermal losses (%)	2%
8. Flue gas temp. (°C)	
Inlet	1,050
Outlet	150

Bag Filter

1. Type	Reverse air bag house
2. Gas flow rate (Nm^3/hr)	27,260
3. Gas temperature (°C)	130–150
4. Outlet particulate loading (mg/Nm^3)	100 maximum

Turbo Alternator

1. Type	Multistage back pressure
2. Inlet steam	
Pressure (bar abs.)	32
Temperature (°C)	350

3. Exhaust steam	
Pressure (bar abs.)	5
Temperature (°C)	190°C
4. Steam flow (kg/hr)	14,000,16,000 after desuperheating station
5. Power output (kW)	900

Total Ash Recovery (kg/hr) 1,000

Space Requirement	40m × 30m × 21m

Utilities

Electricity (kw)

1. Operating	535
2. Connected	1100 (including 200 kW for emergency cooling fan)

Steam (kg. hr)

1. 5 bar (abs.)	8850 (including atomization, evaporation and heating)

Water (m^3/hr)

1. Boiler feed	14.5
2. Cooling	
(a) Circulation	400
(b) Make–up	20–40

Instrument Air (Nm^3/hr)

(Dew point-15°C)	75

Fuel (tonnes/hr) Required only for start-up

Note: 1. The values given are indicative only and may change slightly after finalizing the exact design parameters.

2. To operate incinerator, by-passing the boiler and downstream system in case of emergency, direct grid supply of 570 kW will have to be provided.

Table 16.8

Brief technical particulars of flue gas cleaning system

1. Type	Reverse air
2. No of compartments	6
3. No. of bags in each compartment	56
4. Bag size	203 mm * x 7000 mm L
5. Area of each bag	4.4 m^2
6. Total filtration area	1478.4 m^2

(*Contd. ...*)

Our Scope of supply includes
1. Frame and casing with necessary structural
2. Necessary filter bags with thimbles and bag fixing arrangmenet
3. Internal and external walkways, if required
4. Inspection access door(s)
5. Reverse air fan, centrifugal-type, complete with drive arrangement, motor and common base frame
6. Pneumatically operated poppet valves
7. Sequence controller
8. Dashing hopper with heating arrangement, if required

Table 16.9
Cost of plant and machinery for concentration-incineration

	₹in lakhs
Spent wash concentration unit	125
Incinerator boiler unit	175
Multi-stage turbo-alternator unit	30
Boiler feed water system	6
Chemical cleaning unit	8
Cooling water system	5
Instrumentation for air supply system	3
Erection and commission expenses	23
Civil works	15
Duties and taxes	70
Total	₹460 lakhs

Table 16.10
Energy from concentration-incineration destrotherm surpluses summary

Particulars	*Produced by destrotherm*	*Consumed by destrotherm*	*Surplus available for distillery and other operations*	*Required by distillery*
Steam (kg/h)	14,500	8,850	5,650	6,900
Electricity (kW)	900	535	365	225
Ash (k/h)	1,000	—	1,000	—
Lime (k/h)	—	420	—	—
Dilution water (kg/h)	42,230	—	42,230	36,000
Boiler feed water (kg/h)	—	14,500	—	6,900

Basis: 1. Distillery capacity : 60,000 LPD
2. Distillery steam requirement : 2.75 kg/1 of alcohol produced
3. distillery power requirement : 90 kWh/kl of alcohol produced

questions with regard to the operation of such a plant, especially about operational difficulties and the possibility of air pollution due to fly ash. The pay-back period, even by any conservative estimate, will not be more than five years. However, one of. the serious constraints in going in for this process is arranging for such huge financial resources. The only incentive available is Rs.25 lakhs from the Government of India, which is nominal in comparison to the total financial requirements.

Some salient points are as follows:

1. Quantity of spent wash generated is assumed to be 960 m^3/day—a ratio of 1:16 per litre of alcohol produced, as is the standard figure for distilleries in India.
2. Initial concentration has been assumed to be 8.6%. It may, however, be noted that the all-India average varies between 9 and 11%.
3. The lower calorific value of dry solids has been taken to be 3380 kcal/kg.
4. The final concentration to be achieved in the evaporation plant will be restricted to 60% only, in view of the very high rise of viscosity anticipated in the range 62–65%.
5. Since the calorific value and concentration of the spent wash may change from season to season, combustion through a burner is avoided and the furnace operates on a pyrolytic principle in which three distinct zones are formed—zone of evaporation, zone of volatile combustion and zone of pyrolysis at the base. The furnace construction is circular with tangential air injection at three zones for complete destruction of organics.

   The furnace is refractory lined and has air insulation. The air required for combustion is passed through the outer jacket, not only for insulation but also for pre-heating for maximum combustion efficiency.

   The feature also permits the attainment of self-sustaining combustion without the necessity for auxiliary fuel at concentrations as low as 50% or at lower calorific values.

   A separate incineration furnace, thus, offers maximum flexibility of operation, especially for burning waste products the properties of which cannot be controlled and may fluctuate from season to season.
6. Once combustion is complete, the gases are taken to a typical waste heat recovery boiler with membrane wall design. The membrane wall construction is normally preferred for flue gases, containing molten salts, due to its self-cleaning feature.
7. At the moment, oil firing, in the furnace, is proposed for initial sintering of the furnace and for start-up of the plant. No provision, however, has been made to independently generate steam from the waste-heat recovery–boiler. The provision can be added on the boiler, if necessary, to generate steam, when the evaporation plant is to be started independent of external steam input. Decision on this can be taken at a later date.

The salient features of the plant are

1. Spent wash flow	80 m^3/h
2. Inlet concentration	3%
3. Initial pH	2–3
4. Evaporation plant	4 Effect-vacuum process without thermo compressor backward feed
5. Concentration achieved	52–56%

6. Further concentration in direct contact venturi	57–58%
7. Steam generation	at 27 bar superheated at 100°C
8. Power generation	1.7 MW
9. Steam generation	Approx. 9 tonnes/hr.

Use of Distillery Effluent as Cattle Feed and Fertilizer

The composition of distillery effluent is clearly indicated earlier. Due to the presence of mineral salts, including potassium, proteins and carbohydrates, distillery effluents are considered suitable both as cattle feed and fertilizer.

In most European countries, concentrated stillage is mostly used as a feed ingredient. In France, however, 50% of the concentrated stillage is used as fertilizer. This form of use is highly seasonal since, for climatic and agronomic reasons, the product must be applied to the soil, during a period of no more than six weeks a year. This characteristic calls for good coordination in stillage stockpiling, transportation and application operations. Costs of these operations vary according to the type of stillage involved and the type of crop it is being used on ; the users pay for the product as finally applied.

For the above reasons, the price of stillage applied to crops oscillates considerably. In certain cases, the FOB price of the product may even be a negative one, meaning that the distillery is actually paying to get the product removed from its plant. The cost of product, applied to crops, may be fairly high, depending on the distance from the distillery to the point of application, the time of year and the characteristics of the stillage.

In France and Germany, 90% of the concentrated stillage is marketed. On certain occasions, concentrated stillage has been exported from France to England, whereas, on others, France has imported from both, Germany and Italy, for use as fertilizer.

The importance of the market for stillage as fertilizer, in France, appears to be connected with the particular agricultural structure prevailing there. In other words, the crops on which application of concentrated stillage has given the best results appear to be grapes, citrus fruits, tobacco, asparagus and hogs, which are more highly developed in France than in other European countries.

The Netherlands produces about 100,000 tonnes of concentrated stillage a year, and Belgium 80,000 tonnes. In these two countries, practically the entire output goes to the feed industry. Quantities incorporated vary from 2% by weight in rations for poultry, to 3.4% for hogs and 10–15% for ruminants.

Although the market for concentrated stillage, in the feed sector, has remained firm with an upward trend, it is believed that, in future, it will develop more along the lines of increased competition in the fertilizer market than in that of cereals, as proteins of vegetal origin are used as feed ingredients since they are renewable.

In the Netherlands, for instance, it is anticipated that the most economical solution to the stillage problem, in future, will be concentration up to 50% TS, followed by incineration for recovery of potassium ash.

The Federal Republic of Germany produces about 100,000 tonnes of concentrated stillage a year, 50% which is exported to other European countries. The remainder is used within the country as an ingredient for rations and for special applications.

In Italy, 40% of the output is exported to France. There is a producer of powdered-beet-molasses stillage that competes with ECF from sugarcane molasses produced by National Chemical Products (NCP) in South Africa. A substantial proportion of the Italian output is incinerated, whereas the stillage from fermentation and distillation of pear and apple mashes is centrifuged. The sludge formed in this operation is used locally as fertilizer.

In England, the market is small, amounting to some 60,000 tonnes per year, of which 40,000 tonnes are imported from the continent to be used in rations and as fertilizer.

In Europe, it would appear that use of concentrated stillage as a feed ingredient has already reached the market limit. Hence, all increases in production may be expected to be used as fertilizer.

The availability of concentrated stillage in Europe, remained stable at levels from 150,000 to 180,000 tonnes a year, until 1972. From 1972 to 1976, supply grew at a uniform rate. The projected figure for 1980 is one million tonnes, while France and Italy should continue being the two major producing countries.

It may be noted that, even if the supply of concentrated stillage reaches the level forecast, it will still amount to only 2% of the rations supply and will be equivalent, at most, to 13% of formulated ration's (containing up to 15% concentrated stillage). Even assuming that all the concentrated stillage used in rations and that the low level of participation would indicate high market potential, cost and quality factors would nevertheless seem to suggest that the participation of concentrated stillage in the European feed market will not rise.

Mineral Salts Content

Although the phosphorus content, in concentrated mandioca stillage, is higher than that of molasses, cane juice or mixed stillages, it is still low

The market for concentrated stillage, for use as a lubricant, in France is purely symbolic and does not amount to 30 tonnes a year.

The most profitable market would appear to be in correcting molasses specifications. As this use has implications on the molasses market, consumption data are not available.

In India, some laboratory experiments have been carried out, but large–scale applications, either as fertilizer or for feeding purposes, are yet to follow.

Conclusion

On the basis of material presented, the urgent need for suitable abatement of environment pollution in distilleries is obvious, especially where some of the parameters, viz., BOD, COD, total and suspended solids are extremely high in comparison to the limit prescribed by UK, USA, the water Pollution Prevention and Control Board, Bureau of Indian Standards and other similar boards in the country. It is also interesting to observe that the prescribed values in other industrially advanced countries are still on the lower side.

Considering the growing concern for environmental degradation and energy crisis, the process of methane generation out of distillery effluent has been suggested and the effects of different parameters has been described.

References

1. Buswell, A.M. and W.D. Hatfields, '*Anaerobic Fermentation*', *Bulletin No. 32*, State of Illinois, Division of State Water Survey, Urbana, Illinois (1939).
2. Bhattacharya, R. C. '*Design and Economy of Gobar (Bio) Gas Plant for Rural India*', *Chemical Age of India,* Vol. 30, No. 10 p. 939 October (1979).
3. Mohan Rao, F.I. Sastry and R.S. Mehta, '*Fundamentals of Anaerobic Digestion*', *Envir. Hlth*., Vol. V. No2, p. 169–188 April (1963).
4. Mitchell, Ralph, '*Water Pollution Microbiology*', Vol. 13, Ecology of Methane Fermentation, 349–374.
5. Nemorrow, N.L. *Liquid Waste of Industry–Themries, Practices and Treatment*, Ch. 13.
6. Rudelfs, W. and H.R. Amberg, '*White Water Treatment*', *Sewage and Industrial Waste*, 24(9), 1108, Sept. 1952.
7. Sen, B.P and T.R. Bhaskaran, '*Anaerobic Digestion of Liquid Molasses Distillery Waste'*, J. Wat. Poll. Cent. Fed., 34,1015 (1962).
8. Southgate, B.A., *Treatment and Disposal of Industrial Waste Water*, Her Majesty's State Office (1942).

17

Environmental Pollution Control in the Cotton Textile Industry

Introduction

The cotton textile industry, with an annual production of about 400 million metres of cloth and approximately 1000 million kg of yarn (as given in Table 17.1), is one of the biggest in the country. It provides employment to nearly a million workers in 691 mills which are scattered in different States of India(12). A Statewise distribution of textile mills is given in Table 17.2. The textile industry also plays an important role in the economy of the country as it is one of the major foreign exchange earners. Despite the decline in exports, a result of both, severe international competition and growing import substitution in markets, earnings from cotton textiles are still the third highest. Figures for the export of cotton textiles from the country during the last five years is shown in Table 17.3.

Cotton mills consume large volumes of water for various processes, e.g., sizing, designing, kiering, bleaching, mercerizing, dyeing and printing, and discharge equally large volumes of waste waters containing different types of pollutants, which naturally require urgent attention. It is estimated that 12–65 litres of water is required for processing one metre of cloth °0) which, produces about 20–30 grams of BOD per metre of cloth processed.

There are 41 textile mills in UP of which 10 are in Kanpur. These mills discharge approximately 25,000 kl of the effluent per day and produce about 10 tonnes of BOD, leading to 13.3% of the total organic load on the river Ganga.

Manufacturing Processes and Sources of Effluent

An integrated cotton textile mill provides yarn from raw cotton. The process includes steps like opening and clearing, picking, carding, drawing, spinning, winding and warping. No water borne pollution originates in this sequence of operations since they are all mechanical.

The entire liquid waste from the textile industries originates from sizing, designing, kiering, bleaching, mercerizing, dyeing and finishing. The procedure of processing of raw cotton to the finished cloth is illustrated in Fig. 17.1.

Sizing

The yarn is sized by loading it with starch or other sizing substances. The purpose of sizing is to give the yarn sufficient strength and abrasive resistance to withstand the stresses and

Table 17.1
Production of cotton yarn and cloth by the mill sector

Year	Yam in 1000 kg	Cloth in 1000 metres					
		Coarse	*Medium B*	*Medium A*	*Fine*	*Superfine*	*Total*
1976	1,005,900	553,400	1,130,000	1,788,000	163,000	246,000	3,880,000
1977	846,000	413,000	921,000	1,001,000	95,000	193,000	3,223,000
1978	912,000	442,000	910,000	1,684,000	86,000	129,000	3,251,000
1979	952,000	414,000	954,000	1,651,000	65,000	122,000	3,206,000
1980	1,058,000	428,000	898,000	1,952,000	70,000	128,000	3,476,000

Table 17.2
Locations of the cotton textile industry (Statewise installed capacity as on January 1, 1981)

	State/Zone	No. of mills			Installed spindles (in thousands)			
		Spinning	*Composite*	*Total*	*Spinning*	*Composite*	*Total*	*Installed looms*
	Andhra Pradesh	29	3	32	614	102	716	1,246
	Assam	2	-	2	37	-	37	-
	Bihar	4	2	6	70	25	95	596
	Gujarat	21	91	112	397	3,593	3,990	63,744
(a)	Ahmedabad City	4	62	66	51	2,627	2,678	47,682
(b)	Rest of Gujarat	17	29	46	346	966	1312	16,062
	Haryana	10	2	12	212	58	270	978
	Jammu & Kashmir	1	-	1	25	-	25	-
	Karnataka	20	12	32	348	477	825	6358
	Kerala	21	5	26	464	90	554	1,168
	Madhya Pradesh	6	18	24	134	612	746	12,962
	Tamil Nadu	190	25	215	3,978	1307	5,285	9,911
(a)	Coimbatore	88	17	105	1,808	727	2335	4,076
(b)	Rest of Tamil Nadu	102	8	110	2,170	580	2,750	5,835
	Maharashtra	27	77	104	687	4,245	4,932	76,635
(a)	Bombay	1	53	54	56	3399	3,455	61350
(b)	Rest of Maharashtra	26	24	50	631	846	1,477	15,285
	Orissa	4	1	5	77	51	128	1,014
	Punjab	7	2	9	208	62	270	1,240
	Rajasthan	8	11	19	174	327	501	2,939
	Uttar Pradesh	24	17	41	533	802	1335	13327
(a)	Kanpur	-	10	10	-	505	505	11,115
(b)	Rest of U.P.	24	7	31	533	297	830	2,212
	West Bengal	23	18	41	430	581	1,011	9,490
	Delhi	-	4	4	-	172	172	3370
	Pondicherry	2	3	5	54	104	158	2,696
	Goa	1	—	1	26	—	26	—
	Total	400	291	691	8,468	12,608	21,076	207,657

Table 17.3
Exports of mill-made cotton textiles-Fiscal year basis

Year	Cotton fabrics		Cotton yam		Cotton apparel value (million Rs)	Cotton hosiery value (million Rs)	Other cotton mfg, value (million Rs)	Total value (million Rs)
	Quality (million sq. metres)	Value (million Rs)	Quality (million kg)	Value (million Rs)				
1976-77	563.31	2,011.80	18.52	310.00	2,571.00	141.10	528.90	5,560.80
1977-78	266.32	1,075.29	10.42	225.30	2,408.60	216.70	561.40	4,487.29
1978-79	310.99	1,342.00	6.25	151.90	3,514.50	139.20	579.60	5,727.20
1979-80	393.72	1,873.80	5.80	150.50	3,651.40	234.10	643.80	6,553.60
1980-81 (P)	300.00	1,644.20	7.00	213.90	4,294.60	461.60	571.60	7,185.90

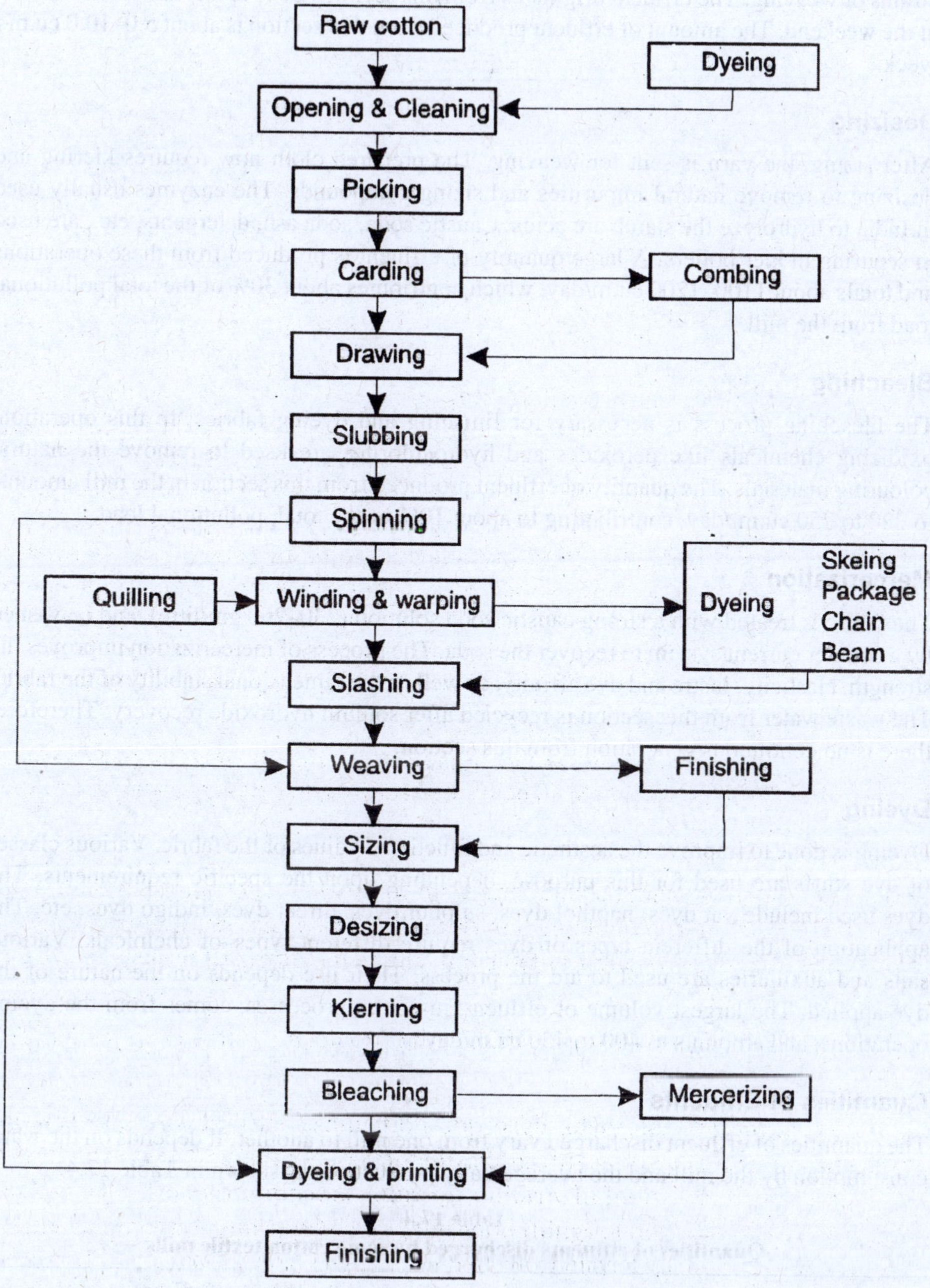

Fig. 17.1 Flow diagram for processing of raw cotton

strains of weaving. The effluent originates from this section due to spills, and floor washing at the weekend. The amount of effluent produced from this section is about 5.0–10.0 cu.m./ week.

Desizing

After sizing, the yarn is sent for weaving. The prepared cloth now requires kiering and desizing to remove natural impurities and sizing compounds. The enzymes usually used in India to hydrolyze the starch are acids. Caustic soda, soda ash, detergents, etc., are used in scouring in kier boilers. A large quantity of effluent is produced from these operations and totals about 1100–1200 cu.m/day, which contributes about 30% of the total pollutional load from the mill.

Bleaching

The bleaching process is necessary for finishing and dyeing fabrics. In this operation, oxidizing chemicals like peroxides and hydrochlorites are used to remove the natural colouring materials. The quantity of effluent produced from this section in the mill amounts to 220 to 250 cu.m./day, contributing to about 10% of the total, pollutional load.

Mercerization

The fabric is treated with a strong caustic soda solution (230–260 gm/litre), and is washed by a counter current system to recover the soda. The process of mercerization improves the strength, elasticity, lustre and dye affinity, as well as the dimensional stability of the fabric. The waste water from this section is recycled after sodium hydroxide recovery. Therefore, there is no continuous generation from this section.

Dyeing

Dyeing is done to improve the aesthetic and functional values of the fabric. Various classes of dye stuffs are used for this purpose, depending upon the specific requirements. The dyes used include vat dyes, napthol dyes, sulphur dyes, direct dyes, indigo dyes, etc. The application of the different types of dyes require different types–of chemicals. Various salts and auxiliaries are used to aid the process. Their use depends on the nature of the dye applied. The largest volume of effluent, in cotton processes, comes from the dyeing operations, and amounts to 400 to 450 cu.m/day.

Quantities of Effluents

The quantities of effluent discharged vary from one mill to another. It depends on the water consumption by the mill and the average daily production, as shown in Table 17.4.

Table 17.4
Quantities of effluents discharged by some cotton textile mills

Production of mill metres/day	*Water consumption kl/day*	*Volume of effluent*	
		kl/day	*l.m of cloth*
2,20,000	13,870	8000	36
1,90,000	2,300	1900	10.0
80,000	3,500	3400	42.5
45,000	1,830	1750	38.8
35,000	1,050	800	22.8

Table 17.5
Characteristics of cotton textile effluent from different sections

Process	*Chemicals used*	*Characteristics of the effluent*								
		pH	*Colour*	*BOD mg/P*	*COD mg/P*	*Total solids mg/P*	*S.S. mg/P*	*Conductivity mho*	*Alkalinity mg/P*	*Chlorine mg/P*
Slashing and Sizing	Starch, Freeh Chalk and Softiers	7.4-8.1	Blue/grey	1800 to 2600	4800 to 5400	46,000 to 58,000	5200 to 6180	—	130 to 320	120 to 160
Kiering	Caustic Soda, Soda Ash, Silicates of Soda or Oils, etc.	0.2-11.0	Dark tan	1200 to 1800	12,300 to 14,500	41,200 to 48,000	5200 to 6180	10.032 to 11.021	400 to 920	180 to 300
Bleaching	Chlorine, peroxide	82-9.3	Cloudy	132 to 830	320 to 810	12,000 to 16,000	3000 to 5800	—	180 to 300	380 to 890
Dyeing	Various dyes, detergents, etc.	3.6-10.4	Colour varies	600 to 1100	1430 to 2140	53,200 to 62,400	8300 to 1250	32.6 to 34.8	120 to 260	230 to 320
Washing	Water	7.6-8.2	Slightly cloudy	400 to 700	900 to 1200	2830 to 3240	830 to 1250	1.35 to 1.668	80 to 160	120 to 230
Mixed	—	10.2-10.9	Coloured	1200 to 1860	2300 to 3800	38,300 to 46,400	12,000 to 23,000	23.8 to 25.6	180 to 390	135 to 330

Table 17.6
Standards for the disposal of industrial effluents

Pollutants	*BIS (IS: 3307, 1965) (IS: 3306, 1965)*			*U.P. Pollution Control Board Act 1974*		
	Into inland surface waters	*Into public sewers*	*On land for irrigation*	*Into inland surface waters*	*Into public sewers*	*On land for irrigation*
PH	5.5-9.0	..5.5-9.0	5.5-9.0	5.5-9.0	5.5-9.0	5.5-9.0
Turbidity	—	—	—	—	—	—
Suspended solids	100	600	—	100	600	—
Total dissolved solids	—	2100	2100	—	2100*	2100
Temperature °C	40	45	—	40	45	—
Sulphates	—	100	100	—	100	100
Chlorides	—	600	600	—	600	600
Ammoniacal nitrogen	50	50	—	50	50	—
Sulphides	2.0	—	—	2.0	2.0	—
Oil and grease	10	100	30	10	100	30
Colour and odour	0	0	0	—	—	—
BOD	30	500	500	30	500	500
COD	250	—	—	250	-	—
Copper	3.0	3.0	—	3.0	3.0	—
Chromium (Hexavalent)	0.1	2.0	—	0.1	2.0	—
Zinc	5.0	15	—	5.0	15.0	—

All values except pH and Temperature have been expressed as mg/l.
a Subject to relaxation or tightening by local authority.
b Relaxable to 750 by local authority.
*These requirements shall apply only where, after treatment, the sewage is disposed off on land for irrigation.

Characteristics of Effluents from Different Sections

The characteristics of the effluents from different sections of the mill is given in Table 17.5. The characteristics of the different process effluents, vary from mill to mill, as they are directly related to water usage.

The effluents have higher values of pH, total solids, TDS, BOD, COD, alkalinity, etc., than the standard values prescribed by the BIS and the Pollutional Control Board. The standard values are given in Table 17.6.

Pollutional Load Contributed by the Mills

The pollution load contributed by the different mills investigated is given in Table 17.7. It clearly indicates that the organic load depends on the volume of the effluent discharged due to the dilution factor.

Harmful Effects of Textile Effluent

The untreated effluents, if discharged into streams, cause rapid depletion of the dissolved oxygen of the receiving streams. The condition is aggravated due to the settlement of die suspended substances and subsequent decomposition of the deposited sludges in an anaerobic condition. The alkalinity and toxic substances like sulphides and chromium affect life and also interfere with the biological treatment processes. Some of the dyes have a toxic effect on aquatic life. The colour, often, renders the water unfit for use for some industrial puiposes in the downstream side9. Streams containing as little as 25 ppm sodium hydroxide have been reported to be deadly for fish8.

Pollutional Control in Textile Industry

The treatment plant set up, for any effluent control, is considered to be expenditure without return. Considering this fact, it is necessary to introduce techniques whose cost of treatment is minimal. This can be best achieved by reduction of pollution at source. For this purpose, good house-keeping, closer process–control and process chemical-substitution are the best solutions. Simultaneously, these steps minimize the cost of treatment. It is also essential to educate the working staff so that they develop a sense of concern for pollution control and realize that it will be in their interest, too.

Table 17.7
Pollution load contributed by a cotton mills

Effluent discharged kl/day	*Effluent discharged per 100 mts. of cloth kl*	*BOD* kg. day	kg/100 mts of cloth
14300	32	4120	9.8
8,000	18	1930	6.4
1,900	38	380	7.2
1,750	32	350	7.25
800	180	225	5.35

Good Housekeeping

The entire drainage system should be thoroughly cleaned and at least 2–3 stage screens should be provided at each entry point. This will prevent any solid material from joining the effluent stream.

The use of water in different sections should be optimized and floor washings and the rest of the water streams should be diverted in such a way that the pollution load is minimized, It will help neutralize acid/alkali present in the effluent.

The solid waste which originates in different sections and eventually joins the effluent stream, should be collected with a proper vacuum collector. This should be done before closing of every shift and should help reduce the pollution load by 10–15 percent.

Closer Process Control

By closer control of processes, the pollution load can be reduced by 30–40 percent. For this purpose, the following measures should be implemented:

Reduction in chemical usage:

1. In the finishing operation, the starch is used in large quantities. The unutilized eventually joins the effluent stream. Its amount should be optimized though it is estimated that it will always remain somewhat in excess of what is required. Obviously, this excess should be diverted to a different route. In summer, it should be sun-dried and in winters, it should be evaporated and the solid material, thus, obtained should be disposed of as solid waste.
2. In bleaching operations, chlorine and peroxides are used. They should be mixed with dyeing effluent in order to decolourise it.
3. In kiering mercerizing processes, caustic soda is used in large quantities. It should be recycled by readjusting its concentration.

Recovery and Re-use of Chemicals: Many chemicals can be recovered and re-used, e.g., caustic soda, starch, etc.

Process Modification: Certain changes in processes can reduce the amounts and concentrations of waste materials, e.g., change in dyeing method (use of standing bath).

Flow or Volume Reduction: The waste flow may be reduced by the re-use of process water, counter flow wastes, segregation of weak waste for disposal without treatment, changes in processes and other similar means.

Process Chemical Substitution

The pollution load in the textile industry can be reduced effectively by process chemical substitution. The following substitutions are suggested:

1. Substitution of low BOD synthetic detergents for soap.
2. Substitution of low BOD sizes, e.g. carboxy methyl cellulose, hydroxy methyl cellulose, polyvinyl alcohol, etc., for high BOD starches.
3. Replacement of acetic acid in dyeing with an inorganic salt, e.g., ammonium sulphate or chloride.
4. Use of low BOD dispersing, emulsifying, leveling, etc., agents in place of high BOD agents.
5. Reduction in the use of caustic soda in kiering.

Ganapati[5] and Masselli6 have reported that the total pollution load of the textile mill can be reduced to a large extent by process chemical substitution.

Souther[4] has also made some suggestion for the abatement of pollution in the textile industry, e.g. process chemical substitution, closer process control and good housekeeping.

Masselli *et al*[7] have emphasized certain preliminary practices to reduce the quantity and strength of the textile effluent. They also observed that closer control of cotton kiering, sizing and the amount of chemicals used in various other processes may reduce the pollutional load up to 30 percent. They have also found process chemical substitution to be an effective means for pollution abatement.

Treatment Methods

Suitable combinations of chemical and biological methods briefly described here are considered essential for proper treatment.

Chemical Treatment

Neutralization and chemical coagulation are the main chemical methods used for the treatment of textile effluent. Alum, ferrous sulphate, ferric sulphate and ferric chloride are generally used as the coagulant for the reduction of BOD and colour from the effluent. Sulphuric acid or lime is used for pH control. Each coagulant, when used with a specific waste, has its own optimum isoelectric point (pH for maximum coagulation). Some coagulant aids are also used in conjunction with the coagulants.

Biological Treatment

The trickling filter, activated sludge and dispersed growth *aeration* are considered suitable for this purpose. Textile effluent has also been treated successfully by the stabilization pond method, in combination with sewage. Trickling filtration is generally desirable due to its flexibility, lower operating cost, and capability of handling shock loads of effluents. Activated sludge treatment leads to greater BOD reduction, but requires large units to provide the long detention periods usually needed and also requires highly qualified supervision. Dispersed growth aeration generally gives a somewhat lower BOD reduction than activated sludge treatment but does away with the sludge problem. It also takes a minimum of operation and maintenance.

Dietrich found that mixtures of electrolytes containing Al^{3+}, Fe^{3+}, Se^{++}, Si^{4+} and Ca^{++} are more effective flocculating agents than those containing only Fe^{3+} *cations*. When the mixture is applied to textile plant sewage at 50 mg/1, it successfully reduces the total pollution load. Nemerow8 enumerated chemical coagulation, trickling filtration, the activated sludge process and dispersed growth aeration for the treatment of textile effluent.

Chamberlain[1] reported the use of chlorinated copper as to oxidize or bleach many dyes and in the reduction of BOD from sulphur dyes. Hazen[5] successfully used the combination of trickling filters and activated sludge for the treatment of a 40–60 percent mixture of textile- finishing-mill waste and sewage. Govindan *et al.*[4] study the treatment of textile effluent in admixture with sewage (1 : 5) by the waste stabilization pond with a detention time of 8–12 days, using acclimated algae culture chlorella pyrenoidosa, microcystis aeruginosa and englena.

In conclusion, a combination of physical-chemical followed by biological treatment for the treatment of textile effluent is considered the most suitable.

References

1. Chamberlain, N. S., "*Application of Chlorine and Treatment of Textile Wastes*", Proc. of 3rd Southern Municipal and Industrial Waste Conference, p. 176, March 1954.
2. Dietric, K.R., "*Simplified Chemical Treatment of Wastewater from Textile Factories with Clarifying, Flocculating and Precipitating Agents*", Text Prax., 22 (2), 126–127 (1967).
3. Ganapati, S.V., "*In-plant Process Control for Abatement of Pollution Load of Textile Wastes*", Env. Health, 8 (3), 169–173 (1966).
4. Govindan, VS. and VS. Sundarlingam, "*Studies on Treatment of Textile Mill Wastewaters by Stabilization Pond Method*", Env. Hlth. 21 (4), 321–331 (1979).
5. Hazen, R., "*Pilot Plant Studies on Treatment of Textile Wastes and Municipal Sewage*". Proc. of 6th Southern Municipal and Industrial Waste Conference, p. 161, April, 1957.
6. Massellin, I. W. and M. G. Burford, "*Pollution Reduction in Cotton Finishing Wastes through Process Chemical Changes*", Sewage Ind. Wastes, 26, 1109,1954.
7. Masselli, I.W. Masselli and M.G. Burford, *A Simplification of Textile Waste Surrey and Treatment, New England Interstate Water Pollution Control Commission*, 1959.
8. Nemerow, N.L., *Liquid Waste of Industry, Theories, Practices and Treatment*, Addison–Wesley Publishing Co., 1979Ind., 225–276,1971.
9. Rao, M.L. and A.K. Dutta. *Waste Water Treatment*, Mohan Primlani, Oxford and IBH Publishing Co., 1979.
10. Souther, RH. and T. A. Alsapaugh, "*Biological Treatment of Mixture of Textile Wastes and Domestic Sewage*". Sew-Industrial Wastes, 29(8), 918,1957.
11. "*Textile Waste Treatment Studies, Proc. of 13th Industrial Waste Conference*, Purdue University, 662–713, May 1958.
12. *The Times of India Directory and Year Book*, 1983, pp. 29–31.

Environment and Transport

It is well established that environment and development are two sides of the same coin, e.g., industrialization, agriculture, transportation, construction, power generation, etc., contribute to environmental degradation. Transportation plays a very important role in energy sector of socio-economic activitics. Both public transport and private .transport are growing exponentially to meet the requirements of human beings both directly and indirectly. Table 18.1 shows the number of automobiles on road in some of the districts of U.P. The availability of proper transportation facilities is considered absolutely essential to meet the requirements. Transport industry contributes significantly to air pollution as well as noise pollution and both are briefly described in this chapter:

Table 18.1
Auto vehicles on road as on 31.3.1983

S.No.	*Districts*	*Heavy vehicles Buses and Trucks*	*Light vehicles*
1.	Allahabad	2712	33,505
2.	Bariely	1433	27,660
3.	Kanpur	4729	64,668
4.	Agra	4224	44,647
5.	Lucknow	3527	63,166
6.	Meerut	3501	29,101

Air Pollution and Transport

Some of the major sources of air pollution have always been the chemical and allied industries, which discharge tons of noxious gases with the increasing standard of living and a growing need for a faster moving life, the numbers of automobiles have been exponentially increasing on Indian roads and simultaneously, so is the pollution from them. The exhaust of automobiles and diesel heavy vehicles contains many harmful gases and the problem of air pollution is more significant at ground level. Since the major activities of human beings are at this level, the pollution from automobiles has been gaining notoriety day and day. It has been determined that they contribute 39 percent of the total air pollutants in terms of tonnes in U.S.A. Table 18.2 shows the various sources of emission of air contaminants to the atmosphere. Table 18.3 shows the relative importance of different sources of air pollution.

Table 18.2
Emission of air contaminants to the atmosphere by source, tons per day

Source	*Organic gases*						*Inorganic gases*	
	Hydro-carbons	*Aldehydes and ketones*	*Other organics*	*Aerosols*	*Oxides of nitrogen*	*Oxides of sulphur*	*Carbon monoxide*	*Other inorganics*
Transportation								
Automobiles (gasoline)	680	10	12	25	250	19	6850	n
Blowby	140	u	u	u	u	n	n	n
Evaporation	145	0	0	0	0	0	0	0
Trucks and buses (gasoline)								
Exhaust	130	3	4	8	80	6	2100	n
Blowby	40	u	u	u	P	n	n	u
Evaporation	45	0	0	0	0	0	0	0
Truck and buses (diesel)	8	n	n	2	8	2	2	n
Ships and Railroads	n	n	n	n	n	n	n	n
Aircraft								
Jet	n	n	n	n	1	0	1	0
Piston	15	n	n	n	5	n	110	0
Petroleum								
Refining	90	2	n	5	1	40	700	4
Marketing	100	0	0	0	0	0	u	0
Production	60	n	0	0	u	n	0	0
Organic solvent users								
Surface costing	190	25	35	7	0	0	0	0
Degreasing	20	n	8	n	40	0	0	0
Dry cleaning	20	n	8	n	0	0	0	0
Plastics and rubbers	17	4	3	n	0	0	0	0
Others	50	14	13	n	0	0	0	0
Combustion of fuel								
Coal	3	1	0	80	20	200	10	0
Liquid	2	1	6	38	187	454	n	0
Gaseous	4	1	2	14	150	13	1	0
Chemical								
Sulphur plants	0	0	0	0	n	30	0	0
Sulphuric acid plants	0	0	0	n	n	20	0	0
Others	16	8	16	8	n	1	0	1
Incineration								
Municipal	n	n	3	3	3	1	3	n
Industrial	n	0	1	n	1	n	1	n
Others	0	0	n	1	n	n	n	0
Minerals	2	0	0	4	6	0	0	0
Miscellaneous	u	0	u	2	0	u	0	u
Total rounded	1777	65	110	198	752	786	9778	5

Note : *n* = negligible (0.05-0.5 tonne per day), *u* = unknown

Table 18.3
Relative importance of different sources of air pollution

Source of air pollution	*Share of total air pollution (%)*
Heating and power plants	27.0
Iron and steel industry	24.3
Non-ferrous metallurgical industry	10.5
Chemical industry	1.3
Mineral oil production, petrochemical industry	15.5
Motor Transport industry	13.1
Building materials industry	8.1
Others	0.2

Note: The position is nearly similar even today.

The estimated population of different vehicles in U.P. to the year 2000–2001 is available. Assuming that the population of vehicles in different cities would increase proportionately, the future emissions were projected. The total annual mass emissions for some of the important cities are shown in Table 18.4.

In many developed countries, the hazards from automobile pollution are recognized well in time, and preventive measures were taken to check them. By, now USA has well defined standards for exhaust concentration and R & D units are sincerely working to achieve them, through engine modification, and exhaust treatment. In India, however, in spite of some cities being flooded with automobiles, this problem has not been given due attention. Smog, a term used to denoted simultaneous formation of smoke and fog, is a very common sight in the contradictory congested cities of Los Angeles (USA) and other cities where millions of vehicles ply on the roads. The main pollutants are shown in table 18.4 along with their amount per 1000 gallons of burnt fuel. The effect of air pollutants on materials is shown in table 18.5. and the effect of gaseous pollutants, on human beings, is shown in table 18.6.

Air pollution caused by motor vehicles can be classified into three types, as discussed below. The severity of their problems depends upon the nature of the contaminant, quantity of emission and meteorological conditions.

1. Nuisance value : smoke, odour and compounds are a cause of nuisance, especially to a person standing next to an idling vehicle.
2. Direct effect from many vehicles : The cumulative effect of many vehicles, plying especially on busy roads during peak hours, has highly deleterious effects. Those residing in the vicinity of such roads are worst affected and they, often, suffer from chronic heart and lung diseases.

Table 18.4 (a)
Pollutants per 1000 gallons of fuel consumed

Pollutant	*Gasoline engine, lb*	*Diesel engine, lb*
Carbon monoxide	2300	60
Hydrocarbons	200	136
Oxides of nitrogen	113	222
Particulates	12	110
Oxides of sulphur	9	40
Acetic acid	4	31
Aldehydes	4	10

Table 18.4(b)
Vehicle emission inventory for some of the important cities Total mass emissions tons/year

Cities	*Type of vehicle*	*1981-82*			*1991-92*			*2000-2001*		
		CO	*HC*	NO_x	*CO*	*HC*	NO_x	*CO*	*HC*	NO_x
Delhi	2-wheelers	17,067	10,651	—	57,025	35,588	—	18,520	73,965	—
	3-wheelers	4,371	2,730	—	13,464	8,409	—	23,609	14,745	—
	Cars/Jeep	25,224	5,282*	1,648	29,937	6,269	1,956	43,008	9,006	2,810
	Taxis	2,756	491*	180	3,485	615	228	5,100	898	333
	Diesel vehicles	8,482	3,285	16,035	16,438	6,351	31,019	40,012	15,496	75,642
	Total	57,900	22,439	17,863	1,20,349	57,232	33,203	230,249	114,110	78,785
Bombay	2-wheelers	4,426	2,762	—	14,788	9,229	—	30,736	19,181	—
	3-wheelers	5,210	3,253	—	16,048	10,020	—	28,140	17,570	—
	Cars/Jeep	35,360	7,405*	2,310	41,967	8,788	2,742	60,219	12,627	3,939
	Taxis	14,193	2,530*	927	17,945	3,166	1,172	26,265	4,621	1,715
	Diesel vehicles	8,428	3,255	15,905	16,304	6,299	30,769	39,757	15,355	75,028
	Total	67,613	19,205	19,142	107,052	37,502	34,683	185,117	69,354	80,682
Calcutta	2-wheelers	2,029	1,266	—	6,779	4,096	—	14,090	8,514	—
	3-wheelers	1,241	755	—	3,823	2,387	—	6,703	4,186	—
	Cars/Jeep	14,370	3,005*	938	17,055	3,566	1,113	24,502	5,123	1,599
	Taxis	3,583	635*	234	4,530	798	296	6,631	11,164	433
	Diesel vehicles	3,176	1,226	5,992	6,144	2,372	11,593	14,982	5,783	28,266
	Total	24,399	6,907	7,164	38,331	13,219	13,002	66,908	34,770	30,298
Madras	2-wheelers	4,223	2,636	—	14,110	8,808	—	29,326	18,306	—
	3-wheelers	1,655	1,033	—	5,098	3,182	—	8,939	5,579	—
	Cars/Jeep	7,373	1,543*	482	8,751	1,832	572	12,571	2,631	822
	Taxis	756	135*	49	956	169	62	1,399	216	91
	Diesel vehicles	2,673	1,033	5,043	5,171	1,999	9,757	12,609	4,873	23,789
	Total	16,680	6,380	5,574	34,086	15,990	10,391	64,844	31,635	24,702

•Includes crankcase blow by and evaporative emissions

Table 18.5
Air pollution effects on materials

No. Pollutant	*Type of effect*	*Materials affected*
1. Ammonia	Deterioration associated with SO_2 and moisture	Damage to varnish and paint sur faces, discolours fabrics
2. Biological aerosols Saprophytic bacteria Fungi	Deterioration of surfaces and food spoilage	All material surfaces in contact with air, most unprotected food
	Deterioration of surfaces	Electronic circuits, leather
3. Carbon dioxide	Deterioration caused by combination of CO_2 and moisture to form carbonic acid.	Building stone
4. Chlorine	Corrosion and discolouration	Metals, paints, textiles
5. Chromium	Corrosion in the form of chromic acid, discolouration.	Metals, paints, building materials, paper, textiles
6. Hydrochloric acid	Corrosion	Most metals and alloys
7. Hydrogen fluoride	Etching	Glass and metals
8. Hydrogen sulphide	Discolouration and tarnishing	Paint (especially lead based), copper, zinc
9. Nitrogen oxides	Cause dyes to fade & whites to turn yellow	Textile
10. Odour-producing-pollutants	Odours that cling to skin, hair, clothing (especially bad near soap plant)	Requires more frequent !laundering and dry cleaning of clothes.
11. Ozone-organics-oxydants	Deterioration, fading of dyes, cracking	Textiles, rubber
12. Particulates	Abrasion and corrosion when combined with gaseous pollutants	Most metals, paint, textiles
13. Phosphorus	Corrosion in the form of phosphoric acid	Most materialst
14. Sulphur oxides	Corrosion	Steel, zinc, electrical equipment, limestone, roofing state, mortar, statues, textiles, leather, book bindings
	Electrochemical deterioration	Iron, aluminium, copper, silver, building materials, leather, paper, textiles

Table 18.6
Effect of gaseous pollutants on man

Pollutants	*Effects*
Sulphur Dioxide (SO_2)	Breathing rate increases. Breathing becomes less deep and a general feeling of air starvation is experienced-some even show signs of Bronchial sparns and asthmatics are badly attected. Any SO_2 which oxideses to SO_3 may dissolve in body fluids to form H_2SO_4, a very strong and corrosive acid.
Carbon Monoxide (CO)	CO combines with haemoglobin of the blood to form carboxy haemoglobin and when about half of the haemoglobin of the blood is used up, death ensues as the carboxy haemoglobin is useless for respiratory purpose. Persons poisoned by carbon monoxide exhibit a characteristic bright pink colour of the flesh due to carboxy haemoglobin.
Oxides of Nitrogen (NO_2)	Prolonged exposure of human beings to even low concentrations of oxides of nitrogen, can cause a chronic irritation of respiratory tract, headache, loss of appetite and nitric oxide reacts with air to form the brown nitrogen dioxide which is very poisonous.

Table 18.7
Particulate emission factors for coal combustion without control equipment

Type of unit	*Particulate per tonne of coal burnt, lb**	*Percent 44 microns*	*Percent 20-44 microns*	*Percent 10-20 microns*	*Percent 5-10 microns*	*Percent less than 5 microns*
Pulverised:						
General	16A	25	23	20	47	15
Dry-bottom	17A	25	23	20	17	15
Wet-bottom without fly ash reinjection	13A	25	23	20	17	15
Wet bottom with ash reinjection**	24A	25	23	20	17	15
Cyclone	2A	10	7	8	10	65
Spreader stoker:						
Without fly ash reinjection	13A	61	18	11	6	4
With fly ash reinjection**	20A	61	18	11	6	4
All other stokers	5A	70	16	8	4	2
Hand-fired equipment	20					100

* The letter A on all units other than hand-fired equipment indicates that the percentage of ash in the coal should be multiplied by the value given. Example : If the factor is 17 and the ash content is 10 percent, the particulate emission ijefore the control equipment would be 10 times 17, or 170 pounds of particulate per tonne of coal.

** Values should not be used as emission factors. Values represent the loading, reaching the control equipment, always used on this type of furnace.

3. *Photochemical air pollution*: Automobiles emit large quantities of both organic compounds and oxides of nitrogen, and under certain favourable conditions of temperature and sunlight, certain photochemical reactions take place. These, as well as other products of photochemical reactions, are highly toxic, irritate eyes and the respirator, system, damage vegetation and impair visibility. Tables 18.7-18.10 show the emission factors and emission rate, respectively for automobile exhaust. The composition of the body of the automobile is shown in Table 18.11 which greatly contributes to air pollution.

Table 18.8
Emission factors for automobile exhaust

Type of emission	*Emissions*		
	Pounds per 1000 vehicles miles	*Pounds per 1000 gallons of gas*	*Pounds per vehicle day*
Aldehydes (HCHO)	0.3	4	0.007
Carbon monoxide	165.0	2300	4.160
Hydrocarbons (C)	12.5	200	0.363
Oxides of nitrogen (NO_3)	8.5	113	0.202
Oxides of, sulphur (SO_3)	0.6	9	0.016
Organic acid (acetic)	0.3	4	0.007
Particulates	0.8	12	0.022

Note: The above values are for uncontrolled automobile exhaust, based on an average rouie speed of 25m. ph in urban areas. Estimated 3.25 trips per day of 8 miles in length each. Average automobile trends about 14.4 miles per gallon of gas consumed. Hydrocarbons add 0.2 pounds per vehicle-day for engine crankcase blowby.

Table 18.9
Generalised emission factors for sulphur dioxide from selected fuels and operations (Modified after NAPCA) publication*)

Source	*SO_2 emission factor*
1. Combustion of coal	0.4536 kg SO_2/1000/Kg coal (38 times percent 5 by weight)
2. Combustion of fuel oil	0.899 kg SO_2/10,000 litre oil (158.8 times percent 5 by weight)
3. Open-burning dumps and municipal incinerators	0 544.fl.907 kg SO_2/ 1000 kg refuse
4. Sulphuric acid manufacture	9.07-31.75 kg/1000 kg 100% acid
5. Copper smelting (Primary)	635.04 kg SO_2/1000 kg concentrated ore
6. Lead smelting (Sccondary cupola)	29.83 kg SO_2/1000 kg metal charged
7. Zinc smelting (Primary)	490.424 kg SO_2/l000 kg concentrated ore
8. Kraft mill recovery furnace	1.088-6.078 kg SO_2/1000 kg air-dried pulp
9. Sulphite mill recovery furnace (assuming 90% recovery)	18.144 kg SO_2/1000 air-dned pulp

* National Air Pollution Control Administration, Control Techniques for sulphur oxide air pollutants, NAPCA Publications No. AP-52, U.S. Government Printing Office, Washington, DC. 1969.

Table 18.10
Average on-the-road emission rates for gasoline-powered motor vehicles (Grams/Vehicle-Mile)

Year	*Hydrocarbon*		*Carbon monoxide*		*Oxides of nitrogen*	
	Urban	*Rural*	*Urban*	*Rural*	*Urban*	*Rural*
1960	21.8	14.6	87.1	34.9	5.72	6.39
1965	20.4	13.2	87.6	35.6	5.76	6.53
1968	17.9	11.4	80.9	33.0	5.92	6.70
1970	14.6	9.49	67.9	28.1	6.27	7.10
1975	7.39	4.78	40.9	17.5	6.84	7.81
1980	4.20	2.65	27.6	11.9	7.08	8.18
1985	3.71	2.18	25.7	10.7	7.08	8.27
1990	3.69	2.18	25.6	10.8	7.06	8.31

Note : Includes cars, trucks and applicable control systems in use as of 1971.

Table 18.11
The composition of the body of an automobile is as follows

Fe	=	85%
Zn	=	3%
Cu		1%
Pb	=	1/2%
Al	=	1%

Other materials, e.g., glass, rubber and plastic = $9\frac{1}{2}$ %. This also contributes greatly to pollution. It may be mentioned that Zn, Cu, AI and lead are pollutants.

Pollutants are exhausted from three major points in an automobile, exhaust gas, crankcase blow by, and fuel tank evaporative losses, though the former is the most important. Only hydrocarbons are emitted from the last two sources as a result of fuel evaporation. Typical emission levels and control standards are given in Table 18.12. A similar figure may be adopted for Indian conditions as well.

Table 18.12
Emission levels and control standards

Sources of emission	*Pollutant*	*Typical emission*	*Emission as wt/% of suppliedfuel*	*Estimated pollution car/day*	*US National Standardfor control equipment 1970*
Exhaust gas	HC	860 ppm	6	237	180 ppm
	CO	3.1%	—	2150 g	1%
i	NOx	1500 ppm	—	114 g	600-800 ppm or 350 ppm as NO
Crankcase blowby	HC	—	2.5	164.0 g	—
Fuel tank	HC	-	-	114.0 g	—

A comparison of three process for the removal of sulphur dioxide, using carbon, is presented. It should be noted that only the low temperature using carbon is presented. It should be noted that only the low temperature scheme is devoid of the severe drawbacks of catalyst decomposition and possible spontaneous ignition common to the others. Although the low temperature in itself is a disadvantage, the process has other possible advantages, such as removing sulphur dioxide in a fixed carbon bed column, and simultaneously producing sulphuric acid or possibly ammonium sulphate in the liquid effluent. Such a process would, hopefully, not require cyclic operation or periodic replacement of carbon. Additionally, there would be little danger of explosion or fire in the system, and no need to preheat or preclean the gas stream.

The role of traffic density and meteorology for air-lead build-up, at cross roads of Ahmadabad, was studied. Lead is a very important pollutant, and present due to addition of tetraethyl lead to improve the octane number of gasoline, and is absent in diesel vehicle exhaust. The summary of this study is given in Table 18.13.

Table 18.13
Seasonal dependence of air concentration as a function of traffic density

Season	*Cone, range (g/m^3)*	*Mean +S.D.*	*Correlation coefficient*	*Regression equation*
Summer	0.59-11.38	3.9 ±2.3	0.05	$Y = 3.47 + 0.00013X$
Winter	2.34-13.34	8.6 ±3.3	8.60	$Y = 0.6 \pm 0.0027X$

where X = traffic density (no./h)
Y = air-lead concentration (g/m^3)

Other studies have not yet been taken up in detail.

Modes of driving do contribute to the emission of varying quantities of hydrocarbon.

Table 18.14 shows the percentage of hydrocarbon contribution by driving modes. Table 18.15 shows the composition of auto exhaust hydrocarbons and Table 18.16 shows the typical exhaust gas concentration.

Table 18.14

Percentage of total hydrocarbon contribution by driving modes

Mode	*Driving time*		*Exhaust vol.*		*EC conc. (C)*	*A × B × C*	*HC contribution*
	Total %	*Time ratio (A)*	*m³/min*	*Vol. ratio (B)*			
Idling	19	1.0	0.224	1.0	800	800	5
Accelerating	19	1.0	1.680	7.5	540	4050	26
Cruising	37	2.0	0.980	4.4	485	4270	27
Decelerating	25	1.3	0.224	1.0	5000	6500	42

Control of Gaseous Pollutants

Though India has only a small fraction of vehicles plying, as compared to the USA, the problem of air pollution is significant here, too, for two reasons:

1. Indian vehicles are generally poorly maintained, and
2. Most automobiles are concentrated in large metropolitan industrialized cities with interaction of pollution from autos and nearby industries. Because of this, auto-exhaust control is considered an important necessity.

An emission control programme aims at reducing the concentration of carbon monoxide, hydrocarbons and oxides of nitrogen. The main approaches which have been used for this purpose are :

1. Engine design modifications
2. Fuel modification
3. Treatment of exhaust gases, and
4. Exhaust gas re-circulation.

Engine Design Modification

Use of linear air fuel ratios resulting in improved fuel distribution and retarded ignition timing, as also the use of lower compression ratio, are some of the modifications in engine design which have proved successful in checking pollution to some extent, though not without a loss in fuel and power economy.

Fuel Modification

Use of fuels lighter than gasoline is a very practical solution for reducing noxious exhaust gases because products of inadequate combustion are eliminated. Methane and steam reformed hexane, or a blend of light hydrocarbons, could be used as fuels but for want of technological progress, we are enable to use them at present. Some additives, e.g., barium salts in fuels have also produced wonderful results and the cost, too, is not high.

Exhaust Gas Treatment

The treatment of exhaust gases, so as to chemically reduce contaminants, has been the topic of most extensive research. The process can be accomplished by using thermal reactors at high temperatures, or the gases can be reduced by catalytic reactions in the exhaust pipe. In case of the latter, nitrogen oxides are reduced, at elevated temperatures, in the presence of some catalyst, usually of noble metals like Ruthenium or some base metal alloys. For oxidizing carbon monoxide and hydrocarbons, oxidizing catalysts of noble metals, or even cobalt, copper or chromium supported or ceramic materials are used in conjunction with suction of additional air, 80 to 90% reduction of pollutant concentration has been observed. Any catalyst in order to be suitable for use in the automobile should be moderately cheap, long lasting and should not be otherwise harmful. Effective catalysts for NO_x, CO and hydrocarbon are given in Tables 18.17 (a), (b) and (c), respectively.

Table 18.15
Composition of auto exhaust hydrocarbons

	Parts per million				*Total*
Saturated	Methane 147.5	Ethane 21.4	Propane 2.2	others 141.8	312.9
Olefins	Ethylene 160	Propylene 58.4	Acetylene 88	others 67.5	374.3
Aromatics	Benzene 21.3	Toulene 49.3	others 30.7	Total 101.3	101.3

Table 18.16
Typical exhaust gas constituents

Pollutant	*Idling*	*Acceleration*	*Crusing*	*Deceleration*
CO%.	4-9	0-8	1-7	2-9
HC as Hexane ppm	500-1000	50-800	200-800	3000-12000
Oxides of N ppm	10-50	1000-4000	1000-3000	5-50

Table 18.17(a)
Effective catalysts for NO, removal

Authors	*Temperature °C*	*Catalyst*	*Removal %*
Roth	320	G-13 (Girdler chromite)	95
Roth	320	Hm 14 (6.8% CuO - 6.8% Cr_2O_3)	95
Baker	200	CuO C_2O_3 (82° o CuO - 17% Cr_2O_3)	90
Ayen	160	Barium Supported Copper Chromite	—
Oxides of Base Metal			
Shelef	350	Copper oxide	90
Shelef	470	Nickel oxide	90
Shelef	510	Iron oxide	90
Noble Metals			
Shelef	480	Platium	—
Shelef	330	Palladium	—
Shelef	240	Ruthenium	—

Table 18.17(b)
Effective catalysts for removal of CO

Authors	*Temperature°*	*Catalyst*	*Removal%*
Thompson and Charls E.	371-871	Ru & Ir in st ratio 10:1-1:10	—
Hara & Hamchi	190-370	190-370	—
Roth & James F	300	Oxides of the Ni, CO, Fe, Cr, Mn	96
Osmanon. M.O.		CuO Cr_2O_3 in ratio 2:1	80

Table 18.17(c)
Catalysts for removal of Hydrocarbons

Author	*Temperature°C*	*Catalyst*	*Removal*
Nicklin and Thompson	650	(Fe oxide + 7NiO + U_2O3) wt %	—
Hirano and Takal	—	Mix of CO and Ni	—
Tiala Josef	—	Cu & Mn salts oxides of Cu, Mn, V, Si, Al, Ni, Zn, Mo	—
Hass & Robert, H	600	CO pelletized with CrO_3	—
Acress and Guy, TK	487-597	4-10% and PtO 2-20.5% Platinum	—

* Tables 18.18 and 18.19 shows details of reducing and 18.20 oxidation catalysts respectively. Table 18.20 shows the effect of constant temperature on NO_x emissions at certain conditions.

Table 18.18
Details of reducing catalysts

S.No.	*Type*	*Manufacturer*	*Special features*
1.	Co oxide, Ni oxide, pd, and alumina	J.M. Maselli	Used in the form of balls, surface area 140 m^2/gm
2.	Copper coated on metal	Toyato, Japan	Thin diffused layer of copper
3.	Fe-Fe oxide or Ag-Ag oxide with mixed oxides	N. Tamora et al	Elimination of NO_x even in the presence of oxygen
4.	Fe oxide sorbents	American gas Association	Removal of NO_x without interference from carbonoxides or water vapour. Also, thermally reactivatable

Table 18.19
Details of oxidative catalysts

S.No.	*Type*	*Manufacturer*	*Special features*
1.	Stabilized Al_2O_3 impregnated with CiO, Cr_2O_3 and Pd	American Cynamide Co.	Stable and active at high temperature operation. Resistant to poisoning by oxides of sulphur.
2.	Mixture of Cu-Mn and Ni-Co oxides on alkaline earth metal aluminate carrier.	W. Vegt.	

(*Contd....*)

(Contd....)

3.	Copper chromite on aluminium support	Mobile oil Co.	
4.	Mixture of Cu oxide, SiO_2 and a group IV element	K.H. Kopernik et al.	Improved abrasion resistance effective oxidation at low temperature
5.	Pt, Pd with Mn oxide and Al_2O_3	R.E. Stephens	
6.	La, Cu, Mn oxides	American Cyanamide Co.	Good oxidation activity, High Thermal Stability

Table 18.20

Effect of control temperatures on NO, emissions at rates conditions 47.5 H.P. at the rate of 2500 RPM

S.No.	*NO_x level ppm*	*%EGR*	*Temp. °C of EGR*	*Percentage reduction No.*
1	1066	Nil	—	—
2	659.7	8.25	148*	38.2
3	434.8	8.25	79	59.3
4	579.2	9.3	158*	45.7

*Uncontrolled temperature EGR.

Tables 18.21 and 18 22 show the standards set for some of the pollutants emitted from automobile exhaust in the United States and other countries. In some countries, legislations have been made for diesel smoke as shown in Table 18.23. Table 18.24 shows ambient air standards in some countries.

Table 18.21

Standards in some states of USA and other countries

Country or states	*CO*	*NO_x*	*Oxidants*	*SO_2*	*Lead*	*Total suspended particles*
California	30 ppm (8 h)	0.25 ppm (1 h)	0.15 ppm (1 h)	0.3 ppm (8 h)	—	—
Colorado	—	0.1 ppm	0.1 ppm	0.1 ppm	—	—
New York	30 ppm (8 h)	—	0.15 ppm (1 h)	0.4 ppm (1 h)	—	100 g/m^3 (1 h)
West Germany	—	0.5 ppm (1 h)	—	0.2 ppm	—	—
USSR	1 ppm (24 h)	0.06 ppm (24 h)	—	0.06 ppm (24 h)	0.7 g/m3 (24 h)	150 g/m^3 (24 h)
Others	5 ppm (8 h)	—	0.02 ppm (8 h)	—	—	—

Table 18.22

Emission standards for specific pollutants from automobiles

Jurisdiction	*Pollutant*	*Source emission*	*Permissible concentration*
Japan	CO	Automobile exhaust	3%
USA	CO	Automobile exhaust	1.5%
USA	CO (100-140 cu. inches)	Automobile exhaust	2%
USA	CO	Automobile exhaust (50-100 cu. inches)	2.3%
USA	Hydrocarbons	Automobile crankness	Not permitted
USA	Hydrocarbons	Automobile exhaust	275 ppm
USA	Hydrocarbons	Automobile exhaust (100-140 cu. inches)	350 ppm
USA	Hydrocarbons	Automobile exhaust (50-100 cu. inches)	410 ppm
California (US)	Nitrogen oxides	Automobile exhaust	350 ppm

Table 18.23

Diesel smoke legislation in some countries

Country	*Year of legislation*	*Smoke meter*	*Maximum allowable level*
Belgium	1966	Hartridge	50
France	1964	Hartridge	40-60 (depending on engine size)
Finland	1960	Bosch	7
Germany	—	Bosch	4.5-6.5 (depending on engine size)
Norway	1964	Hartridge Bosch	5.5
Sweden	1965	Bosch	3.5-4.5 (for used vehicles)
Switzerland	—	Acceptable limit	Determined visually
UK	—	-do-	-do-
USA	1970	Public Health service smokemeter	40% reduction in light during acceleration & 20% reduction in light during bugging

Table 18.24

Ambient air standards in some countries

Pollutant	*Country*	*Long term*			*Short term*		
		mg/m³	*ppm*	*Average time*	*mg/m³*	*ppm*	*Average time*
Sulphur	USA	0.08	0.03	1 yr	—	—	—
dioxide	USA	0365	0.14	24 hr	—	—	—
(SO_2)	USSR	0.05	0.02	24 hr	0.5	0.2	30 min.
	Japan	0.1	0.04	24 hr	0.26	0.1	1 hr
	West Germany	0.15	0.06	24 hr	0.5	0.2	30 min.

(*Contd. ...*)

(*Contd. ...*)

	Argentina	0.07	0.03	30 days	—	—	—
	Brazil	0.05	0.02	24 hr	—	—	—
	Bulgaria	0.05	0.02	24 hr	—	—	—
	Canada	0.03	0.11	24 hr	0.9	0.34	1 hr
	East Germany	0.15	0.06	24 hr	0.5	0.2	30 min
	France	1.0	0.38	24 hr	—	—	—
	Israel	0.26	0.1	24 hr	0.78	0.3	30 min
	Italy	0.38	0.15	24 hr	0.75	0.3	30 min
Carbon monoxide (CO)	USA	10.0	8.6	8 hr	40.0	34.6	1 hr
	USSR	1.0	0.9	24 hr	3.0	2.7	30min.
	Japan	23.0	20.0	8 hr	—	—	—
	Japan	11.5	10.0	24 hr	—	—	—
	West Germany	10.0	8.6	24 hr	40.0	34.6	30 min
	Argentina	11.5	10.0	8 hr	57.7	50.0	1 hr
	Canada	17.3	15.0	8 hr	46.1	40.0	1 hr
	East Germany	1.0	0.9	24 hr	3.0	2.7	30 min
	Israel	11.5	10.0	8 hr	34.6	30.0	30 min
	Italy	22.5	20.0	8 hr	57.2	50.0	30 min
Nitrogen dioxide (NO_2)	USA	0.1	0.05	1 yr	—	—	—
	Japan	0.04	0.02	24 hr	—	—	—
	West Germany	0.1	0.05	30 min	0.3	0.16	30 min
	Argentina	—	—	—	0.85	0.45	1 hr
	Canada	0.02	0.01	24 hr	0.04	0.02	1 hr
	Finland	0.2	0.1	24 hr	0.56	0.3	30 min
	Romania	0.1	0.05	30 min	0.3	0.16	30 min
Hydrocarbon (HC)	USA	0.16	0.24	3 hr	—	—.	—
	Canada	0.125	0.19	3 hr	—	—	—
	Israel	2.0	3.0	24 hr	5.0	7.5	30 min
	Italy-	26.6	40.0	24 hr	53.3	80.0	30 min
Suspended particulate matter (SPM)	USA	0,15	—	24 hr	—	—	—
	USSR	0.15	—	24 hr	—	—	—
	Japan	0.1	—	24 hr	0.2	—	1 hr
	West Germany	0.2	—	24 hr	—	—	—
	Argentina	0.15	—	30 days	—	—	—
	Bulgaria	0.15	—	24 hr	0.5	—	20 min
	Canada	0.06	—	1 yr	—	—	—
	France	0.35	—	24 hr	—	—	—
	Israel	0.2	—	24 hr	—	—	—
	Italy-	0.3	—	24 hr	—	—	—
	East Germany	0.15	—	24 hr	0.5	—	30 min
Photochemical oxidants	USA	—	—	—	0.16	0.08	1 hr
	Japan	—	—	—	0.12	0.06	1 hr

(*Contd. ...*)

(*Contd. ...*)

	Canada	0.05	0.025	24 hr	0.16	0.08	1 hr
	Israel	0.2	0.1	24 hr	0.1	0.05	1 hr
	Romania	0.03	0.15	24 hr	0.01	0.005	30 min
Lead (Pb)	USA	0.0015	—	30 days	—	—	—
	USSR	0.007	—	24 hr	—	—	—
	Canada	0.015	—	24 hr	—	—	—
	East Germany	0.007	—	24 hr	—	—	—
	Israel	0.005	—	24 hr	—	—	—
	Italy	0.01	—	8 hr	0.05		30 min

Table 18.25
Air pollution standards

Pollutant	*Country*	*Long term*			*Short term*			*Remarks*
		mg m^3	*ppm.*	*Average time (min)*	*mg m*^{3}	*ppm.*	*Average time (min)*	
Acetone	Bulgaria	0.35	0.15	24	0.35	0.15	30	
	Hungary	12.0	5.0	24	18.00	75	30	
	E. Germany	0.35	0.15	24	1.0	0.42	30	
	India							
	Israel	7.2	3.0	24	24	10	30	
	Romania	2.0	0.83	24	5.0	2.1	30	
	USSR	0.35	0.15	24	0,35	0.15	30	
	W. Germany	120.0	50.0	1 2	360.0	150	30	
	Yugoslavia	0.35	0.15	24	0.35	0.15	30	
Aceetophenone	Bulgaria	0.35	0.07	24	0.35	0.07 .	30	
	E. Germany	0.003	0.0006	24	0 01	0.002	1	
	India	—	—	—	—	—	—	
	USSR	0.003	0.0006	24	0.003	0.0006	30	
	Yugoslavia	0.003	0.0006	24	0.003	0.0006	30	
Acrolein	Bulgaria	0.1 .	0.04	24	0.3	0.12	30	
	Czechoslovakia	0.1	0.04	24	0.3	0.12	30	
	E. Germany	0.01	0.004	24	0.02	0008	30	
	Hungary	0.1	0.04	24	0.3	0.12	30	
	India							
	Israel	0.1	0.04	24	0.25	0.1	30	
	Romania	0.1	0.04	24	0.3	0.12	30	
	USSR	0.03	0.012	24	0.03	0.012	30	
	W. Germany	0.01	0.005	1 2	0.025	0.01	30	
	Yugoslavia	0.1	0.04	24	0.3	0.12	30	
Ammonia	Bulgaria	0.2	0.28	24	0.2	0.28	30	

(*Contd. ...*)

(*Contd....*)

	Czechoslovakia	0.1	0.14	24	0.3	0.43	30	
	E. Germany	0.1	0.14	24	0.3	0.43	30	Highly protected Area
	Hungary	0.2	0.28	24	0.2	0.28	30	
	India	0.5	0.71	24	1.5	2.14	30	
	Romania	0.1	0.14	24	0.3	0.43	30	
	USSR	0.2	0.28	24	0.2	0.28	30	
	Yugoslavia	0.2	0.28	24	0.2	0.28	30	
Amyl Acetate	Bulgaria	0.1	0.019	24	0.1	0.019	30	
	E. Germany	0.1	0.019	24	0.3	0.057	30	
	Hungary	0.1	0.19	24	0.1	0.019	30	
		30	5.7	24	90	17.1	30	
	India	—	—	—	—	—	—	
	Israel	5.25	1.0	24	15.75	3.0	30	
	USSR	0.1	0.019	24	0.1	0.019	30	
	FRG	30.0	5.0	1/2	90	15	30	
	Yugoslavia	0.1	0.019	24	0.1	0.019	30	
Amyl alcoeol	W. Germany	20.0	5.0	1/2	60.0	15.0	30	
Aniline	Bulgaria	0.03	0.008	24	0.05	0.013	30	
	Czechoslo vakia	0.03	0.008	24	0.05	0.013	30	
	E. Germany	0.03	0.008	24	0.05	0.013	30	
	India							
	Romania	0.02	0.005	24	0.05	0.013	30	
	USSR	0.03	0.008	24	0.05	0.013	30	
	W. Germany	0.8	0.2	1/2	2.4	0.6	30	
	Yugoslavia	0.03	0.008	24	0.05	0.013	30	
Aresenic	Bulgaria	0.003	—	24	—	—	—*	
	Czechoslovakia	0.0003	—	24	—	—	—	
	E. Germany	0.003	—	24	—	—	—	
	India	—	—	—	—	—		
	Israel	0.006	—	24	—	—	—**	
	Poland	0.003	—	24	0.01	—	20	
		0.002	—	24	0.005	—	20	
	Romania	0.01	—	24	0.03		30	
	USSR	0.003	—	24	—	—	—	
	Yugoslavia	0.003	—	24	—	—	—	
	* Including inorganic compounds except arsinc, AsH,							
	** Tentative standards							
Benzene	Czechoslovakia	0.8	0.25	24	2.4	0.75	30	
	E. Germany	0.8	0.25	24	1.5	0.46	30	

(*Contd....*)

(*Contd....*)

	Hungary	0.8	0.25	24	1.5	0.46	30*	Highly protected areas
		3.0	0.94	24	10.0	3.42	30	
	Israel	1.6	0.5	24	4.8	1.5	30	
	India							
	Poland	0.3	0.09	24	1.0	0.31	20	
	Romania	0.8	0.25	24	2.4	0.25	30	
Butane	Bulgaria	—	—	—	200	85.0	30	
	E. Germany	50	21.0	24	200	85.0	30	
	India							
	USSR				200	85.0	30	
	Yugoslavia				200	85.0	30	
Butanol	Bulgaria	—	—	—	0.3	0.1	30	
	E. Germany	0.1	0.03	24	0.3	0.1	30	
	India							
	USSR	—	—	—	0.1'	0.03	30	
	W. Germany	15.0	5.0	1/2	45	15.00	30	
	Yugoslavia	—	—	—	0.3	0.1	30	
Butylene	Bulgaria	3.0	1.2	24	3.0	1.2	30	
	E. Germany	2.0	0.8	24	3.0	1.2	30	
	India	—	—	—	—	—	—	
	USSR	3.0	1.2	24	3.0	1.2	30	
	Yugoslavia	3.0	1.2	24	3.0	1.2	30	
Cadmium	India	—	—	—	—	—	—	
	Yugoslvia	0.003	—	24	0.01	—	30	
Caprolactam	Bulgaria	0.06	0.013	24	0.06	0.013	30*	
	E. Germany	0.06	0.013	24	0.1	0.022	30	
	USSR	0.06	0.013	24	0.06	0.013	30*	
	Yugoslavia	0.06	0.013	24	0.06	0.013	30*	
	* Fumes and aerosols							
Carbon disulphide	Bulgaria	0.01	0.0033	24	0.03	0.01	30	
	Czechoslovakia	0.01	0.0033	24	0.03	0.01	30	
	East Germany	0.003	0.001	24	0.03	0.01	30	
	India	—	—	—	—	—	—	
	Israel	0.15	0.05	24	0.45	0.15	30*	
	Poland	0.015	0.005	24	0.045	0.015	20**	
	Romania	0.01	0.0033	24	0.03	0.01	30	
	USSR	0.005	0.0016	24	0.03	0.01	30	
	Yugoslavia	0.01	0.033	24	0.03	0.01	30	

* Tentative

** Protected areas in Poland

Noise Pollution and Environment

Although of a different nature, as for pollutant emission control, trade-offs between conflicting objectives relating to. motor vehicles, noise control requires an analysis of the problems and related factors, prior to defining control levels, involving different technological approaches. Determination is required on the part of authorities to define priorities and to tackle environmental problems in relation to noise. In this respect, decision makers should bear in mind the following considerations :

(*i*) Particularly in metropolitan areas, noise directly affects senses, and consequently, the quality of the urban environment, more than any other nuisance stemming from technical progress. Urban noise is an erratic combination of "Peak noise" and background noise of a lower intensity, ranging from about 50 to 70 dBA, for which motor vehicles are regarded as one of the major contributors. This is in spite of the significant progress achieved in the last decades in silencing exhausts and reducing mechanical noise. Noise disturbs sleep and may be a cause of stress.

(*ii*) Four-wheeled vehicles((passenger cars, public transports and commercial vehicles) and two-wheeled vehicles (motor cycles and mopeds) present different characteristics, as far as their acoustic energy emission and radiation are concerned. Experience has shown that, especially in urban areas, commercial vehicles and motor cycles are responsible for the majority of "Peak noise" emission recorded in traffic.

(*iii*) Concerning the four-wheeled vehicles, both acoustic energy generation and radiation should be considered. For these vehicles, the noise control levels enforced in Europe, Japan and the United States of America, generally, result in a minimum exhaust pipe noise, achieved by means of advanced silencers, using gas expansion and noise frequency interference techniques. It may be difficult technically to further reduce this source of noise. Conversely, exploration of ways and means should continue to reduce the following acoustic energy emissions and radiations which are unrelated to exhaust:

— fan aerodynamic noise, particularly from air-cooled engines,

— mechanical noise from the engine cylinder block and crank case, gear box transmission and alternators,

— rolling noise from tyres in contact with the road.

Fig. 18.1 and 18.2 taken from VDA "Urban Traffic and noise" show the respective average sound level attribution from car and truck rolling and engine sources at various constant driving speeds. The substitution of larger engines, with low er RPM for engines of smaller cubic capacity and higher RPM coupled with higher transmission ratios, should also be considered in association with related parameters which may be included in vehicle taxation criteria. Many industrialized countries are considering the possibilities of progressive reduction in noise emission levels of motor vehicles of 5 to 10 dBA according to the vehicle type. Attention is drawn to the fact, however, that different noise measurement methods are used in different parts of the world.

(*iv*) Diesel equipped vehicles are noisy by the nature of the engine combustion, under very high compression. Public transport and heavy commercial vehicles require special consideration, and authorities should pay particular attention to their proper maintenance and periodic inspection, including their silencing devices. Authorities should also encourage research and development on advanced diesel engine technology, and appropriate engine and transmission encapsulation which, when applied at the vehicle design stage, may reduce their acoustic energy emission and radiation. Incentives should also be given to implement "quiet truck and bus" demonstration programmes where the cost-effectiveness of the solutions demonstrated would be the major aspect to be considered. Such programmes could be complemented by appropriate durability tests,s to provide data on degradation of noise emission as a function of use, age and service. Concerning buses, the interior noise issue should also be considered.

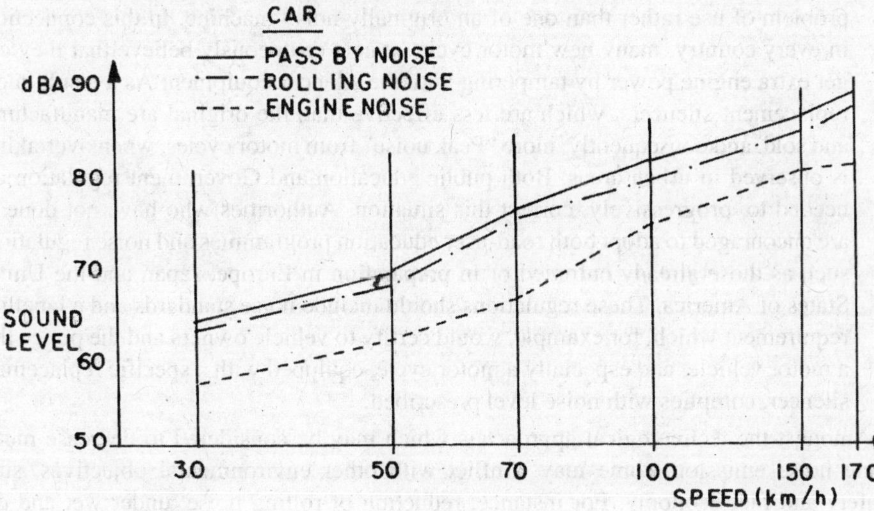

Fig. 18.1

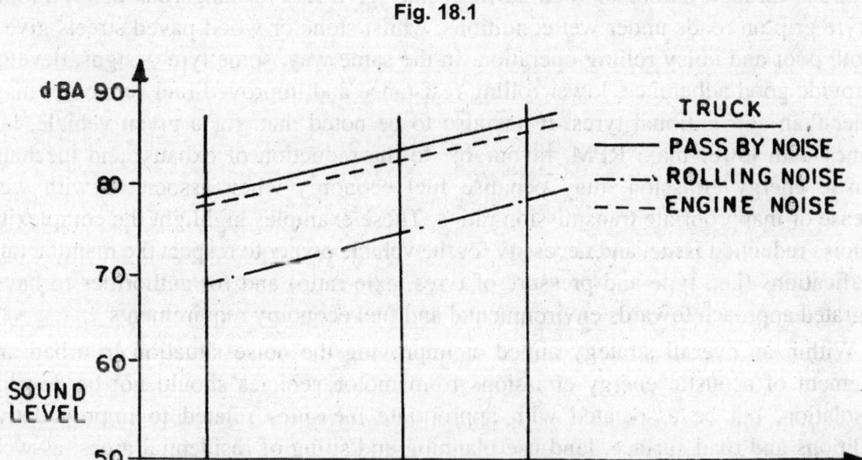

Fig. 18.2

Fig. 18.1 and 18.2 Sound level of car and 3.5t truck pass-by and rolling noise on dry concrete pavement, according to Frietzche 1/, and calculated sound level of engine noise as a function of speed. (Mean of 13 types of car, and 11 types of truck—Unaccelerated runs in direct gear on level road. Pass-by with microphone at 7.5 meters).

(*v*) Noise control for motor cycles appears to be one of the most complicated issues amongst those relating to environmental protection and motor vehicle use. Owing to the weight limit, high engine power/ cubic capacity ratio, resulting in high engine RPM for maxi torque, have to be used on most motor cycles. Moreover, since, for reasons of cooling and handling in cross-winds, the engine and gear box cannot easily be encapsulated or protected by sound proofing cover, the problem of their acoustic energy radiation remains difficult to solve. However, more than other current road transportation noise problems, the motor cycle noise issue may be seen more as a problem of use rather than one of an originally noisy machine. In this connection, in every country, many new motor cycle owners erroneously believe that they can get extra engine power by tampering with the silencer equipment As a result, more replacement silencers, which are less effective than the original are manufactured and sold, and consequently, more "Peak noise" from motor cycles, when overtaking, is observed in urban areas. Both public education and Government regulation are needed to, progressively, correct this situation. Authorities who have not done so are encouraged to adopt both road-user education programmes and noise regulations such as those already enforced or in preparation in Europe, Japan and the United States of America. These regulations should include noise standards and a labelling requirement which, for example, would certify to vehicle owners and the police that a motor vehicle, and especially a motor cycle, equipped with a specific replacement silencer, complies with noise level prescribed.

Amongst the technological approaches which may be considered to decrease motor vehicle noise emission, some may conflict with other environmental objectives, such as safety and fuel economy. For instance, reduction of rolling noise, under wet and dry conditions through smoother road surface; may give rise to dangerous deterioration of the tyre grip on roads under wet conditions, whilst stone or wood-paved streets give rise to both poor and noisy rolling operation. In the same way, some tyre designs, developed to provide good adherence, lower rolling resistance and improved fuel economy, may be noisier than conventional tyres. It has also to be noted that, for a given vehicle, larger engines with lower maxi RPM, favourable to the reduction of exhaust and mechanical acoustic energy emission, may penalise fuel economy when associated with weight increase or inappropriate transmission ratios. These examples highlight the complexity of the noise reduction issue, and necessity for the vehicle owner to respect the manufacturers' specifications (i.e., type and pressure of tyres, axle ratio) and for authorities to have an integrated approach towards environmental and fuel economy requirements.

Within an overall strategy aimed at improving the noise situation in urban areas, abatement of acoustic energy emissions from motor vehicles should not be developed in isolation, but be associated with appropriate measures related to improved traffic conditions and road surface, land use planning and siting of residential areas, as well as to the progressive use of sound absorbing materials in buildings and in sound barriers along major highways in urban areas. In this respect, for example, the possibility of two people holding a conversation at normal levels, between 2 and 3 metres apart in a dwelling, along any urban road, should be, amongst others, a reasonable and practicable objective. This implies that peak noise should be eliminated and background noise level during the daytime should be less than 60 dB A (as measured at the facade of the building).

As for pollutant emission control, there is a need for an internationally acceptance test procedure for noise measurement, and efforts should be to evolve an acceptable test procedure for noise measurement and efforts should be addressed to reaching agreement on the definition of a common noise testing procedure which, in any case, would better reflect traffic noise than the existing SAE J 986 and ISO R 362 test procedures currently in use. Proposals have been made by the United States of America Environment Protection Agency and the Committee of the Common Market Constructors (CCMC), whilst the Group of Experts on the construction of Vehicles of the UN/ECE has recently adopted a slightly modified and more appropriate version of the ISO R 362 method. However, these solutions differ significantly, mainly with regard to vehicle approach speed and acceleration and position of microphones in the measurement area. No agreement has yet been concluded as regards the adoption of a common and appropriate noise testing procedure. At the same time, new trends are being observed in the evolution of the car market, where there is an increased registration of smaller and lower powered cars in the United States of America. Furthermore, the trend for more diesel equipped cars in Europe is being followed in the United States of America. Both of these trends may change progressively the traffic noise conditions.

19

Conservation of Material Resources and Energy Through Recycling

Environmental pollution not only creates health hazards and causes deterioration of the qualify of the surroundings but also affects overall production and, thus, the economy, when examined in a larger perspective.

Since pollution generation is a combined result of population, industrialization and specific technological developments, it is difficult to estimate exactly how fast the exponential curve for total pollution air, water, etc., is rising. We might estimate that if 7 billion people living in the year 2000 have a GNP per capita as high as that of present day Americans, the total pollution load on environment would be at least ten times of its present value.

Before adopting any measure to control pollution, both the capital and energy expenditure involved should be studied at, the quality of the commodity obtained or service provided, examined and an assessment made to see whether it is indeed "a good measure" or not. For this, the concept of resource should be clarified, the rate of its depletion determined, the life style, as reflected in the waste, we produce, and its composition, should be analyzed to assess what can be reclaimed/recovered from it. A detailed examination of the refuse will, then, enable assessment to be made of the recovery or conversion potential.

On of the most economical methods of controlling pollution seems to be the recycling arrangement, i.e., one in which the pollutants are, by and large, processed at the place of their generation itself, and converted into products which could be used there or as raw material for more useful products.

Recycling is a much abused term, generally taken to mean getting something back from waste, e.g., newspaper recovery by de-inking, followed by repulping, to make more newsprint.

In fact, recycling falls into three main categories:

1. Re-use
2. Direct recycle
3. Indirect

Re-use is typified by the returnable bottle or tin; it means several steps from the bottler to the consumer and back again, where it is cleaned and refilled. Once it is unfit for re-use, it may be cleaned and broken down for cullet, i.e., glass which is remelted at the glass works and used to make new bottles. The latter process comes under the heading of direct recycling, which is dependent on the quality of recycled material and on its cost, which should not exceed that of the fresh raw material. It is quite probable that the bottle may eventually end up in domestic refuse, where it can be extracted by screening and separation in conjunction with other bottles. These bottles will probably be of different colours, and at varying degrees of cleanliness, which might render them unsuitable for cullet, unless optical sorting is opted which would, however, raise costs. The bottles may, however, be ground and used for a highly skid-resistant and durable road surfacing material. This is an example of indirect recycling. Other examples are: (a) the conversion of refuse to combustible gases by pyrolysis (b) direct heating by means of incineration with heat recovery.

Energy Resource Conservation

Increasing use of use energy by mankind is also related to pollution. The process of economic development, is, in effect, the process of utilizing to increase the productivity and efficiency of human labour. In fact, one of the best indicators of the wealth of a human population is the amount of energy it consumes per person. Per capita energy consumption, in the world, is increasing at a rate of 1.3 percent per year, which means a total increase, including population growth, of 3.4 percent per year.

At present, 97 percent of industrial energy production comes from fossil fuels, i.e., coal, oil and natural gas. Current global production of oil is tending to flatten out at around 20 billion barrels/year at the moment, due to energy economy measures adopted following the major 1972 price increase. However, viewed against man's life-time, this curve is cause for anxiety as it means that the industry has to find 20 billion barrels/year just to maintain the current production rates. Should the finding rate fall further, the reserves will be consumed and eventually decline to zero. Now, the current finding rate is 18 billion barrels/year and proven reserves total 600 billion barriers. Thus, the global problem is likely to become serious before the turn of the century Coal reserves have a cycle of production, which tails off around the year 2300. India has only 0.8 percent of the total world coal reserves.

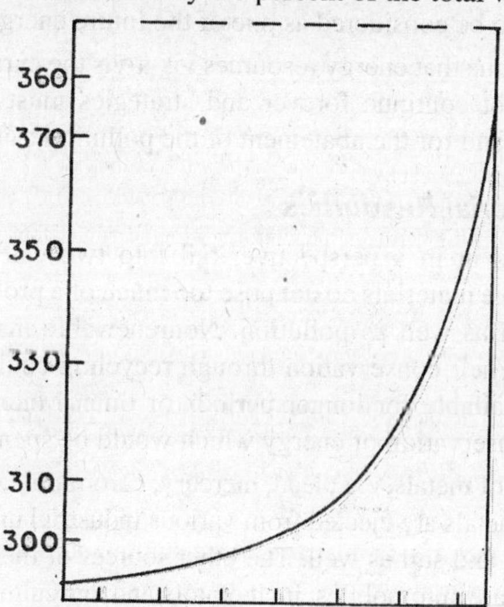

Fig. 19.1 Amount of CO_2 going into the atmosphere

For extracting energy out of fossil fuels, they are burned. In the process, they release, among other substances, carbon dioxide and carbon monoxide into the atmosphere. Currently, 20 billion tonnes of CO_2 are being released from fossil fuel combustion every year. Figure 19.1 shows that the amount of CO_2 in the atmosphere is increasing exponentially, at the rate of 0.2 percent per year. One half of this CO_2 actually appears in the atmosphere, while the other half is apparently absorbed, mainly by the surface waters/oceans.

The reserves of oil, natural gas and coal have started depleting. Their use as the source of energy will not only create a pollution problem but also complicate the growth of petrochemical industries. Already, cases are being made for reservation of these resources for chemical synthesis, in order to prolong the time-span available for the construction of synthetic oil and gas plants using the still abundant coal reserves as raw material.

Efforts are being made to develop technology for large scale power generation, especially fast breeder nuclear reactors. The use of nuclear energy will decrease the CO_2 concentration in the atmosphere and abolish other complexities which arise when fossil feels are used. Nuclear reactors produce unused fissionable material as waste, the reprocessing of which is always superior to the direct disposal of spent fuel in terms of economy, material conservation and environmental protection. Recycling of unused fissionable material, through reprocessing, is very important as the process of reusing can be repeated until 40 times as much energy has been extracted from the raw material as can be done in conventional reactors. Recycling and reprocessing permit the use of synthetic fissionable material, and conserves natural fissionable material. Nuclear energy can also be converted into electrical energy, which is pollution free. Another side-effect of the use of this energy which is independent of fuel sources, is its dissipation as heat. If the energy source is something other than incident solar energy (e.g., fossil fuel or nuclear energy), that heat results in warming the atmosphere. Locally, waste heat or thermal pollution in stream causes disruption in the balance of aquatic life. Thermal pollution may also have serious worldwide climatic effects, when it reaches some appreciable fraction of energy, normally absorbed by the earth from the sun. The natural sources of energy, prime amongst which is the sun, can also be considered as one of the future energy sources.

Therefore, it is obvious that energy resources vis-a-vis the current rate of consumption are finite. Growth cannot continue forever and strategies must be adopted for a more economic use of energy and for the abatement of the pollution caused thereby.

Conservation of Material Resources

Resources, when looked at in a perspective, fall into two categories : renewable and nonrenewable. Renewable materials do not pose too much of a problem both from the point of view of conservation as well as pollution. Nonrenewable materials, however, create problems of pollution. Their conservation through recycling could reduce such problems and also make them available for longer periods of time. Material recycling can, thus, substantially and the conservation of energy which would be spent on its extraction.

The harmful effects of metals, e.g., lead, mercury, chromium, arsenic, copper, zinc, etc., are well known. These metals are ejected from various industrial units into the environment, thus, polluting air, water and soil as well. The other sources of their release into waterways and into the atmosphere are automobiles, incinerators and agricultural pesticides.

The mercury pollution of water because of the use of mercury cells in caustic soda manufacture is responsible for reduction in the application of these cells in spite of their many advantages over diaphragm cells. Japan has had serious problems of mercury pollution which ultimately resulted in the issue of an ordinance for discontinuation of the use of mercury cells.

The world's known reserves of chromium are about 775 million m. tonnes, of which 1.85 million. tonnes are mined annually at present. Thus, at the current rate of use, the known reserves would last about 420 years. The actual world consumption of chromium is increasing at the rate of 2.6 per cent annually. If the exponential relationship in an increased rate of consumption is assumed, the reserves would last for only 95 years. If the undiscovered reserves increase the present reserves by five times, this would extend the life time of reserves only from 95 to 150 years. The lifetime of aluminium is estimated to be 100 years using a static index, 31 years with an exponential index, 55 years with a five-fold increase in reserves.

Copper, with a life time of 3 6 years at the present usage rate, would actually last only 21 years at the present rate of growth, and 45 years if reserves are multiplied by five. Table 19.1 gives the position of reserves of nonrenewable natural resources and their life time using static and exponential indices.

Table 19.1
Nonrenewable natural resources

Resources	*Known global reserves*	*Static index* (yrs)*	*Average rate of growth % per year*	*Exponential index (yrs)*	*Exponential index ** using 5 tonnes blown reserves*
Nickel	147×10^9 lbs	150	3.4	53	96
Chromium	7.75×10^5 tonnes	420	2.6	95	154
Aluminium	1.17×10^9 tonnes	100	6.4	31	55
Copper	308×10^6 tonnes	36	4.6	21	48
Lead	91×10^4 tonnes	26	2.0	21	64
Iron	1×10^{11} tonnes	240	1.8	93	173
Mercury	3.34×10^4 flasks	13	2.6	13	41
Tin	4.36×10^6 tonnes	17	1.1	15	61
Zinc	123×10^6 tonnes	23	2.9	18	50

$$* \text{ Static index} = \frac{\text{Total reserve}}{\text{Current annual consumption}}$$

$$** \text{ Exponential index} = \frac{\ln(rS) - 1}{r}$$

where r = average rate of growth

s = static index

Taking into account economic factors such as increased prices with decreased availability, it would appear at present that the quantities of platinum, gold, zinc, lead, etc., are not sufficient to meet demand. At the present rate of expansion, silver, tin and uranium may be in short supply even at higher prices by the turn of the century. By the year 2050, several more minerals may be exhausted if the current rate of consumption continues.

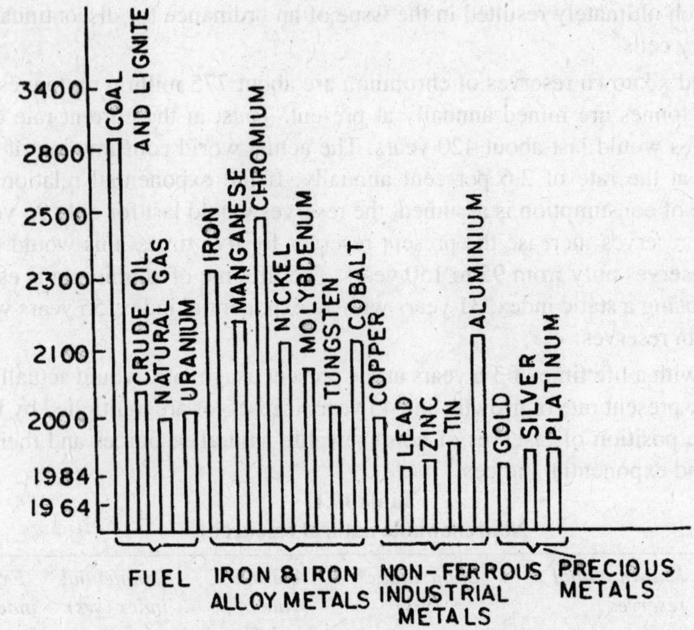

Fig. 19.2 Life of estimated recoverable reserves of mineral resources

Taking the example of lead, in 1960 global demand had risen to 4.5 m. tonnes year, but reserves had risen to 90 million tonnes due to farther discoveries. However, extrapolation as a paper exercise show- that by the year 2020 there would be a demand of 25 m. tonnes/ year, which if an R: P ratio of 20 were the norm require 500 m. tonnes of reserves which are just not there. The lifetime of estimated recoverable reserves of mineral resources is shown in Figure 19.2.

The consumption of these minerals, in a more efficient manner, would help in minimizing pollution and conserving materials as well as the energy spent on them. Recycling appears to be one of the best ways to meet this end. This is illustrated by the following relationship:

$$\text{Demand on reserve} = P(1-R)$$

Let annual production P be constant and the Recycled fraction be R.

Thus, the life time of reserves is extended by

$$\frac{P}{P(1-R)} = \frac{1}{1-R}$$

i.e., for a recycling factor of 50 percent, the life time is doubled; for a recycling factor of 99 percent, the life time is extended by 100.

The production curves being exponential to reserves, depletion would be faster and the effect of recycling will have less impact due to the time lag between raw material production and its arrival back to scrap cycle. Figure 19.3 shows the total and recycled material consumption. From Fig. 19.3, it is obvious that the adoption of recycling in an exponential growth situation can only mildly assist the inexorable march of resource depletion. Obviously, a static consumption situation is required with maximum recycling to conserve resources in on long-term and not short-term basis.

Thus recycling can aid both energy and material conservation. It alone cannot assure a steady state situation but it can buy time, conserve resources and. if properly applied, minimize both energy consumption and environmental impact.

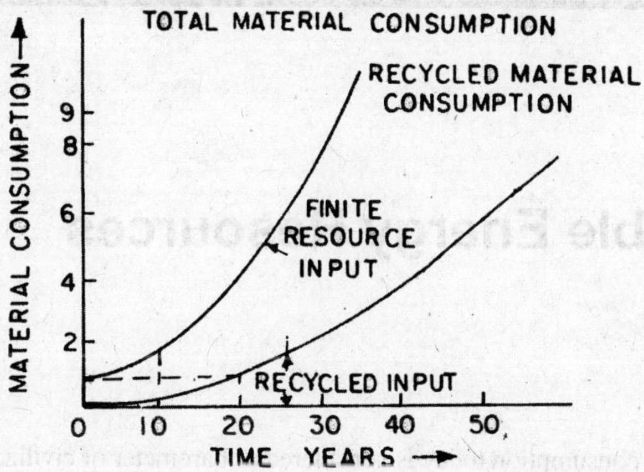

Fig. 19.3 Total and recycled material consumption

The problems associated with adopting recycling may be the cost factor, obtaining of proper know-how, etc., which could be overcome by proper planning. The problems of cost could be tackled by legislature, tax relief, cash incentives, development rebate, etc. This would encourage industries to even invest in setting up of plants for waste processing and encourage conscious industrialists to come forward with new ideas of controlling pollution. The chain reaction, so started, will go a long way in conserving energy and materials, minimizing pollution and providing a better environment to mankind to live in.

20

Renewable Energy Resources

The rate of energy consumption today is considered as barometer of civilization. The energy consumption is also linked with socio-economic development. The average rate of growth of energy consumption has been observed just double to average growth rate of economy from the first five year plan to the seventh five year plan. At present, the total installed capacity for power generation in India is about 48000 MW while installed capacity for hydroelectric power generation is only about 12000 MW, while is only 25% of the total. Thus, a major share is contributed by thermal systems. It has been recognized that thermal generation of electricity contributes significantly to suspended particulate matters, CO_2, CO, SO_2, etc. With the increasing percentage of ash in coal, the problem of suspended particulate matters, especially, where a thermal power plant is located in the heart of city, is turning severe.

Some of the major problems, for example, green house effect, and effect on ozone layer, which are developing because of air pollution are as follows:

Green House Effect

The green house effect, once a subject of purely scientific enquiry, is rapidly emerging as an important public policy issue. A precise definition of green house effect is difficult, but in simple terms, it is the heating effect, exerted by the atmosphere upon the earth by absorbing and re-emitting long wave radiation from the earth; it will disturb the climate of the earth. This, in turn, will aggravate existing problems such as drought, desertification and soil erosion in some regions. This effect on earth has to be checked by reducing the amount of fossil fuel burnt, by filtering CO_2 from the emissions of power stations and by disposing off the green house gases.

The CO_2 in the atmosphere effectively shields the earth's surface from the cosmic radiation of the outer space. Increase in CO_2 content of the atmosphere would reduce the shielding effect making the surface warmer. The build up of CO_2 in the atmosphere will produce the so-called green house effect as the increased concentration of CO_2 will absorb the infrared radiation emitted by the earth.

The Ozone Shield

Ozone (O_3) produced in the lower atmosphere is a serious pollutant in that it is poisonous to both plants and animals. At the same time, paradoxically ozone is absolutely essential in the stratosphere (upper atmosphere) in that it acts as a shield against ultraviolet radiation (UV). Ultraviolet is a part of natural radiation from the sun; the wavelengths are just slightly shorter and have higher energy content than those of visible light. However, when UV penetrates living tissues, it is preferentially absorbed by proteins or nucleic acids such as DNA, and its high energy enables it to actually break the chemical bonds of these molecules. UV is extremely destructive to biological tissues and is capable of causing mutations.

Some UV docs penetrate to the surface of Earth. It is responsible for sunburn and is involved in some 200,000 to 600,000 cases of skin cancer per year in the U.S. However, we are spared the worst effects of UV because most of it is absorbed and, hence, screened out by the ozone in the stratosphere. Without this ozone "shield", the biological damage to both plants and animals would be disastrous. Indeed, it is doubtful whether life could even exist on land without the protection of the ozone layer.

The stratosphere O_3 layer varies reasonably in thickness between 2.4-2.6 mm at the equator and 3.1-4.3 mm at 70°-m latitude. O_3 layer exists only because our atmosphere contains O_2. Without O_2, it could not have produced O_3 and formed the protective O_3 layer. The ozone layer is generally located between 15 km and 40 km above the earth, but its highest density is at 25 km. Between 200 and 290 mm range, UV is destructive to life but is efficiently absorbed by O_2 and O_3 in the atmosphere.

Certain pollutants diffusing gradually into the stratosphere from the lower atmosphere have damaging effects on the ozone layer. In particular, chlorine atoms catalyze the breakdown of ozone. A single chlorine atom can break down millions of molecules of ozone, upsetting the natural ozone balance. A major potential source of chlorine, reaching the stratosphere is the chloroflurocarbons such as freon ($CFC1_3$) used as a propellant in aerosol cans and as refrigerants. Some 300 million tonnes of chlorine are released into the atmosphere every year by the evaporation of sea water which contains salt (sodium chloride). Large amounts of this chlorine reach the stratosphere, through the pumping action of thunderstorms, hurricanes, typhoons and other cyclonic activity which also break up the sodium chloride molecules. There are 4.2 million tons of chlorine gases produced by the burning of biomass, largely due to slash and burn agricultures methods.

Nitrogen oxide produced by high altitude aircraft, such as the supersonic transports, nitrogen fertilizers and automobile exhaust, can break down ozone in a manner similar to chlorine.

Because of this fact and due to heavy depletion of nonrenewable energy sources like oil and coal and due to increasing demand for energy, there is obvious need for the search of alternative renewable sources of energy such as sun, wind, biomass, etc. A brief status report on the availability of Alternative Energy Sources is presented in this chapter.

The exhaustible energy resource is one which is a nonaugmentable stock ; when used up, it is gone. The renewable energy resource is an augmentable resource flow, one can tap into the resource flow at any time without reducing the amount available in the future. Hydro, solar and wind energy are augmentable in the broadest sense; the amount of flowing water is given, as is wind speed and the level of insolation, but knowledge of total annual flows, from these sources, offers little guidance to future energy supply unless the resource concept is given an economic dimension. Once this part is over, augmentation is possible through improved technology or higher prices.

The energy potential of a nation has direct correlation with economic growth and prosperity. The stage of development is well reflected by the per capita energy consumption of a country. The deepening energy crisis, with which the world community is confronted has led to the formulation of an energy policy framework within which the rate of growth and pattern of energy consumption could be regulated. In this context, a transition may be considered necessary. The required transition is to shift from fossil and non-renewable sources such as petroleum, coal and uranium to renewable energy sources like hydroelectric, solar, wind, biogas, etc.

The main energy sources of a country have been usually decided into commercial and non-commercial sources. Commercial sources consist of coal, oil, natural gas, hydroelectric power and nuclear fuel. Under non-commercial category, the main sources are livestock, forest, vegetable waste which mainly consists of crops residue and cowdungs. Besides, there are some important non-conventional sources as well. These are solar, biogas, wind mill and tidal. India has sufficient potential of all these energy sources.

The following discussion reviews the potential contribution of solar thermal energy, photovoltaic energy, wind energy, hydro energy and bio energy, which may be considered as most potential renewable energy sources in India.

Solar Thermal Energy

Solar radiation has become an attractive energy source because of its many features: its global distribution, its high thermodynamic quality, its inexhaustible energy supply, and its pollution free nature. On the other hand, some characteristics have made its use limited at large scale. The daily and seasonal variations in available solar energy may require the use of energy storage facilities. The dispersed nature of the resource itself alfects the economics of power generation. The average amount of solar energy, striking an area, including direct and diffuse radiation, can vary from 2 kwh per square meter to as much as 7-8 kwh/m^2 in sunny regions. The average energy available (in kwh/m^2 year) to a tracking surface is 0.5 to 0.7 times the number of sunshine hours. As a world wide average, 1.500 kwh/m^2 year is available on a tracking surface and 1,150 kwh/m^2/year on a horizontal surface. Solar radiation is currently being used to generate electricity via two technologies : solar thermal and photovoltaics.

Solar Thermal Electric Conversion

There are a number of possible systems for solar thermal electric conversion : parabolic trough, parabolic dish, satellite, total systems (heat and electricity), control receiver and solar ponds. Based upon research to date, the most viable method for large scale conversion is the central receiver. In this method, sunlight, falling on flat two axis tracking mirrors, is focused on a central boiler. The absorbed energy produces superheated steam or hot gases to drive a Rankine-Steam cycle. Projected sizes of solar thermal energy conversion systems range to 150MW.

Technical Limitations

Solar thermal energy conversion is a concentrating system; it must rely solely on the direct insolation component, the highly collimated solar radiation. This stands in contrast to photovoltaic and other flat plate collectors which can use both diffuse and direct insolation. Thus, solar thermal energy conversion can be considered to be very much successful in arid region where there is less diffusion by clouds, dust, pollution, etc.

Land requirements, although significant, are not a limiting factor, particularly in the light of land availability in hot arid areas where solar thermal energy conversion is most likely. A thumb rule is that a square mile will supply 100 MW at a 40 percent load factor.

Solar Energy in the form of heat

Energy in the form of heat is one of the main energy requirements in domestic, agricultural, industrial and commercial sectors. In the domestic sector, thermal energy is needed for cooking, for heating water and for drying purposes. The agricultural sector needs thermal energy for growing of plants under controlled environment, using green houses. Drying of agricultural products is required for their preservation.

In the industrial sector, there is a need for hot water, heated air, gases and liquids and low temperature steam. Also the commercial sector, viz., hotels, hospitals offices, needs thermal energy for variety of applications. Generally, these requirements are being met by burning of coal, oil, wood, animal dung and use of electricity. Many of these conventional energy sources can be replaced by solar energy. Due to its geographical position, India is blessed with plenty of sunshine, with an annual average insolation, varying from 4 to 7 kwh per m^2 per day with 250-300 clear sunny days, per year. The entire temperature range required by the applications can be covered with the available technologies of conversion of solar energy to thermal energy. The available technologies can be categorized as follows:

Temperature range	*Applications*
1. Low thermal energy (below 100 °C)	Water heating, air heating, drying, refrigeration, space heating, desalination, etc.
2. Medium grade thermal energy (100 to 300 °C)	Cooking, steam generation, drying, power generation, etc.
3. High grade thermal energy (above 300 °C)	Power generation.

Photovoltaic Energy Conversion

Photovoltaic devices convert light to electricity, using solar cells comprised of semiconductive materials such as silicon. The process works at ambient temperature and produces byproducts other than heat from the sunlight, which is not converted into electricity.

Solar photovoltaic has an immense potential in a developing country like India where maximum part of landmass receives sunshine almost throughout the year. Photovoltaic systems are now in widespread use in India in remote villages, islands and hill tops performing a variety of function including lighting communication. The primary R and D efforts are directed towards cost reduction because this is the most significant determinant of application. Several studies have projected cost reduction of upto two orders of magnitude; under such circumstances, potential application of photovoltaics is substantial in both central generation and distribution energy systems. Power from solar photovoltaics has already been shown to be cost effective in India for many applications when it is deployed at distance 4-40 km from the transmission network. Solar photovoltaic is one of the interesting possible ways for meeting the electrical energy needs of remote villages in India, having no access to utility grids.

Constraints

Even at the low efficiencies associated with current technology, photovoltaic devices require little land relative to other sources. The materials intensity is low compared with other alternative energy sources, although it is higher than that of conventional technology. Studies of material availability of cell inputs, have shown that the elements of silicon, zinc, copper, tin, sulfur and phosphorous impose no limits on photovoltaic cell production.

The primary emphasis of current R and D work, with single-crystal silicon, is on reducing the costs of preparing materials. Thin-film, continuous ribbon technology offers promise of very low cost cells. At present, thin film cells have efficiencies below 9 percent. Both, cost reduction and efficiency improvements, are viewed as equally probable components in the move toward economic viability. Studies have shown concentration to be on economic option until the year 2000, when higher cell efficiencies will prove low concentration system to be less costly. Tracking has been considered to be uneconomical because of the use of diffuse as well as direct insolation.

Wind Energy

Because of the comparatively long term experience in the use of wind plants, future contributions and cost of this source are more certain than those of other renewable sources.

In projecting the significance of Wind Energy conversion-system's contribution, as an energy source, account must be taken of the highly localized quality of the wind resource. Although the resource is large, site selection is a critical and limiting factor in forecasting potential.

The annual-average hourly-mean wind-speed is, generally, used to reveal the wind energy potential for a particular location. In India, at most places, this falls in the range 9-17 km/h. The rated wind speed at which full rated power is generated is normally higher than the annual average-speed. Therefore, in order to maximize energy availability during a year, a rated speed in the range of 20-25 km/h would correspond to 9-17 km/h annual average-speed.

The number of hours during any year, when wind speed would equal or exceed this rated wind speed at a given place, would probably be between 1000-2000 hours, though not equitably distributed throughout the year. During the period March to August, the winds are uniformly strong over the whole of Indian peninsula except the eastern peninsular coast. The months of May, June and July account for nearly half of the annual energy availability. Wind speeds during, November to March, are weaker. Therefore, unless the wind energy availability and the demand are matched, a wind mill designed to operate in windy months would deliver only a fraction of output in the less windy months or if it is designed to operate in a less windy months, it would utilize only a fraction of energy available during the windy season.

It has been estimated that in windy areas (18-20 km/h), the potential for wind power generation is about 5 MW/sq km and, in less windy areas (15-18 km/h), about 2 MW/sq km. Such wind conditions, according to the present information, are available in, atleast, 5 percent of the land area of the country. On the basis of available wind information, it is estimated that there exists a potential of the order of 20,000 MW in the country for wind generated electricity.

Wind and Solar energy can not be a replacement for the presently available commercial sources of energy, in terms of the total power delivered. They can play an important role as a decentralized source, in regions where commercial power is not available and where good wind and sunshine prevail, particularly in the development of integrated energy systems in many rural areas in India.

Micro-Hydel Power

Hydropower is one of the most attractive sources of renewable energy. In the realization of harnessing hydro energy both, major and mini/micro hydro sources, are to be developed. It has been realized uniformly that large hydro projects involve several .environments and social consequences. Hence, there is increasing interest in small hydro projects. The Central Electricity Authority (CEA) has classified the small hydro plants into three classes.

(1) Small Hydro Plants

The plants with individual unit ranging between 1MW and 5 MW and total installed capacity is less than 15 MW.

(2) Mini Hydro Plants

Total installed capacity is less than 2 MW with individual unit capacity ranging between 100 KW to 1 MW.

(3) Micro Hydro Plants

Those plants which are of less than 100 KW installed capacity with individual capacity ranging between a few KW to 100 KW.

In Indian conditions, small hydro can be broadly categorized into two types as

I. Small hydroelectric project sites in the hilly regions where small streams are available.

II. Small hydro especially in the plains where the canal falls, utilizing regulated discharges for irrigation and water supply to towns.

The total number of small hydroelectric schemes in operation at the end of 1988 was 89 with an installed capacity of more than 171 MW. The on-going small hydro schemes numbered 87 with an aggregate installed capacity of 198 MW. About 255 small hydro projects were under investigation in various parts of the country.

The north and north eastern areas of India are hilly and mountainous. These areas are sparsely populated and accessible with difficulty. Extension of grid lines from plains is very difficult and expensive. Setting up of diesel based stations is also difficult and uneconomical because of high cost of transportation. But these areas are blessed with a number of hilly streams which can be utilized for generation of electricity through microhydel. The energy can be distributed to the surrounding villages through isolated grids.

Biogas Technology in India

Biogas is an important renewable source of energy, produced from materials like cattle dung, human wastes and different types of biomass. Biogas has revolutionized the style of living in many rural areas of India. This programme has now spread to almost all parts of the country. A total of over 1.05 million biogas plants had been setup by March 1988. Assuming that about 85% of these plants are working, at a given time, at 80% rated capacity with an average of 4 cubic meter gas production per day, these plants are estimated to produce 1020 million cubic meters of biogas equivalent to a saving of 3.7 million tonnes of fire wood valued at Rs.1485 million per year. At the same time, 17 million tonnes of enriched manure, valued Rs.1477 million, can also be produced.

21

Conservation of Energy

It is well known that energy saving could be obtained to the extent of 15%, without an additional input and with proper modification addition of equipments both, for generation of power, especially boilers of about 3 3 % efficiency. Using fluidized bed techniques, it is possible to save energy to the extent of 30%. The organized sector, especially industries, transport, etc., could take lead in this direction. The other sector especially agriculture could very well make use of alternate energy sources including biogas, wind energy, and photovoltaic which is considered extremely suitable for remote areas including hills because of distribution problems as with conventional energy.

It is well known that any additional generation of power, especially through thermal will lead to further environmental degradation. It is, therefore, obvious that conservation of energy will also reduce environmental degradation. Hence, any effort on energy conservation will automatically contribute to control of environmental pollution as well as ecorestoration. Energy conservation techniques are briefly described in this chapter.

Power Shortage

The rise in demand of power against supply may hamper the growth of industry and agriculture. At the end of sixth plan, a gap of 5,444 MW between demand and supply, may become as wide as 10,000 MW during seventh plan. In the first year of the seventh plan (1985-86) the addition to the utilities was 4072 MW including 2,830 MW in the thermal sector. The power position in the country worsened in 1985–86 with a 7.9% shortfall in power supply. In 1984–85, the power deficit was around 6.7%. The expected annual growth rate in the demand for the electricity in the seventh plan is 12.2%.

There has been substantial increase in cost per megawatt of power. This has gone up from Rs.24 lakhs in the first plan to Rs.159 lakhs at the end of the sixth plan. Transmission and distribution losses were as high as 21 percent in 1985-86, while in Japan and in the Federal Republic of Germany, the loss was about 5.3% and 4.7%, respectively.

As the thermal and hydel energies are very costly and are also location based, so the gap, in demand and supply can be reduced to some extent by non-conventional energy sources, such as solar, wind, biomass, etc.

Energy, through other sources, is being looked into but we are not in a position to tap other sources which are not very much efficient. Efficient use of energy, therefore, has to be given more importance, wastage has to be minimized and maximum utilization of capacity is the need of the hour. It is obvious that there is no alternative to conservation of energy. Thus, any innovation contributing to the saving of energy should be welcomed and effort in this area should be encouraged.

Energy Conservation in Steel and Allied Industries

The iron and steel industry in India, involving high temperature processes, consumes as much energy as 9-10 million cal per tonne of crude steel which is about 58% more than that in USA and is about 38% more than the lowest energy consumed in the world. Energy consumption costs in an integrated steel plant account for as much as 25% of total production costs. Indian steel Industry alone consumes about 50% energy consumed by the Industrial sector.

Global Scenario

To explain the reasons for high energy consumption in Indian steel industry, a shop-wise comparison with that of a developed country may give better insight. The following observations were made from a comparison between energy usage in Indian steel plant and steel plant in Japan during 1980:

(*i*) Specific energy consumption in the Indian steel plant is twice that of the Japanese steel plant.

(*ii*) In both the cases, about 72% of the energy consumed is upto the iron making stage.

(*iii*) The fuel utilization efficiency, in the steel making and reheat furnaces, is poor in the Indian steel plants. In these areas, the specific energy consumption is twice that in the Japanese steel plant.

Action Areas For Energy Conservation

In the operation of steel industries, maximum attention should be given to the optimum utilization of energy by use of appropriate technologies. The following areas maybe easily observed where conservation efforts should be focussed:

(*i*) The consumption of petroleum fuels contributes to about 13% of the total fuel bill of the steel plants. So, reduction in consumption of petroleum products is really advisable at this stage.

(*ii*) A high priority should be given to the energy conservation efforts in the iron making areas where about 72% of the total energy is consumed.

The energy conservation measures can be categorized as follows:

1. Equipment improvements
2. Operational improvements
3. Modernization

1. Equipment Improvements

This category of measures may give quite high return with marginal investment. The following areas may be recognized easily :

A. Insulation of cold blast main

B. Minimizing leakages of hot blast

C. Improvement in combustion systems

D. Insulation of furnaces by ceramic fiber may reduce the heat loss to an extent of 5-7%.

E. Modification of water cooled spide in the reheating furnaces.

2. Operational Improvements

This category does not require any capital investment that have to be followed on a continuous routine basis. Some areas of improving operational aspects are: To minimize leakage of oil, air, steam, etc. To analyze fuel gases regularly

To maintain proper quality and size of input raw materials.

Modernization

A huge amount of investment is required for this purpose. Leisure is an essential requirement for efficient plant and failure to modernize the plant at the right time leads to steep deterioration in the plant output.

Energy Conservation in Textile Industry

It is estimated that textile industry consisting of a little over 700 mills consumes energy worth Rs.490.00 crores per year (1982 figures). This, in other word means that energy alone forms 8 to 10% of the total production cost of the textile produced by them. Effective conservation measures can save us as much as 10% of the energy cost. In the past, the power and utility cost of the textile sector was only 3 to 4% of the total cost structure. The hike in coal and other fuel prices has led to this cost going up to 8 to 10%. Obviously our efforts should be effected towards a more economical use of our fuels. The more instant energy conservation measures specifically suggested for some industries are as follows:

(*i*) Use of premium efficiency electric motors and correct motor and load sizing.

(*ii*) Regular inspection of transformers for distribution lines, prevention of leakages, prevention in abnormal rise of temperature and working transformers over 85% of the rated load.

(*iii*) Use of static condensers to improve power factor.

(*iv*) Roof level reduction to reduce lighting load.

(*v*) Optimum speed of spindle to produce most economic yarn.

(*vi*) Proper motor maintenance to prevent loose cotton and dust accumulation and burn out of motors.

(*vii*) In the heat energy side, proper boiler operation and maintenance, good insulation of steam lines, feed water recycling and waste heat recovery can be economically carried out.

(*viii*) Solar energy in textile industry can be used for

(*a*) Steam generation

(*b*) Preheating of motor

(*c*) Air cooling and humidification

(*d*) Cooking and dish washing in the canteen

(*e*) Drying of cloth.

Energy Conservation in the Railways

Energy accounts for 22-23 percent of the operating expenses of the Railways. Over the years, the railways have taken systematic steps towards reduction in energy consumption and this is manifest in the changeover from steam to diesel and now electric traction. The Railways consume, annually about 7.25 million tonnes of coal, 1550 million litres of HSD oil and about 3250 million kwh of electricity for traction alone. Any measure which promotes more efficient use of energy in the Railways would greatly add to measures of reducing in operating costs in Railways and to be a trend setter in energy utilization in the rest of the economy. The study of the following aspects may contribute somewhat in the area of energy saving:

1. Better Track

   The consumption of energy is directly related with the surface on which the movement of the body takes place. A road vehicle gives less kilometrage per unit of fuel on a rough road. The same phenomenon occurs in railway system, too, and, hence, the design, construction and maintenance of track are important factors to be taken care of, if energy has to be conserved.

2. Fuel Economy in Diesel Engines

   The primary aim of the diesel engine designers has been to achieve fuel economy. Considerable economy in fuel consumption has been achieved using assemblies/ components of improved designs and optimizing energy performance parameters based on these changes. However, some fuel economy can be achieved by minor modifications and adjustments on the engines.

Energy Conservation in Other Areas

Domestic consumers can be motivated to curtail energy consumption on many household goods. These include fan regulators, lighting fluorescent chokes, pressure cookers, etc. Introduction of high technology will help in conservation and in minimizing wastage. Advancement in electronics, in general, and semiconductor technology, in particular, has opened avenues for improving energy efficiency in almost all sectors of industry. For transmission of high voltage electrical energy, the use of high power semiconductors can contribute to better cost effectiveness.

Use of Electronic Controls

One area for energy conservation is the use of electronic controls for a wide variety of electrical motor operated systems, where speed is required to be maintained at level significantly lower than full rated speed over reasonably prolonged periods. If an electronic regulator is used in place of resistance type regulators in fans, about 12 watt per fan can be saved easily. Thus, 6 MW for 5.5 million fans, now being manufactured in India, per year, can be saved. Power semiconductors will also be effective for light dimmers, room coolers, sodium lamps, radios, TVs and other equipments.

Considering the existing dismal power scenario, a concerted campaign needs to be mounted on conservation and efficient use of energy industry. Industry needs motivation to discard inefficient use of power. Appropriate legislation containing a package of incentives would induce manufactures of equipment, using energy, to switch over to modern technology including electronics.

22

Environmental Management

There is a growing concern in developed nations about the ever-increasing environmental degradation due to industrialization. Even though the level of environmental pollution is much less in developing nations, it a cause for alarm there, too. There is total agreement throughout the world that any further environmental degradation should be effectively and completely checked. Heavy pollution in some of the larger cities in the world, e.g., London, New York, Los Angeles, Bombay, Istambul, Ankara, etc., has already taken a serious turn and the necessity to control ever growing pollution is obvious. There are main two approaches for environmental management:

1. Management based on standards
2. Management based on best practicable means.

The first approach requires statutory provision for standards for each pollutant for air, water, noise and soil pollution. In this approach, each polluter could choose a suitable technique for pollution control, based on their evaluation for technical feasibility and economic viability. A regular monitoring of each relevant pollutant and its comparison with prescribed limit will indicate the amount of pollution to be removed by pollution control. However, should there be any deviation from the prescribed limits, penal action could be taken against the polluter. The standards indicating the permissible limits for liquid effluents discharge on land and into water streams including lakes and rivers are given in Table 22.1. It should be appreciated that the permissible limits are higher for disposal on land because, due to percolation, there will be significant reduction in their values before their joining the water systems and, in case where effluent is discharged directly into river system, the effect will be direct and naturally the permissible limits are lower.

Regarding air pollution, the standards for ambient air quality are given in Table 22.2 which indicates that the permissible limits are highest for industrial areas but lowest in the case of sensitive areas including Agra-Mathura region, due to location of Taj Mahal, and the entire hill area including Kumaon and Garhwal region of the state.

The standards for noise pollution are being finalized. World Health Organization (WHO) standards for drinking water are given in Table 22.3.

The second approach is based on best practicable means . In this case, the industry is free to adopt any suitable method which is technically feasible as well as economically viable. Such a system is prevalent in the United Kingdom. It may also be emphasized that the Environmental Protection Agency for the United States shifted the time bound standards for a specific period of time when confronted with the energy crisis.

The developing nations have also started organizing effective checks and controls on environmental pollution. In some case, suitable standards for water pollution have also been prescribed. However, detailed standards, for different industrial environments as well as for waste disposal, noise, air pollution, radioactive materials, etc., are yet to be developed. In each case, it is necessary to have a time bound programme for implementation of effluent treatment plan to meet the prescribed limits, and to consider the calculation of depth columns for dumping of radioactive waste, which will not come into contact with permanent water levels of the land. The site should be selected so that permeability and possibly of cap rock including container are fairly low to enable any appreciable diffusion. In case of tanneries, for example, the BOD of effluent varies from 7000 to 10,000 mg/l depending upon whether they are dealing with vegetable or chrome tanning or a combination of both the tanning operations. It is obviously difficult to immediately reduce BOD to 30 mg/*l*, which is the permissible limit for BOD, when the effluents are to be discharged into natural streams. Similarly, the situation in the case of distilleries is still worse because the BOD of the effluent is about 50,000 mg/l. In such cases, a suitable grace period is needed to enable tire industry to develop suitable treatments for effluent disposal with prescribed limit.

The following suggestions could be helpful in proper environmental management:

With regard to implementation, there are three possibilities. The first is to have statutory provisions and to declare that the level of pollutants, discharged into open streams beyond the desired limit, will invite criminal proceedings or other suitable actions by the state. Thus, it will be mandatory to have as an integral part of each plant, a suitable device to reduce the level of each pollutant below the desired limit. The second possibility is to leave the matter entirely to the industry, with certain guidelines so that they may adopt the best practicable methods available. There is a third alternative which incorporates the advantages of both the methods but in any case a time bound programme will be needed.

1. There is no doubt that the 'best practicable means' approach offers a lot of freedom and has built-in flexibilities, which could be fully utilized for the benefit of the industry, and in the case of environmental management based on slandards, it is essential for industry to follow the standards to avoid penal action.
2. In developing countries. about 80% people live in villages and are engaged in agriculture. The sanitary conditions prevalent ;n villages are far from satisfactory. A large migration of rural people from rural to urban areas due to 'urban pull' and 'rural push' is also responsible for poor collection of solid wastes on a large number of them donot have regular accommodation in the city. Sometimes, this collection does not even exceed 30%. Obviously, this balance creates the problem of soil pollution and, subsequently, water pollution due to run off, eventually joining a natural stream, and air pollution due to favourable meteorological conditions in tropical countries. Even climatic conditions are favourable to biodegradation of waste materials left outside in tropical countries. It is, therefore,, obvious that the situation in developing countries is different from that prevalent in developed nations, especially cold countries.
3. In the case of developing countries, there is increasing emphasis on small scale/ cottage/village industries, specially to contain unemployment. However, it is very difficult for small scale industries to have effective effluent treatment plant to meet prescribed limits of state pollution control board. They do not have expertise either for monitoring or for abatement of effluent. Further, they have resource constraint which also comes in their way in timely implementation of pollution control.

4. There is apparently some relationship between the size of the plant and the profit likely to be earned, especially due to scale economy. This also discourages the small-scale industry from going in for pollution abatement.
5. Extensive instrumental facilities to measure concentration of each pollutant are required, irrespective of the size of the industry, especially when the materials involved are the same. The expenses involved also prevent the small-scale industry from going in for scientific monitoring of each pollutant at regular interval.
6. Pollution abatement measures, except in the case of odour and noise, may not increase productivity, which is considered a plus point in favour of pollution abatement. The awareness, about loss in hearing, due to constant noise levels, has not yet been fully appreciated in developing countries, as this process is slow and its harmful effect has not yet been fully realized, *i.e.*, it takes a fairly long time before hearing loss is appreciable.
7. The general standard of living is fairly low in developing countries. Hence, the flexibility offered by the 'best practicable means' approach may not be fully appreciated. On the other hand, it is likely to be misused. Even today, in most of the developing countries, statutory provisions for the monitoring of air, water, soil, noise and radioactive materials have not been laid down. In some countries, there is a provision for monitoring of important water streams at regular interval throughout a year. Surprisingly, scientific water treatment plants are not available everywhere, especially in third world countries. The absence of sophisticated instruments, required for proper monitoring of some of the pollutants, is another parameter responsible for delay in scientific monitoring.
8. What happened at Swansea Valley (England), where due to concentration of similar industries, especially with identical characteristics of effluent led to water and soil pollution and, consequently, the industrial activities came to a halt. This should be an eye opener to the scientific community and planners and should be kept in view while formulating policies for environmental management. Once pollution is left unchecked, there will be several closures like Swansea Valley industries.
9. The flexibility of the 'best practicable means' approach may lead to unnecessary litigation, causing delay and wastage of money in developing countries, due to difficulty in agreeable quantification of technical feasibility and economic viability, especially with relatively poor civic responsibility.
10. In the last five years, the standards for hexavalent chromium, mercury, lead, arsenic, cadmium, etc., have been reduced by several-fold. Obviously, this has been done due to better scientific understanding about their effects on human health. The studies conducted on a few important and common fishes, e.g., Mirgala Singala (Sihii), Mysturs Mystus (Tangri), Hetroponeust (Singhi), and Channagachua (Giri), have revealed that the distribution of heavy metals in different parts is not uniform.
11. As far as industrialization is concerned, there has not been geographical uniformity due to several constraints. Hence, the degree of pollution, which is directly linked to industrialization, is far from uniform. Thus, the total pollution load on each natural stream, at places, is different, suggesting different action in different situations. For example, in a region where there are a few industries, there is no point in being rigid about the concentration of different pollutants in the effluents being discharged into natural streams or in air. But in the case of heavily industrialized areas, the discharge of each industry should be carefully analyzed because the total

load on the natural stream would consist of individual loads. Hence, the idea of enforcing a uniform standard for different pollutants discharged into the natural stream in different areas does not appear to be scientifically and economically sound.

Here, again it is necessary to have different standards for different zones. In fact, wherever assimilation capacity is still available, further industrialization may be encouraged. But wherever the assimilation capacity has been surpassed due to heavy pollution, further industrialization, without-polluting industries, should be encouraged.

The state could be divided into three parts, Red, Grey and Green. Red area may be considered as that area where pollution load is more than assimilation capacity. Gray area maybe considered for the part of the state where pollution load is less than 50% of the assimilation capacity. Green area maybe considered that area where pollution load is within 25% of the assimilation capacity.

12. The ecosystem consists of the physical and biotic environment. The biotic environment consists of the animal kingdom, plant kingdom and human beings. The dynamic interaction among the three is very complex. Similarly, the impact of the physical environment on biotic environment is not yet well-understood. In the absence of any quantification of interactions between the physical environment and the biotic environment and different degree of pollution load, it is difficult to suggest realistic standards for different pollutants which are acceptable to polluters as well.
13. There is no proper justification for carrying out a detailed physico-chemical and biological analysis at different points in natural water streams. For example, in Uttar Pradesh, there is practically no point in finding out the radioactivity as there is practically no source. Secondly, there is no justification for carrying out a detailed chemical analysis as there is no source for some of the heavy metals, e.g., hexavalent chromium, lead, mercury, etc., at many places. The total biological analysis, as suggested in the prescribed standards, may not lead to meaningful information and may not effectively convey the position of a body of water, i.e., river or lake, with regard to its pollutants.

In view of the points enumerated earlier, the following conclusion are obvious:

1. There should be statutory standards for air, water, noise, radioactive materials, etc. But due to the difficulties mentioned earlier, they should be implemented keeping in view the special situation, i.e., circumstances associated with the industry and natural streams involved. Total pollution load on the river, its assimilation capacity and self-purification constant should be invariably considered.
2. The standards should serve as guidelines and there should be complete flexibility so that the pace of industrialization may be maintained or accelerated as far as possible. The global and regional requirements, and also economic conditions, may be kept in view while making statutory provision for the standards to be maintained by each industry. The practice of 'best practicable means', as adopted in the United Kingdom, and shifting of standards set by the Environmental Protection Agency of the United States are outstanding examples.
3. Wherever suitable technical know-how is not available, a grace period may be allowed and, in the meantime, suitable know-how may be developed with assistance from the polluting industry on the principle 'polluter should pay'. Further, as mentioned

earlier, certain guidelines with regard to the desirable limits are necessary to know the exact position.

4. As an incentive, tax concessions may be given to those industries which are maintaining the standards, and a suitable penalty may be imposed on those which are well above the prescribed limit, depending upon the degree of deviation from standards prevailing in the industry.

Thus, a flexible approach to environmental management, based on standards, should be adopted with, provision for detailed evaluation of technical feasibility and economic viability, jointly by polluters as well as enforcement agencies, so that both have faith in the evaluation, and the systems for effluent treatments, thus finalized, are implemented with full confidence.

Table 22.1

Standards for the disposal of industrial effluents

Pollutants mg/l	*BIS*		*WHO*		*UP Pollution Control Board*	
	A	*B*	*A*	*B*	*A*	*B*
1	*2*	*3*	*4*	*5*	*6*	*7*
Arsenic (as As)	0.2		0.05	0.05	0.2	—
Ammoniacal nitrogen	50	—	—	—	50	—
Anionic detergents	—	—	0.2-1	0.2-1	—	—
BOD at 20 °C for 5 day	30	500	—	—	30	500
Boron	•	2	—	—	—	2
Colour & odour	—	—	5-50	5-50	—	—
COD	250	—	—	—	250	—
Cyanides	0.2	—	0.05	0.05	0.2	—
Cadmium	2.0	—	0.1	0.01	2	2 —
Chromium (hexavalent)	0.1	—	—	—	0.1	—
Copper	3.0	—	0.05-1.5	.05-1.5	3.0	3.0
Chlorides	—	600	200-600	200-600	—	600
Calcium	—	—	75-200	75-200	—	—
Fluorides	2.0	—	0.8-8.7	0.8-8.7	2	—
Hardness	—	—	100-500	100-500	—	—
Insecticides	—	—	—	—	0	—
Iron	—	—	0.1-1	0.1-1	—	—
Lead	0.1	—	0.1	0.1	0.1	—
Mercury	0.01	—	0.001	0.001	0.01	—
Magnesium	—	—	30-150	30-150	—	—
Manganese	—	—	0.05-0.5	0.05-0.5	—	—
Nickel	3	—	—	—	3	—
Nitrate	—	—	11.3-22.6	11.3-22.6	—	—

(Contd. ...)

Oil & grease	10	30	0.01-0.3	0.01-0.3	10	30
PH	5.5-9	5.5-9	7-8.5	7-8.5	5.5-9	5.5-9
Phenolic compounds	1	—	0.001 -0.002	0.001 -0.002	1	—
Percent Sodium	—	60	—	—	—	60
Radioactive materials						
i) Alpha emitters μc/ml	10"7	10"'	3 nci/l	3/nci/l	io-7	to-'
ii) Beta emitters μc/ml	10"6	to 8	30 nci/l	30 nci/l	10-6	—
Suspended solids	100	—	5-25	5-25	100	—
Sulphides	2	—	—	—	2	—
Selenium	0.05	—	0.01	0.01	0.05	—
Sulphates	—	1000	200-400	200-400	—	1000
Total dissolved solids (inorg.)	—	2100	500-1500	—	—	2100
Temperature, °C	40	—	—	—	40	—
Total residual chlorine	1	—	200-600	200-600	1	—
Total hardness mg/1 $CaCO_3$	—	—	100-500	100-500	—	—
Turbidity	—	—	5-25	5-25	—	—
Zinc	5	—	5-15	5-15	5	

A = Into inland surface waters,

B = On land for irrigation

Subject to relaxation or tightening by the local authority

Relaxable to 750 by the local authority

These requirements shall apply only where, after treatment, the sewage is disposed of on land for irrigation.

Table 22.2
Ambient air quality standards

The concentration for the following pollutants shall be 95% of the time within the limits prescribed below:

Area Category	*Concentration in microgrammes per meter cube*			
	Suspended Particulate Matter	*Sulphur Dioxide (SO_2)*	*Carbon Monoxide (CO)*	*Nitrogen Dioxide (NO_2)*
1. Industrial & mixed use	500	120	5000	120
2. Residual & rural	200	80	2000	80
3. Sensitive	100	30	1000	30

Sensitive Areas : Hill stations, Tourist resorts, Sanctuaries, National parks, Nation monuments etc (Agra-Mathura region in the form of trapezium and Doon valley are sensitive areas in U.P.)

Table 22.3
World Health Organization standards for potable water

Constituent	*Criteria*	
Lead (as Pb)	0.1 mg/1	
Selenium (as Se)	0.05 mg/1	Maximum allowable concentration
Arsenic (as As)	0.2 mg/1	
Chromium (as Cr^{6+})	0.05 mg/1	
Cyanide (as CN)	0.01 mg/1	
	Permissible	*Excessive*
Total Solids	500 mg/1	1,500 mg/1
Colour	5 units	50 units
Turbidity	5 units	25 units
Taste	Unobjectionable	
Odour	Unobjectionable	
Iron (Fe)	0.3 mg/1	1.0 mg/1
Mangnese	0.1 mg/1	0.5 mg/1
Copper (Cu)	1.0 mg/1	1.5 mg/1
Zinc (Zn)	5.0 mg/1	15 mg/1
Calcium (Ca)	75 mg/1	200 mg/1
Magnesium (Mg)	50 mg/1	150 mg/1
Sulphate (S04)	200 mg/1	400 mg/1
Chloride (CI)	200 mg/1	600 mg/1
PH	7.0-8.5	(6.5 or) 9.2
(Mg + Na) SO_4	500 mg/1	1,000 mg/1
Phenolics	0.001 mg/1	0.002 mg/1
α emitters	10^{-9} c/ml	—

23

Planned Industrial Development

The industrialization has not been done uniformly throughout the country. In order to have well balanced industrial development, several concessions are being given to those who are interested to put up their industries in backward areas. These incentives include loan at reduced rate of interest. This could be defended on the basis of socio-economic considerations. But there is a scientific basis for having much higher standard in backward area which is practically more than half of the total area in every state of this country, due to the fact that total pollutional load whether organic or inorganic or both is much less than the assimilation capacity of receiving stream. On the other hand, there are several places, viz., Kanpur, Bombay, Madras, Delhi, Calcutta and Varanasi. where pollution load is much more than the assimilation capacity and, consequently, the receiving streams are badly affected. Such places should be declared as restricted area for any further industrial development. There should be an inbuilt provision for a time-bound action-programme. It is, therefore, obvious that a distinction has to be made between the region where there is practically no industrialization, *e.g.*, Gazipur, Jaunpur, Gonda, Chamauli, Garhwal, etc., from those which have several industries, contributing to a large amount of industrial effluents such that assimilation capacity has been surpassed.

The world management congress at its last meeting at New Delhi projected the concept of eventual sharing of resources that are available. This would amount to possible exploitation of all the available resources as far as possible. For example, both distillery and tannery have fairly high BOD content in their effluents. Hence, their collective discharge always leads to serious consequences from pollutional point of view. The ideal location for distillery/tannery will be a remote place, where there is no additional effluent containing high BOD. There is no dearth of such suitable locations in India.

Combination of Industrial Effluents

A summary of industrial waste, its origin and character is given in Table 23.1. The characteristics of effluents from different industries are different. The characteristics of effluents from some selected industries are given in Table 23.2, which clearly indicates that their characteristics also could be used as a suitable basis for planned industrial development, e.g., liquid effluents of tannery are acidic in nature while the effluents from Textile and Jute mills are alkaline. Secondly, BOD of tannery effluent is between 6000 and 10,000 ppm, depending upon whether the effluents are coming from chrome tanning or vegetable tanning or a combined unit of both, while the BOD effluent from cotton textile is only about 350. Hence a combination of these two effluents would involve much less investment. Similarly, the effluents from pulp and paper craft process is generally alkaline and BOD is about 375. On the other hand the BOD of distillery is about 40,000 to 70,000 and is acidic in nature. Therefore, a combination of these two could require much less investment. Even a combination of these two could require fertilizer and that of distillery would result in considerable saving.

Low Pollution Technology

There has been shift from high technology to low technology which could be used for development of village and small scale industries in developing countries but in view of the deterioration of environment even in developing countries, it is imperative to go in for development of pollution technology which could be adopted without much contribution to environmental pollution.

Use of Process Chemicals

There are several chemicals including heavy metals which are used in industry. The degree of harm that can be caused and the nature of pollution are different in different areas. The contribution of some of the important pollutions is given in Table 23.3. In the light of Table 23.3, each process in operation should be reviewed with a critical evaluation on substitution of every chemical by a low pollution chemical including solvent, heavy metals, etc. Efforts have been made successfully to develop substituent chemicals used as solvents with low pollutional level in a tannery.

Disposal of Industrial Effluents

It is a general observation that most of the industrial effluents either join the river directly or through an aqueduct. Hence, the introduction of an effluent into any natural stream is only through laminar sub-layer, where the flow is practically longitudinal which does not permit any axial mixing. This is the only reason why a large number of fish are found dead with the input of concentrated amount of effluent either organic or inorganic. A suitable arrangement for disposal of effluent, especially away from tine bank of river, which is accessible for drinking purposes, would definitely eliminate the possibility of such a large scale killing of living beings. Even those animals, which provide milk, also consume water for drinking purposes from such polluted sources. During festive days, tens of thousands of people use river water for drinking purposes, from this laminar zone, which is heavily polluted. Hence, proper disposal of industrial effluents, at appropriate points, in the receiving stream could go a long way to fully utilize the assimilation capacity.

Conclusion

The following guidelines could be of assistance for further industrial development:

1. There should be continuous monitoring, at strategic points, at regular intervals, to quantitatively determine the pollution load.
2. The assimilation capacity and recovery constant should be determined on the basis of experimental data collected.
3. The list of programmes for monitoring should be reviewed every year, depending upon the nature of effluents from new industries.

4. Table 23.1 and Table 23.2 could be used to assess quantitatively and qualitatively the incoming pollution load.
5. The data available from monitoring of natural stream should be used for preparing the guidelines for development of new industries.
6. A time-bound programme, based on suitable incentive, should be developed for each group of industries, e.g., distillery, textile, tannery, etc., and be strictly adhered to.
7. The values for each parameter should be reset industrially developing and developed areas in every state.
8. Suitable guidelines for industrial development, for each district, in the light of interacting parameter, e.g., population, agriculture, agricultural inputs, fertilizer, pesticides, etc., should be evolved. Forest industries already in production and total pollution load should be prepared and made available.
9. Research and Development should be geared to develop low pollution technology.
10. A check list for recycle should be prepared and circulated in industry for implementation. The indirect saving on energy, due to recycle of materials, should be emphasized.
11. A detailed study should be conducted in critical process industries for substitution of high pollution chemicals by low pollution ones.
12. Development of low pollution technology should be given proper place in R & D efforts.

Table 23.1

Summary of Industrial waste : Its origin and character

	Industries producing wastes	*Origin of major wastes*	*Major characteristics*
1.	Textile	Cooking of fibers, desizing of fabrics	Highly alkaline, colour, high BOD
2.	Leather goods	Dehairing, soaking and deliming of hides	High total solids, hardness, salt, sulphides, chromium, pH, precipitated lime and BOD.
3.	Laundary Trade	Washing of fabrics	High turbidity, alkalinity, and organic solids.
4.	Canned goods	Trimming, culling, juicing and blanching of fruits and vegetables	High in suspended solids, colloidal and dissolved organic matter.
5.	Dairy product	Dilution of wholemilk, separated milk, butter milk and whey.	High in dissolved organic matters, mainly protein, fat and lactose.
6.	Brewed distilled beverages	Steeping and pressing grain residue from distillation of of alcohol	High in dissolved organic solids, containing nitrogen, chlorine and fermentated or their products.
7.	Meat and poultry products	Stock yards, slaughtering of bones and fats, residues in concentrated grease, wash water and pickling of chikens.	High in dissolved suspended organic matter, blood, other proteins and fats.

(*Contd. ...*)

8. Animal feed	Excreta from animal	High in organic suspended solids and BOD
9. Beet sugar	Transfer, screening and juicing water, drainage from lime.	High in dissolved and suspended organic matters containing sugar and protein.
10. Pharmaceutical products	Mycelium, spent filtrate and wash-waters.	High in suspended and dissolved organic matter including vitamins.
11. Yeast	Residue from yeast filtration	High in solids (mainly organic and BOD)
13. Coffee	Pulping and fermenting of coffee bean	High BOD and suspended solids.
14. Fish	Rejects from centrifuge, evaporators and other wash-water wastes	Very high BOD, total organic solids and odour.
IS. Rice	Soaking, cooking and washing of rice	High BOD, total and suspended solids (mainly starch)
16. Soft drinks	Bottle washing, floor and equipment cleaning, syrup storage, tank drains	High pH, suspended solids and BOD
17. Bakeries	Washing and greasing of pans, floor washings	High BOD, grease, floor washing, sugars, flours, detergents.
18. Water product	Filter backwash, lime soda, sludge, brine, alum sludge.	Minerals and suspended solids.
19. Pulp and pepers	Cooking, refining, washing of fibres, screening of paper, paper pulp	High or low pIT, colour, high suspended, colloidal and dissolved solids.
20. Photographic	Spent solution of developer and fixer	Alkaline, containing various organic and inorganic reducing contents.
21. Steel	Coking of coal, washing of blast furnace, flue gases, pickling of steel	Low pH, acids, phenol, and ore, cokes, limestone, alkali oils, and fine suspended solids.
22. Metal plated	Stripping of oxides, cleaning and plating of metals	Acid metals, toxic low volume, mainly, mineral matter.
23. Iron Foundry	Wasting of used sand by hydraulic discharge	High suspended solids, mainly sand, some clay and coal.
24. Oil fields and refineries	Drilling muds, salt, oil and some natural gas, acid sludge and miscellaneous oils from refining	High dissolved salts from high BOD odour, phenol and sulphur compounds from refining.
25. Fuel oil use	Spills from fuel tank filling waste, autocrank case oils	High in emulsified and dissolved oils.
26. Rubber	Washing of latex, coagulated	High BOD, odour, high suspended

(*Contd. ...*)

	rubber, exuded impurities from crude rubber.	solids, variable pH, high chlorides.
27. Glass	Polishing and cleaning of glass	Red colour, alkaline, nonsettleable suspended solids.
28. Naval stores	Washing solvent recovery	Acid, high BOD and oil recovery water
29. Glue manufacturing	Line wash acid, extraction of non-specific proteins	High COD, BOD, pH, chromium, periodic strong mineral acids.
30. Wood preservation	Steam condensates	High in COD, BOD, solids, phenols.
31. Candle mfg.	Wax spills, stearic acid condensates, dilute acids.	Organic (fatty) acid, low pH, low organic content.
32. Ply wood mfg.	Glue washing	High BOD, pH, phenols, potential toxicity.
33. Acid	Dilute wash-waters dilute acids	Low pH, low organic contents.
34. Detergents	Washing and purifying soaps and detergents	High BOD and soponified soaps.
35. Corn starch	Evaporator condensate or bottoms, when not re-used or recovered syrup final washes.	High BOD and dissolved organic matter, mainly starch and related materials
36. Explosives	Washing TNT and gun cotton for purification, washing and pickling or cartridges	TNT colour, acid odorous and contains organics acids and alcohol from powder and cotton, metals acids, oils and soaps
37. Pesticides	Washing and purification of products, such as 2, 4, D & DDT	High organic matter, benzene, ring structure, toxic to bacteria and fish acid.
38. Phosphate and Phosphorous	Washing and screening of floating rock	Clays, slimes and tails, oils low pH, high suspended solids, phosphorous, silica and fluorides.
39. Formaldehyde	Residues from manufacturing synthetic resins and from dying synthetic fibers	Normally high BOD and HCHO, toxic to bacteria in high concentrations
40. Plastic and Resins	Unit operations from polymer preparations and use, spills and equipment wash downs	Acids, caustic dissolved organic matter such as phenols, formaldehyde, etc.
41. Coal processing	Cleaning and classification of coal leaching and sulphur started with water.	High suspended solids, mainly coal, low pH, high H_2SO_4 & D_2SO_4
42. Steam power	Cooling water, boiler low down, coal drainage	Hot, high volume and high inorganic and dissolved solids.
43. Nuclear power and radio-active materials	Processing ores, laundering of contaminated clothes, research lab wastes, processing of fuel, power plant, cooling water.	Radio active elements can be very acid "hot".

Table 23.2
Characteristics of waste water from selected industries in India

Industry	*Flow*	*pH*	*Suspended Solids mg/l*	*B.O.D. mg/l*	*C.O.D. mg/l*	*O.D. O.D.*	*B.O.D. load per % product*	*Other important characteristics*
1	*2*	*3*	*4*	*5*	*6*	*7*	*8*	*9*
Dairy	$7m^2/m^3$ milk	—	690	816	—	6.6	5.7	Oil and putrescibility
Distillery	$14m^3m^3$ rectified spirit	4.0-4.5	—	40,000	80,000	0.5	560	High TDS, Cl, SO_4, colour and putrescibility
Cotton Textile	$25m^3$/1000 meter cloth	7-10	375	350	525	0.66	8.75	TDS 300mg/l% sodium and colour
Viscose Rayon	$570m^3$/tonne	2.08-4.1	200	—	210	—	—	Zinc, 6.18mg/l, Polysulfides
Tannery	$3.2m^3$/100 kg hide	8.0	1900	1000	3500	0.48	5.4	Cr^{+3} 0.35-0.45 kg/100 kg hide, Cl 4600mg/l tannin, colour
Pulp and paper craft process	$310m^3$/tonne	6.5 - 8.2	375	160	610	0.26	50	Lignin, colour, suspended fibre
Primary polymers Polyethylene		1.44-5.8	200	4000	—	—	—	Solids
Coke Oven	$3m^3$/tonne of coke	3.6- 11.2	82	1200	2900	0.41	3.6	NH3, Phenol, CN, CNS, Tar and oil
Refinery	$1.7m^3$/tonne oil processed	—	300	200	—	—	0.34	Free oil, 2500mg/l emulsified oil, 100mg/l mercaptan 115mg/l
Phenol formaldehyde Resin	$30.0m^3$/tonne	4.0-7.0	—	23,600	32,160	0.73	7.1	Phenol, 7900mg/l HCHO 4360mg/l
Parathion	—	2.0	—	700	3,000	0.23	—	TS 27,000mg/l parathion 20mg/l
Carbaryl	—	7.0-10	—	—	10,000	—	—	TS 40,000 mg/l No Carbyl, Low Toxicity
Poly Propylene	—	1.44-5.8	—	200	—	400		

1	*2*	*3*	*4*	*5*	*6*	*7*	*8*	*9*
Polystyrene	—	1.8-5.6	—	200	—	3000	0.05 - 0.25	
Polyvinyl Chloride		5.5-11	50 - 500	1000	—	2000	0.05 - 0.25	
Cellulose Acetate	—	0.036 - 0.72	500 - 2000	1000	—	5000	0.4 - 0.5	
Butyl Rubber	—	7.2-21.6	800 - 2000	2500	—	5000	0.32 - 0.4	
Tributyl Phophate	—	3.6-14.4	500 - 2000	1000	—	3000	0.5 - 0.67	Phophorous

Table 23.3
Characteristics of waste water from selected industries in India

Industry	*Flow* m^3*/tonne*	*B.O.D.* *mg/l*	*C.O.D.* *mg/l*	*B.O.D./C.O.D.*	*Other Important Characteristics*
Dyes and pigments	180 - 900	200 - 400	500 - 2000	0.2 - 0.4	Heavy metals, solids, colour, pH
Primary Petrochemical Ethylene	0.18 - 5.4	100 - 1000	500 - 3000	0.2 - 0.33	Phenol, Oil, pH
Propylene	0.36 - 7.3	100 - 1000	500 - 3000	0.2 - 0.33	Phenol, pH
Toluene	1.1 - 11.0	300 - 2500	1000 - 5000	0.3 - 0.05	
Xylene	0.72 -11.00	500 - 4000	1000 - 8000	0.5	
Methanol	1.1 - 11.0	300 - 1000	500 - 2000	0.5 - 0.63	Oil and solids
Ethanol	0.72 - 7.2	500 - 4000	1000 - 8000	0.5	Heavy metals
Ethyl Benzene	1.1 - 11	500 - 3000	1000 - 7000	0.83 - 0.5	Heavy metals
Chlorinated hydrocarbons	0.18 - 3.6	50 -150	100 - 500	0.3 - 0.5	Oils, solids, pH

24

The Environmental Audit

The environmental audit is a review of activities affecting the environment to determine the status of a corporation's compliance with central, state and local environmental laws and regulations. It also provides the corporation with data and other information on which environmental decision and planning could be based.

The environmental compliance audit can be company-wide and comprehensive, or it can be limited either to particular facilities owned by a corporation or to determining compliance with specific regulatory programmes. Whatever the audit's scope, the basic principles and considerations related to the conduct of an audit will remain the same.

An environmental audit is a management tool for taking inventory of a company's environmental assets and liabilities. As such, the audit provides information on a company's compliance status at a given point in time, analysis of the perceived implications of the information gathered and, if management so chooses, options that arise from this information and analysis. In short, an audit provides a snapshot of one segment of management's responsibility.

1.1 Responding to Enforcement actions

Understanding a company's actual compliance status not only enables corporate management to take steps to avoid being the target of litigation, it also renders the company better prepared in the event of an enforcement action. When an action is brought, ready knowledge of the company's overall environmental situation may be a key element in responding. Without an orderly and usable reporting system and access to the broad data-base that the audit procedure provides, a period of chaos may ensue, disrupting the company's business activity and impairing its ability to assess its position.

The term "snapshot" should not be misunderstood. While the data collected will focus on compliance status at a given point in time, an effective and useful audit must look back to past particles in some areas, e.g., waste management and should also identify potential liabilities arising from past or current practices. The audit should also establish the basis for continued reporting and making management systems to ensure rational, responsive decision-making in the future. To accomplish this, the audit should be designed to present information in a format that will allow efficient integration with subsequent compliance monitoring activities.

The audit itself does not necessarily entail development of management reporting systems or engineering drawings for construction of new pollution control equipment. Nor need it entail developing cost estimates for such construction or equipment. These actions may be appropriate management responses after completion of an initial audit.

2. Reasons to Undertake an Environmental Audit

There could be a number of reasons for undertaking an audit and the benefits associated with the audit process are described below.

2.1. Determining Compliance Status

A fundamental reason for undertaking an environmental audit is to determine the status of a company's compliance with central, state, and local environmental laws and regulations. More than a decade of major environmental legislation regulating air and water pollution, chemicals, hazardous substances and waste disposal has imposed a complete scheme of obligations on business, industry and local bodies. Environmental compliance represents a significant aspect of doing business- both, in terms of the effort and cost, necessary to achieve compliance and in terms of the fines, penalties and liabilities that maybe incurred as a result of noncompliance.

Understanding the applicability and impact of environmental regulation has become necessary for informed corporate planning and decision-making. The audit is a vehicle to help management identify environmental problems that could adversely affect an otherwise normal business activity, and avoid or minimize liability for costly remedial work, fines or damage claims before enforcement actions are brought.

Where corporate management does not know of a problem until it becomes serious, of substantial duration, and difficult to clean up, enforcement actions, involving substantial sums, may result. Some cases involving substantial civil and criminal penalties have developed because of concealment of problems, sometimes, by lower-level employees, acting - usually erroneously-from the belief that management did not want to hear the bad news. Possible enforcement actions can be avoided by an environmental audit that identifies "skeletons in the close," thereby, enabling the company to take steps, in advance of government action, and to focus its efforts on specific problem areas of plant operations.

An environmental audit can also help in maintaining a corporation's compliance status in an efficient and cost-effective manner. Frequently, facilities can be control technologies including equipment, and management practices may be available to, control a particular waste or discharge. The capital and operating costs associated with tlje different options may vary substantially. By identifying the applicable regulatory requirements, an environmental audit can assist the business manager in focusing on potential problems and selecting, in a timely and organized fashion, the most efficient and cost-effective approach. An audit can also help management recognize if there is a need for change in operating or administrative procedures to improve the company's system for compliance assurance and internal reporting.

2.2 Crisis Management

Information obtained in an audit can be of enormous value in crisis situations. Such information can help a company respond quickly to a spill or other release of a hazardous substance or to other pollution incidents the impacts of which may have been exaggerated by the press or others. Conversely, such information can help companies avoid making claims or assertions that, upon further investigation, prove to be understatements by saying nothing, but this course may subject it to significant negative publicity. Generally, a far better approach is to understand one's compliance status from the beginning, and, thus, to be able to make informed, sensitive judgements about how to handle problems when they arise.

It is absolutely essential in the environmental area to be prepared for emergencies. Failure to respond promptly and appropriately to a spill of a hazardous substance, for example, can result in loss of life, damage to property, contamination of drinking water, fire or explosion, or other injuries. Further, the costs of cleaning up a spill after it has been initially mismanaged can often be many times greater than the cost of initial containment and removal.

3.1 Planning and Conducting the Audit

An environmental compliance audit should be tailored to fit the company's circumstances and needs. Though each corporation is different, the basic elements of a successful audit are the same. These elements include:

- Defining the purpose and scope of the audit, resolving policy issues and establishing priorities;
- Assigning departmental responsibility for the audit function and ensuring in-house cooperation;
- Choosing the audit team;
- Reviewing central, state and local laws and regulations to identify regulatory programmes applicable to company operations;
- Selecting elements of analysis on which to base data collection;
- Beginning the audit;
- Preparing compliance profiles;
- Conducting a site visit;
- Analyzing and presenting the Results of the audit; and
- Evaluating the audit.

3.2 Establishing the Authority for the Audit: Purpose, Scope and Policy Issues

Before a company begins an environmental audit, its Board of Directors or senior management should issue a resolution or directive to initiate and legitimize the audit. This step is necessary to achieve the maximum level of cooperation from within the corporation. Such cooperation is essential in providing the information senior management needs to obtain a clear picture of the company's compliance status.

This directive should authorize the creation of the audit team and state1 clearly the nature and purpose of the audit as well as any limitations on the audit due to legal considerations or internal management policy.

4. Conducting the Audit

Once the regulatory programmes, potentially applicable to company operations, have been identified and the elements on which to base data collection and analysis have been selected, the audit may begin. Collection of audit data should be organized into two stages: Preliminary data collection prior to the site visit, and data collection at the site.

4.1. Preliminary Data Collection

Three questions must be addressed in designing the preliminary data gathering process:

- Who should collect the information?
- How should it be collected?
- What basic information does the audit team need about the site to determine whether a specific audit element is subject to regulation?

Index